political participation in france and germany

Edited by
Oscar W. Gabriel, Silke I. Keil
and Eric Kerrouche

© Oscar W. Gabriel, Silke I. Keil and Eric Kerrouche 2012

First published by the ECPR Press in 2012

The ECPR Press is the publishing imprint of the European Consortium for Political Research (ECPR), a scholarly association, which supports and encourages the training, research and cross-national cooperation of political scientists in institutions throughout Europe and beyond. ECPR Press, ECPR Central Services, University of Essex, Wivenhoe Park, Colchester, CO4 3SQ, UK

All rights reserved. No part of this book may be reprinted or reproduced or utilised in any form or by any electronic, mechanical, or other means, now known or hereafter invented, including photocopying and recording, or in any information storage or retrieval system, without permission in writing from the publishers.

Typeset by ECPR Press
Printed and bound by Lightning Source

British Library Cataloguing in Publication Data
A catalogue record for this book is available from the British Library

Hardback ISBN: 978-1-907301-31-5

www.ecprnet.eu/ecprpress

ECPR – Studies in European Political Science

Series Editors:
Dario Castiglione (University of Exeter)
Peter Kennealy (European University Institute)
Alexandra Segerberg (Stockholm University)
Peter Triantafillou (Roskilde University)

ECPR – Studies in European Political Science is a series of high-quality edited volumes on topics at the cutting edge of current political science and political thought. All volumes are research-based offering new perspectives in the study of politics with contributions from leading scholars working in the relevant fields. Most of the volumes originate from ECPR events including the Joint Sessions of Workshops, the Research Sessions, and the General Conferences.

Books in this series

The Domestic Party Politics of Europeanisation: Actors, Patterns and Systems
ISBN: 9781907301223
Edited by Erol Külahci

Interactive Policy Making, Metagovernance and Democracy
ISBN: 9781907301131
Edited by Jacob Torfing and Peter Triantafillou

Perceptions of Europe: A Comparative Sociology of European Attitudes
ISBN: 9781907301155
Edited by Daniel Gaxie, Jay Rowell and Nicolas Hubé

Personal Representation: The Neglected Dimension of Electoral Systems
ISBN: 9781907301162
Edited by Josep Colomer

Political Trust: Why Context Matters
ISBN: 9781907301230
Edited by Sonja Zmerli and Marc Hooghe

Please visit www.ecprnet.eu/ecprpress for up-to-date information about new publications.

contents

List of Figures and Tables vi

Contributors xi

Preface xv

Chapter One: Political Participation in France and Germany – Traditions, Concepts, Measurements, Patterns and Explanations
Oscar W. Gabriel 1

Chapter Two: Mapping Political Participation
Kristina Kuhne and Oscar W. Gabriel 33

Chapter Three: Conventional Political Participation
Jürgen Bauknecht 71

Chapter Four: Local Electoral Participation
Angelika Vetter and Vincent Hoffmann-Martinot 113

Chapter Five: Local Democracy – A Comparison of Mayoral Perceptions
Björn Egner and Eric Kerrouche 137

Chapter Six: Initiatives and Referendums
Christophe Premat 161

Chapter Seven: Social Participation
Silke I. Keil 189

Chapter Eight: Turnout in Parliamentary Elections
Kerstin Völkl 209

Chapter Nine: Political Protest
Emmanuel Rivat/Matthias Stauer 237

Chapter Ten: New Forms of Citizen Involvement
Ortwin Renn and Pia-Johanna Schweizer 273

Index 297

| list of figures and tables

Figures

Figure 1.1: Approaches to the explanation of political participation   11

Figure 3.1: Party membership in France and Germany   78

Figure 3.2: Determinants of conventional political participation   80

Figure 4.1: Explanatory factors affecting turnout   114

Figure 4.2: Local electoral turnout in France and Germany 1950-2007   117

Figure 4.3: Hypotheses on turnout effects from different contexts   119

Figure 4.4: Municipal size and local turnout in France and Germany   121

Figure 4.5: Local and National Electoral Participation in France and Germany   126

Figure 7.1: Social Participation in France and Germany, 2002/03, 2006/07   199

Figure 8.1: Voter turnout percentages in French and German parliamentary elections (1949–2007)   215

Figure 9.1: Potential of civil disobedience 1990–1999–2000   245

Figure 9.2: Perceptions of political systems   257

Figure 9.3: Opportunity structures and political protest   260

Tables

Table 1.1: Types of political participation according to Verba and Nie (1972)   8

Table 2.1: Strong and weak systems of participation   39

Table 2.2: Comparison of the participative systems of Germany and France according to four criteria   65

Table 3.1: Five forms of conventional political participation and their characteristics   76

Table 3.2: Levels of conventional political participation (percentage)   77

Table 3.3: Political participation in Germany (percentage)   77

Table 3.4: Determinants: socio-economic characteristics 81

Table 3.5: Determinants: microenvironment 85

Table 3.6: Determinants: political attitudes 87

Table 3.7: Determinants: media use 89

Table 3.8: Ten value types and four higher order value types 90

Table 3.9: Determinants: values 92

Table 3.10: Country effects 93

Table 3.11: The strongest determinants 95

Table 4.1: Local turnout in France and Germany 1999–2002 116

Table 4.2: Municipal size and local turnout in France and Germany 122

Table 4.3: Votes for national parties, free lists, list combinations and independent candidates in German local elections 125

Table 4.4: Local and national electoral turnout percentage in Germany by states, 1949–2006 132

Table 5.1: Statements on the functioning of local democracy 145

Table 5.2: Basic regression for the importance of election results 147

Table 5.3: Regression for the importance of election results including controls 147

Table 5.4: Basic regression for the importance of generating consensus 148

Table 5.5: Basic regression for the importance of generating consensus with controls 148

Table 5.6: Basic regression for the importance of residents making their views known 149

Table 5.7: Basic regression for the importance of residents making their views known with controls 149

Table 5.8: Basic regression for the importance of active and direct participation 150

Table 5.9: Basic regression for the importance of active and direct participation with controls 150

Table 5.10: Statements on the role of parties and local referendums 151

Table 5.11: Basic regression for the role of parties 152

Table 5.12: Regression for the role of parties with controls 152

Table 5.13: Tools of communication with local people 153

Table 5.14: Overview of regressions for tools of communication with
local people with controls 155

Table 5.15: Regression on the statements about the functioning of local
democracy 156

Table 6.1: Types of direct democratic procedures 163

Table 6.2: The institutional set-up for local referendums and popular
initiatives in Germany (quorum and deadlines) 165

Table 6.3: Number of popular initiatives and local referendums in
Germany 170

Table 6.4: Frequency of popular initiatives in the German Länder
(1956–2005) 171

Table 6.5: Frequency of local popular initiatives in Baden-Württemberg
(1996–2006) 172

Table 6.6: Local referendums in Baden-Württemberg (1995–2004) 174

Table 6.7: Communal referendums in Baden-Württemberg between
1956 and 1987 175

Table 6.8: Local referendums in the old Länder 177

Table 6.9: Reworked popular initiative referendums in Baden-Württemberg
(1975–2006) 179

Table 6.10: Topics, turnout and approval rates of French local
referendums (1992–2004) 182

Table 6.11: Popular initiative topics in Germany (1975-2007) 183

Table 6.12: Topics, turnout and approval rates of local referendums in
Baden-Württemberg (1975–2006) 184

Table 7.1: Registered associations in Germany: 2001, 2003, 2005 (entries
in absolute numbers) 196

Table 7.2: Registered associations in France: 1999, 2005 (entries in
absolute numbers) 197

Table 7.3: Country effects 200

Table 7.4: Determinants of membership in France and Germany,
2002/03–2006/07 (in Exp (B)) 201

Table 7.5: Determinants of active social participation in France and
Germany, 2002/03–2006/07 (in Exp(B)) 201

Table 8.1: Voter turnout percentages in parliamentary and presidential
elections in France (1958–2007) 218

Table 8.2: Voter turnout percentages in German Bundestag elections (1949–2005)	218
Table 8.3: Determinants of vote abstention in France and Germany (2002/03–2004/05–2006/07 (in Exp(B))	224
Table 9.1: Typologies of political protest	240
Table 9.2: Percentage level of political protest (1990–2004)	244
Table 9.3: Levels of political protest as per cent (2002–2007)	247
Table 9.4: Countries as determinants of political protest	249
Table 9.5: Protest and individual political participation	255
Table 9.6: Characteristics of open and closed states	258
Table 9.7: Patterns of political opportunity structures	259
Table 9.8: Determinants of context analysis	261
Appendix: Dimensions of political protest participation (1999–2000)	268
Table 10.1: Characteristics of policy-making styles	283

contributors

JÜRGEN BAUKNECHT is a researcher at the Department of Political Systems and Political Sociology at the University of Stuttgart. His scientific focus lies in political attitudes and behavior, political participation and welfare state research. Furthermore he specialises in methods of empirical social science. He was chief executive officer of the German partial study of the European Social Survey.

BJÖRN EGNER leads the Department of Methods of Political Science at the Technical University of Darmstadt. He researches on fields of local politics and local elites. Besides numerous contributions to these topics, his most important monographs are *Einstellungen deutscher Bürgermeister: Lokale Eliten zwischen Institutionen und Kontext* (Nomos, 2007) and, together with Michael Haus, Hubert Heinelt and Christine König, *Partizipation und Führung in der Lokalen Politik* (Nomos, 2005).

OSCAR W. GABRIEL is professor of political systems and political sociology at the University of Stuttgart and Chercheur Associé at the IEP Bordeaux. His main research interests include political attitudes and political behaviour, political culture and methods of comparative political science. In addition to his teaching assignment, he is involved in certain national and international research programmes and leads a project on citizen and political representation in Germany and France. Oscar Gabriel also belongs to the German coordination team of the European Social Survey. Two of his latest (co-)edited publications are *Deutschland, Österreich und die Schweiz im Neuen Europa: Bürger und Politik* (Nomos, 2010) and *Kommunale Aufgaben im Europäischen Binnenmarkt* (Nomos, 2010).

VINCENT HOFFMANN-MARTINOT is professor of political science and director of Sciences Po Bordeaux (University of Bordeaux). Inter alia, he served on the executive committee of the International Social Science Council (2000–2004) and was a member of the executive committee of the European Consortium for Political Research (ECPR) (1997–2003). From 2003 to 2009, he was the chairman of the research committee on comparative study of local government and politics of the International Political Science Association. He is the author of numerous professional articles and contributions to edited books, and has written and (co-)edited a number of books and major studies. These include *State and Local Government Reforms in France and Germany: Divergence and Convergence* (VS Verlag, 2006) and *Le gouvernement des villes: Une comparaison internationale* (Coll. Logiques politiques, 2007).

SILKE I. KEIL is a research assistant at the Department of Political Systems and Political Sociology at the University of Stuttgart. She works on comparative political culture research, especially the fields of social capital, participation, inequality and electoral research. She was also chief executive officer of the German partial study of the European Social Survey. As well as her contributions, which are published in certain edited volumes, she is also involved in other publications, for instance *Deutschlands Metamorphosen: Einheit und Differenzen in Europäischer Perspektive* (Nomos, in print) and *Society and Democracy in Europe* (together with Oscar W. Gabriel), which is a work in progress.

ERIC KERROUCHE is professor at the Institute d'Etudes Politiques de Bordeaux. He is one of the persons responsible for the LEA-CODE, a co-operative project between the University of Stuttgart and the IEP to analyse European democratic systems in the context of the enhancement of the European Union. His main research interests range from local politics, elected officials and territorial reforms to the methods of social science. He is the author of several contributions to journals and edited volumes, together with a number of published monographs, for example: *L'intercommunalité en France* (Montchrestien, 2008) and *Qui sont les députés français? Enquête sur des élites inconnues* (Presses de Sciences-Po, 2007).

KRISTINA FADEN-KUHNE is researcher at the Department of Political Systems and Political Sociology at the University of Stuttgart. Her research interests encompass political attitudes and behaviour, political psychology and methods in the field of empirical social research. Currently, she is working on her dissertation about the meaning of emotions for political judgments.

CHRISTOPHE PREMAT is French co-operation attaché at the Embassy of France in Sweden. Before that he was trainee at the European Parliament. He studies German-French relations, international co-operation, and the comparison of the French and German political systems. He is the author of *La pratique du référendum local en France et en Allemagne: Le moment référendaire dans la temporalité démocratique* (Editions Universitaires, 2010) and also a contributor to *Handwörterbuch der Deutsch-Französischen Beziehungen* (Nomos, 2009).

ORTWIN RENN serves as full professor and chair of environmental sociology and technology assessment at Stuttgart University. He directs the Interdisciplinary Research Unit for Risk Governance and Sustainable Technology Development at the University of Stuttgart and the non-profit making company DIALOGIK, a research institute for the investigation of communication and participation processes in environmental policy making. He is primarily interested in risk governance, political participation and technology assessment. He has published more than thirty books and 250 articles, most recently the monograph *Risk Governance* (Earthscan, 2008).

EMMANUEL RIVAT finished his masters in international relations at Sciences Po Bordeaux. He holds a doctorate in political sciences and works with Sciences Po Bourdeaux and the University of Amsterdam. His dissertation addresses the antinuclear movement in France and the Netherlands from the 1970s to the present. In line with this, he deals primarily with topics such as social movements, ecology and nuclear power, civil disobedience, non-violence. In his studies of international relations, he follows a constructivist perspective.

PIA-JOHANNA SCHWEITZER is a research assistant at the Department of Environmental Sociology and Technology Assessment at the University of Stuttgart. In 2008, she completed her dissertation on the subject of discursive risk regulation. She researches questions of risk governance and risk sociology. Her latest publication in collaboration with other researchers is *Precautionary Risk Appraisal and Management: An Orientation for Meeting the Precautionary Principle in the European Union* (Europäischer Hochschulverlag, 2009).

MATTHIAS STAUER was a student at the Department of Political Systems and Political Sociology at the University of Stuttgart (chair of Oscar W. Gabriel). He worked on participation, especially social capital.

ANGELIKA VETTER is researcher at the Department of Political Systems and Political Sociology at the University of Stuttgart. She teaches and writes on political sociology, comparative politics and empirical social science. Especially she is interested in the political system of Germany and the analysis of local politics. Among her (co-)edited books are: *Lokale Politikforschung heute* (VS Verlag für Sozialwissenschaften, 2008), *Erfolgsbedingungen lokaler Bürgerbeteiligung* (VS Verlag für Sozialwissenschaften, 2008) *and Local Politics: A Resource for Democracy in Western Europe? Local Autonomy, Local Integrative Capacity* (Lexington Books, 2007).

KERSTIN VÖLKL is a researcher at the Department of System Analysis and Comparative Politics at the University of Halle. She researches in the field of political attitudes, political participation and social participation, local politics, political sociology, and also parliamentarianism. Kerstin Völkl has published lots of contributions in national and international journals and edited volumes. One of her latest works is *Reine Landtagswahlen oder regionale Bundestagswahlen? Eine Untersuchung des Abstimmungsverhaltens bei Landtagswahlen 1990–2006* (Nomos, 2009).

preface

This book results from a longstanding scientific cooperation between the Institute of Political Studies (Bordeaux) and the Institute of Social Science (Stuttgart). Since 2005, the cooperation has been embedded in a Laboratoire Européen Associé 'Comparing Democratic Societies in Europe (LEA-CODE)' initiated and supported by CNRS with the aim to stimulate research cooperation between France and other European countries. As a part of the LEA-CODE network activities, some fields of joint research were established and several research meetings were held in Bordeaux and in Stuttgart during the preceding years. Comparative analysis of political participation in France and Germany was one of the selected research topics. Since 2009, a second large project on Political Representation in France and Germany supported by the French and German Research Associations (ANR, DFG) was initiated including not only researchers from Bordeaux and Stuttgart, but also from the Institute of Political Science, University of Halle Wittenberg and SciencePo Paris.

Strengthening institutionalised research cooperation between France and Germany is not the only rationale underlying this publication. If French German comparative research on politics in general is rather poorly developed, this applies particularly to the field of political behaviour and participation. Up to the beginning of the 1990s, this was mainly due to a lack of appropriate data. But since then, broad data on the French and German publics have been gathered in several comparative surveys such as Eurobarometer, European Values Survey, International Social Survey and European Social Survey and made available for secondary analyses.

Since comparative empirical analyses of the French and German publics are now feasible, having a closer look at the two countries has become attractive for several reasons. The first reason is simply curiosity. According to a widely held cliché, French publics are more prone to (illegal) political protest than most Europeans and – particularly – Germans, the latter are well known for casting their votes at the Election Day, belonging to voluntary associations or donating money for good causes. But how far do these clichés correspond to political reality? This question can only be answered by systematic cross-national and longitudinal empirical analysis.

The second reason is the increasing role of citizen participation in political life. As already stated by Gabriel Almond and Sidney Verba, but also by Daniel Bell some time ago, European publics have become increasingly active in political life during the last few decades. In particular, political protest and claims for a direct say in the making of authoritative political decisions seem to have become more widespread. Is there really a trend towards more and different forms of political participation in France and Germany and what are the underlying reasons for it, if it can be validated empirically?

Finally, as founding members of the European Community, France and Germany are included in a system of European multi-level governance for more than half a century. While the impact of Europeanisation on national public policymaking has been extensively investigated, it is far less clear whether being embedded in the European political system has also impacted on peoples' political attitudes and behaviours. Answering this question also requires systematic empirical research.

This book presents an overview over various aspects of political participation in France and Germany, ranging from electoral turnout to participation in legal and illegal protest activities. Beyond describing patterns and trends, the authors also examine the most important explanatory concepts in order to find out what makes the difference between political participation in the two countries under observation.

For the successful finishing of the project and this volume we want to express our gratitude towards a number of people and institutions. We would thank the Fritz-Thyssen-Stiftung (Cologne) for generous support of several meetings of the authors in France and Germany. Furthermore we are very grateful for the support of the translation work and language editing provided by IEP Bordeaux. In practice, that meant the turning of all chapters from diverse versions of Continental English into something which deserves to be called proper English. We would thank Susanne Kaliwe for her timely and efficient help in producing the final script. Finally, and most importantly, we are very grateful to all colleagues, who contributed to this project.

Stuttgart and Bordeaux, Spring 2012
Oscar W. Gabriel
Silke I. Keil
Eric Kerrouche

chapter one | political participation in france and germany – traditions, concepts, measurements, patterns and explanations

Oscar W. Gabriel

> Citizen participation is at the heart of democracy. Indeed, democracy is unthinkable without the ability of citizens to participate freely in the governing process.
>
> (Verba, Schlozman and Brady 1995)

Political participation and democracy

Almost all contributions to modern democratic theory agree with the view that democracy is a political regime based upon the idea of popular sovereignty. Accordingly, as all citizens are entitled to play an active role in political life, they should have free and equal access to the political process. Moreover, their political activity needs to have an impact on the decisions made by political leaders (Dahl 1971). Regardless of either the specific rules defining citizens' participatory rights, or the appropriate procedures for exerting political influence in various nations, participation as a universal civic right is an indispensable principle of a democratic regime.

The basic idea of a close interrelationship between democracy and participation is by no means novel. It was emphasised in the classical studies of Lipset (1981), Almond and Verba (1989), Cnudde and Neubauer (1969), Rokkan (1971) and Dahl (1971).[1] In his seminal analysis, Dahl (1971) characterised the transition from a closed hegemony to a polyarchy as a process of institutionalising participation (inclusiveness) on the one hand and competition (liberalisation) on the other. In his research on societal and political modernisation, Rokkan (1971) emphasised the solution of the crises of participation and distribution as final stages in the transition from pre-modern to modern, democratic structures. In his view, a fully-developed modern society is characterised by universal and equal citizen participation (democracy) as well as citizens' access to welfare state provisions. From a cultural perspective, Almond and Verba (1963) focused on the attitudinal prerequisites of a stable and well-performing democracy. 'Civic culture' as the cultural basis of a democratic regime entails a strong participatory component, thereby laying the ground for responsive government. One decade later, Daniel Bell (1973)

---

1. All quotations from Lipset refer to the revised edition of *Political Man* published in 1981; all those from Almond and Verba refer to the revised edition of *The Civic Culture* published in 1989.

pointed to the idea of political participation as the axial principle of the political life of the emerging post-industrial society. A related view on modernisation was made popular in political science by Ronald Inglehart's analysis of the transition from traditional (material) to modern (participatory and self-actualisation) values (Inglehart 1971; 1977; 1990; 1997; Inglehart and Welzel 2005).

Although attributing a key role to citizen participation in political life, the approaches outlined so far emphasise different aspects of civic engagement: *institutionally*, political participation is regarded as a basic civic right, anchored in the constitution and laws, which sets a framework for the political life of a modern democracy. In order to enable the citizenry to use these rights, appropriate procedures and organisations need to be implemented in any political system with, for example, free and equal elections, political parties, and pressure groups. As a *cultural value* and *norm*, political participation is part of the normative model of a good society and a good citizen. In order to have an impact on political life, these norms and values need to be internalised by at least some of the members of the political community. In short, political participation is a particular form of *political behaviour* used by citizens in order to exert influence in political life.

Irrespective of its prominent position in democratic theory, the concept of political participation is by no means clear and uncontested. Even when the behavioural component is focused on, these different empirical phenomena are matters for investigation. Initially, political participation was largely equated with casting one's vote to elect political leaders. Regarded from a normative and institutional perspective, the struggle for the institutionalisation of universal, equal and free elections was the main research topic, with behavioural analysis being more strongly interested in the use of the available participative rights. As we will show below, the scope of participative activities has considerably broadened in the post-World War II era. In spite of these changing patterns of political behaviour, normative theories of participation, as well as empirical analyses, were faced with new problems.

After a long-lasting struggle for a democratic franchise and related civic rights, most Western countries – and an increasing number of political regimes outside the Western hemisphere – have developed a more or less participatory style of citizen politics. But, even in modern times, the ideal of universal political participation seems to be more characteristic of formal constitutional arrangements than of peoples' real-life political behaviour. The question of how France and Germany can be situated in the world of participatory political communities makes up the substance of this book. In this introductory chapter, we will set the historical and theoretical framework for the comparative analysis of the forms, patterns, trends and determinants of citizen participation in France and Germany. We will start with an outline of the participatory traditions of the two respective countries. Thereafter, we will turn to the theoretical foundations of empirical research regarding the role of political participation in modern democracies and give an overview as to how the perception of political participation has changed over the years. This chapter will conclude with a short summary of the current position of the research into political participation in France and Germany, and an overview of the topics analysed in this book.

Political traditions and developments

When listing the nations characterised by strong traditions of civic participation, neither France nor Germany would spring immediately to mind. While countries such as Switzerland and the United States serve as textbook examples of strong participative traditions, this is surely not the case with the two nations under observation here. Despite their stable democracy characterisation in contemporary research (Lijphart 1999), the political heritage of France and Germany stands, by and large, for ideas that do not fit into the concept of an active civic community. Although universal male franchise was institutionalised in the two countries earlier than in most other contemporary democracies – 1848 in France and 1871 in Germany – this political achievement was not considered an important contribution to democratic development by most observers. A strong and paternalistic state, characterised by a powerful and efficient bureaucracy and a highly-fragmented political community, was long considered more important to political life in France and Germany than active participation by the community (see, for example, Almond 1956).

Such an assessment is underlined by a short review of the political development of France and Germany since the beginning of the nineteenth century. During the nineteenth century, as well as the early twentieth century, France and Germany were highly fragmented and polarised social and political communities. Socially and politically, the public of both nations was divided into various camps. The most important dividing lines ran between religious and secular, liberal (republican, constitutionalist) and monarchist, working class and bourgeois subcultures. The respective societal cleavages found their political expression in a corresponding system of political parties, interest groups and voluntary associations, which were 'pillarized' in the various political subcultures and thus did not promote the idea of a civic community (see, for example, Greiffenhagen and Greiffenhagen 1993; Holtmann 2005; Christadler 2005; Münch 2005). This entanglement of societal and political conflicts, encouraging antagonistic and disruptive rather than co-operative types of political participation, persisted into the first two decades after World War II, and traces can still be found in French and German political life today. Nevertheless, the impact on contemporary political systems is described as being stronger and more persistent in France than it is in Germany (Lane and Ersson 1987: 39–179; Lijphart 1999: 62–89, 171–184; Schain 2000: 237–252; Dalton 2000: 296–309; Gallagher *et al.* 2001: 171–270).

In both countries, political elites tried to overcome the existing political cleavages by 'inventing' the ideology of a strong, unified state and nation. In the French conception of statehood, a negative approach to interest pluralism is rooted in the antithesis between the *'volonté générale'* on the one hand, and the *'volonté de tous'* on the other. A similar view is implied in the German ideology of the state as the institution representing the common good ('community'), while particularistic and egoistic forces are incorporated in the notion of society.

These ideological notions became particularly powerful since they were closely bound up with an important achievement of modern government. In both countries, an effective and non-partisan bureaucracy – alongside a strong legalistic approach to political problem-solving – was institutionalised at an earlier stage of political development compared with many other nations. Seen in terms of participative politics, a strong bureaucratic tradition comes as a mixed blessing. On the one hand, well-performing bureaucratic institutions contribute to the efficient production and distribution of collective goods. On the other hand, the reduction of political problems to mere technical questions to be resolved by finding and applying the appropriate legal provisions, generates not only a division between (bureaucratic) experts and laymen (politicians, citizens), but also impedes the articulation and accommodation of different interests in favour of a seemingly pre-given optimal solution. On the basis of an alliance of a bureaucratic-legalistic approach to politics with an anti-pluralist ideology, active citizen involvement in political life could easily be discouraged, with citizens being denied the political competence required to play such a role and the common man's demands criticised as expressing merely egoistic interests that interfere with the common good. Again, these characteristics of political life have persisted for a long time and have left their traces in the behaviour of the post-war publics of both countries. Co-operative political activities transcending the boundaries of the existing subcultures were largely missing; political participation other than voting in elections was limited; and having a stake in politics was understood as being a matter for the elite rather than for citizens (Schild and Uterwedde 2006:19–34; Greiffenhagen and Greiffenhagen 1993: 67–85; Holtmann 2005).

While the systemic attributes described above seem to be common to France and Germany, specific national traditions that prevent civic engagement also exist in both countries. As regards France, political traditions seem to have had an ambiguous impact on actual civic involvement in politics. Let us start with the positive aspects: France was the first state in modern Europe where a broad popular movement overthrew the absolutist monarchy. The democratic creed of *'liberté, égalité et fraternité'* was the leading principle of the French Revolution, which, in its early stages, could be regarded as embodying the European enlightenment. However, the French Revolution did not evolve towards a modern, participatory democracy. The ideas of the French Revolution were seldom incorporated into regime structures and political practice, and were often interrupted by authoritarian backlashes. The regime installed by Napoleon by the end of the eighteenth century fitted into the absolutist legacy of strong political and administrative centralisation. Moreover, centralisation accounts for a lack of local and regional autonomy, both of which are conditions for widespread, meaningful social and political participation (Hoffmann-Martinot 2003). Unless citizens perceive political engagement as salient and effective in the shaping of public affairs, they are unlikely to become politically active. Such a perception of the political circumstances is highly probable if the competencies of local and regional governments are as weak as they have long been in France.

A low level of civic involvement also stems from the weakness of the system of interest intermediation in France. For various reasons, voluntary associations, pressure groups and political parties do not play an important role as points of access to the political system. Until now, the French party system has served as an instrument of the power-seeking aspirations of the political elite rather than as an effective vehicle of citizen participation. As a consequence, party-related and social participation have so far remained low in France, particularly in comparison with neighbouring countries (Bréchon 2006: 65–78; Schain 2008: 220–234).

In some respects, the German political tradition seems to be more conducive to active civic involvement. This assumption does not so much refer to its national political system, but to local politics, with local autonomy going back to medieval times, and being strongly rooted in the German political tradition. Earlier than in most other European nations, and quite unlike France, the German *Reichsstädte* developed a rudimentary system of civic self-government. The large merchant cities united in the *Die Hanse* Federation were the most prominent examples of local self-administration. In 1807, following defeat in the Napoleonic wars, large-scale administrative reform, particularly concerning local government, was implemented in Prussia. From that date on, Prussian cities commanded a broad array of competencies in the provision, regulation and administration of local services. Citizens were entitled to take part in local policy making, at least as regards electing their representatives. More liberal community charters were enacted somewhat later in the south German states of Bade, Württemberg and Bavaria. However, the prevailing concept of self-government as a part of society – which was thought to be strictly separated from the state – prevented a spillover of participatory ideas from local to national politics. Moreover, local self-government in Prussia suffered from a strong backlash in the 1830s. The broad competencies of the city council were severely and successively restricted, and the municipal council was not elected according to democratic principles, but on the basis of a three-class ballot. As a consequence, the strong participatory potential of the German system of local self-government was undermined by the prevailing ideology, as well as by the institutional setting of imperial Germany (Gunlicks 1986).

Throughout the nineteenth and the early twentieth century, democratisation in Germany did not prove successful: the liberal revolution of 1848 failed. Despite the constitutional provision of universal male franchise and a certain degree of civic freedom, the Prussian Empire was an authoritarian regime, not a liberal one. After military defeat in the First World War, the first experiment with a truly democratic constitution ended up with the disaster of the Nazi regime. The wide-ranging civic rights and instruments of direct democracy granted by the Weimar Constitution did not evolve as parts of a strong democracy, but were abused in order to overthrow democratic government.

Regardless of Germany's long-standing, strong decentralist tradition, civic culture and a corresponding pattern of behaviour did not develop before the foundation of the Federal Republic. Even then, attempts to avoid confrontation once more with the shortcomings of the first democratic constitution led to the inauguration of a strictly representative-type government, albeit authoritarian traditions remained strong in the early stages of the Federal Republic. When the participatory revolution began to spread throughout the modern world, neither France nor

Germany was well equipped to meet the new challenges.

The era following the World War II was considered as a participatory revolution by many observers (Almond and Verba 1989). In its first stage of development, an increasing number of citizens made use of their legally stated right to take an active role in political life, e.g. by casting their votes on Election Day, or joining organisations and actively working within them. Subsequently, legal and non-legal protest and other types of collective political action were used as means of political influence by small but active minorities, and soon they became part of the political action repertoire of a broader public. The so-called 'unconventional forms' of political participation raised the question as to whether elements of direct democracy, such as initiatives and referendums, should be strengthened as complements to the participatory institutions of representative democracy. Meanwhile, direct popular participation had become widespread, at least at the local level. Finally, the potential of the digital revolution cannot be overlooked, since it offers unprecedented possibilities for bridging the gap between the governed and the governors. Nowadays, formalised civic rights concerning participation in political life, as well as the informal opportunities to play an active role in the decision-making process, are far more widespread throughout the world than ever before (see Chapter Ten). This applies to France and Germany as well as to other modern societies (Almond and Verba 1989; Barnes and Kaase 1979; Norris 2002; LeDuc 2002; Cain *et al.* 2003).

The concept of political participation and the changing view on citizen involvement in political life

Mainly due to limitations of data, the first empirical studies of political participation conducted in the 1930s equated political participation with voting in elections (Asher *et al.* 1984: 27–30). A slightly broader approach was chosen in the early studies, using survey data as the basis of analysis. Although Lazarsfeld *et al.* (1944) and Campbell *et al.* (1954; 1960) were mainly interested in the explanation of party preference, they devoted some sections of their books to the question why some people went to the polls at the Election Day, while others abstained from voting. The concept of political participation underlying the empirical analyses conducted by them also encompassed activities 'surrounding' electoral participation, such as political communication, campaigning and party activity. However, a clear concept of political participation was lacking. Rather than looking for a common denominator for all activities under observation, the researchers simply listed the forms of behaviour they were interested in (Campbell *et al.* 1960: 90–115; Lipset 1981: 184).

In this first stage of empirical research on political participation, various indicators – if multiple indicators were used at all – were seen as building a continuum of activities based on the necessary 'amount' of initiative and effort required to become involved. In drawing a parallel with the gladiatorial spectacles in ancient Rome, Lester W. Milbrath (1965) grouped the public of modern democracies into three different segments: the apathetic, who remained outside political life or restricted themselves, at best, to reading about politics in newspapers; the spectators, who followed the political game in a passive way (discussing, wearing stickers, etc.); and the gladiators, the active players in the political game, participating in electoral campaigns, working in political parties and running for political office. In most instances, this assumption of a one-dimensional structure of participatory activities was not empirically tested. This view of political participation prevailed during the 1950s and 1960s, but was increasingly challenged by changing patterns of citizen behaviour in the modern world. In their important studies on political participation in the United States (Verba and Nie 1972) and six additional, strongly varying political nations (Verba *et al.* 1978), a research group under Sidney Verba proposed a new vision of political participation. The group introduced an explicitly nominal definition of the phenomenon by stating: 'Political participation refers to those legal activities by private citizens that are more or less directly aimed at influencing the selection of government personnel and/or the actions they take' (Verba and Nie 1972: 2).

On the basis of this definition, the Verba group rejected the idea of political participation as a one-dimensional phenomenon. For them, there is no single way of influencing politics; instead, people choose varying forms of access to the political process, depending on their specific goals. In their efforts to identify different systems of political participation, the researchers first specified the criteria involved by distinguishing between the various systems of participation. In line with traditional approaches, they used the 'effort' required to become politically active as the first criterion. Additionally, they wanted to discover whether participation was primarily aimed at conveying information to the elites or exerting pressure on them; whether the outcomes of participation were merely relevant to participants and/or their group or to society as a whole; and the extent of any conflict involved in these respective activities. By combining three of these four criteria,[2] they differentiated between four systems of political participation, each characterised by its own distinct combination of the characteristics mentioned above. Two of these systems – participation in national and local elections, and campaign activities – were already known from prior research, but were now regarded as qualitatively different systems of political participation. Attending political meetings and trying to persuade others how to vote were considered as typical campaign activities. The other two – co-operative activity and citizen-initiated contacts – were characterised as non-electoral; they took into account forms of access to the political process that had evolved outside party politics and elections. Co-operative activities, such as participating actively in the work of local single-issue groups, were solidly anchored in the American political system, and so were citizen-initiated contacts with local or national representatives. The characteristics of these modes of political participation are shown in Table1.1.

---

2. The characteristic of 'pressure' versus information was dropped from the final classification.

Table 1.1: Types of political participation according to Verba and Nie (1972)

	Electoral activity		Non-electoral activity	
	Voting	Campaign activity	Co-operative activity	Citizen-initiated contacts
Conflict dimension	Conflictual	Conflictual	Usually non-conflictual	Non-conflictual
Scope of outcome	Collective outcome	Collective outcome	Collective outcome	(Collective or) particularised outcome
Initiative required	Little	Some	Some or a lot	A lot

Source: Verba/Nie 1972: 54; parentheses inserted by the author.

The Verba group went further than most previous empirical analyses by empirically testing the validity of the assumptions underlying the classification of systems of political participation. The result of factor analyses conducted for this purpose largely supported their *a priori* – theoretical – classification. The only modification referred to non-electoral activity: here, the main difference was whether the activity aimed to resolve a societal problem or a personal concern of participants, but not whether citizens themselves initiated contacts with the public. As a result of empirical validation, non-electoral activities were regrouped in the following way: communal activity was seen as one sort of non-electoral participation, aimed at achieving collective goods; particularised contacting was the other form, directed at obtaining private goods by political contacting (Verba and Nie 1972: 73, Tables 4–6). This revised classification served as the basis of a description and explanation of four types of participants. In addition to specialists of one of the four types mentioned above, two further groups existed: the completely inactive and the fully active (Verba and Nie 1972: 73–93).

The research conducted by the Verba group stimulated a new look at political participation by pointing to the existing possibility of exerting political influence beyond purely electoral activities. The problem with the concept of political participation, however, was the exclusion of non-legal forms of exerting political influence. This was surely justified as regards violent political actions, but was not appropriate for other types of political activity that had become increasingly important in political life, e.g., forms of peaceful protest, as well as certain kinds of civil disobedience.

It cannot be said that protest activities as such were completely unknown; indeed, ever since the nineteenth century they had been used in many countries as a way of exerting political influence. In the 1960s, however, protest activity became a more widespread form of political behaviour and the Civil Rights Movement in the United States was to become a catalyst for a worldwide protest movement. This was followed, in turn, by the Students' Movement in Europe, the United States and Japan and other so-called New Social Movements. Initially, participation research lagged behind this very real political development, not according sufficient attention to all these new forms of political behaviour. The work of the Political Action Group,[3] in its truly innovative research approach, focused on describing and explaining these new, unconventional or elite-challenging forms of political participation and finding out how they would fit into the general patterns of political activity (Barnes and Kaase 1979; Inglehart 1983; Jennings and van Deth 1990).

Initially, the broadening of the research agenda required a new definition and a different concept of political participation. Compared to the previously cited definition proposed by Verba and Nie (1972: 2), the new concept by the Political Action researchers entailed only a slight modification, omitting the word 'legal' in the description of the relevant activities. Whereas the Verba group excluded 'non-legal activities', the Political Action researchers used the concept of legality as a criterion in its classification of different forms of political participation. In a later contribution, Kaase defined political participation as a class of political activities encompassing all kinds of voluntary activities aimed at influencing political decisions made at various levels in the political system (Kaase 1997: 160; similarly, Verba *et al.* 1995: 38–9).

Now it was a matter of how traditional (conventional) and new (unconventional) forms of political participation could be differentiated from each other. In the conceptual work of the Political Action researchers, three criteria were used – whether or not the respective activities are:

- institutionalised;
- legal; and
- legitimate.

Using these criteria, Kaase and Marsh (1979a: 42–45) equated conventional participation with those legal activities that were considered as highly legitimate and referred to institutionalised elements of the political process. On the other hand, activities not conforming to the legal or behavioural norms regulating the political process were considered unconventional forms of political participation. In a somewhat more systematic way, we can attribute the characteristics of being institutionalised, legal and legitimate to conventional activities, while unconventional activities are non-institutionalised, legal or non-legal and not considered as legitimate by the greater part of the public.

The Political Action researchers, like the Verba group, demonstrated that the differentiation between conventional and unconventional activities was not simply an analytical one, but could be validated empirically (Marsh and Kaase 1979). Regarding conventional activities, the concepts of the two research groups overlapped considerably. The campaign-related activities (persuading, attending

---

3. Barnes *et al.* (1979) developed a new concept, which was present in eight different countries that they empirically tested.

meetings) and co-operative activities (working in local problem solving groups) analysed by Verba *et al.* were also included in the Political Action study, but were considered as being located on a single dimension. On the other hand, unconventional activities included actions such as petitioning and demonstrating, as well as illegal ones like joining wildcat strikes and blocking traffic. The Political Action project, unlike the work of the Verba group, did not take voting in elections into account, because it did not fit into the general structure of behaviour. Finally, the typology of political action proposed by Kaase and Marsh (1979b) was re-proposed on the same idea as that developed by Verba and Nie: some people decide to stay out of political life (inactive), while others use the complete repertoire of political activities in order for their voices to be heard (full activists). Other groups were thought to specialise in a more or less limited set of actions: the conformists, who rely on conventional means alone; the protestors, who restrict themselves to unconventional activities; and the reformists, who combine conventional and legally unconventional means of influence.

This is not the place to go into a detailed discussion of the merits and shortcomings of the existing concepts. Irrespective of some need for clarification and more theoretical rigour, the work of the Verba group and the Political Action group should be greatly appreciated for their research breakthroughs in several areas:

1. Political participation as a particular type of social activity was now clearly defined by the following characteristics: it was understood as an (observable) action of private citizens (neither carried out by professional or elected political officials, nor simply an attitude), referring to political objects (and not to private or social concerns), carried out voluntarily, aimed at influencing political decisions (and not merely communicating with others, or supporting political leaders or organisations).
2. The various forms of political activities were differentiated from each other on the basis of theoretical criteria, subsequently validated by empirical analyses.

Empirical research conducted since then has focused on modifying, differentiating and broadening the concepts used in empirical analyses of political participation. The main modifications of the concept are as follows:

1. Additional activities, particularly consumerism, engagement in the New Politics movement and chequebook activities, were included in research on participation, and a stronger emphasis was placed on the interrelationship of social and political participation, and vice versa. In some contributions, the lines between activities formerly considered as political or social were blurred.
2. The systems of conventional and, particularly, unconventional political participation, were differentiated further. In the first instance, voting, contacting, co-operative and campaign activities turned out to be the most important sub-dimensions of conventional participation. Political protest was seen as composed of two different sets of activities: legal and illegal.

Sometimes, the use of violent action was analysed as an additional strategy for influencing politics.

3. Over time, the boundaries between conventional and unconventional activities have become increasingly fluid. Some forms of political behaviour, initially not considered as legitimate, have evolved into normal forms of political participation. In more recent studies, the most important division is between party-related and single-purpose activities (see, for example, van Deth 2001; 2008; van Deth *et al.* 2007; Gabriel 2002; 2004; Gabriel and Völkl 2008; Parry, Moyser and Day 1992; Pattie *et al.* 2004; Uehlinger 1989; Zukin *et al.* 2006).

Research strategies and explanations: why do people become involved in politics?

As discussed in the preceding section, the forms of political participation have changed considerably over time. Not only has citizen participation in politics become more widespread in the democratic world, but the range of political action has widened. Although casting one's vote at elections is still the most widely-used form of political participation, several alternative – or complementary – modes of exerting political influence have become 'normal' activities in political life. Explaining these changes in political behaviour has been one of the crucial aims of theories of societal and political modernisation, but testing such theories is no easy task. However, we will not go into this question more deeply since our main focus is on the description and explanation of the differences and similarities of citizen participation in two modern societies, France and Germany (although in studying the two countries, some theoretical concepts are more relevant for explanatory purposes than others). Nevertheless, we provide a short overview of the relevant approaches used in explaining political participation.

Explanatory variables → Level of analysis↓	Institutional	Socio-economic	Psycho-cultural
Micro (individual)	Institutional affiliation	Resources, status, networks	Socialisation, motivation, derivation
Macro (system)	Neo-institutionalism, political modernisation	Social structure, societal modernisation	Political culture, value change, social capital

Figure 1.1: Approaches to the explanation of political participation

Source: Author's presentation

The first decision to be made in developing research design concerns the level of analysis. In this respect, we find three different strategies in political participation research:

1. macro-level analyses, focusing on characteristics of the respective societies and political systems;
2. micro-level analyses, aimed at exploring the individual antecedents of individual political participation; and
3. multilevel analysis, situating individual characteristics within a larger societal and institutional context (Norris 2002).

In the observation of just two cases – France and Germany – macro-level approaches can only be applied when analysing sub-national units such as regions or local communities (see Chapters Four and Six). The same applies to multilevel analyses: when nations are the units of analysis, the institutional setting and the social structures of the respective communities are the most important explanatory variables. Irrespective of the rich explanatory potential of macro-level and multilevel analysis, micro-level research – by choosing the individual instead of the polity or the society as its unit of observation and analysis – is clearly more common, and the only appropriate strategy to be applied in most of the subsequent chapters.

Most contributions to this book focus on the micro-level, i.e., groups of individuals as the unit of observation, although a few have chosen a macro-level strategy of research. But, irrespective of the level of analysis, the general explanatory strategy remains the same: empirical research aims to examine empirical hypotheses ('laws') stating a (causal) relationship between at least two variables describing particular states of political reality. Additionally, the variables representing the characteristics under scrutiny need to be suitable for direct or indirect observation. The state or behaviour to be explained is the dependent variable (y), while the antecedents of the respective state or behaviour are the independent variables (x1, x2 ... xn). A causal relation between y and x can only be assumed if:

1. the two variables correlate with each other;
2. x precedes y in the course of time; and
3. the relationship between y and x persists, even if third variables $z_1, z_2 ... z_n$ have been controlled.

In this book, we want to explain different forms of individual and/or collective participation in France and Germany. At the micro-level, the type and degree of individual political participation constitute the dependent variable; at the macro-level, the distribution of individual participation in French and German local communities is considered the dependent variable. These individual or societal characteristics will not only be described and compared but, moreover, explained by various antecedents.

Subsequently, we will give a short overview of some approaches to the explanation of political participation. As in other fields of political analysis, three sets of variables are regarded as relevant to the explanation of political participation: political, socio-economic, and personality or cultural factors (Norris 2002). Sometimes, they are derived from general theories of political behaviour, but most often from middle-range theories of political participation. We will commence our outline of explanatory theories with the most important general theories of political behaviour, before considering the relevant middle-range approaches.

General theories: rational choice and social psychology

The first general theory of political behaviour was presented by Anthony Downs (1957). Originally, the focus of *An Economic Theory of Democracy*, or the 'rational choice approach', was on the explanation of party choice in two-party and multiparty systems. The question of whether and why people would be willing to take part in elections at all was a crucial topic of rational choice theory from the very beginning. Over the last few years, this approach has become increasingly popular among political scientists, being applied not only to the explanation of voting participation (Riker and Ordeshook 1973), but also to activity in pressure groups (Olson 1969), as well as to legal and illegal protest activities (Muller 1979).

The explanatory concept of rational choice models is very parsimonious in its use of a restricted set of assumptions and related variables. The decision of an individual to become politically active instead of staying outside of politics can be derived from a cost-benefit calculation. The basic assumptions of the model are as follows:

1. Individuals have fixed political preferences.
2. They are able to establish an ordering of their preferences according to the expected benefits attributed to them.
3. When confronted with the necessity to decide among alternative political options, they always choose the alternative ranking highest on the preference order.

In deciding on the choice of political alternatives, individuals have not only to take into account the payoff or benefit provided, but also the costs resulting from the activities needed to achieve a desired goal. Only if the marginal benefits of an action exceed the marginal costs, will the respective action be carried out, otherwise people remain passive. The first attempt to apply the theory of rational choice to political participation was conducted in the context of elections (Downs 1957). A rational political actor will cast his vote on election day if he expects that the electoral success of party A will bring him a larger material benefit than the success of competing party B. However, the rational actor is well aware of the fact that his vote – as one of millions of other votes – will scarcely have a decisive influence on the electoral outcome. Regardless of the benefit attributed to an electoral victory of the preferred political party, going to the polls becomes irrational if minimal costs of voting, such as acquiring political information, going to the polling station and so on, are incurred. Hence, rational citizens will normally abstain from voting. As shown by Olson (1969), not only is passivity a typical characteristic of rational voters, but it also turns out to be the most rational of all forms of collective behaviour, particularly in the case of large groups.

We do not need to conduct a complicated empirical analysis in order to see that the assumptions of rational choice theory do not correspond to political reality. Contrary to the predictions of the theory, most people do cast their votes in elections. Some engage actively in trade unions and political parties, and certain protest activities mobilise large numbers of citizens. In order to resolve this voting paradox, rational choice theorists proposed including additional – exogenous – variables in their explanatory models: feelings of citizen duty and the long-term benefit of living in a democracy (Downs 1957: 261–76; Frohlich and Oppenheimer 1978: 97–116).

Irrespective of its parsimony and elegance, rational choice theory falls short of providing an empirically-valid explanation of political participation. We are not going so far as to say that cost-benefit calculations are completely irrelevant to citizens' decisions to become active in politics, but they can be considered as only part, and not the whole, of the story. In spite of its shortcomings, the rational choice approach is still sometimes used as background theory in the interpretation of empirical data. Moreover, certain scholars have proposed modified variants of the rational choice approach, which come closer to political reality. One of the most interesting general theories of social behaviour derived, at least in part, from rational choice theory is the 'theory of planned behaviour' developed by Icek Ajzen and Martin Fishbein (Ajzen and Fishbein 1980; Ajzen 1988). This theory also offers a very parsimonious explanatory model, differentiating between endogenous and exogenous determinants of political choices. Accordingly, only four sets of variables are needed in explaining whether and why people chose particular forms of social action rather than others (or, indeed, no action at all). Substantially, some of these variables come very close to the constructs used by Downs. The first set of variables – 'attitude toward behaviour' – refers to 'the individual's positive or negative evaluation of performing the particular behaviour of interest' (Ajzen 1988: 117). Additionally, the choice of a particular form of behaviour is assumed to depend on subjective norms or on a 'person's perception of social pressure to perform or not to perform the behaviour under consideration' (Ajzen 1988: 117). A first assumption regarding the determinants of people's behavioural choices can then be stated as follows: 'Generally speaking, people intend to perform a behaviour when they evaluate it positively and when they believe that important others think they should perform it' (Ajzen 1988: 117).

According to Ajzen and Fishbein, positive evaluations of a particular form of behaviour, and the subjective norms supporting it, do not directly lead to political behaviour, but to behavioural intentions. As is the case in our daily lives, political intentions do not always lead to corresponding form of behaviour. As Ajzen admits, factors such as information, skills and abilities, emotions and compulsions, opportunities and dependence on others all play an important role in bringing about particular activities (Ajzen 1988: 127–32). In order to take these factors into account, Ajzen and Fishbein included in their model an additional variable that they considered influenced both behavioural intention and behaviour – the degree of perceived behavioural control. This type of attitude concerns 'the perceived ease or difficulty of performing the behaviour and is assumed to reflect past experience as well as anticipated impediments and obstacles' (Ajzen 1988: 132).

Although the theory of planned behaviour seems to be a convincing approach in explaining many types of political action (see, for example, Kühnel 2001; Lüdemann 2001; Muller 1979; Opp 1984), its application in empirical research is confronted with at least one fundamental difficulty. In research practice, political participation cannot normally be measured directly, but only by asking for behavioural intentions or self-reports of past behaviour. In such a situation, empirical analysis needs to be restricted to the explanation of intentions to participate, or to past behaviour. The first alternative does not allow a test of the complete model, while the second is not elegant from a logical point of view, since the second principle of causality described above is violated: thus neither of these two solutions is convincing.

Nonetheless, compared to other explanatory approaches, the theory of planned behaviour does offer an attractive alternative, since it is a parsimonious, straightforward, general theory of human action. From a political science perspective, this theory also presents another advantage; having only rarely been applied in the explanation of political participation, it can, therefore, be regarded as an innovative approach in this field of research.

Middle-range theories

Although the approaches presented so far have been employed in the empirical analysis of political participation on couple of occasions, most empirical research is less ambitious regarding its theoretical foundations and starts from middle-range theories. These are well established in the tradition of behavioural theory and simply assume that social and political environment characteristics, as well as personality factors, have an impact on political participation. Generally, no effort is made to specify clearly the type and degree of interrelationship between the relevant variables (Milbrath and Goel 1977). Depending on the emphasis accorded to particular components of the respective models, middle-range approaches can be classified into a three-fold division: political, socio-economic and psychological.

The analyses of the research group of Sidney Verba (Verba and Nie 1972; Verba *et al.* 1978; Verba *et al.* 1995), and those of the Political Action researchers (Barnes and Kaase 1979), are good examples of middle-range theories. Since the work of the Verba group is particularly innovative and inclusive, theoretically ambitious and more consistent in linking theory and empirical analysis together, we will use it in order to present the logic of micro-level behaviourism middle-range approaches. Interesting ideas found in other research will subsequently be added to the assumptions and variables of the Verba group.

Resources and institutions: Verba, Nie and Kim

In three important studies of political participation, Verba and his associates presented straightforward explanatory models that included the most important variables already used in empirical research; they also incorporated additional innovative ideas. The first of their books dealing with political participation in the United States (Verba and Nie 1972), refined some ideas outlined in two articles published three years earlier (Nie *et al.* 1969a; Nie *et al.* 1969b). Here, participation was largely regarded as a result of people's social position and related resources. Socio-economic status (SES) was assumed as a direct antecedent of the type and level of political participation (voting, campaigning, communal activity and particularised contacting). Moreover, the researchers supposed a path travelling from SES via civic orientations to political participation. Three of the four different modes of political participation were convincingly explained by their model; particularised contacting was the exception, with only a modest amount of variance in participation attributable to civic orientations and SES. Moreover, the influence of SES mediated by civic orientations was slightly stronger than direct influence in the cases of voting, campaigning and participation in communal activities (Verba and Nie 1972: 125–35). In addition to the Standard Model, variables such as the position in the life cycle, party alignments and so on were examined as antecedents of political participation. Nevertheless, the SES-Standard Model remained the theoretical core of the study of *Participation in America: political democracy and social equality*.

The basic idea of the book was re-adopted in the comparative analysis of political participation in seven nations published by Verba, Nie and Kim (1978) a few years later. In this study, covering a set of nations strongly differing in the political, cultural and socio-economic settings, the authors emphasised citizens' institutional affiliations as mediators between social status on the one hand, and political participation on the other. Socio-economic factors were summarised in a variable called 'socio-economic resource level' (SERL), encompassing material (income) as well as intellectual resources (education). In line with broad empirical evidence, the authors supposed a positive effect of the SERL on political participation.

Neither this assumption, nor its support by the empirical analysis conducted by the Verba group, is particularly spectacular and innovative. However, they did not terminate their analysis by simply stating that the better-off are more inclined to become politically active. Going a step further, they reasoned about the meaning of such a result for a democratic polity and possible solutions to the respective problem. Evidently, high levels of political participation among the resourceful segments of the public and a correspondingly low level among the 'have-nots', challenge the democratic value of equality and the respective political norms. Hence, it should be asked how social bias among the activist groups of citizens could be successfully neutralised in a democracy.

According to Verba, Nie and Kim, political institutions should be designed so as to contribute to the mobilisation of the hitherto inactive parts of the citizenry. Since political institutions can play a mobilising role only when people are affiliated to them in some way, the authors used the concept of 'institutional affiliation' in order to find out how institutions might affect the impact of socio-economic resources on political participation. This characteristic was operationalised by an index built on the basis of party identification and politicised membership in voluntary associations.

Verba, Nie and Kim did not assume that institutional affiliation would always have an impact on the above-mentioned relationship. Even if an effect of this type did exist, it would not always contribute to reducing political inequality. Accordingly, weak institutions would leave the relationship of SERL to political participation unaffected, or only change the level of participation in the relevant status groups without changing the basic relationship of these variables (weak effects or additive effects). On the other hand, dominant institutions would completely neutralise the impact of SERL on political participation: all institutionally affiliated people would participate strongly, while all the unaffiliated would remain largely passive. Additionally, some hybrid effects of institutions were described: in mobilising institutional systems, all affiliated segments of the public would strongly participate, irrespective of their SERL, while the impact of SERL on participation would remain unchanged or even strengthened among the unaffiliated. In restrictive institutional systems, all the unaffiliated would be passive, but the strong influence of status on participation would continue to exist or even increase among the organisationally affiliated.

The empirical test of these models did not lead to clear results, since the effect of the institutional variable varied from one nation to another, and also according to the various forms of participation (see, for details, Verba *et al.* 1978: 63–142). Moreover, Verba, Nie and Kim had not stated clear expectations about the conditions under which institutions would impinge in a certain way on the relationship of resources to participation. It may be that the interesting approach developed by the Verba group needs to be elaborated further, by differentiating between types of involvement and types of organisation with regard to their equalising effects. At first glance, at least, it does not seem reasonable that being active in a football club has the same political impact as being an active member of either a union or a religious group with a stake in political life.

Resources, socialisation, and mobilisation: Verba, Schlozman and Brady

Several years later, the Verba group published another important contribution to the explanation of political participation (Verba *et al.* 1995). In some respects, they used parts of their previously developed models, but they also added some new components and developed some alternative operationalisation of existing constructs. The starting point of their analysis of political participation was as follows:

> In thinking about *why some people are active* while others are not, we find it helpful to invert the usual question and to ask instead why people do not take part in politics. Three answers immediately suggest themselves: *because they can't; because they don't want to or because nobody asked*
>
> (Verba *et al.* 1995: 15, italics in original).

Three classes of variables are included in this hypothesis: resources, motivation and mobilising networks. Of these variables, only motivation was not directly entailed by the older explanatory model, but it was included in the work on participation in the United States. These variables, moreover, have played an important role in the explanation of political participation from the very beginnings of research. The attitudes (motivations) considered as most relevant to political participation include the level of political information or knowledge, political interest and subjective political competence (Nie et al. 1969a; Nie et al.1969b; Milbrath and Goel 1977; Verba and Nie 1972). Additionally, some other – hitherto neglected – attitudinal variables have proven to play a role as determinants of political participation, particularly participative norms (Pattie et al. 2004; Gabriel 2004; Armingeon 2007), support of democratic principles (Sniderman 1975) and postmaterialist values (Inglehart 1979; 1983). On the other hand, assumptions regarding a negative impact of political distrust and discontent on political participation were not confirmed in empirical analyses (Finifter 1970; Muller 1979; Muller and Williams 1980; Muller et al. 1982).

The modifications to the approach of Verba, Nie, and Kim by Verba, Schlozman and Brady did not so much refer to the general explanatory strategy, as to the scope and meaning of the relevant variables. Regarding resources, they added such new components as free time and civic skills, but these variables did not have a major impact on political participation when other factors remained constant. The role of mobilising networks as facilitators of political participation had already been demonstrated in the analysis of Nie, Powell and Prewitt (1969a; 1969b), but social networks became more prominent as predictors of political participation during the last two decades when research on social capital flourished (see the next section).

The model of Verba, Schlozman and Brady fulfils several important functions in research on political participation. In the first instance, it provides a good summary of the micro-level explanatory factors of political participation used in empirical research so far. With few exceptions, later research has not added substantially different theoretical constructs to the explanation of political participation (see, for example, Armingeon 2007; Gabriel and Völkl 2008; Norris 2002; Pattie et al. 2004; Zukin et al. 2006). Moreover, instead of simply including a more extended or different set of variables in their models, the authors elaborated the theoretical arguments concerning the reasons why some people become active in politics, while others do not. From the viewpoint of the individual, access to resources, the existence of motivation and inclusion in mobilising networks are the most important incentives for political participation. Disposing of these factors encourages political activity; lack of them prevents participation.

Mobilising agencies: elites and networks

In one respect, the model of Verba, Schlozman and Brady remained incomplete. Although they included the mobilising activities of an individual's environment in their considerations and found empirical evidence for the contribution of mobilising agencies in encouraging political participation, they dealt with only one part of the whole story. If an individual faces a decision about whether or not to participate in politics, he will probably not only be mobilised by friends, but also by members of the organisations to which he belongs or by workplace colleagues. Politicians themselves may play an important role in shaping the kind and level of political participation: this is evident as regards campaigning and protesting, which are often directly or indirectly induced by party elites or other types of political entrepreneurs (Rosenstone and Hansen 1993). Moreover, certain local elites may develop a particular style of action and a political climate that encourages/discourages people disposed to engage in local politics. An analysis of the way elites and citizens interact in the process of politicisation and mobilisation would surely constitute essential progress in research on political participation, but currently we are facing a serious gap in the research. The elites' attitudes and behaviour, particularly at local level, may shape the degree and pattern of political participation considerably. Whether or not mayors and councillors consider political participation favourably is not only relevant to the participatory climate in the respective communities, but also plays a decisive role as to whether the available tools of citizen involvement in the political process – citizen assemblies, agenda 21 processes, round tables, future workshops, civic juries and so on – will be used in practice (for details, see Chapter Ten). The way elites provide and handle participatory tools of this kind may eventually play at least the same role in mobilising local political engagement, as do the individual characteristics of participants. However, analysis of the interplay of elites and citizens in the political mobilisation process requires much more complex research designs than mass surveys that, at present, represent the most important data source for studies of political participation.

Social capital, civic engagement and political participation

In 1993, Robert Putnam published a study on 'making democracy work', which has had a strong and lasting impact on research into political participation. According to Putnam, social capital – which he defined as 'such features of social organisation as trust, norms, and networks' (Putnam 1993: 167) – is an important determinant of a large set of civic attitudes and forms of behaviour, including that of political participation. In rather pessimistic tones, he blames the long-term decline of social capital in the United States for having produced a political demobilisation of the American public and of citizens elsewhere in the world (Putnam 2000: 31–47; Putnam 2001).

Although the thesis concerning the decline of social capital in modern societies was criticised as being overly pessimistic and poorly supported by empirical evidence gathered outside the United States, the idea of social capital was broadly accepted by scholars as an important contribution to research on various kinds of political attitudes and behaviour. The assumption of a strong impact of membership and activity in voluntary associations as a determinant of political participation had already been supported by some studies conducted in the 1950s and 1960s (see, for example, Nie *et al.* 1969a; 1969b; Verba and Nie 1972), but the concept of social capital provided a sounder theoretical basis for the interpretation of the respective results. Allied to their role in instilling civic virtues and co-operative behaviour, voluntary associations encourage their members to become active in other domains of civic life as well. Beyond the well-known studies of the role of social engagement as an antecedent of political participation, the concept of social capital stimulated additional research into the determinants of political participation. Analyses of the joint impact of social engagement, social trust and civic norms on political participation led to the conclusion that trust and norms do not substantially contribute to explaining political participation, once social engagement has been controlled for (Armingeon 2007: 373–6; Gabriel *et al.* 2002: 159–74; somewhat differently, Dalton 2008; Gabriel 2004; Roller and Rudi 2008). As some other studies conceptually linked to research on social capital found, social engagement impacts differently on political participation, depending on the type of organisation and the kind of behaviour under observation. However, the respective studies did not lead to general insights into the contribution made by these organisational characteristics concerning active engagement in political life (Stolle 2003; Stolle and Rochon 1998). Unfortunately, some interesting studies on 'small democracy' – participation in health care and educational institutions – did not investigate the impact of these new types of social engagement on political participation (Kriesi and Westholm 2007; Westholm and von Erlach 2007). Ultimately, research on social capital has led to the fundamental question as to whether the traditional distinction between social and political participation still makes sense or should it be replaced by a new view of civic engagement, encompassing both types and including such additional ones as boycotting and buying products for ethical reasons (van Deth 2004; 2009; van Deth *et al.* 2007; Zukin *et al.* 2006).

Neo-institutionalist explanations of political participation

As macro-political studies of voting participation show, institutional arrangements may be important as determinants of political participation in general (Jackman 1987). If certain ways of exerting an influence on politics – particularly voting in elections and referendums, or primaries in candidate selection – are not available, they cannot be used. On the other hand, political participation only becomes active on specific occasions. If campaigns are not held, the question of campaign activities simply does not arise; if political decisions always conformed to public expectations, there would be no reason to engage in protest activities. Although these are rather trivial statements, they should be taken into account when analysing fluctuations of political participation across time and space. Certainly, the incentives and restrictions set by institutions and leaders always need to be perceived and evaluated by individuals if their behaviour is to become meaningful. Research on political participation should be aware, however, that these factors represent political participation determinants which, though beyond the individual's control do – as exogenous factors – shape individual attitudes and behaviour. Systematic empirical research on the interrelationship of institutional arrangements, features of social organisation, political events and characteristics of individual participants on the level and type of participation are still in an early phase of development (Norris 2002; Roller and Rudi 2008).

Research on political participation in France and Germany

As previously shown above, research on political participation has focused on different political activities and developed different research strategies and explanatory models over the years. A good deal of this research was carried out in the United States, but comparative analyses of political participation had already developed by the late 1950s. We now turn to the empirical research on French and German political participation. Although the overview will be limited to the time span after the World War II, it should be borne in mind that neither France nor Germany is a nation with a strong tradition of citizen participation.

Limitations of research on participation in France and Germany

Summarising the findings on political participation in France and Germany is relatively difficult for a number of reasons. While Germany has been included in almost all comparative research projects on political culture and political participation conducted so far (Almond and Verba 1989; Barnes and Kaase 1979; Jennings and van Deth 1990; van Deth *et al.* 2007), this does not apply to France. International surveys such as Eurobarometer, World Values Surveys and ISSP (International Social Survey Programme), which are regularly conducted in France as well as in Germany, include only a limited set of questions on political participation (Topf 1995a; 1995b). This situation only changed recently with the start of the European Social Survey programme, and when the ISSP programme ran a module on 'Citizenship' in 2004. As a consequence, truly comparative micro-level data on political participation in France and Germany are in short supply. A limited set of items on political protest activities has been available for both countries since 1981, but for other kinds of activities (contacting, party-related activities), the data situation is even poorer than it was before 2002. Apart from analysing voting participation for which official statistical data are available, the opportunities for truly comparative research on political participation in France and Germany are very limited for the pre-2002 period.

If data from comparative surveys are not available, using national survey data as a basis of comparison could be the next best solution. However, this presupposes a data situation that is simply not available for the nations under observation here. Unlike in the United States and certain other democracies, a continuously conducted national election study, including items that allow comparisons over time, is neither available for France nor for Germany (Kaase and Klingemann 1994; Klein *et al.* 2000; Ysmal 1994). Although election studies have been conducted for all German elections since 1961, they were directed by different research teams and therefore lack continuity (lack of continuity is also typical of electoral research in France). Moreover, items on political participation have only rarely been included in the surveys. The German General Social Survey (ALLBUS) has, in addition to its electoral studies, incorporated a module on political participation from time to time (1988; 1998). However, as the German data series starts in a late post-war development period, the time span between these surveys is rather long. For France, a general social survey is simply not yet available.

Specific surveys of political participation in France and Germany are infrequent; this is particularly so in France, which means that here the data basis is too small to present a comprehensive, long-term report on political participation. Some information can be found in general studies of political attitudes and behaviour in France (Bréchon 2003; Bréchon 2006; Boy and Mayer 1997; Grunberg *et al.* 2002; Mayer and Perrineau 1992; Perrineau 1994). The situation in Germany is similar, although to a lesser extent; and in addition to the comparative surveys mentioned above, some studies on political participation in Germany do exist but, due to a lack of research continuity, they can hardly be used as a basis for studying long-term political participation patterns and trends (Reigrotzki 1956; Ellwein *et al.* 1975; Radtke 1976; Uehlinger 1989; Bauer 1993; van Deth 1997; Schmitt-Beck and Weins 1997; Koch *et al.* 2001; Gabriel 2002; 2004; Bertelsmann Foundation 2005; Gabriel and Völkl 2005). Furthermore, not only is there a shortage of data, but the measures of participation used in these various studies differ too much to convey information about the long-term development of political participation in Germany. If all these difficulties arise when the political participation trends and patterns of just one nation are being analysed, this is even more the case in comparative studies, due to the sheer diversity of measurements, sampling procedures, time points, and so on.

Findings

The research situation described above provides little sure ground for an assessment of political participation research topics and findings in France and Germany. Nevertheless, the findings available do furnish some fragmentary insights concerning the level, type and determinants of political participation in the nations under observation.

Ever since the end of World War II, West Germany seems – somewhat more rapidly and vigorously than France – to have moved away from the traditional top-down relationship between citizens and the state towards a more participatory system. Regarding electoral participation, the level in Germany was – until the 1980s – about 20 per cent higher than in France and even though the gap between the two countries has narrowed since, it has not disappeared (Dalton 2006: 38–43). Membership and active work in political parties, as well as engagement during election campaigns, is far more widespread in Germany than in France, and the same applies to membership in social and political organisations (Dalton 2006: 43–50; Norris 2002: 168–87; Scarrow 2000: 86–91). The extremely uneven development of party membership figures in the two countries deserves particular attention. Whereas Scarrow (2000: 89) enumerates enormous temporal fluctuations in France, the figures are much more stable in Germany – despite a period of enormous growth in membership figures between 1970 and 1980. In the mid-1990s, 1.88 million Germans were members of a political party, against only 582,000 in France (see also Niedermayer 2005: 219–49; Bréchon 2006: 65–73). In contrast, legal and illegal forms of protest play a much more important role in France than in Germany (Westle 1994; Dalton 2006: 64–9; Norris 2002: 188–212; Schild

1998, 2000; Gabriel and Völkl 2008). Consultative forms of political participation have not been investigated in any depth so far. Apart from a few legal-institutional analyses and case studies, no quantitative studies have been conducted as yet (Ansell and Gingrich 2003). In sum, comparative research provides only rudimentary information about the levels and development of political participation in France and Germany.

The story is much the same as regards the available national studies that highlight the different forms of participation. While the whole spectrum of participatory activities analysed in the international research literature is covered more or less exhaustively by German research, the interest of French researchers has focused on voting participation and protest: findings on campaigning and communal activities are not available in the recent literature (see references above). However, the respective studies do document particular activities by which citizens try to exert influence on political decisions, showing that the style of action preferred by the French differs somewhat from the patterns of behaviour prevailing among Germans.

With regard to an explanation of participation, similarities as well as differences between the research in the two countries can be observed. Socio-economic and socio-cultural resources play a decisive role in explaining voter turnout and other electoral activities. In the German studies, these resources are normally interpreted within the framework of the socio-economic standard model explaining political participation (Nie *et al.* 1969a; Nie *et al.* 1969b; Verba and Nie 1972). In contrast, French research is prevalently based on Bourdieu's theory of social and cultural differentiation (Bourdieu 1979; Mayer and Perrineau 1992; Boy and Mayer 1997), which does not play a role in German research. A couple of recent German studies refer to Ajzen and Fishbein's theory of planned behaviour (Ajzen 1988) and to its modification by Opp (1992) (see also Lüdemann 2001; Gabriel 2004). However, this theory has not been adopted by French research. Due to the diverse research focal points, periods of analysis and explanatory approaches, national studies provide few comparable insights into the determinants of political participation in both countries. Empirical analyses systematically comparing participatory behaviour in France and Germany have hitherto scarcely been available. Two books by Schild (1998; 2000) provide rare exceptions, but even these focus only on political protest.

In a comparative analysis of participation patterns in four Western democracies, including France and Germany, conducted by Dalton (2006), the prevailing pattern showed broad similarities and only slight differences between the two countries under observation here. Most factors accounting for political activism did not greatly differ among French and German citizens. Some core variables contributing to the explanation of participation in the two countries were supplemented by a small number of country-specific variables: political efficacy, age, and party attachment were the most important predictors of voting participation in France and Germany. In Germany, education also played a role, and the direction of influence is in conformity with a well-established body of knowledge: the advantaged and cognitively-involved segments of the public are most active in political life. Much the same can be said about political protest, most common among young, well-educated male citizens. In France, leftism, and attachment to unions were additional antecedents of protest. Only participation in campaign activities showed slightly different national profiles. Not surprisingly, party attachment boosted participation in these activities, both in France and in Germany. While well-educated, middle-aged and older citizens and dissatisfied people were also most prone to political activity, political efficacy was the only substantially meaningful additional factor in Germany.

Although the measurements used by Dalton are open to dispute, as is the political context in which the participatory activities under scrutiny were situated, the results reported by him are in line with findings in other countries and other contexts. Apart from a few insignificant exceptions, political participation – in whatever form – is primarily an instrument of citizens on the 'sunny side of life'. Most of the public in the less-privileged sector choose to stay out of politics – whether in France and Germany, or in other contemporary democracies.

Conclusion

Irrespective of the advances in comparative analysis of political participation, the question as to whether the citizens of France and Germany differ in the way they participate in politics – in what respect, why and with what impact – has not been a prominent topic in comparative empirical research to date. We have to admit that comparative knowledge of political participation in the two countries is poor. Several reasons account for this situation: political science in France and Germany is embedded in different intellectual traditions; and, in both countries, a good deal of research was initially legal and/or institutional, historical and philosophical. In such research contexts, the questions of how, why and with what results did people become active in political life were simply irrelevant. Consequently, the number of empirical studies dealing with political behaviour is very small, with none providing comparative information on political behaviour patterns in the two countries. The lack of French-German research co-operation in the discipline has compounded the problem, while studies of political participation conducted by US or international research teams offer no solution, since France was not included.

Systematic empirical analyses of political behaviour and an acceptance of US research methods formed part of the professionalisation process of the discipline, but this process did start until the late 1960s in Germany and considerably later in France. Empirical research on various aspects of political attitudes and behaviour has been established and a handful of studies on patterns, trends and determinants of political participation have been published, but empirical evidence still remains fragmented. As far as a comparison between France and Germany is concerned, research has not really progressed from the situation three decades earlier.

A review of the available publications allows some preliminary conclusions on political participation in France and Germany to be validated in the subsequent chapters of this book. A sizeable majority of voters in the two countries take part in national elections, but less so in local electoral contests. As far as the poor state of research makes any generalisations possible, Germans are more active in using conventional forms of political participation, while the French rely more strongly on protest as a way of exerting influence. Forms of direct democracy are more widespread in Germany than in France, but they do not play a major role in either of the two countries. If the contours of a participatory democracy have become visible in France and Germany during the last few decades, the citizens of each country seemingly choose different strategies to make their voices heard. In the subsequent chapters of the book, we will validate this assumption by more in-depth analysis of citizen participation patterns in France and Germany.

References

Ajzen, I. (1988) *Attitudes, Personality and Behaviour*, Chicago: Dorsey.
Ajzen, I. and Fishbein, M. (1980) *Understanding Attitudes and Predicting Social Behaviour*, Englewood Cliffs, N.J.: Prentice Hall.
Almond, G. A. (1956) 'Comparative political systems', *Journal of Politics*, 18 (3): 391–409.
Almond, G. A. and Verba, S. (1963) *The Civic Culture: Political attitudes and democracy in five nations*, Princeton: Princeton University Press.
— (1989) *The Civic Culture: Political attitudes and democracy in five nations*, London: Sage Publications.
Ansell, C. and Gingrich, J. (2003) 'Reforming the administrative state' in B. E. Cain, R. J. Dalton and S. Scarrow (eds) *Democracy Transformed? Expanding political opportunities in advanced industrial democracies*, Cambridge: Cambridge University Press.
Armingeon, K. (2007) 'Political participation and associational involvement' in J. W. van Deth, J. R. Montero and A. Westholm (eds) *Citizenship and Involvement in European Democracies: A comparative analysis*, London: Routledge.
Asher, H. B., Richardson, B. M. and Weisberg, H. F. (1984) *Political Participation: An ISSC Workbook in comparative analysis*, Frankfurt/Main: Campus Verlag.
Barnes, S. and Kaase, M. (eds) (1979) *Political Action: Mass participation in five western democracies*, Beverly Hills: Sage Publications.
Bauer, P. (1993) *Ideologie und politische Beteiligung in der Bundesrepublik Deutschland: Eine empirische untersuchung politischer überzeugungssysteme*, Opladen: Westdeutscher Verlag.
Bell, D. (1973) *The Coming of Post-Industrial Society: A venture in social forecasting*, New York: Basic Books.
Bertelsmann Foundation (2005) *Politische Partizipation in Deutschland*, Gütersloh: Bertelsmann.
Bourdieu, P. (1979) *La Distinction: Critique sociale du judgement*, Paris: Minuit.
Boy, D. and Mayer, N. (eds) (1997) *L'électeur a ses Raisons*, Paris: Presses de Sciences Po.
Bréchon, P. (ed.) (2003) *Les Valeurs des Français*, Paris: Armand Colin.

— (2006) *Comportements et Attitudes Politiques*, Grenoble: Presses Universitaires.
Cain, B. E., Dalton, R. J. and Scarrow, S. E. (eds) (2003) *Democracy Transformed: Expanding political opportunities in advanced industrial democracies*, Oxford: Oxford University Press.
Campbell, A., Converse, P. E., Miller, W. E. and Stokes, D. E. (1960) *The American Voter*, New York: Wiley.
Campbell, A., Gurin, G. and Miller, W. E. (1954) *The Voter Decides*, Evanston, Ill.: Row, Peterson and Company.
Christadler, M. (2005) 'Frankreichs politische Kultur auf dem Prüfstand' in A. Kimmel and H. Uterwedde (eds) *Länderbericht Frankreich*, 2nd edn., Bonn: Bundeszentrale für Politische Bildung.
Cnudde, C. F. and Neubauer, D. E. (eds) (1969) *Empirical Democratic Theory*, Chicago: Markham.
Dahl, R. A. (1971) *Polyarchy: Participation and opposition*, New Haven: Yale University Press.
Dalton, R. J. (2000) 'Politics in Germany' in G. A. Almond, G. B. Powell, R. J. Dalton and K. Strøm (eds) *Comparative Politics Today: A world view*, 7th edn., New York: Longman.
— (2006) *Citizen Politics: Public opinion and political parties in advanced industrial democracies*, 4th edn., Washington, D.C.: CQ Press.
— (2008) *The Good Citizen: How a younger generation is reshaping American politics*, Washington, D.C.: CQ Press.
Downs, A. (1957) *An Economic Theory of Democracy*, New York: Wiley.
Ellwein, T., Lippert, E. and Zoll, R. (1975) *Politische Beteiligung in der Bundesrepublik Deutschland*, Göttingen: Schwartz.
Finifter, A. W. (1970) 'Dimensions of political alienation', *American Political Science Review*, 64 (2): 389–410.
Frohlich, N. and Oppenheimer, J. A. (1978) *Modern Political Economy*, Englewood Cliffs, N.J.: Prentice Hall.
Gabriel, O. W. (2002) 'Bürgerbeteiligung an der Kommunalpolitik' in 'Enquete-Kommission, Zukunft des Bürgerschaftlichen Engagements' Deutscher Bundestag (ed.) *Bürgerschaftliches Engagement und Zivilgesellschaft*, Opladen: Leske and Budrich.
— (2004) 'Politische Partizipation' in J. W. van Deth (ed.) *Deutschland in Europa: Ergebnisse des European Social Survey 2002–2003*, Wiesbaden: VS Verlag für Sozialwissenschaften.
Gabriel, O. W., Kunz, V., Roßteutscher, S. and van Deth, J. W. (2002) *Sozialkapital und Demokratie: Zivilgesellschaftliche ressourcen im vergleich*, Wien: WUV-Universitätsverlag.
Gabriel, O.W. and Völkl, K. (2005) 'Politische und Soziale Partizipation' in O.W. Gabriel and E. Holtmann (eds) *Handbuch Politisches System der Bundesrepublik Deutschland*, 3rd edn., München: Oldenbourg.
— (2008) 'Politische und Soziale Partizipation' in O.W. Gabriel and S. Kropp (eds) *Die EU-Staaten im Vergleich*, 3rd edn., Wiesbaden: VS Verlag für Sozialwissenschaften.

Gallagher, M., Laver, M. and Mair, P. (2001) *Representative Government in Modern Europe: Institutions, parties and governments*, 3rd edn., New York: McGraw-Hill.

Greiffenhagen, M. and Greiffenhagen, S. (1993) *Ein Schwieriges Vaterland: Zur Politischen Kultur Deutschlands*, München: List.

Grunberg, G., Mayer, N. and Sniderman, P. M. (eds) (2002) *La Démocratie à l'Épreuve: Une nouvelle approche de l'opinion des Français*, Paris: Presses de Sciences Po.

Gunlicks, A. B. (1986) *Local Government in the German Federal System*, Durham: Duke University Press.

Hoffmann-Martinot, V. (2003) 'The French republic, one yet divisible?' in N. Kersting and A. Vetter (eds) *Reforming Local Government in Europe: Closing the gap between democracy and efficiency*, Opladen: Leske and Budrich.

Holtmann, E. (2005) 'Die deutsche Tradition und das politische System der Gegenwart' in O. W. Gabriel and E. Holtmann (eds) *Handbuch Politisches System der Bundesrepublik Deutschland*, 3rd edn., München: Oldenbourg.

Inglehart, R. (1971) 'The silent revolution in Europe: intergenerational change in post-industrial societies', *American Political Science Review*, 65 (4): 991–1017

— (1977) *The Silent Revolution: Changing values and political styles among western publics*, Princeton, N.J.: Princeton University Press.

— (1979) 'Political action: The impact of values, cognitive level, and social background' in S. Barnes and M. Kaase (eds) *Political Action: Mass participation in five western democracies*, Beverly Hills: Sage Publications.

— (1983) 'Changing paradigms in comparative political behaviour' in A. W. Finifter (ed.) *Political Science: The state of the discipline*, Washington D.C.: American Political Science Association.

— (1990) *Culture Shift in Advanced Industrial Society*, Princeton, N.J.: Princeton University Press.

— (1997) *Modernization and Postmodernization: Cultural, economic and political change in 43 societies*, Princeton, N.J.: Princeton University Press.

Inglehart, R. and Welzel, C. (2005) *Modernization, Cultural Change and Democracy: The human development sequence*, New York: Cambridge University Press.

Jackman, R. (1987) 'Political institutions and voter turnout in the industrial democracies', *American Political Science Review*, 81 (2): 405–23.

Jennings, M. K. and van Deth, J. W. (1990) *Continuities in Political Action: A longitudinal study of political orientations in three western democracies*, Berlin: Gruyter.

Kaase, M. (1997) 'Vergleichende politische Partizipationsforschung' in D. Berg-Schlosser and F. Müller-Rommel (eds) *Vergleichende Politikwissenschaft: Ein einführendes Studienbuch*, 3rd edn., Opladen: Leske and Budrich.

Kaase, M. and Klingemann, H. -D. (1994) 'Electoral research in the Federal Republic of Germany', *European Journal of Political Research*, 25 (3): 343–66.

Kaase, M. and Marsh, A. (1979a) 'Political action: A theoretical perspective' in S. Barnes and M. Kaase (eds) *Political Action: Mass participation in five western democracies*, Beverly Hills: Sage Publications.

— (1979b) 'Political action repertory: Changes over time and a new typology' in S. Barnes and M. Kaase (eds) *Political Action: Mass participation in five western democracies*, Beverly Hills: Sage Publications.

Klein, M., Jagodzinski, W., Mochmann, E. and Ohr, D. (eds) (2000) *50 Jahre empirische Wahlforschung in Deutschland: Entwicklungen, Befunde, Perspektiven, Daten*, Opladen: Westdeutscher Verlag.

Koch, A., Wasmer, M. and Schmidt, P. (eds) (2001) *Politische Partizipation in der Bundesrepublik Deutschland: Empirische Befunde und theoretische Erklärungen*, Opladen: Leske and Budrich.

Kriesi, H. and Westholm, A. (2007) 'Small-scale democracy: The determinants of action' in J. W. van Deth, J. R. Montero and A. Westholm (eds) *Citizenship and Involvement in European Democracies: A comparative analysis*, London: Routledge.

Kühnel, S. (2001) 'Kommt es auf die Stimme an? Determinanten von Teilnahme und Nichtteilnahme an politischen Wahlen' in A. Koch, M. Wasmer and P. Schmidt (eds) *Politische Partizipation in der Bundesrepublik Deutschland: Empirische befunde und theoretische erklärungen*, Opladen: Leske and Budrich.

Lane, J. -E. and Ersson, S. O. (1987) *Politics and Society in Western Europe*, London: Sage Publications.

Lazarsfeld, P. F., Berelson, B. and Gaudet, H. (1944) *The People's Choice: How the voter makes up his mind in a presidential campaign*, New York: Columbia University Press.

LeDuc, L. (2002) 'Referendums and initiatives: The politics of direct democracy' in L. LeDuc, R.G. Niemi and P. Norris (eds) *Comparing Democracies 2: New challenges in the study of elections and voting*, London: Sage Publications.

Lijphart, A. (1999) *Patterns of Democracy: Government forms and performance in thirty-six countries*, New Haven: Yale University Press.

Lipset, S. M. (1981) *Political Man: The social bases of politics*, Baltimore: The Johns Hopkins University Press.

Lüdemann, C. (2001) 'Politische Partizipation, Anreize und Ressourcen: Ein Test verschiedener Handlungsmodelle und Anschlusstheorien am ALLBUS 1998' in A. Koch, M. Wasmer and P. Schmidt (eds) *Politische Partizipation in der Bundesrepublik Deutschland: Empirische befunde und theoretische erklärungen*, Opladen: Leske and Budrich.

Mabileau, A., Moyser, G., Parry, G. and Quantin, P. (eds) (1989) *Local Politics and Participation in Britain and France*, Cambridge: Cambridge University Press.

Marsh, A. and Kaase, M. (1979) 'Measuring political action' in S. Barnes and M. Kaase (eds) *Political Action: Mass participation in five western democracies*, Beverly Hills: Sage Publications.
Mayer, N. and Perrineau, P. (1992) *Les Comportements Politiques*, Paris: Armand Colin.
Milbrath, L.W. (1965) *Political Participation: How and why do people get involved in politics?*, Chicago: Rand McNally College Pub. Co.
Milbrath, L. W. and Goel, M. L. (1977) *Political Participation: How and why do people get involved in politics?*, 2nd edn., Chicago: Rand McNally College Pub. Co.
Muller, E. N. (1979) *Aggressive Political Participation*, Princeton, N.J.: Princeton University Press.
Muller, E. N., Jukam, T. O. and Seligson, M. A. (1982) 'Diffuse support and antisystem political behaviour: a comparative analysis', *American Journal of Political Science*, 26 (2): 240–64.
Muller, E. N. and Williams, C. J. (1980) 'Dynamics of political support-alienation', *Comparative Political Studies*, 13 (1): 33–59.
Münch, Richard (2005) 'Grundzüge und Grundkategorien der staatlichen und gesellschaftlichen Entwicklung Frankreichs', in A. Kimmel and H. Uterwede (eds): *Länderbericht Frankreich: Geschichte, Politik, wirtschaft, gesellschaft*, Schriftenreihe: 462, Bonn: Bundeszentrale für Politische Bildung.
Nie, N. H., Powell, G. B. and Prewitt, K. (1969a) 'Social structure and political participation: developmental relationships', Part I, *American Political Science Review*, 63: 361–76.
— (1969b) 'Social structure and political participation: developmental relationships', Part II, *American Political Science Review*, 63: 808–832.
Niedermayer, O. (2005) *Bürger und Politik: Politische orientierungen und verhaltensweisen der Deutschen*, Eine Einführung, 2nd edn., Wiesbaden: VS Verlag für Sozialwissenschaften.
Norris, P. (2002) *The Democratic Phoenix: Reinventing political activism*, Cambridge: Cambridge University Press.
Olson, M. (1969) *Die Logik des Kollektiven Handelns: Kollektivgüter und die theorie der gruppen*, Tübingen: Mohr Siebeck.
Opp, K. -D. (1984) *Soziale Probleme und Protestverhalten: Eine empirische konfrontierung des modells rationalen verhaltens mit soziologischen und demographischen hypothesen am beispiel von atomkraftgegnern*, Opladen: Westdeutscher Verlag.
— (1992) 'Legaler und illegaler Protest im interkulturellen Vergleich', *Kölner Zeitschrift für Soziologie und Sozialpsychologie*, vol. 44: 436–60.
Parry, G., Moyser, G. and Day, N. (1992) *Political Participation and Democracy in Britain*, Cambridge: Cambridge University Press.
Pattie, C., Seyd, P. and Whiteley, P. (2004) *Citizenship in Britain: Values, participation and democracy*, Cambridge: Cambridge University Press.

Perrineau, P. (1994) *L'Engagement Politique: Déclinou Mutation?*, Paris: Presses des la FNSP.
Putnam, R. (1993) *Making Democracy Work: Civic traditions in modern Italy*, Princeton: Princeton University Press.
— (2000) *Bowling Alone: The collapse and revival of American community*, New York: Simon and Schuster.
— (2001) *Gesellschaft und Gemeinsinn: Sozialkapital im internationalen vergleich*, Gütersloh: Bertelsmann.
Radtke, G. D. (1976) *Teilnahme an der Politik: Bestimmungsgründe der bereitschaft zur politischen partizipation: Ein empirischer beitrag*, Leverkusen: Heggen Verlag.
Reigrotzki, E. (1956) *Soziale Verflechtungen in der Bundesrepublik: Elemente der sozialen teilnahme in kirche, politik, organisationen und freizeit*, Tübingen: Mohr.
Riker, W. H. and Ordeshook, P. C. (1973) *An Introduction to Positive Political Theory*, Englewood Cliffs, N.J.: Prentice Hall.
Rokkan, S. (1971) 'Die vergleichende Analyse der Staaten- und Nationenbildung: Modelle und Methoden' in W. Zapf (ed.) *Theorien des Sozialen Wandels*, 3rd edn., Berlin: Kiepenheuer u. Witsch.
Roller, E. and Rudi, T. (2008) 'Explaining level and equality of political participation: The role of social capital, socioeconomic modernity and political institutions' in H. Meulemann (ed.) *Social Capital in Europe: Similarity of countries and diversity of people: Multilevel analyses of the European Social Survey*, Boston: Brill.
Rosenstone, S. J. and Hansen, J. M. (1993), *Mobilization, Participation, and Democracy in America*, New York: MacMillan.
Scarrow, S. E. (2000) 'Parties without members? Party organisation in a changing electoral environment' in R. J. Dalton and M. P. Wattenberg (eds) *Parties Without Partisans: Political change in advanced industrialized societies*, Cambridge: Cambridge University Press.
Schain, M. A. (2000) 'Politics in France' in G. A. Almond, G. B. Powell, R. J. Dalton and K. Strøm (eds) *Comparative Politics Today: A world view*, 7th edn., New York: Longman.
— (2008) *The Politics of Immigration in France, Britain and the United States: A comparative study*, New York: Palgrave Macmillan.
Schild, J. (1998) 'Wertewandel und politischer Protest: Die wachsende Bedeutung direkter Partizipationsformen' in R. Köcher and J. Schild (eds) *Wertewandel in Deutschland und Frankreich: Nationale unterschiede und europäische Gemeinsamkeiten*, Opladen: Leske and Budrich.
— (2000) *Politische Konfliktlinien, Individualistische Werte und Politischer Protest: Ein Deutsch-Französischer vergleich*, Opladen: Leske and Budrich.
Schild, J. and Uterwedde, H. (eds) (2006) *Frankreich: Politik, wirtschaft, gesellschaft*, 2nd edn., Wiesbaden: VS Verlag für Sozialwissenschaften.
Schmitt-Beck, R. and Weins, C. (1997) 'Neue Soziale Bewegungen und

politischer Protest in Ostdeutschland' in O.W. Gabriel (ed.) *Politische Orientierungen und Verhaltensweisen in Deutschland,* Opladen: Leske and Budrich.

Sniderman, P. M. (1975) *Personality and Democratic Politics,* Berkeley: University of California Press.

Stolle, D. (2003) 'The sources of social capital' in M. Hooghe and D. Stolle (eds) *Generating Social Capital: Civil society and institutions in comparative perspective,* New York: Palgrave Macmillan.

Stolle, D. and Rochon, T. (1998) 'Are all associations alike? Member diversity, associational type and the creation of social capital', *American Behavioural Scientist,* 42 (1): 47–65.

Topf, R. (1995a) 'Beyond electoral participation' in H. -D. Klingemann and D. Fuchs (eds) *Citizens and the State: beliefs in government,* Oxford: Oxford University Press.

— (1995b) 'Electoral participation' in H.-D. Klingemann and D. Fuchs (eds) *Citizens and the State: Beliefs in government,* Oxford: Oxford University Press.

Uehlinger, H.-M. (1989) *Politischer Protest in der Bundesrepublik: Strukturen und erklärungsmodelle,* Opladen: Westdeutscher Verlag.

van Deth, J. W. (1997) 'Formen konventioneller politischer Partizipation: Ein neues Leben alter Dinosaurier?' in O.W. Gabriel (ed.) *Politische Orientierungen und Verhaltensweisen im vereinigten Deutschland,* Opladen: Leske and Budrich.

— (2001) 'Soziale und politische Beteiligung: Alternativen, ergänzungen oder zwillinge?' in A. Koch, M. Wasmerand, P. Schmidt (eds) *Politische Partizipation in der Bundesrepublik Deutschland: Empirische befunde und theoretische erklärungen,* Opladen: Leske and Budrich.

— (2004) 'Soziale Partizipation' in J. W. Van Deth (ed.) *Deutschland in Europa: Ergebnisse des European Social Survey 2002–2003,* Wiesbaden: VS Verlag für Sozialwissenschaften.

— (2009) 'Politische Partizipation' in V. Kainaand and A. Römmele (eds) *Politische Soziologie: Ein studienbuch,* Wiesbaden: VS Verlag für Sozialwissenschaften.

van Deth, J. W., Montero, J. R. and Westholm, A. (eds) (2007) *Citizenship and Involvement in European Democracies: A comparative analysis,* London: Routledge.

Verba, S. and Nie, N. H. (1972) *Participation in America: Political democracy and social equality,* New York: Harper and Row.

Verba, S., Nie, N. H. and Kim, J. -O. (1978) *Participation and Political Equality: A seven-nation comparison,* Cambridge: Cambridge University Press.

Verba, S., Schlozman, K. L. and Brady, H. (1995) *Voice and Equality: Civic voluntarism in American politics,* Cambridge, Mass.: Harvard University Press.

Westholm, A. and von Erlach, E. (2007) 'Small-scale democracy: The consequences of action' in J. W. van Deth, J. R. Montero and A. Westholm (eds) *Citizenship and Involvement in European Democracies: A comparative analysis*, London: Routledge.

Westle, B. (1994) 'Politische Partizipation' in O. W. Gabriel and F. Brettschneider (eds) *Die EU-Staaten im Vergleich: Strukturen, Prozesse, Politikinhalte*, 2nd edn., Opladen: Westdeutscher Verlag.

Ysmal, C. (1994) 'The history of electoral studies in France', *European Journal of Political Research*, 25(3): 367–85.

Zukin, C., Keeter, S., Adolina, M., Jenkins, K. and Carpini, M. X. (2006) *A New Civic Engagement? Political participation, civic life and the changing American citizen*, Oxford: Oxford University Press.

chapter two | mapping political participation
Kristina Faden-Kuhne and Oscar W. Gabriel

Introduction

Research on the behavioural and the institutional aspects of political life had, for several decades, taken separate intellectual paths, but over recent years political scientists have invested increasing efforts into integrating these two perspectives of political analysis. This is mainly due to the insight that individual political behaviour is influenced, to a greater or lesser extent, by the institutional context of a given political system. Political institutions provide restrictive measures as well as incentives for political behaviour; some institutional arrangements – such as a low referendum quorum – may encourage citizens to become active in political life, while others – like the need to register before voting in an election – prevent them from doing so. The institutional setting as a macro-variable needs, therefore, to be taken into account in the explanation of micro-level, individual behaviour. It should be borne in mind, however, that political institutions can only set up a political life framework ready to be fleshed out by individual or collective forms of political behaviour (Carmines and Huckfeldt 1996; Dunleavy 1996; Rothstein 1996; Sniderman 2000).

Do institutions matter in explaining political participation?

Attempts at integrating institutional and behavioural variables have become more important over the years in many areas of political research. As regards political participation, using institutional arrangements to predict political behaviour follows a well-established tradition going back to the earliest empirical studies (Gosnell 1930; Tingsten 1937). Gosnell emphasised the role of party and elite mobilisation, and also certain electoral rule characteristics, as determinants of electoral turnout. In the post-war era of research on political participation, the role of political institutions and party mobilisation as electoral turnout determinants was emphasised by Rokkan (1962). More recently, Jackman (1989) studied the impact of several institutional arrangements on electoral turnout, although this was at the expense of competing explanatory approaches. Norris (2002: 64–82), however, managed to take a step further by integrating macro-, meso- and micro-level variables. She focused on electoral system types, electoral rules – districts, frequency of contests, compulsory voting, etc. – party system characteristics, and presidential vs. parliamentary executives as the principal institutional determinants of turnout. Her main finding was that 'political institutions and legal rules proved to be strongly and significantly associated with voter participation' (Norris 2002: 82).

In what respect are political institutions important as regards the kind and level of political participation? As a type of behaviour aimed at influencing political decisions at various levels of the political system, political participation impacts on the distribution of political power between the governing and the governed. The question of 'who governs' is strongly influenced by the regulations concerning who is entitled to participate and with what result; which types of decision are open to direct citizen participation; which procedures can legally be applied in the political process; whether the respective provisions are set by the constitution or by law, and so on. The role of civic participation in political life does not, therefore, merely depend on an individual's decision to become politically active; it also depends on the characteristics of the participative tools put at their disposal. Participatory institutions either enhance or hamper civic participation by respectively proposing specific incentives or else imposing certain restrictions. Regarded from this point of view, an analysis of the strength of the participatory institutions in France and Germany should specify some systematic criteria accounting for citizens' influence in political life. The main criteria for this – formalisation/institutionalisation, inclusiveness, scope and multiplicity, and the decisiveness of participatory rights – are examined below.

Formalisation/institutionalisation

Formalisation/institutionalisation refers to the existence and nature of formal rules regulating political participation, rules that are to be found in the constitution, in specific laws, or else in governmental and administrative provisions. What is laid down in the national constitution enjoys a more prominent symbolic status than is the case for some mere administrative rule applying to a specific policy regulation. Legal status also impacts on the protection, stability and reliability of participatory rights. Unlike simple administrative procedural changes, constitutional changes need to be supported by a sizeable majority in the parliament. In several countries, constitutional referendums are required and even if this not the case, broad popular support of changes to the political rules of game seems to be desirable.

A second characteristic of institutionalisation refers to the specific content of formal regulations. This usually refers to the segment of the public entitled to participate, the requirements to be met in order to initiate a participatory process, the matters to which political participation refer, and the procedures and results of the respective participatory activities. The election of representatives at various levels of the political system is the most prominent and universally-implemented formalised participatory right (Gallagher *et al.* 2001: 300ff.). See below (*Binding political decisions: the institutions of elections and referendums*) and Chapter Eight for more detail on the national election process and the right to vote. In the case of voting, the preconditions, the process, issue, and the final result of participation are regulated in almost every detail by constitutional or electoral law. At the other end of the formalisation spectrum, certain ways of influencing political decisions are either not formalised at all (contacting politicians), or only rudimentarily (legal demonstrations). Formalisation, contrary to the assumptions of the Political Action researchers (Kaase and Marsh 1979), does not differentiate between conventional and unconventional participation, since some forms of unconventional participation, such as demonstrations, are more strongly regulated than conventional ones, such as contacting politicians (see Chapter Three).

Formal rules that prescribe the way people can influence policy choices play an important part in the practice of political participation, in as much as they can either encourage or restrict people's active involvement in politics. Restrictive political institutions build up barriers for citizens who want to participate in political decisions. The need to register before being entitled to vote in general elections, a high quorum required for organising referendums and a limited number of political issues susceptible to citizen participation are, for example, barriers that make political participation a costly and demanding activity.

On the other hand, the fact of being automatically enrolled on voter registers, enjoying a low referendum quorum, and benefiting from a large number of issues to be decided by popular vote all have the opposite effect on potential participants. Formal regulations about the number of public offices subject to popular vote, the length of an electoral term, the size of electoral districts, the specific characteristics of the electoral system, and the conditions to be respected by successful referendums make a considerable difference when the effectiveness of a participatory system in the process of shaping and sharing political power is to be asserted (Franklin 2001; LeDuc 2002; Norris 2002).

Why is formalisation an important characteristic of participatory systems? Basically, formal rules make the outcome of collective political participation binding on everyone, be they citizens or the elite. Little or no discretion is left to participants about accepting, or not, the outcome of the various decisions. Although many French voters were not enthusiastic about the majority vote in the presidential election of 2007, they had, nevertheless, to accept it. This sort of obligation, however, does not apply to such activities as contacting politicians or demonstrating: representatives are not obliged to grant requests, nor do activists have to agree on the final decisions of the representatives in the respective cases.

A strong participatory system is characterised by at least some degree of formalisation. This requirement is particularly vital regarding basic civic rights – these need to be granted and protected by the constitution. Formalisation is also required when the outcomes of participatory activities – voting in elections or referendums – are binding on the whole political community. Other types of political activity require less regulation because of their weaker impact on the political community.

Inclusiveness

Inclusiveness, another important criterion of a system of participation, involves the number and characteristics of the people entitled to participate in either social or political life. The question underlying this characteristic is as follows: Who is entitled to claim the idea of popular sovereignty and thus have the full rights of participation in the civic life of a particular community?

In the early stages of democratisation, only a small segment of the people living within the boundaries of a sovereign nation state – the well-educated, wealthy, white adult males – enjoyed the status of full citizens. In some nations with universal male franchise, the votes were unequally weighted. Later, as the democratisation process in the modern nation states progressed, participatory rights were successively universalised and made more equal by including women and previously excluded minorities. Being a citizen became increasingly tantamount to residing in a country. One consequence was that every female or male inhabitant having reached adulthood became a full citizen of their country. Nevertheless, as shown by Dahl (1971), a fully inclusive participatory system has not yet been attained in many modern states, even in some of the most democratically-advanced ones. The main reason for the newly-emerged disparity between citizens and inhabitants, and the related differentiation between universal human rights and more restricted civic rights, owes much to worldwide migration. The number of immigrants living in the European Union member states averaged 7 per cent in 2006 but, in some nations, the figure is considerably higher and amounts to a sizeable proportion of the public.[1] Although such human rights as free expression of opinion are granted to immigrants in all EU member states, the formal participatory status of these immigrants varies strongly from one nation to the next. In some countries, immigrants have the right to cast their votes in national or, at least, municipal elections, they may set up voluntary associations, join political parties, and so on; in others, these rights are expressly reserved for the citizens of EU member states. In yet other countries, even EU-citizens are still excluded from participation in national elections, and citizens who arrived from nations outside the EU enjoy even lower status.

Since political participation is a universal principle bestowing the right to participate in the political life of one's country of residence, the inclusiveness of full citizenship is a second criterion to be employed in analysing the strength of the national system of participation. In comparing the institutional political settings of France and Germany, we have to examine whether, and to what degree, full participatory rights are reserved to citizens or open to their adult populations as a whole.

Scope

Over the years, the range of participatory activities has expanded considerably. Many channels of access to the political system have been opened up to citizens in order to give them more say in the shaping of public policies. Beyond voting in elections and joining voluntary associations, the forms of influence actually used by the citizenry of modern democracies also encompass participating in legal or non-legal protest activities (see Chapter Nine); buying or boycotting products for ethical reasons; using the internet to send messages to political leaders; becoming active in various forms of problem-solving groups, and so on (Zukin *et al.* 2006).

The actions aimed at influencing politics can be classified in several ways.

---

1. Source: *Bundesagentur für Arbeit 2006*, www.arbeitsagentur.de

Substantially, we can distinguish between participation in the selection of political leaders on the one hand, and decisions concerning public policies on the other. Procedurally, political participation entails the right to articulate individual or collective demands, set the political agenda, exert influence on the authoritative decisions to be made by political leaders, participate directly in choosing among political alternatives, and also to have a say in the way political decisions become implemented. Sometimes, exerting influence means voting in a decisive way; at other times, participation may take the form of consultation or bargaining. In some instances, citizens act at an individual level; at other times they may join with others and become active in formal organisations to make their voices heard. Various factors – institutional changes, the use of new technologies for political purposes, the presence of politics in citizens' daily lives, increased individual capabilities to become active in politics and so on – mean that the available forms of political participation have never been as diverse as they are today. As Scharpf (1970) claimed several decades ago, the offer of opportunities to participate in politics for everyone who wants to become active has considerably improved over the years. But that is not all; since diverse forms of political participation serve a multitude of aims – conveying specific demands to leaders or exerting pressure on them, taking part in collective choices or raising individual issues, influencing the choice of issues or of political leaders, acting individually or else with others, bargaining with political leaders or competing with others over scarce political resources – the repertoire has not only become extended, but also offers more specific instruments to achieve specific political goals. The broader and more differentiated the range of participatory tools, the more efficient the participatory system as a whole.

Political participation has not only differentiated vertically, but also horizontally. This means that the range of institutionalised, semi-institutionalised and non-institutionalised means of exerting influence on political choices is available at various levels of the political system. In this respect, the degree of decentralisation of state authority and the territorial fragmentation of a political system both enter the stage as parts of the territorial map. As already emphasised by Dahl (1971), participation becomes more effective if autonomous political units, endowed with a substantial degree of decisional discretion, exist at the sub-national level, whether regional or local. In assessing the strength of the participatory systems institutionalised at these levels, one must bear in mind that a large number of autonomous political units may either enhance political participation, since it is easier to organise, or else devalue it if the matters to be influenced become trivial. This readily becomes the case if the sub-national units are too small or lack substantial competencies (Dahl and Tufte 1973; Petterson and Rose 1996). As will be shown in subsequent chapters, France and Germany serve as good examples of the varying forms of horizontally-differentiated systems of political participation. Germany is a federal system, France a unitary one; Germany has a strong system of local government, France does not; Germany has some 15,000 autonomous local municipalities, France more than twice that number (for more details, see Chapters Four, Five and Six).

Impact

Most scholars agree that the levels and forms of political participation are important characteristics of the distribution of power between citizens and authorities. In order to have an impact on the way a country is governed, participative rights need to vest the citizenry with a certain degree of decisional authority. Formalised and direct decisional citizen competencies characterise a strong system of participation. It should be borne in mind, however, that the diverse forms of political participation vary widely in this respect. The place of participatory rights in the process of setting up binding political decisions constitutes a decisive power resource for the citizenry. Some activities, such as joining voluntary organisations and participating actively in organisational life (see Chapter Seven), are located at the periphery of the decision-making system, while others, such as voting in elections or in referendums, are situated at the centre of the respective system. Hence, participatory activities and systems of political participation can be compared both as regards their closeness to authoritative decisions, and their relevance to the distribution of power between citizens and elites. To a certain extent, this aspect is bound up with formalisation. Activities directly entailing authoritative decisions are more formalised than those that are only loosely related to decisional authority. These loosely-related activities can be arranged on a continuum. At the one end, we find individual rights, which whilst allowing specific political preferences to be voiced, also leave considerable discretion to the authorities as regards their reactions. Organisational rights, such as setting up political organisations, joining them and using collective resources in order to achieve certain goals that are common to a broader segment of the electorate, are somewhat closer to the centre. Rights explicitly aimed at exerting political influence, such as taking part in the intra-party nomination of candidates for public leadership positions, give participants an even greater share of power. Casting one's ballot in the election of political leaders or in the choice of public policies means direct participation in the establishment of authoritative decisions, thereby dispossessing political elites of their discretionary powers.

Strong participatory systems are characterised by the allocation of considerable decision-making power to the citizens. This occurs if civic participation is encouraged and made easy by low institutional barriers or effective participative tools; it also occurs if the political elite is favourable to civic participation and willing to share decision-making power with citizens. This does not necessarily imply extensive use of the available participatory rights by the majority of citizens; indeed, in most advanced democracies, participation rights that go beyond simply voting in national elections are only used by a minority of citizens. This is not so much due to restrictive institutional arrangements, as to diverse sociostructural or cultural factors.

Strong and weak participatory systems

On the basis of the four criteria introduced above, one can easily imagine political regimes, even if they are democratic, differing considerably in the leeway accorded to effective civic participation. Completely closed political systems – characterised by limited inclusiveness, a narrow range of participation opportunities and a lack of decisional power by the average citizen – are scarcely compatible with the idea of democracy (Dahl 1971); nonetheless, the specific institutional arrangements that set the frame for effective civic engagement can – and do – vary from one nation to another. As shown in Table 2.1, weak participatory systems attribute a very limited role to citizen participation, while strong ones emphasise the role of civic participation in the conduct of governmental activities. In the first case, great decisional power resides in the political elite; in the second, the distribution of power is shifted in favour of the general public. Most modern political systems do not stand at either one of these extremes, but can be found somewhere between the two.

In the subsequent sections of this contribution, we will compare the institutional framework of the French and German political systems as regards the strength of their participatory systems. We will examine their various participative rights, whether laid down in the national constitution, or in their 'simple laws'. The focus will be on elections and voluntary associations as points of access to the political process, as well as on various kinds of individual rights to participate in the making of authoritative decisions.

Table 2.1: Strong and weak systems of participation

	Formalisation	Inclusiveness	Scope	Impact
Weak system of political participation	Negligible: merely informal civic rights	Limited: restricted and unequal access to the political process	Narrow: limited range of opportunities to influence politics	Weak: merely consultative forms of participation
Strong system of political participation	Significant: constitutionally and legally granted civic rights	Extensive: all adult inhabitants endowed with the whole range of civic rights	Wide: broad range of formal and informal opportunities to influence politics	Strong: outcome of participatory activities is binding on the political community

Source: Author's presentation

Institutionalised individual participative rights: constitutional and legal

Exerting influence on political decisions is one of the most important civic rights in modern democracies. Details of the respective participatory rights – such as the concrete forms of political influence at citizens' disposal, the procedures involved, or the eligibility criteria for participation – are therefore often explicitly stipulated in a nation's constitution. Some rights of participation, e.g. the right to vote in democratic elections, are part of the bedrock of all modern democracies. Others, such as petitions or referendums, vary between countries: they are common practice in some democracies, but not in others. When it comes to these characteristics of political participation, differences – as well as similarities – do exist between France and Germany. In this section, we explore those individual participative rights that are either drawn up institutionally or else regulated by law. There are several ways of influencing the political process other than via institutionally-organised forms of participation. Although the constitution and legislation do not govern all types of conventional participation, all of them are based on institutional civil rights (Gabriel and Völkl 2005: 543). France and Germany differ regarding the degree of institutionalisation of participative forms.

The principle of popular sovereignty

The Constitution of the Fifth French Republic (enacted in 1958) and the Federal Republic of Germany (enacted in 1949), which serve as a basis for participative rights, both establish the sovereignty of the people as a fundamental principle of political rule (art. 20, para. 2 of the German Constitution, and art. 4 of the French Constitution). Thus, the idealised will of the citizens is given as the ultimate foundation of political rule. Political authority is not regarded as legitimate unless it is directly or indirectly derived from the citizens' will of consent. Political participation is the most important expression of popular sovereignty; accordingly, the basic laws of both countries place great significance upon the participative rights of their citizens. However, who are the members of the public to whom the respective constitutions assign this important role? In both countries, only persons aged eighteen or over can make use of their formally-granted participative rights.[2]

In all modern democracies, a distinction is made between human rights and civil rights. Human rights – such as the protection of human dignity, personal freedom, or freedom of opinion, which are laid out in articles 1–5 of the Basic Law (the German Constitution), and as a reference to the Declaration of Human and Civil Rights of 1789 in the French Constitution – apply to all persons permanently or intermittently living in a state. Likewise, the right to set up or participate in trade unions applies to 'everybody' in both countries and is not reserved to citizens alone (see art. 9 of the Constitution, preamble of the 4th Republic). Civil rights, however, apply exclusively to citizens of the state. As participative rights are cat-

---

2. This applies only to formally-granted participative rights. However, persons younger than 18 can use non-formalised forms of participation.

egorised as civil rights, this means they do not apply to residents.

Differentiating between citizens and residents, less relevant once French and German politics had become fully democratised, has now become important again with, among other things, the increase in international migration. Being classified as a 'citizen' is now crucial for the opportunity to fully participate in the political process. The legislation in France and Germany defines explicitly those residents who acquire citizenship automatically and who are entitled to apply for it (see also the German Law of Citizenship StAG and the French Law No. 98-170 or arts 21–15 of the *Code Civil*).

In Germany, a child born to foreign parents automatically acquires German citizenship if he or she is born in Germany, as long as one of the parents has been ordinarily resident in Germany for eight years and has unlimited right of residence (art. 4, StAG). In France, a child automatically acquires citizenship at birth if he or she is born in France and one of the parents was also born in France, irrespective of whether or not the parents are French citizens. This shows a significant difference to the situation in Germany, where access to citizenship is more difficult. Since 1st September 1998, every child born in France to immigrant parents is granted French citizenship as soon as he or she reaches the age of eighteen, provided that he or she is resident in France at the time and has spent at least five years in the country since his or her eleventh birthday. France, therefore, goes one step further than Germany, as a potential citizen is naturalised automatically on his or her eighteenth birthday, without having to take further steps to ensure this; in Germany, such a person would be automatically 'denaturalised' (Brubaker 1992). There are further differences between the two countries regarding the naturalisation of adult immigrants. An adult immigrant who has been ordinarily resident in Germany for *eight* years can apply for and will be granted naturalisation if he or she meets certain criteria (art.10, StAG). In France, the number of years during which an applicant must have been resident in the country is *five*. It is therefore possible to acquire citizenship more quickly in France than in Germany.

Basic participatory rights

Which individual participative rights are set out in the constitutions of democracies? The French Constitution does not include a charter of basic rights defining human and civil rights. Instead, in its preamble, it refers directly to the Declaration of Human Rights of 1789, as well as to the Charter of Basic Rights of the 4th Constitution. The German Basic Law, however, lists all basic human and civil rights. This underlines the central position of participative rights in the country's legislation, and demonstrates a major distinction between France and Germany regarding the constitutional position of participative rights. The basic rights described in articles 1 to 19 of the German Constitution include, for example, freedom of association and assembly, as well as the right of petition. Freedom of opinion is also a key component of political participation, as it is the cornerstone of freedom of association and the right of petition. It also grants the right to express one's opinions publicly and thus participate in the political process. Freedom of opinion is established as a human right in the constitutions of both countries and is, therefore, granted to all residents (art. 5 of the Basic Law and arts 10 and 11 of the Declaration of Human and Civil Rights of 1789). However, as will be shown below, the institutional guarantee of further basic rights differs considerably between France and Germany.

The right of petition is part of the basic rights section in the German Basic Law. Article 17 gives all Germans 'the right to address individually or jointly with others written requests or complaints to competent authorities and to the legislature'. This provision, rooted in the right of subjects to address petitions to their ruler has, in modern times, been transformed into the custom of addressing pleas or complaints to the Federal President, the Federal Chancellor, individual ministers or Members of Parliament (Patzelt 2005: 207). Furthermore, article 45c of the Constitution states that the *Bundestag* must appoint a petition committee to deal with all petitions. Therefore, the Constitution not only protects the right of petition, it also stipulates the provision of a committee to process petitions. Since 2005, all petitions that have been signed by a minimum of 50,000 people within a time period of three weeks are discussed in a public committee meeting. Since that time, too, petitions can also be handed in, discussed and signed via email or on the government web page (Ismayr 2009: 525). In France, the right of petition is not explicitly mentioned in the Constitution. The law only sets out the terms and conditions under which voters can apply to use the right of petition (art. 72-1).

Freedom of association and freedom of assembly are equally granted by the German Constitution. Article 8 states that all Germans have 'the right to assemble peacefully and unarmed without prior notification or permission'. Article 9 governs the freedom of association and gives all Germans 'the right to form associations and other societies' and, furthermore, 'to form associations to safeguard and improve working and economic conditions'. This legitimises volunteer organisations and interest groups, as well as professional associations such as unions. The French Constitution of the Fifth Republic does not feature anything of the sort. Trade unions have only been tolerated in France since the 1870s, being officially authorised and added to the basic rights of the 4th Constitution in 1884. Freedom of association was acknowledged in 1901, after a long period of hesitation, in the shape of a law that has never been included in the constitution (Mény 2005: 287).

Elections

From many points of view, voting in elections at various levels of the political system is a basic civic right and forms a focal point in the struggle for the democratisation of political regimes (Rokkan 1962). The right to vote is the most important and, often, the only form of active participation in political life for many citizens. The prominent status of electoral participation is also mirrored in the French and German constitutional provisions.

In both countries, the right to vote and the election process are guaranteed by their constitutions and various legal texts. In France, citizens have two national votes: one to elect the members of the National Assembly, the other to elect the

President. In Germany, only the *Bundestag* is elected directly by the people (art. 38 of the Basic Law). The section below (*Binding political decisions: the institutions of elections and referendums*) will focus in more detail on the national election process and the right to vote, as will Chapter Eight. The election process at the regional level of the political system will be investigated in Chapter Four.

Direct democracy

Direct democratic practices are only mentioned in the Basic Law to the extent that they apply to the restructuring of Federal Territory according to article 29. Apart from this, such procedures are not in place at the national level, but are part of the constitution of the *Bundesländer* and municipal charters (Ismayr 2009: 517). In France, elements of direct democracy are implemented more prominently at the national level. Referendums are discussed below and Chapter Six.

Participative rights at different political levels

Decisional authority is differently allocated to the various tiers of the French and German political system, as the French system is unitary and the German system is federal. Since the German Basic Law states explicitly that democratic principles are constitutive elements of the state and local political organisation (art. 20), it comes as no surprise that Germany and France differ in terms of the horizontal distribution of individual participative rights at different levels of the political system.

France is classed as a 'unitary centralist state', in which municipalities have very limited influence on central decisions (Schild 2006: 111). As a result, French citizens can only exercise genuine political influence at the national level. They can participate regionally via the elections of communal, departmental and regional councils, but these political units have only limited influence on central politics, which means that civil participation at this level has only a limited degree of political leverage.

Germany, on the other hand, is a federal state and distributes authority horizontally amongst its political units. The German *Bundesländer* (Federal States) enjoy a high degree of autonomy. They have their own constitutions and government bodies, and article 70 of the *Grundgesetz* grants them the right of legislation. They also administer their own finances and influence central decisions through the *Bundesrat* (Federal Council). German citizens, therefore, have the opportunity to influence national politics through the parliaments of the federal states. This gives them an additional option to participate in the political process (Ismayr 2009: 552; Kropp 2005a: 377).

We have seen that France's centralism offers fewer opportunities for citizen participation than is the case of Germany's federalism. Schild (2006: 110) argues that active participation in municipal politics, a key component of political socialisation in other systems, is hindered by the limited authority of local political subdivisions in France. A federal system such as that of Germany offers more opportunities for participation, as civil bodies and organised groups have easier access to national and regional institutions, not least because their physical vicinity is closer (Kropp 2005a: 377).

Summary

Regarding the criteria concerning strong or weak citizen participation set out above, there are a number of points to be made about legally-stipulated participative rights. With regard to the criteria of *formalisation*, Germany displays signs of a strong participatory system, as its civic rights are guaranteed both in the Constitution and by federal law. By contrast, these rights are not explicitly specified in France. Although the French Constitution refers first to the preamble of the Fourth Republic, only the right to organise unions is explicitly mentioned there. Therefore, with respect to the criteria of formalisation, France displays a rather weak participatory system, Germany a rather strong one.

Regarding the criterion of 'inclusiveness', the conclusion is somewhat different: at first glance, there appear to be no differences between France and Germany, as in both countries only citizens can use their institutionally-granted participative rights. However, in France, it is easier than in Germany to become a legal citizen; residents can be naturalised after living five years in France compared to eight years in Germany. Equally, children living in France automatically become citizens on attaining their majority, which is not the case in Germany; France therefore shows more inclusiveness concerning such rights.

Germany and France differ in the strength of the participatory system with reference to the criterion of 'scope'. Germany has an advantage in this respect; as a federal state it displays strong local self-administration, which provides its citizens with access to diverse opportunities of participation at different levels of the political system. In France, only very limited opportunities for citizens to influence decisions exist at different levels of the political system. However, the scope of national participative rights is wider in France as stronger elements of direct democracy are present, which is not the case for Germany at the national level. As we will show below, electoral democracy is also more developed in France than in Germany, while Germany offers more participative opportunities to its citizens as far as parties and voluntary associations are concerned.

As to the 'impact' of the forms of participation, it can be noted that, as France has more elements of direct democracy – like the direct election of the president and the possibility of national referendums – French citizens have more binding decisional competencies than German citizens. However, Germany has significantly more formalised rights of association, e.g. the *Grundgesetz* stipulates that the *Bundestag*, via the petition committee, must deal with incoming petitions.

Binding political decisions: the institutions of elections and referendums

The various forms of participation can be differentiated into those that are more consultative in nature (such as petitions) and those resulting in binding decisions for the entire political community (such as elections and referendums). Both types of process involve a decision of the electorate that is binding on the political community and its representatives. As referendums and elections are of particular importance, they are explored in more detail below.

Elections are an indispensable element of any representative democracy. Citizens collectively select representatives who have, for a fixed period of time, to make binding decisions on their behalf. Elections are the only form of participation used by a majority of citizens. This can be attributed to several factors: elections take place relatively rarely; eligible voters can participate without much effort; and voting entails only low opportunity costs.

The right of citizens to participate in the selection of their political leaders is set out in all democratic constitutions and is considered as a crucial element of democracy and the principle governing popular sovereignty. In addition, the struggle for the democratic right to vote has been a key element of the process of democratisation and modernisation in many countries.

When it comes to other forms of political participation, however, opinions differ considerably. This is especially so as regards a referendum, in which a decision on specific policies is made by the citizens themselves. Such procedures are implemented in some democracies, but not in others. There are certain differences between Germany and France in this respect. The advantages and disadvantages of direct democracy and the question of how direct democracy can be combined with a representative democratic system are the subject of lively debates in political research, especially in normative democratic theory. Opponents of direct democracy are generally of the opinion that its elements are irreconcilable with a representative democratic system and, what is more, they are too time-consuming, inefficient and expensive, and lead to a blurring of responsibilities. Supporters of direct democracy, however, praise their legitimacy, transparency and responsiveness (Walter-Rogg 2008: 243).

Elections

The right to vote and eligibility for office

In order to exercise one's active and passive electoral rights (i.e. right to vote and right to run for office) in either France or Germany, one must be a legal citizen of the respective country, as these rights are included within civil rights (Haensch and Tümmers 1993: 135). In both countries, however, foreign EU citizens have the right to vote and to run for office at the European and municipal level.

The minimum age of eighteen in order to vote for a political representative at the national level applies to both France and Germany. This means that any person of that age or over can vote in any political election: there are no differences between France and Germany in this respect. There are, however, some federal states[3] (*Bundesländer*) in Germany in which citizens of sixteen or over are allowed to cast their vote in local elections; this is not the case in France.

The minimum age required to run for political office is eighteen in Germany (*BWahlG* (law on elections) art. 15). In France, citizens must be aged eighteen to be elected in municipal, general or regional elections; to be elected for the president or to the National Assembly, only persons aged twenty-three or over are eligible. In order to be elected as a senator, a French citizen must be at least thirty years old. All in all, a citizen generally has to be older in France than in Germany in order to be eligible to run for office. This means that fewer citizens can make use of this form of participation in France than they can in Germany.

Which government bodies are elected?

In France, the following government bodies at all levels are elected by popular vote: the presidency and the National Assembly, municipal councils, general councils, regional councils and the European Parliament (Kempf 2009: 372). The different councils are mainly elected by means of the 'first-past-the-post' election system. Those councils then elect the president of the council or the mayor, as posts with most power at this level (Schild 2006: 123; Kempf 2009: 395). The Senate (the second house of parliament) is elected indirectly by the representatives of communities, regions and departments, who have themselves been elected. The direct election of the president was incorporated into the Constitution in 1962 – following a referendum on this subject (previously, the president was elected indirectly). The direct election of the French President underlines this important position in the French political system, which is frequently characterised as 'semi-presidential' (Kempf 2009: 355).

Germans directly elect the *Bundestag* (lower house of the Federal Parliament), the sixteen different *Landtage* (parliaments of the *Bundesländer*), the members of the European Parliament, municipal and county councils, as well as mayors and – in some *Länder* – the district administrator. The *Bundesrat* (second house of parliament) consists of irregularly alternating members of state governments, who appoint or remove them from this position.

It might seem, after close examination of the voting system in both countries, that French citizens have more influence on the political process, as they elect both the National Assembly and the president directly, whereas Germans *only* elect the members of the *Bundestag*. One must not forget, however, that the political power of the French Parliament was weakened in the transition to the Fifth Republic, with most political power now resting with the government and the president, who himself appoints the government. The government is not elected by the parliament, as is the case in Germany.

---

3. Lower Saxony, Schleswig-Holstein, Saxony-Anhalt, North Rhine-Westfalia, and Mecklenburg-West Pomerania.

Which basic principles apply to the election process?

The Constitutions of France and Germany state that elections must be direct, free, equal, general and secret (art. 38 of the Basic Law and art.3 of the French Constitution of the Fifth Republic). The principle of directness refers to the fact that citizens elect their political representatives directly and not via an electoral college. The principle of freedom means that the voting process must not be influenced by pressure from outside. The principle of equality refers to the premise that all adult citizens are entitled to vote and that every vote carries the same significance ('one man, one vote'). The principle of confidentiality secures the principle of freedom, as it ensures that no direct or indirect pressure or force is applied to voters.

Duration of legislative periods

In France, the president and the National Assembly are currently elected for a period of five years. The duration of the presidency was reduced in 2002 to five years (previously seven years), with deputies – men and women – being elected six weeks after the presidential election. This decision strengthens the position of the president even more. It can be assumed that – having just elected the president – voters are unlikely to trigger off a parliamentary situation that is counterproductive for their newly-elected president (Kempf 2009: 353). The Senate and the councils of all political sub-divisions are elected or appointed for a period of six years (Haensch and Tümmers 1993: 208).

In Germany, the *Bundestag* is elected for a period of four years. The parliaments of the *Bundesländer* are elected for a legislative period of four or five years, whereas municipal councils remain in office for five years. Mayors are elected for five to eight years, depending on the *Bundesland*, while a member of the European Parliament remains in office for five years.

It can, therefore, be said that as German citizens have the opportunity to confirm or recall a newly-elected government within a relatively short period, they consequently participate in the political process more frequently than the French.

Which laws apply to elections?

The exact election process is not set out in the French Constitution. This means that laws governing elections can be altered by simple parliamentary majority. As a result, changes in the electoral law are not uncommon in France. For example, proportional representation has tended to be replaced by majority voting. Majority representation is currently in place at virtually all levels of the political system as, for example, in the election of the National Assembly. In this two-round election, 577 constituencies elect their 577 representatives. A candidate must obtain more than 50 per cent of the votes, as well as a minimum of one quarter of the registered votes in the first ballot; if not, a second ballot is held after one week and a relative majority then suffices to win. All candidates with 12.5 per cent or more of the votes are entitled to participate in this round, which means that the second round usually comprises no more than two to four candidates (Kempf 2009: 37, Schild 2000: 56). In the case of the presidential elections, if a candidate does not receive an absolute majority of votes, a second ballot is held after 14 days: according to article 7 of the Constitution, only the two candidates with most votes in the first ballot can then go through to the second round (Pütz 2004: 45).

The electoral process in Germany is only partly outlined in the Constitution and stipulates temporal guidelines, the duration of the electoral period and details regarding the dissolution of parliament (art. 39); other details are set out in federal legislation. The 598 delegates in the *Bundestag* have, since 1949, been elected in accordance with the system described below (BWahlG art.1). Each voter has two votes in the *Bundestag* elections. The first vote allows citizens to elect representatives from 299 constituencies as part of a first-past-the-post election system (BWahlG art.5). The second, more important, vote is used according to the principle of party-list proportional representation; it determines the distribution of all *Bundestag* seats amongst those political parties obtaining at least 5 per cent of the votes cast. It is this vote which, in fact, determines the formation of the government (BWahlG art.6). Each party is allocated a number of seats in the *Bundestag* in proportion to the number of votes it has obtained. When the total number of mandates won by a party has been determined, those mandates are then distributed between the sixteen states. The first of the mandates allocated to each state goes to the candidates who have won direct mandates in that state. The rest are assigned in order of the position of the candidates on the state party organisation tickets. Additionally, there are circumstances in which certain candidates win what is referred to as an 'overhang seat'.[4] The election of state parliaments uses basically the same election system – with a few minor differences between individual states (Ismayr 2009: 536; Rudzio 2006: 161).

Institutional facilitation or restriction

The French election system presents a certain number of obstacles for citizens to overcome on their way to the ballot box. Voters must register in their electoral district before an election; in order to do so, they must have been living in the electoral district for at least six months. The lists of voters compiled by the electoral districts serve as the basis for the distribution of voting cards. Since November 1997, all citizens have been automatically added to the voting lists in their electoral district as soon as they turn eighteen. Nevertheless, even with this new, much easier system of automatic registration, the arrangement remains problematic, as citizens must register on their own initiative when they move to a new electoral district. Owing to the mandatory registration of voters, observers assume that be-

---

4. If a party has gained more direct mandates in one state than it is entitled to according to the results of the second vote, it keeps these mandates because all directly-elected candidates are guaranteed a seat in the *Bundestag* (for further information, see Rudzio 2006: 161).

tween 6 per cent and 10 per cent of potential voters are not registered to vote. In addition, France does not offer the possibility of a postal vote since this was abolished in 1975 in order to avoid fraud. The postal vote was replaced by the *vote par procuration*. This 'substitutional' vote, which is also available to French expatriates, allows a person who is unable to vote to send another person from their borough to cast the vote in their stead (Appelton 2000: 207; Kempf 2007: 235).

In Germany, voters are not required to register prior to an election, as they are registered and notified automatically. Furthermore, citizens have the option of a postal vote (BWahlG art. 14 para. 3 and art. 36).

Summary

What do the constitutional and legal arrangements imply for the characteristics of voting as part of a participatory system in France and Germany?

Elections and their basic principles, procedures and the particular political units to be elected are precisely regulated by the constitutions of both countries, and also federal law in Germany. Therefore, there are only a few differences between France and Germany concerning the degree of election 'formalisation'.

Regarding 'inclusiveness', France and Germany differ most notably with regard to their passive electoral rights (right to run for office). While active electoral rights (right to vote) at the national level apply to all citizens of full age (except for local and European elections, in which EU-foreigners also have the right to vote), passive electoral rights are more restricted in France than in Germany, which can thus be regarded as more inclusive than France with respect to passive electoral rights. Additionally, France and Germany differ with regard to active electoral rights at state level. In some German federal states (*Bundesstaaten*), citizens of sixteen or over have the right to vote in local elections, whereas in France, citizens have to be eighteen or over to be allowed to cast their vote, at whatsoever level of election.

With regard to 'scope', it should be noted that different bodies are elected in both countries at different levels of the political system. French citizens elect their president via direct elections, and it is they who subsequently elect the National Assembly; at the national level, German citizens only elect the members of the *Bundestag*; those members then go on to elect the chancellor. In Germany, citizens cannot elect the president or chancellor directly but, as the legislative periods for parliaments are shorter, more elections take place than in France. Hence, German citizens have the chance, via elections, to participate in the political system more often. This also shows the differences with regard to the 'impact' of these forms of participation. As the political leaders are selected through elections, these can be seen as direct decisions of the citizens; by definition, then, elections have a large impact. French citizens, however, benefit from having a greater number of national leadership positions open to popular elections.

Referendums

As regards referendums, it seems appropriate to define a few relevant terms. Melanie Walter-Rogg (2008: 239) distinguishes three types of direct democratic practices:

- *mandatory referendums* – required and normally concern constitutional reforms or amendments;
- *plebiscites* – public ballots that are held on the initiative of the appropriate authorities, whether the government, parliament or the head of state;
- *initiatives, petitions* or *facultative referendums* – initiated by the citizens themselves and usually subject to a quorum to ensure representativeness.

National referendums

In France, direct democratic practices are employed at all levels of the political system (see Walter-Rogg 2008: 248). The French president has the option of initiating a national referendum, if this is proposed by the government or by the two houses of parliament (art. 11 of the Constitution). The discrepancy between the constitutional premise and reality is shown by the fact that, with one exception – the referendum on the status of New Caledonia in November 1988 – referendums have always been initiated by the president himself, rather than by the government or one of the parliamentary houses. Basically, a referendum of this kind constitutes a vote of confidence for the head of state (Kempf 2009: 355). Historically, apart from direct election, the referendum has also been the president's main means of communication with his people. This applied particularly to President Charles de Gaulle, who used referendums mainly, if not exclusively, for this purpose. According to the constitutional reform of 21st July 2008, it is now possible for the parliament to initiate a referendum in conjunction with the electorate. Article 11 states that such a procedure requires the support of one fifth of all Members of Parliament and one tenth of all registered voters (Kempf 2009: 399). This means that the electorate is unable to instigate a referendum without the support of a certain proportion of parliamentary delegates. Article 89 of the Constitution also allows a referendum in order to instigate constitutional changes or amendments. However, if the president decides to present a legislative proposal to the parliament, no referendum is held.[5] In France, referendums are part and parcel of national politics and are included in the Constitution in various forms. Christine Pütz argues, however, that 'the plebiscitary character of the Fifth Republic has lost most of its significance' (Pütz 2004: 44, authors' translation).

In Germany, although referendums do not form part of national politics, they can be used for regional politics within the *Bundesländer*. The only scenario that would call for a *mandatory national referendum*, according to article 29 of the

---

5. The draft for changing the constitution is considered officially accepted by the parliament if it is subsequently supported by at least three-fifths of the votes of parliament.

Grundgesetz, is a restructuring of the Federal Territory. Other direct democratic measures are theoretically enabled by art. 20, para. 2, but are not stipulated by the *Grundgesetz* (Gabriel and Völkl 2005: 542).

Referendums at the regional level

Ever since the French constitutional reform on state decentralisation was passed in 2003/04, regional and local political units have been able to hold binding referendums; previously, these decisions were merely consultative. Additionally, the reform gave voters the right of petition, thereby enabling them to have issues added to the agenda of council meetings in their municipality, which can then lead to a referendum to determine an issue (art. 72-1 of the Constitution). Petitions and initiatives are therefore possible in all local municipalities – but not often found in practice. The referendum, as a powerful democratic instrument, is still in the hands of elected local politicians and cannot be initiated by the public (Schild 2006: 115; Kempf 2009: 395).

Germany is one of those countries with a political system that strictly adheres to the principle of representative democracy. This becomes particularly obvious if one considers the lack of direct democratic measures at the national level. Until 1989, only seven states made use of the referendum as a decision-making instrument. After reunification, however, the rise of direct democracy began. Ever since 1998, various forms of referendums have been possible in all German states (Gabriel and Völkl 2005: 542; Zintl 2005: 108). Bills can be introduced at state level at citizens' initiative: this is classified as a *facultative referendum.* Although the quorum varies, it never drops below 10 per cent. If a State Parliament accepts a proposal put forward by such an initiative, the new legislation comes into force; if it does not accept the proposal, a referendum is then held, with a quorum of not less than 25 per cent of the voters. The same procedure is used for constitutional reforms and amendments. Some states place more importance on the direct democratic component (i.e. art. 76 of the Bavarian Constitution, or art. 123 of the Hessian Constitution): in such cases, a referendum is obligatory for constitutional reforms or amendments. In other states, it is entirely up to the representative authority as to whether or not a referendum is held (e.g. arts 100 and 101 of the Saarland Constitution; see also Ismayr 2009: 553; Zintl 2005: 108). Some state constitutions also allow for 'civil initiatives' (or 'civil petitions'), which serve to put an issue forward for discussion within the representative body (e.g. Brandenburg, art. 76; Mecklenburg-Western Pomerania, art. 80; Lower Saxony, Art. 47; Saxony, art. 71, etc.). Even the dissolution of the State Parliament itself may be the object of such a petition.

At the third administrative level of the Federal Republic of Germany, that of municipalities, there is a wide range of municipal charters, but they do not lend themselves readily to any simple synthesis. One common feature is that the mayor is elected directly in all German *Länder.* In 1990, direct democratic measures were introduced at the municipal level in all states. A civil petition requires 3 to 17 per cent of agreement amongst citizens of the community. The quorum for actual decisions via communal referendums is relatively high at 20–30 per cent (Ismayr 2009: 553; for further details, see Chapter Six).

Summary

What can be stated about the four criteria of a strong participatory system concerning referendum regulations in Germany and France?

With regard to formalisation, France displays more signs of a strong participatory system than does Germany, at least at national level. In France, national level referendums are more formalised, being stipulated in the constitution. By contrast, in Germany, referendums are mentioned in the Constitution only with respect to the reorganisation of German territory (boundary modifications of the *Bundesstaaten*). However, at the regional level, referendums in France have only provided an opportunity to participate since the 2004/05 decentralisation reform; previously, referendums were only of a consultative nature. In Germany, referendums – indubitably important instruments of civic participation – have existed at the local level since 1990 and are stipulated in the constitutions of the German federal states (*Bundesländer*). In short, while France displays a higher degree of referendum formalisation at the national level, Germany has more formalised rights for referendums at local and regional levels.

France and Germany differ only slightly regarding the inclusiveness of referendums. In both countries, those citizens who are eligible to vote in elections are also allowed to vote in referendums. Sometimes in Germany more people are allowed to vote at the local level than in France because some of the German federal states accord active electoral rights to their citizens from the age of sixteen. This is not the case in France; in this respect, Germany's referendum regulations appear to be more inclusive than those in France.

With regard to scope, Germany is the front runner in terms of territorial organisation, providing more opportunities to participate at the various sub-national levels of the political system than in France. At the national level, however, France displays wider scope, as plebiscites[6] exist as an option at the national level in France but not in Germany.

As for referendums, it should be noted that referendums *per se* have a strong impact, being direct decisions emanating from citizens. In France, however, referendums at the regional level are sometimes of a consultative nature. In Germany, facultative as well as mandatory referendums are to be found at both regional and local levels.

---

6. Plebiscites are public ballots decided on and initiated by the authorities (the initiator can be the government, the parliament or the head of state).

Constitutional and legal foundations of collective action: political parties, interest groups and voluntary associations

There are many ways for a country's citizens to influence the political process: they can do so directly via elections, petitions and referendums, or indirectly via actively participating in intermediate organisations such as parties or interest groups. By using the immediate forms of political participation described in the previous sections, citizens can exert a binding influence on politics in varying degrees. The indirect means of political participation that citizens have at their disposal are further explored in this section. Citizens are free to set up and support associations, parties, or interest groups, all of which play an active role in the political process and represent citizens' interests. By supporting or actively joining these organisations – which act as intermediaries between citizens and the political system – citizens can collectively influence politics in ways additional to those measures available to individual citizens. Sometimes parties or interest groups are officially involved in the political decision-making process and hold positions on different political committees and panels. Participating in a party or interest group increases citizens' opportunities to be elected to office in various sectors of public life.[7] In this way, intermediate organisations offer citizens another, albeit indirect, means of political participation. France and Germany show some differences, but also similarities, in this respect and the section below investigates the institutions of collective civil action – intermediate organisations, such as parties, lobby groups or voluntary associations – that mediate between the individual citizen and the political system.

In France, parties and interest groups were not incorporated into the Constitution before the founding of the Fifth Republic; this was due, in part, to a traditionally individualist and republican way of thinking, inherent in French society. This is a view that closely resembles the idea proposed by Rousseau, which sees citizens joining together in a civil society through the social contract. It was assumed that intermediate organisations only represented particular individual interests, instead of the common welfare pursued by the state (*volonté générale*). In France, therefore, collectively-organised political participation plays only a minor role. This effect applies also to political parties, being frequently described as an 'anti-party effect'.

Another reason for the late development and weakness of French political parties lies in the social structure of the country – predominantly rural-agricultural until the middle of the twentieth century, with industrialisation and urbanisation progressing only slowly. Neither of these processes, however, has similarly exacerbated the emergence of political parties in other countries (Pütz 2004: 47; Schild 2005: 269). Compared to other contemporary democracies, the French party system shows a lesser degree of organisation and stability, while it is also more ideo-

---

7. Participation in political parties is often classified as conventional political participation (see the chapter by Bauknecht). On the contrary, participation in interest groups and volunteer associations is classified as social participation (see Chapter Seven of this book).

logically fragmented (Haensch and Tümmers 1993: 280). Other bodies that can act as agents between citizens and state (such as associations, lobby groups and trade unions) are less powerful and important in France than in Germany (Pütz 2004: 47; Schild 2006: 38). In Germany, such organisations have emerged out of a long-standing tradition: not only are they incorporated into the *Grundgesetz,* but they also constitute an integral part of the German political system. Parties and interest groups in Germany are well-organised and efficiently structured, and play an active part in the political process. They are closely connected to the government, as administrative legislation requires the government to officially contact them 'when formulating new policies that may affect their interests' (Dalton 2000: 296).

Parties

The constitutional position of political parties

The Constitution of the Fifth Republic gave France's political parties a constitutional position for the first time, but the role of those parties is limited to their participation in elections and does not extend, as it does in Germany, to an active contribution in political decision-making (art. 4 of the Constitution; see also Haensch and Tümmers 1993: 148; Schild 2005: 271). France does not have any specific legislation regarding political parties (Kempf 2007: 173) and the public funding of parties has only been in place since 1988. Nevertheless, the law on party funding passed in 1988 was the first to define the role and function of political parties in detailed fashion. Article 8 states that political parties are not restricted in their activities, can be set up by any citizen, and have the right to accept donations (Kempf 2009: 376; Schild 2005: 271).

In Germany, political parties are a more prominent element of the Constitution and article 21, paragraph 1 of the Basic Law stipulates their role and function in the political system as active contributors to the decision-making process. This gives parties there a larger field of activity, going beyond the mere electoral participation set out in the French Constitution (Ismayr 2009: 538). Furthermore, article 21, paragraph 1, states that parties must themselves be internally structured in accordance with democratic principles, which is not the case in France. Setting up a political party is, however, open to all citizens in both countries. In Germany, the legal status of political parties is not only laid down in article 21 of the Basic Law, but also by the law on political parties (*Parteiengesetz*) and election regulations (*Bundeswahlgesetz*). The law on political parties assigns them such indispensible functions as mediation between citizens and the political system, the formation of public policies and the recruitment of political leaders. A party, however, must take part in an election for the national or a regional parliament within six years of being set up, if it is to be allowed to continue its work (art. 2 of the Law on Political Parties). Article 6 of the same law dictates that every party must ensure that its manifesto and statutes are written, as this secures its status and defines its rights and duties (Ismayr 2009: 538; Tsatsos 1997: 148).

Membership of political parties

According to the German Constitution, all citizens are lawfully entitled to join a political party. Membership can only be denied if granting it would endanger the party's existence. As for the party, it has certain rights when it comes to accepting new members, being generally free in its decision to accept or refuse a particular citizen as a party member. Only if the refusal to accept new party members was general policy, would this be a breach of regulations (art. 10, para. 1, *Part G*). It is possible for foreign citizens or persons not yet enfranchised to become members of a political party,[8] so long as they do not constitute the majority of members (Tsatsos 1997: 150; Ismayr 2009: 541). In France, party membership is not institutionally regulated; every individual organisation is free to decide who should be accepted. Since it is not just every citizen, but every resident who can become member of a political party both in Germany and France, party membership provides one of the few opportunities foreign residents have for participating in the political process, albeit at an intermediate level.

The influence of political parties

There are obvious differences between France and Germany regarding the influence of parties on the political process. In France, a political party suffers from a relatively weak position due to the two-headed structure of its executive authority, and the imbalance in power between government and parliament (Jun 2000: 124). The significant position that the French political system assigns to its president has a notable effect on political competition, leading to a personalisation of election campaigns: these tend to focus more on candidates than on the parties that they represent. So far, all presidential candidates elected to office have received the support of a party represented in parliament at the time. Political parties have gradually gained more importance due to the fact that presidential candidates depend on their affiliated party for financial support, and also the support of its most prominent figures (Pütz 2000: 83; Schild 2005: 273). The way political parties are structured and organised internally has been 'presidentialised': parties are often characterised by a great concentration of power at their head, which means that they can be more easily used strategically by presidential candidates (Schild 2005: 274). The result of this is the typically French phenomenon of the *parti presidentiel* – a political party that makes winning the presidential election its chief priority, with all its long-term measures being devoted to achieving this objective (Pütz 2000: 86; Jun 2000: 133).

Nevertheless, parties do play a certain part in the political decision-making process in France. The Fifth Republic was originally intended to minimise the

---

8. The statutes of each party stipulate the minimum age required to become a party member. The organisational statutes of the SPD (Social Democratic Party), Art.2, for example, allow persons to join from the age of 14; for the CDU (Christian Democratic Party), the minimum age is 16 (Party statutes of the CDU, Art.4).

influence of political parties.⁹ It was decided that the directly-elected president should be enabled to govern both parliament and parties by means of a strong executive branch. Once the presidency of Charles de Gaulle had ended, however, parties were able to re-establish their influence, and they remain a major factor in the structuring of political competition. It is their responsibility to organise elections and to appoint political personnel. Furthermore, they can influence the formation of the government and its policies, as coalitions are formed on the basis of party political factors (Pütz 2004: 48). Depending on the political majority at the time, the influence of political parties on the formation of the government has fluctuated considerably in the past. A congruent political majority party in the presidential election and the National Assembly puts the executive branch in a dominant position (Jun 2000: 137), leaving parties with less influence than they would enjoy in the case of 'cohabitation'.¹⁰ If there is a conflict between party heads and the government, the upper hand lies with the government in the context of rationalised parliamentarianism, even in the case of cohabitation.¹¹ Political parties have also gained more influence over the recruitment of administrative staff and public service personnel (Pütz 2000: 93).

When directly compared to the situation in Germany, however, the role and function of political parties in the Fifth Republic seems rather limited, due to two institutional factors. One is the direct election of the French president, whose central position provides a barrier against a possible upgrading of parties in the political process, especially when it comes to government policies and decisions. The other important factor is the possibility of reaching political decisions by means of a national referendum, the outcome of which cannot possible be controlled by the parties (Schild 2005: 273). All in all, French parties – relatively weak when compared to their German equivalents – are not entirely powerless (Pütz 2000: 98).

In Germany, the situation is different. The law on political parties, passed in 1967, gives them clear responsibilities including developing manifestos and agendas, recruiting political personnel, forming the government, influencing parliamentary and governmental politics, aggregating and articulating opinions and interests, as well as ensuring political communication. Parties decide on the composition of parliament and government, and enjoy a considerable degree of influence over the decision-making process in both authorities. Most of the time, members

---

9. Charles de Gaulle intended to circumvent parties as intermediate organisations between citizens and the state by introducing direct democratic elements; the fact that solid majorities were something of a rarity in the parliamentary system of the 4th Republic (1946-1958), prevented a stable political process (see Haensch/Tümmers 1993: 276; Jansen 2001: 127; Pütz 2000: 77; Schild 2005: 269).

10. This refers to a situation in which the executive is split into two, with the President being part of one political tendency and the government representing another.

11. The term 'rationalised parliamentarianism' mainly refers to the use of a so-called 'vote bloqué'. The prime minister can attach the vote on a legislative proposal to a vote of confidence. The proposal is considered to be accepted unless a motion of no confidence is brought forward and accepted within 24 hours (Jun 2000: 125ff.).

of the *Bundestag* can only exercise their rights as members of a parliamentary party. Parliamentary groups are given a dominant function in boards and committees, whereas individual delegates have only a few rights. Additionally, the election system gives German political parties a major say in the decision as to who joins the *Bundestag,* by requiring that parties put forward their lists of candidates prior to the election (Dalton 2000: 306; Ismayr 2009: 538; Rudzio 2006: 93). As a consequence, the German political system has often been characterised as a party state or party democracy.

The role of parties at different levels of the political system

Since, even after the regional reform of 1982/83, France can be defined as a predominantly centralist political system, there is no necessity for an efficient organisation of political parties at the local and regional level. Party organisations in rural areas are often little more than election committees or mere instruments of the local notables (Haensch and Tümmers 1993: 148).

In comparison, Germany's federal system grants regional party branches a great deal of autonomy. The national representation of a party has relatively few rights to intervene in the organisation of one of its state branches, as far as policies and personnel issues are concerned. According to the *Bundeswahlgesetz*, only the nomination of constituency delegates can be vetoed at the national level, and this seldom happens. The position of parties in the system is stressed by the Constitution, but it is also expressed through the parties' participation in the political process in Germany, where the parties play a prominent part (Dalton 2000: 309; Rudzio 2006: 138).

Summary

After careful examination of the criteria for evaluating the participatory systems in Germany and France, the following points can be made about the participation of parties.

With regard to 'formalisation', Germany displays many elements of a strong participatory system, as parties are institutionalised by the *Grundgesetz* as well as by federal law. In France, reference to parties is now stipulated in the Constitution, but only as regards their involvement in elections. In Germany, significantly more functions are assigned to parties and, furthermore, Germany has a specific law concerning political parties, which is not the case in France.

There is, however, no difference as regards the criterion of 'inclusiveness': parties in both countries can themselves decide to whom membership may be granted or denied. Even under-age and foreign persons can, in principle, become members of parties.

As for the 'scope' of opportunities to participate via parties, Germany – with its essentially autonomous regional party branches – shows strong territorial organisation, whereas in France the regional organisation of parties is often merely in the form of informal election committees. With respect to scope at national level, parties in Germany have greater formal opportunities to influence politics, and are also assigned more functions. In France, the opportunities of parties to influence politics are rather limited.

The 'impact' of political parties is definitely greater in Germany than in France. Parties in Germany determine the composition of the government and parliament, recruit the political personnel and significantly shape the decision-making process in the different political entities. A party's right to participate in decision-making processes is also legally recognised and, hence, more binding than in France. For parties in Germany, the aggregation and articulation of opinions and interests perform an important function and, consequently, strongly influence the priority and presence of different topics on the political agenda (agenda-setting) and, hence, the formation of citizens' opinions. The situation is quite the opposite in France, where the parties have a rather weak institutional position in the governmental system due to the dominance of the government over parliament and the strong position of the president. In the context of rationalised parliamentarianism, the government always prevails over party leaders. In addition, political parties are less often associated with that important function of aggregation and articulation of opinions and interests that is credited to parties in Germany.

In conclusion, as regards indirect participation via parties, Germany shows a stronger participatory system than France, where the parties are assigned a less central role.

Interest groups and voluntary associations

Position under constitutional law

The French Constitution does not mention groups, societies or volunteer associations. Only trade unions are included in the preamble to the Constitution of the Fifth Republic, which refers to the Declaration of Human and Civil Rights. It states that all citizens are entitled to defend their rights and interests by joining a trade union. Article 4 of the Constitution, which defines the role and function of political parties, refers to 'political groups' more generally; hence, trade unions and other interest groups can be subsumed under this definition. Unlike in Germany, however, neither trade unions nor interest groups are explicitly mentioned in the Constitution.

Freedom of association was first institutionalised in France by means of a law passed in 1901. Previously, associations were not considered as bodies with legal status. The specific freedom of 'coalition' (the right to set up associations to protect economic and working conditions), was implemented in 1884 – previously, trade unions were merely tolerated. The right to implement collective labour agreements was introduced in 1919. Until then, trade unions and employers' associations had not enjoyed any legal status and were not acknowledged as negotiating parties. Even today, only organisations legally classified as 'representative' are truly acknowledged as negotiating or consultative partners by the state.[12] The basic notion of common welfare (*volonté générale*) still determines the relationship between the state and associations. Using the rule of representativeness, the state decides which organisations to acknowledge as legitimate representatives of interests by giving them a voice in consultative meetings and committees. Consequently, the state still has the option of excluding some associations, whilst establishing relations with others (Jansen 2001: 125; Kempf 2009: 387; Mény 2005: 287).

The German *Grundgesetz* underlines the important position of interest groups and associations within the administrative system by explicitly mentioning the right of association in article 9 (Kropp 2005b: 665): this grants all Germans 'the right to form associations and other societies'. Paragraph 3 states that 'the right to form associations to safeguard and improve working and economic conditions is guaranteed to everyone and to all trades and professions'. Associations and interest groups in Germany enjoy a status that is secured and formalised by the Constitution; this is not the case in France.

In Germany, the official status of interest groups and associations is legally established,[13] albeit not in the same way as it is for political parties. This is because the Constitution does not define the functioning of interest groups in the same way as it does for political parties, such as participation in the political decision-making process (Kropp 2005b: 666). Moreover, interest groups are not legally required to have an internal democratic structure (Tsatsos 1997: 147). Nevertheless, associations and interest groups are institutionalised to a greater extent in Germany than in France,[14] as the constitutional freedom of association and the freedom of coalition can be considered as providing the necessary basis; this, however, is not the case in France.

Membership of interest groups and volunteer associations

In France, there are no regulations in place stating who can join an association and who is prohibited from doing so; consequently, societies and associations can decide freely whom to accept. Equally, the German law on associations does not limit or regulate access (*VereinsG* art. 2, para. 1), although clubs, associations and societies are not obliged to accept every citizen (Kropp 2005b: 665). In fact, any

---

12. The criteria for representativeness stated in the legislation on employment since 1946 are: number of members, independence, income, experience and age, as well as patriotic beliefs during the time of occupation in WW II. These criteria were originally developed for trade unions, but have been applied to other professional associations since the 1950s (Jansen 2001: 129).

13. According to article 2 of the law on associations and groups, an association (German: *Verein*) is the voluntary union of persons or corporate entities for a common purpose, regardless of whether they are vested with legal capacity. A club has legal capacity if its particulars are listed in the official register of associations. Such clubs must have statutes defining their name, location, and aims (BGB art. 21–79).

14. This also regulates their status and authority under the rules and regulations of parliament, government and ministries (Reutter 2001: 78).

person, not just any citizen can, in principle, become a member of an association and as such participate in the political process in an intermediate fashion.

The influence of interest groups and volunteer associations

As we have seen, there are considerable differences between France and Germany regarding the legal status and political influence of interest groups and associations. As discussed in the section above on political parties, only organisations that are legally acknowledged as 'representative' can act as negotiators with the state. To achieve this, organisations have to orientate themselves towards the public good (Jansen 2001: 129; Mény 2005: 297). Such representative organisations are legally entitled to become involved in various consultative bodies. Their opinions are consulted by members of the central government, the department or the community, before important decisions are made (Jansen 2001: 148; Kempf 2009: 269). However, in return for their prominent role, the state involves itself in the daily organisation of groups and associations, creating a relationship of dependency through regulations that control their administration and funding. It is difficult, considering their financial dependence on state funding, for associations to assert their independence (Jansen 2001: 144).

Since the early days of the Fifth Republic, the manner in which interests are voiced has changed considerably. During the Third and Fourth Republics, representatives of organisations preferred to contact delegates of the National Assembly if they had any requests.[15] When parliament lost much of its political power in the Fifth Republic, interest groups tried to apply pressure directly on ministries and the bureaucracy (Kempf 2007: 283). These days, there has been a strong increase in the number of interest groups, which does not necessarily mean that they also enjoy greater political influence; this rise tends, on the contrary, to reflect their relative weakness. This trend is supported by the relative ease with which a group or quasi-group can gain legal capacity thanks to the law on associations of 1901 (Mény 2005: 292).

Interest groups in Germany are an integral part of the political process. The German system of interest intermediation can be classified as 'corporatist', as there is close co-operation between government, bureaucracy, political parties and interest groups (Reutter 2001: 75). German interest groups are well-organised and efficiently structured, and benefit from frequent communication with the government (Dalton 2000: 296). They participate in the shaping of political decisions and exercise varying degrees of influence on parliament, government, administration, parties and the general public at all levels of the federal system.[16] Interest groups do not take part in political competition in the same manner as parties. Their field

---

15. They were the correct people to address, due to the chronic instability of French governments and the resulting concentration of political power in parliament (Kempf 2007: 269).
16. The most important interest groups are those that protect working and economic conditions. They emerged during the second half or the nineteenth century and were, until the beginning of the Weimar Republic, closely associated with political parties (Ismayr 2009: 544).

of activity is more differentiated and specialised – according to the particular function and social group they represent – and they are designed to operate at a level that is much closer to people. Parties, on the other hand, tend to pursue a more generic political function (Schiller 2005: 459).

Administrative laws require the government to officially contact groups 'when formulating new policies that may affect their interests' (Dalton 2000: 296). The regulations under which the ministries operate (shared rules and regulations) require that representatives of interest groups be included in the preparation of legal bills. National groups as well as special interest associations that operate at a national level must be consulted in good time, in order for a bill to pass through parliament. The first ports of call for all associations in this respect are the specialised boards within the ministries, as this is where legal propositions are drafted. Ministries also have advisory boards, which give interest groups the opportunity to formulate their ideas. Representatives of interest groups comprise a considerable proportion of advisory board members and, as such, benefit from a more long-term influence on the executive branch. The overall aim of interest groups is to influence the creation of legal propositions in order to obtain alterations or amendments before a bill is put to the vote (Kropp 2005b: 682; Ismayr 2009: 546).

The intense interweaving of interest groups and Members of Parliament is particularly obvious in the *Bundestag* committees. Representatives of the agricultural association, for example, are members of the Committee for Agricultural Issues, in the same way as employee organisations are present in the Committee for Labour and Social Affairs. Interest groups strive for permanent influence on parliamentary decisions through their close links with party groups (Kropp 2005b: 680f; Reutter 2001: 94; Rudzio 2006: 73).[17] It is a specific feature of the German system of associations that, compared with what applies in other nations, interest groups and political parties collaborate to a significant extent and that many associations are in a beneficial position for any type of interaction, participation or negotiation regarding central areas of politics (Schiller 1997: 474).

Summary

The four criteria previously used in connection with the other forms of participation are now used in the summary, that follows, to evaluate the opportunities of participation offered via interest groups and volunteer associations.

In Germany, the 'formalisation' and 'institutionalisation' of interest groups and volunteer associations is significantly stronger than in France. The *Grundgesetz* stipulates the right to set up associations and other groups, thereby providing voluntary associations with a statutory basis. Further, there are several federal laws in Germany concerning such organisations (e.g. association legislation). In France, interest groups and volunteer associations are not mentioned in the constitution.

---

17. During the 12th legislative period, approx. 40 per cent of all delegates exercised a function within an interest group.

There is a law of association, but it is the state that decides which groups are to be considered 'representative' and, therefore, accepted as discussion and negotiation partners.

As for 'inclusiveness', it can be established (as was said above in the conclusion dealing with parties) that, in both Germany and France, associations can themselves decide who can become a member. In principle, even young people and foreign persons are allowed to join an association.

With respect to 'scope', Germany, with its federal system, provides more opportunities to exert influence at different levels of the political system. Besides influencing national politics, citizens in Germany can wield influence on the subnational level as regards regional and local politics. In France, however, opportunities at the regional level are rather limited. With regard to the criterion of scope at the national level, Germany provides more formal opportunities for interest groups and voluntary associations to influence politics than France, where the inclusion of these groups in the political process depends on their recognition by the government as being representative. In Germany, by comparison, as some members of interest groups or associations are also parliamentary members, those interest groups and voluntary associations have additional means of influencing politics.

As to the 'impact' of interest groups and voluntary associations, Germany exhibits more features of a strong participatory system than France. In France, as mentioned above, only associations considered as 'representative' by the government have a right to a say in political matters. These groups have to be consulted before important decisions are made. However, as the state interferes very much in associations' activities, the influence of these associations cannot be called strong or autonomous. On the contrary, in Germany, where interest groups and associations constitute an integral part of the political process, the German interest intermediation system can be classified as 'corporatist'. If the government sees the need to pass new laws and regulations, the appropriate interest groups have to be consulted.

Conclusion

So far, we have established that Germany and France differ not only in terms of the informal individual forms of political participation that are part of political life, but also as regards those participative methods that are collective and those which are binding. If the above-mentioned criteria for political participation are applied, these differences can be summarised very clearly (see Table 2.2).

Regarding the criterion of 'formalisation', Germany exhibits more characteristics of a strong participative system than does France, where civil rights such as freedom of assembly or the right to petition are not protected by the Constitution. In addition, intermediate organisations, like parties and voluntary organisations, have a more formalised status in Germany. Forming the political will of citizens, for instance, is – according to the German Constitution – a function of political parties, whereas their only legally-prescribed function in France is their involvement in politics.

The French Constitution does not assign intermediate organisations a particular political function; in fact, for a long time, they had no legal existence and could therefore not be officially accepted. In Germany, besides what is to be found in the Constitution, formal federal laws, such as the law on political parties, precisely regulate the role of intermediate organisations in the political process (see Table 2.2).

In France, direct democratic processes such as referendums are implemented more prominently at the national level, which is not the case in the German political system. As for the election systems of both countries, these are regulated by law.

Germany and France share further common factors if one considers the criterion of 'inclusiveness'. Citizens of both countries can make unlimited use of the participative forms offered by the political system, in addition to their right to vote. Furthermore, both countries set the voting age at eighteen years. However, acquiring full citizenship is easier and quicker to acquire in France – children living in France are automatically granted French citizenship when they attain their majority age; in Germany children would be expelled (if they do not submit their request for naturalisation). Furthermore, adult foreigners living in France can request their naturalisation after only five years, while in Germany they have to wait eight years before making this request.

However, there is also a difference regarding the minimum age required to run for office; since this is higher in France, citizens here are unable to participate in the political process to the same extent as their German neighbours. In what concerns parties and associations, neither country restricts access to any of these organisations; the organisations are free to decide who to accept. Consequently, these interest groups provide foreign residents or under-age persons with a platform for participation (see Table 2.2).

In terms of the 'scope' of associations and interest groups, there are marked differences between France and Germany. France, as a unitary centralist state, whose municipalities enjoy only limited political influence, offers its citizens essentially national-level participation. The federal system of Germany, however, with its authority distributed horizontally amongst political subdivisions, allows greater participation in the political process via its regional parliaments; it also provides easy access to its local institutions, helped by their physical vicinity (Kropp 2005a: 377). This difference is reflected in the political parties – in France, rather informal election committees exist; in Germany, the regional branches of political parties are mostly autonomous. Elections, which also lead to binding decisions, take place more frequently in Germany, on account of shorter legislation periods, which translates into more opportunities for citizen participation.

However, the scope of national participative rights also plays an important role. France offers wider scope as, on the one hand, the president is elected directly and, on the other hand, plebiscites at the national level are stipulated in the Constitution. In Germany, there are no equivalent provisions; the rights of associations, however, are more strongly codified in Germany, while this is less the case in France (see Table 2.2).

When it comes to the 'impact' of both nations' forms of participation and the obligation of the political community to adhere to their signals, different types of participation must be distinguished. Parties and associations, for example, enjoy more political power and influence in Germany than they do in France, and the same goes for the way in which citizens use them to participate in politics. Furthermore, parties in Germany also have a strong influence on political agenda-setting. An important function in the aggregation and articulation of opinions and interests (agenda-setting) is ascribed to them. This means that parties in Germany have a strong say in what politicians or citizens consider important or unimportant; this gives parties great influence in political proceedings. In France, political parties do not perform this function in the same way, and thus they do not have this kind of influence. With regard to agenda-setting, French parties wield less influence than German ones. Referendums, which by definition lead to binding decisions, are implemented more strongly at the national level in France than in Germany, where they are not used. However, they are more strongly supported by German institutions at the regional level (see Table 2.2).

All in all, Germany exhibits more characteristics of a strong system of participation than France, especially with regard to the criterion of 'formalisation' and, in part, as regards the 'scope' at a sub-national level.[18] France, however, shows a wider scope at the national level in what concerns its participative rights, as the procedures of direct democracy (such as direct election of the president and the possibility of national-level plebiscites) are more strongly institutionalised. Germany does not have any of these procedures at the national level.

As far as 'inclusivity' and 'impact' are concerned, the system in Germany should be classified as relatively participative. France shows features of a medium or weak participatory system in almost all respects, except as regards scope, which is stronger at the national level.

At the beginning of this chapter, the question of the participative impact of institutions was raised. Formal regulations created in an institutional system render certain decisions, regulations or certain forms of behaviour binding on every citizen in a political community. These regulations guarantee the rights – including the participative rights – and set out the duties of citizens. Individual behaviour is influenced to a greater or lesser extent by this institutional context. Institutions can, therefore, either foster or hinder political participation (by creating incentives or restrictions for certain forms of participation), as Norris (2002) already pointed out. Hence, a strong participatory system can foster the increased participation of its citizens significantly, whereas a weak participatory system tends to hinder this. The preceding discussion has shown the importance of the four criteria – formalisation, inclusiveness, scope and impact – with regard to providing the opportunity for citizens to participate and revealed how different the French and German institutional systems are concerning these criteria. However, the institutional context only provides the framework, which then has to be fleshed out with individual behaviour.

---

18. This underlines the extent of possible participation in the country.

Table 2.2: Comparison of the participative systems of Germany and France according to four criteria

	Formalisation	Inclusivity	Scope	Impact
Germany	– Forms of participation granted by civil rights section in the Constitution – Parties, societies and interest groups legitimised by the Constitution – Election system is defined by the Constitution and legislation	– All citizens can use their civil rights and right to vote – Right to vote and right to run for office at the age of 18 – No restrictions on party membership or on joining associations	– Access to forms of participation at different levels of the political system (Federal Republic) – More frequent elections due to shorter legislative periods	– Parties have great political influence – Referendums not in use at national level, but implemented at regional level
France	– Forms of participation are not mentioned in the civil rights section of the Constitution[1] – Parties, groups, etc. have limited influence – Election system regulated by the Constitution and legislation	– Right to vote and forms of participation apply to all adult citizens – Right to vote from the age of 18 – Right to run for office from the age of 23 or 30 – No restrictions on joining parties or associations	– Limited possibilities of influencing politics at different levels of the political system (unitary centralist state)	– Parties have only limited political influence – Referendums implemented at the national level, but only weakly at the municipal level

Source: Author's illustration.
Note: 1 Nor in the preamble of the Fourth Republic or the Declaration of Human and Civil Rights of 1789.

On the basis of the knowledge gained about the participatory systems of Germany and France, it can be expected that, first and foremost, forms of participation that are stipulated in the Constitution and legislation – voting, writing petitions, participating in referendums, or being a member of a party or voluntary association – will be influenced by the institutional arrangements of a country. Forms of participation that are not institutionally regulated, either in Germany or in France – different sorts of political protest, for example – are, accordingly, less influenced in practice by institutional arrangements. Hence, it can be assumed that in Germany – which in many aspects displays a stronger participatory system than France – the institutionally stipulated forms of participation would be more strongly practised by citizens than in France. On the other hand, in France, non-institutionalised forms of political participation such as political protest might be practised more often by citizens, as these are not institutionally restricted. This expectation can only be confirmed by empirical research and contributions in the subsequent chapters do just that, by examining how various forms of participation are actually practised in Germany and France.

References

Appelton, A. M. (2000) 'The France that doesn't vote: Nonconsumption in the electoral market' in M. S. Lewis-Beck (ed.) *How France Votes*, New York: Chatham House Publishers.
Brubaker, R. (1992) *Citizenship and Nationhood in France and Germany*, Cambridge: Harvard University Press.
Bundesrecht Deutschland. Online. Available http://bundesrecht.juris.de/index.html (accessed 26 April 2011).
Carmines, E. G. and Huckfeldt, R. (1996) 'Party politics in the wake of the Voting Rights Act' in B. Grofman and C. Davidson (eds) *Controversies in Minority Voting*, Washington, D.C.: Brookings Institution.
Dahl, R. A. (1971) *Polyarchy: Participation and opposition*, New Haven: Yale University Press.
Dahl, R. A. and Tufte, E. R. (1973) *Size and Democracy: The politics of the smaller European democracies*, Stanford: Stanford University Press.
Dalton, R. J. (2000) 'Politics in Germany' in G. A. Almond, G. B. Powell, R. J. Dalton and K. Strøm (eds) *Comparative Politics Today: A world view*, 7th edn., New York: Longman.
Dunleavy, P. (1996) 'Political behavior: Institutional and experimental approaches' in R. E. Goodin and H.-D. Klingemann (eds) *A New Handbook of Political Science*, Oxford: Oxford University Press.
Franklin, M. N. (2001) 'How structural factors cause turnout variation at European Parliament elections', *European Union Politics*, 2(3): 309–328.
French Constitution. Online. Available http://www.botschaft-frankreich.de (accessed 26 April 2011).
Gabriel, O. W. and Keil, S. (2005) 'Wählerverhalten' in O.W. Gabriel and E. Holtmann (eds) *Handbuch Politisches System der Bundesrepublik Deutschland*, 3rd edn., München: Oldenbourg.
Gabriel, O. W. and Völkl, K. (2005) 'Politische und Soziale Partizipation' in O. W. Gabriel and E. Holtmann (eds) *Handbuch Politisches System der Bundesrepublik Deutschland*, 3rd edn., München: Oldenbourg.
Gallagher, M., Laver, M. and Mair, P. (2001) *Representative Government in Modern Europe: Institutions, Parties and Governments*, 3rd edn., New York: McGraw-Hill.
Gosnell, H. F. (1930) *Why Europe Votes*, Chicago: University of Chicago Press.
Haensch, G. and Tümmers, H. J. (1993) *Frankreich*, München: Beck.
Ismayr, W. (2009) 'Das politische System Deutschlands' in W. Ismayr (ed.) *Die politischen Systeme Westeuropas*, Wiesbaden: VS Verlag für Sozialwissenschaften.
Jackman, R. (1989) 'The politics of economic growth: once again', *Journal of Politics*, 51(3): 646–661.
Jansen, P. (2001) 'Frankreich: Verbände – eine Rechnung mit vielen Unbekannten' in W. Reutter and P. Rütters (eds) *Verbände und Verbandsysteme in Westeuropa*, Opladen: Leske and Budrich.

Jun, U. (2000) 'Parteien im Parlament: Die institutionell schwache Stellung der Fraktion' in S. Ruß, J. Schild, J. Schmidt and I. Stephan (eds) *Parteien in Frankreich: Kontinuität und wandel in der v. republik,* Opladen: Leske and Budrich.

Kaase, M. and Marsh, A. (1979) 'Political action: A theoretical perspective' in S. Barnes and M. Kaase (eds) *Political Action: Mass participation in five western democracies,* London: Sage Publications.

Kempf, U. (2007) *Das Politische System Frankreichs,* Wiesbaden: VS Verlag für Sozialwissenschaften.

— (2009) 'Das Politische System Frankreichs' in W. Ismayr (ed.) *Die politischen Systeme Westeuropas,* Wiesbaden: VS Verlag für Sozialwissenschaften.

Kropp, S. (2005a) 'Föderale Ordnung' in O. W. Gabriel and E. Holtmann (eds) *Handbuch Politisches System der Bundesrepublik Deutschland,* 3rd edn., München: Oldenbourg.

— (2005b) 'Interessenpolitik' in O. W. Gabriel and E. Holtmann (eds) *Handbuch Politisches System der Bundesrepublik Deutschland,* 3rd edn., München: Oldenbourg.

LeDuc, L. (2002) 'Referendums and initiatives: The politics of direct democracy' in L. LeDuc, R. G. Niemi and P. Norris (eds) *Comparing Democracies 2: New challenges in the study of elections and voting,* London: Sage Publications.

Lewis-Beck, M. S. (2000) 'The enduring French voter' in M. S. Lewis-Beck (ed.) *How France Votes,* New York: Chatham House Publishers.

Mény, Y. (2005) 'Interessengruppen in Frankreich: Von Pluralismus keine Spur' in A. Kimmel and H. Uterwedde (eds) *Länderbericht Frankreich: Geschichte, Politik, Wirtschaft, Gesellschaft,* Schriftenreihe: 462,Bonn: Bundeszentrale für Politische Bildung.

Norris, P. (2002) *The Democratic Phoenix: Reinventing political activism,* Cambridge: Cambridge University Press.

Patzelt, W. J. (2005) 'Der Bundestag' in O. W. Gabriel and E. Holtmann (eds) *Handbuch Politisches System der Bundesrepublik Deutschland,* 3rd edn., München: Oldenbourg.

Petterson, P. A. and Rose, L. E. (1996) 'Participation in local politics in Norway: Some do, some don´t; some will, some won´t', *Political Behavior,* 18(1): 51–97.

Pütz, C. (2000) 'Rolle und Funktion der Parteien in der V. Republik' in S. Ruß, J. Schild, J. Schmidt and I. Stephan (eds) *Parteien in Frankreich: Kontinuität und Wandel in der V. Republik,* Opladen: Leske and Budrich.

— (2004) 'Wahlen und Parteien', *Informationen zur Politischen Bildung* (285): 44–48.

Reutter, W. (2001) 'Deutschland: Verbände zwischen Pluralismus, Korporatismus und Lobbyismus' in W. Reutter and P. Rütters (eds) *Verbände und*

Verbandssysteme in Westeuropa, Opladen: Leske and Budrich.
Rokkan, S. (1962) 'The comparative study of political participation: Notes toward a perspective on current research' in A. Ranney (ed.) *Essays on the Behavioral Study of Politics,* Urbana, Illinois: University of Illinios Press.
Rothstein, B. (1996) 'Political institutions: An overview' in R. E. Goodin and H. -D. Klingemann (eds) *A New Handbook of Political Science,* Oxford: Oxford University Press.
Rudzio, W. (2006) *Das Politische System der Bundesrepublik Deutschland,* 7th edn., Wiesbaden: VS Verlag für Sozialwissenschaften.
Schain, M.A. (2000) 'Politics in France' in G. A. Almond, G. B. Powell, R. J. Dalton and K. Strøm (eds) *Comparative Politics Today: A World View,* 7th edn., New York: Longman.
Scharpf, F. W. (1970) *Demokratietheorie Zwischen Utopie und Anpassung,* Konstanz: Universitätsverlag Konstanz.
Schild, J. (2005) 'Politische Parteien und Parteiensystem im Wandel' in A. Kimmel and H. Uterwedde (eds) *Länderbericht Frankreich: Geschichte, politik, wirtschaft, gesellschaft,* Schriftenreihe: 462, Bonn: Bundeszentrale für Politische Bildung.
— (2006) 'Politik' in J. Schild and H. Uterwedde (eds) *Frankreich: Politik, wirtschaft, gesellschaft,* 2nd, Wiesbaden: VS Verlag für Sozialwissenschaften.
Schiller, T. (1997) 'Parteien- und Interessensverbände' in O. W. Gabriel, O. Niedermayer and R. Stöss (eds) *Parteiendemokratie in Deutschland,* Opladen: Westdeutscher Verlag.
Sniderman, P.M. (2000) 'Taking sides: A fixed choice theory of political reasoning' in A. Lupia, M. D. MacCubbins and S. L. Popkin (eds) *Elements of Reason: Cognition, choice and the bounds of rationality,* New York: Cambridge University Press.
Tingsten, H. (1937) *Political Behaviour: Studies in election statistics,* London: PS King and Son.
Tsatsos, D. T. (1997) 'Die politische Parteien in der Grundgesetzordnung' in O. W. Gabriel, O. Niedermayer and R. Stöss (eds) *Parteiendemokratie in Deutschland,* Opladen: Westdeutscher Verlag.
Walter-Rogg, M. (2008) 'Direkte Demokratie' in O. W. Gabriel and S. Kropp (eds) *Die EU-Staaten im Vergleich,* 3rd edn., Wiesbaden: VS Verlag für Sozialwissenschaften.
Zintl, R. (2005) 'Die Verfassungsordnung' in O. W. Gabriel and E. Holtmann (eds) *Handbuch Politisches System der Bundesrepublik Deutschland,* 3rd edn., München: Oldenbourg.
Zukin, C. et al. (2006) *A New Engagement? Political participation, civic life and the changing American citizen,* Oxford: Oxford University Press.

chapter three | conventional political participation
Jürgen Bauknecht

Introduction: participation, responsiveness and equality

Voting is the form of conventional political participation that, by enabling citizens to exert the greatest pressure on political actors, ultimately allows citizens to select their leaders (Fuchs and Klingemann 1995: 436), thereby affecting, albeit indirectly, future political decisions. However, the policy focus of voting is uncertain (Dalton 2006: 36) and the expression of detailed demands impossible (for voting at local and national levels see, respectively, Chapters Four and Eight). There are, nonetheless, other forms of conventional political participation which allow citizens to indicate which issues are important to them.

While most citizens in France and Germany vote in national elections, a minority of citizens, by doing more than just voting, have more than one vote (Verba *et al.* 1995: 46), which means that their influence exceeds that of ordinary voters. Though this could mean unequal influence (Lijphart 1997:1) if the democratic condition of governmental responsiveness (Verba *et al.* 1995:1) was fulfilled, the implications of this inequality would be negligible if participants were randomly drawn from the whole citizenry. But the stronger the bias – the more certain life circumstances increase or reduce the probability of participation – the less representative participants are of the whole citizenry. This, in turn, means that political influence is unevenly distributed over various societal groups. This unequal influence is critical if the political demands of over-represented groups deviate significantly from the unexpressed wishes of those not participating.[1] In that case, 'The violation of the democratic principle of political equality leads to the implementation of non-representative interests and jeopardises, in the long run, democracy's survival chances' (van Deth 2009: 155; author's translation).

Over- or under-representation may cause distortions in favour or disfavour of the enforcement of interests, since unarticulated interests have a lower

---

1. On the other hand, in Gabriel's (2000: 111ff.) study of thirteen countries, voters' or protesters' policy preferences merely deviate to small degrees from the policy preferences of non-voters respective to non-protesters. However, deviations are bigger between active and inactive citizens in protests than in elections. This is partly the case, because in protests a bigger proportion of the population is inactive.

probability[2] of being considered during the process of policy making (Gabriel 2000: 101). This may be regarded as unfair, particularly if distortions in representation can be attributed to a lack of either ability or opportunity and not to a lack of willingness (Verba *et al.* 1995: 280; 1997: 1053). Therefore, while governmental responsiveness is a democratic condition and results from participation (Almond and Verba 1989: 343), responsiveness to the unrepresentative expression of interests violates democratic principles.

In this chapter, the frequency and determinants of conventional political participation in France and Germany will be analysed, using data from the European Social Survey (ESS). While the two countries differ in the nature of their political systems,[3] they are, in fact, Europe's core nations (Huntington 1998: 135) and belong to the four 'major powers among Western democracies' (Dalton 2006: 4). Furthermore, both countries are driving forces behind European integration propelled by the European Union (EU), a transnational political system neglecting responsiveness in favour of effectiveness through its lack of openness for citizen participation (Dahl 1994: 28ff.). If the EU is to be more responsive to citizen demands, one might expect that pressure has to come from its core.

Analyses of the frequency of political participation other than in elections provide a clue about forced responsiveness between elections. Analyses of the determinants of these activities should reveal whether there are inequalities of representation and, if so, whether those inequalities are voluntary or not.

Analysing conventional political participation

In contrast to the elite-challenging unconventional political participation, conventional political participation is elite-directed and 'sanctioned and encouraged by political elites and by the rules of a democratic regime' (Marsh 1990: 1).[4] Another way to separate conventional from unconventional participation is the assumed strong legitimacy of the former (Kaase 1992: 148). Obviously, based on these

---

2. Though unarticulated interests may be taken into consideration by politicians who want to fulfil citizens' wishes before they give voice to them, there is no reason to believe that politicians will adopt a strategy towards groups generally known to stay silent in order to 'keep them from becoming active' (Almond and Verba 1989: 353).

3. In France, both the president and the representatives of the national parliament are directly elected by the citizens. In Germany, voters directly elect one half of the representatives; the other half is assigned on the basis of a proportional system and party lists. The representatives elect the Federal Chancellor. Further, in Germany's federal system, more decisions are made at sub-national levels than in France (Dalton 2006: 4ff.).

4. One of the basic rights accorded by the German constitution (article 8) is that of taking part in a demonstration. So demonstrations are sanctioned, on the one hand, by the rules of the democratic regime (conventional), but may challenge the élite (unconventional). The same applies to the signing of a petition (article 17), or when writing letters to public officials. Even going to the polls may be elite-challenging, if someone deliberately casts an invalid ballot, or votes for a protest party, to express their dissatisfaction.

definitions, no clear boundary can be drawn between the two categories of political participation.[5]

There are five major forms of political participation:

1 party membership;
2 working in a political party or action group;
3 contacting a politician or governmental official;
4 signing petitions; and
5 taking part in lawful public demonstrations.

As these forms are legal and, in most cases, legitimate (Gabriel and Kunz 1999: 372ff.), it is appropriate to label them as conventional.[6] The five forms are brought together in an index, but neither the scope of this chapter, nor the multitude of explanatory factors, allows for more detailed analysis.

Party membership

Party membership – understood here as simple fee-paying membership – is a form of political participation (Gabriel 2004: 319; Scarrow 2007: 645). However, it may be objected that there is no activity involved and, for van Deth (2003: 171), it is 'activity' that is constitutive of political participation. Furthermore, alongside public subsidies and donations, membership fees constitute another source of income for political parties (Scarrow 2007: 647), increasing their capacity to campaign and, by winning elections, to push through their policies (Klein 2006: 38).

The policy focus on simple fee-paying membership in political parties is as uncertain as that on voting. Being a non-active member indicates no detailed policy preferences, but merely shows support for a basic political or ideological orientation. It is, hence, not certain whether simple membership can be considered as exerting influence over policy issues (Gabriel and Völkl 2005: 543). No large variations in volume are possible because parties do not allow their own members to be members of other parties.

Obviously, time, skills or personal contacts are not needed for passive chequebook membership (Scarrow 2007: 637); only money and recruitment (being asked) may be relevant. Being a chequebook member does not require any co-operation with others.

Working in a political party or action group

Unlike voting or party membership, this activity offers more possibilities to express personal views and demands. In the case of political parties, political work

---

5. Another way of solving the problem of classification is to assert that the distinction between conventional participation and political protest is outdated (Norris 2002: 190ff.).
6. Gabriel *et al.* (2002: 155) state: 'Nowadays there are hardly any persuasive reasons to call one of these participation forms [among others, demonstrations and petitions] "unconventional"' (author's translation).

enables participants to exert indirect influence over political, and therefore generally binding, decisions[7] (Widfeldt 1995: 143; Scarrow 2007: 652). Legislators may consider their party members' opinions, or even let party activists vote if important basic decisions about the party's stance are necessary. Furthermore, political parties often recruit officeholders for parliaments from their active membership base (Dalton and Wattenberg 2000: 7; Scarrow 2007: 649), so participants in parties have a far greater chance of occupying positions of political power[8] (Wiesendahl 2006: 75). Variations in volume are high, ranging from 'occasional' to 'seasonal' or even 'daily activity'.

Political work 'requires more initiative, and there is greater need to coordinate participation with others' (Dalton 2006: 43). That is to say, civic skills and time are needed to perform these acts satisfactorily: considerable effort is required (Gabriel and Kunz 1999: 374; Klein 2006: 56). Lastly, which particular action groups are political and which are not, depends on the respondent's definition.

Contacting a politician or governmental official

In this 'expressive' (Putnam 2000: 45) form of political participation, the opportunity of conveying detailed information is huge. Variations in volume depend on sophistication: one can send the same email to lots of different representatives, but attending their consultation-hours comes with more requirements.

While the attribution by Zuckerman and West (1985: 123) of great intellectual costs to this activity is plausible, this is probably wrong in terms of financial costs, at least if done legally. As was the case with 'political' action groups, it all depends upon the respondent's definition as to which person is a politician or a governmental official. In both the French and German questionnaire, the local level is explicitly included, in which case, even local council members may be considered as politicians, and policemen as public officials. No co-operation with others is needed for this activity.

Signing petitions

Petitions and demonstrations are explicitly mentioned as basic rights in both the French and German Constitutions, although somewhat less explicitly in the former

---

7. Widfeldt (1995: 137) defines people who are 'formally enrolled in a political party' as party members. However, exerting influence over political decisions does not come automatically with mere chequebook membership. One has at least to show up for internal votes, or to take part in mail ballots (Scarrow 2007: 649). Therefore, to take part in generally binding decisions, one has to do more than just be a member, although less than what might be called 'work'.

8. Norris and Lovenduski (1993: 396) revealed that supply-side factors (i.e. members of some groups trying less than those of other groups) are more relevant for biases in the socio-economic composition of the House of Commons, rather than demand-side factors (parties avoiding candidates from some groups). This shows the significance of bias among party workers: in nominating candidates, parties build on biases created some steps further down the recruitment ladder.

case.[9] Marsh's (1990: 1) condition that conventional political participation should be sanctioned and encouraged is, accordingly, met. Furthermore, we can assume that both activities are generally regarded by most French or German citizens as legitimate (Gabriel and Kunz 1999: 372; van Deth 2003: 184), which is itself another characteristic of conventional political participation (Kaase 1992: 148). Early on, Fuchs (1991: 151ff.) described petitions and demonstrations as 'legal unconventional actions', and stated that these activities have 'almost become a normality' in Western Germany, so petitions may be regarded as conventional (see also Dalton 2006: 65).

The opportunities for conveying detailed information are mixed. Petitions concern definable issues, but the person who signs neither chooses the topic nor formulates the statement. Variations in volume are medium. The opportunities for signing petitions on the street occur randomly, but one can look for online petitions and sign many of them.

In some cases, if carried out *en passant* or online, the costs of signing a petition are even lower than those of voting. The amount of time, cognitive demands or civic skills may be extremely low; at most, some amount of trust is needed that the signature and data will not be misused. Petitions are partly 'non-committal' (Fuchs and Klingemann 1995: 436); in other cases they are to be handed in and then have legal effects.

Taking part in lawful public demonstrations

Although Barnes and Kaase (1979: 31) have described demonstrations as being considered illegitimate by a majority of the public, one may argue that perceptions of what is legitimate or not are subject to change. However, this form of political participation has gained legitimacy and, in most cases, is legitimate (Gabriel and Völkl 2005: 531ff.). Furthermore, and in contrast to some forms of civil disobedience, this form of participation is established by article 8 of the German constitution, and legality is explicitly mentioned in the questionnaire.

Someone attending a demonstration can express more or less detailed demands by carrying a sign or chanting slogans (Verba *et al.* 1995: 45). Variations in volume are limited; one cannot attend more demonstrations than take place within reachable distance. This activity, which cannot be done alone, is costly in terms of time. In Table 3.1, characteristics of the five forms of conventional political participation are summarised. The term 'mixed' indicates that it depends on circumstances.

Conventional political participation: France and Germany in Europe

Since political participation other than voting may foster the responsiveness of political systems, comparing the frequency of such acts to those of other European

---

9. In the Preamble of the French Constitution of 1958, the basic rights of 1789 are incorporated. Article 6 allows every citizen to take part in law-making, which may be interpreted as a right to address or sign a petition. Article 11 refers to the free communication of ideas and opinions, which may be interpreted as a right to demonstrate.

countries may show to what extent the French and Germans try to affect policy outputs. Table 3.2 shows the frequency and recent development of these forms of conventional political participation.[10]

About a third of French respondents reported having taken part in a petition in the 12 months previous to the survey. Far fewer respondents took part in demonstrations or contacted a politician. Only a small minority of respondents was engaged in political work in that time frame; about 2 per cent of French respondents reported being party members.

In Germany, petitions are also the most frequent forms of participation. In contrast to France, the second most frequent form is not demonstrations, but contacting politicians. While all three activities are less popular in Germany than in France, political work and party membership are more frequent.

As can be seen, party-related forms of political participation are more frequent in Germany than in France. Conversely, party-unrelated forms of political participation like petitions and demonstrations are far more common in France than in Germany (see also Chapter Nine).

The comparison with the average value of the other countries participating in the ESS shown in Table 3.2 reveals that citizen engagement in party-related activities is below average in both countries. Participation, however, in petitions and demonstrations is higher. This is especially true in France with regard to demonstrations: 'A call to the barricades stirs the hearts of many French citizens' (Dalton 2006: 62). In general, French and German citizens seek responses from government through less formalised communication channels than other Europeans.

Table 3.1: Five forms of conventional political participation and their characteristics

Type of participation	Capacity for conveying information	Variation in volume	Requirements	Alone /group
Party membership	Low	Low	Money	Alone
Political work	Mixed	High	Time, skills	Group
Contacting	High	Medium	Time, skills	Alone
Petition	Mixed	Medium	Time	Mixed*
Demonstration	High	Medium	Time	Group

Source: Table mainly based on Verba *et al.* 1995: 48.

Note: * Petitions constitute 'a political activity that require face-to-face contact' (Dalton 2006: 66), but people do not have to coordinate with others before signing them.

---

10. Consistent with previous findings (Gabriel 2004: 319), there are far more similarities than differences between Eastern and Western Germany. Therefore, they have not been shown separately.

Table 3.2: Levels of conventional political participation (percentage)

Type	France			Germany			Europe*
	2003	2004/5	2006/7	2002/3	2004/5	2006/7	2006/7
Party member	2.3	1.8	2.1	3.6	3.0	4.2	5.8
Political work	4.5	4.3	3.5	3.9	3.2	3.8	4.4
Contacting	16.8	15.0	15.1	12.8	10.9	12.3	14.2
Petition	33.8	31.4	33.9	30.5	32.4	27.5	20.4
Demonstration	16.9	12.3	16.5	10.6	8.5	7.0	5.1
N	1,503	1,806	1,986	2,909	2,870	2,916	38,097

*Europe: ESS mean, with every country being equally weighted: Austria, Belgium, Bulgaria, Cyprus, Denmark, Estonia, Finland, Hungary, Ireland, Netherlands, Norway, Poland, Portugal, Russian Federation, Slovakia, Slovenia, Spain, Sweden, Switzerland, UK, Ukraine. All calculations were conducted with d weight.
Source: European Social Survey 2002/2003; 2004/2005; 2006/2007; author's calculations.

Since the question is about participant behaviour in the last twelve months, seasonal effects (Rosenstone and Hansen 1996: 127) could be circumvented; but cross-national comparisons have to take into account the fact that nation-specific circumstances affect the participation level analysed at a given point in time. However, the time series shows that fluctuations between ESS rounds are small.

Even though the effects of social desirability may cause a distorted reflection of actual behaviour (Gabriel and Völkl 2005: 560), it is to be expected that, due to 'the lack of a social obligation to participate in campaigns' (Jankowski and Strate 1995: 94) and the other activities analysed here, over-reporting seldom occurs. The same can be said for under-reporting, since the activities concerned are legal and generally legitimate.

Table 3.3: Political participation in Germany (percentage)

	Western Germany						Germany		
	1974	1980	1981	1985	1986	1988	1989	1990	1997	2004
C	27	12	–	–	31	26	29	–	–	21
P	31	18	46	29	–	26	43	58	64	55
D	9	5	14	11	–	11	13	26	25	30

Notes: C = Contacting; P = Petitions; D = Demonstrations.
Sources: Gabriel 1990: 38; 1995: 181; 1999: 122, 124; Gabriel et al. 2002: 156. 2004: ISSP 2004, author's calculations.

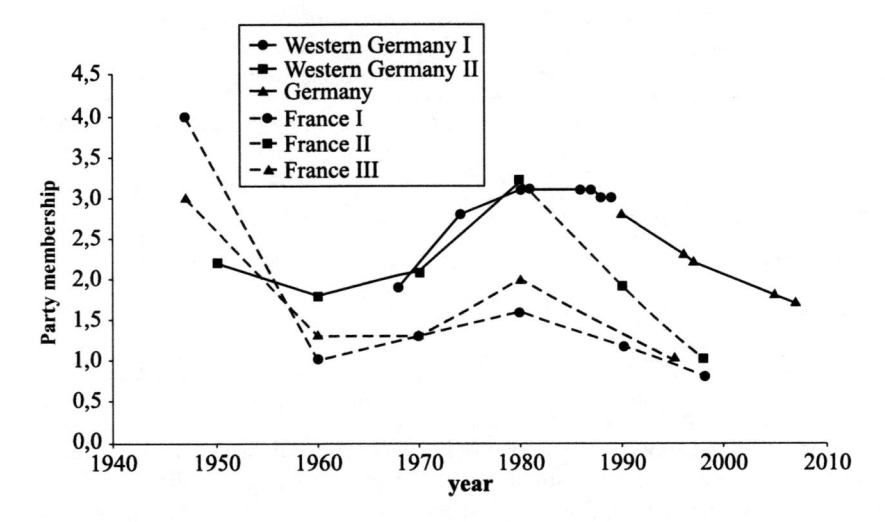

Figure 3.1: Party membership in France and Germany (percentage of population)

Notes: France I: calculated from party membership figures adapted from Knapp (2002:121). Annual party membership numbers were calculated as a mean of previous/following years. France II: calculated from figures taken from Mair and van Biezen 2001: 11. France III: calculations based on figures from Scarrow 2000: 89. Western Germany I: calculated from party membership figures of the SPD, CDU, CSU, FDP, Bündnis 90/Die Grünen and PDS (1968–2005: Wiesendahl 2006: 84; 2007: http://www.polwiss.fu-berlin.de/people/niedermayer/docs/AHOSZ13.pdf) and population figures.* Western Germany II: Calculations based on figures from Scarrow 2000: 89.[11]

The absence of clear trends can also be attributed to the somewhat short observation period. Older empirical results may give an impression of long-term trends. As regards party membership, the patterns are shown in Figure 3.1. For both countries, three different calculations were conducted, since party member numbers could often not be determined exactly. Unlike the figures given in Table 3.3, which show the answers of respondents aged 15 or more, Figure 3.1 shows the proportion of party members among the whole population.[12] As a comparison between

---

11. Population figures for France taken from Pison 2008: 3; 1995 from http://www.destatis.de-/jetspeed/portal/cms/Sites/destatis/Internet/DE/Content/Publikationen/Fachveroeffentlichungen/Laenderprofile/Content75/Frankreich,property=file.pdf.

    Results for East and West Germany were weighted according to population. Source: http://www.destatis.de/jetspeed/portal/cms/Sites/destatis/Internet/DE/Content/Statistiken/Zeitreihen/LangeReihen/Bevoelkerung/Content75/lrbev03a,templateId=renderPrint.psml.

    1980: in both Western Germany II and France II, party membership figures stand at 3.2 per cent.

12. Considering that, in 2007, 13.9 per cent of the German population were 14 years old or younger, 1.7 per cent of party members represent 1.9 per cent of the whole population among the over-

conventional political participation | 79

the rows containing Members I, II and III shows, the results for France should be viewed with a degree of scepticism. However, the overall tendency stands out quite clearly: party membership dropped in the period from the late 1940s until 1960.[13] Afterwards, membership numbers rose until the above-mentioned decline, which started in 1980 (Scarrow 2000: 89ff.).

In Germany, a similar pattern emerges: membership fell until about 1960, though not as dramatically as in France. Membership numbers then rose and peaked in 1980; this was followed by a long-term decline, attributable only in very small measure to lower party membership in East Germany.[14] In Table 3.2, the ESS questions concerning contacting, petitions, and demonstrations refer to respondent activities in the previous twelve months. The data in Table 3.3 is based on questions about the activities of respondents during the course, so they are not comparable.

Both petitions and demonstrations were on the rise in Germany in the last three decades. However, a rise in the number of people having attended even one demonstration or signed one single petition does not necessarily imply that these activities occur more often. In contrast, the number of people having contacted a politician even once seems to fluctuate, but with no clear trend emerging.

Explaining conventional political participation

According to the Civic Voluntarism Model (Verba *et al.* 1995: 269ff.), the three relevant factors for explaining political participation are resources, engagement, and recruitment. Many life circumstances influence the existence of not just one of these three factors, but of two or all three. For example, having a paid job may provide skills (resources), further one's interests because of one's position as employee or employer (engagement), and enhance the likelihood of being asked to join in political action (recruitment). Therefore, to avoid repetition, this article will be structured in terms of life circumstances, and not in terms of the resulting factors.

Though every explanation of political participation is necessarily far from complete (Verba *et al.* 1995: 273), the following analysis does combine the effects of five 'life spheres'. Each of these spheres has possible effects on a person's level of resources, engagement and chances of recruitment, each of which, in turn, is relevant for political participation (see Figure 3.1).

14s. This contrasts sharply with the 4.2 per cent of ESS3 respondents describing themselves as party members. One reason for this is a possible over-representation of politically-interested respondents in surveys.

13. This is due to a huge drop in the number of communist and socialist party members, as well as the difference between the high number of 'claimed' Gaullists (280,000) and the low estimated number (2,000). Knapp (2002:121) uses this low number to calculate the total.

14. The number of party members in relation to the whole population in 2005 resembles that of 1968, but the composition has changed remarkably. In 1968, roughly 64 per cent of party members were Social Democrats and 31 per cent Conservatives; in 2005, this had changed to 39 per cent of Social Democrats and 49 per cent Conservatives.

Life spheres	Resources	Conventional political participation
– Socio-economic characteristics	Time Money Skills	
– Microenvironment	→ Party Membership Political Work	→ Party Membership Political Work
– Political attitudes	Contacting Petition	Contacting Petition
– Media use	Demonstration (Index)	Demonstration (Index)
– Values		

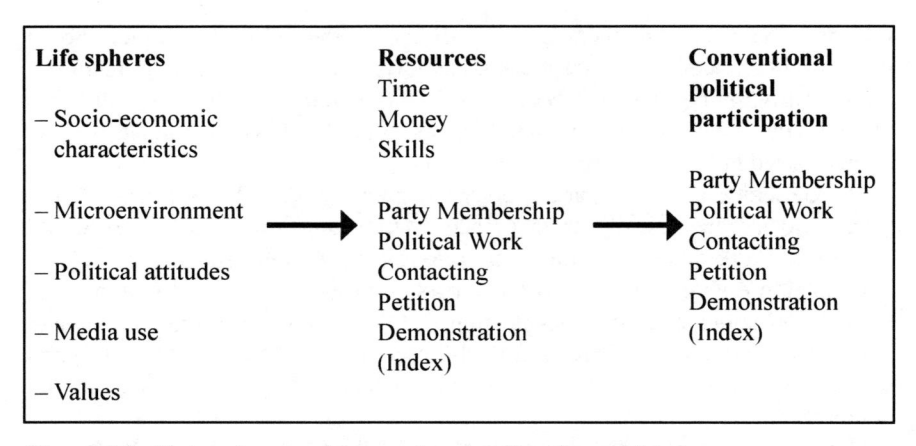

Figure 3.2: Determinants of conventional political participation
Source: Author's presentation

Socio-economic characteristics

There may be an independent effect of gender on political participation by a 'constructed preference' of men for politics, i.e. an over-representation of men (Verba et al. 1997: 1053), resulting from and causing a dominance of male role models in politics (Lane 1964: 212; Verba et al. 1997: 1064; Dalton 2006: 51).

Education belongs to the immaterial resources available to a person (Gabriel and Völkl 2005: 562). It is plausible that, with rising education, people are more capable of expressing their personal views and demands, and of knowing where to turn with their concerns.

Income, a material resource (Gabriel and Völkl 2005: 562) is only essential for party membership and donations. However, subscription fees for party members depend in many cases on income and as low wage-earners pay the same percentage of their income as those with higher salaries, this may mitigate income effects.

The influence of age on political participation may be inversely U-shaped (Lüdemann 2001: 54) because of life-cycle effects (Bowler et al. 2003: 1125) resulting from the 'social and psychological involvements of the young and the aged' (Rosenstone and Hansen 1996: 137). These cohorts may be distracted from political participation by their life circumstances. According to the life-experience hypothesis, there is a linear effect of age caused by the accumulation of skills, political knowledge and social contacts. Equally, generational effects,[15] referring to certain attitude-shaping circumstances, which members of a cohort experience in their early life phase, may occur (Rosenstone and Hansen 1996: 137ff.). This may apply particularly to petitions and demonstrations, activities that became common after the primary socialisation of the oldest cohorts.

---

15. According to Putnam's (2000: 283) estimation, the replacement of the 'civic generation' by the 'baby boomers' is the most important factor behind the US decline in civic engagement.

Erratum: *Political Participation in France and Germany*
Please note that Figure 3.2 on page 80 should read:

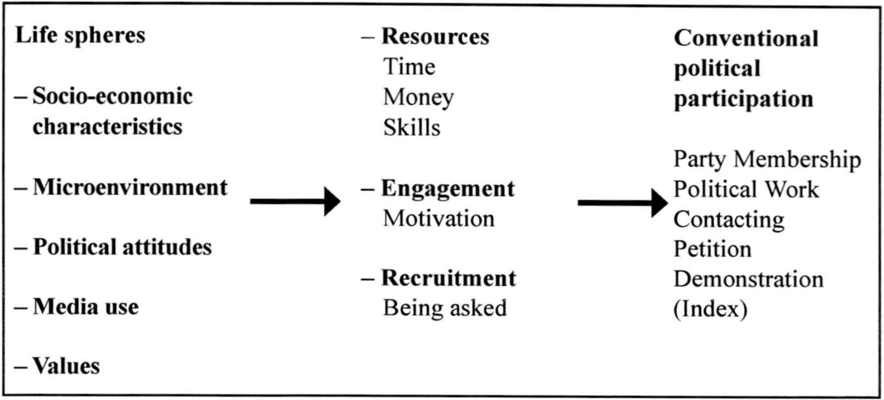

Life spheres	– **Resources** Time Money Skills	**Conventional political participation**
– **Socio-economic characteristics**		
– **Microenvironment**	→ – **Engagement** Motivation →	Party Membership Political Work Contacting Petition Demonstration (Index)
– **Political attitudes**		
– **Media use**	– **Recruitment** Being asked	
– **Values**		

Figure 3.2: Determinants of conventional political participation

Source: Author's presentation

Table 3.4: Determinants: socio-economic characteristics

	France				Germany			
	ESS1		ESS3		ESS1		ESS3	
	B	Beta	B	Beta	B	Beta	B	Beta
Gender (fem.)	-.11	-.06[c]	-.16	-.08[a]	-.03	-.02[n]	-.02	-.01[n]
Age	-.01	.01[n]	-.00	-.01[n]	-.03	.04[n]	.01	.02[n]
Education	.13	.27[a]	.13	.26[a]	.16	.18[a]	.15	.18[a]
Income	-.00	-.05[d]	-.01	-.03[n]	.02	.05[c]	.04	.09[a]
constant	.57[a]		.65[a]		.08[n]		-.25[c]	
R^2adj.	.08		.07		.04		.05	
N	1,494		1,732		2,315		2,087	

Significance: [a] ≤ 0.001; [b] ≤ 0.01; [c] ≤ 0.05; [n] = not significant at the 5% level.
Source: European Social Survey 1 and 3; author's calculations.

Table 3.4 shows the strong positive effects of education on political participation. Gender effects are only significant in France; age and income are relatively irrelevant in both countries.

Microenvironment

The factors to be analysed in the 'microenvironment within which people live, work, and play' (Kenny 1993: 237) are citizens' participation in voluntary associations, their informal social interactions, familial integration and the workplace. Effects on political participation are to be expected because:

> the various institutions with which individuals are affiliated […] – among them, the family, school, workplace, church, and voluntary association – operate in multiple ways to produce the factors that foster participation […] three categories of factors – resources, attitudes and psychological predispositions.
>
> (Schlozman *et al.* 1999: 32)

Voluntary organisations

Involvement in voluntary organisations and informal activities are components of structural social capital and are believed to enhance political participation (Gabriel and Kunz 1999: 361). Being active, or having friends in voluntary associations, could matter for political participation (Gabriel 2004: 327ff.). While our data does not contain the latter, it is plausible that the former is far more important for participation than formal membership (Gabriel and Kunz 1999: 377).

As argued by Verba *et al.* (1995: 369ff.), voluntary organisations are 'training grounds for civic skills' and a 'site for political recruitment'. Whereas voluntary organisations do not differ from certain workplaces in these respects, Ayala (2000: 111) attributes far greater mobilising power to voluntary organisations because of the fact that they are more voluntary. Furthermore, participation in voluntary associations may strengthen democratic virtues, 'broaden individuals' interest and concerns', or increase the sense of belonging to the community (Kwak *et al.* 2004: 644).

Conceivably, participation in groups 'overlapping with the political arena' (Bowler *et al.* 2003: 1124), like environmental or human rights groups,[16] or economic organisations like trade unions[17] or business associations, has a stronger effect on political participation than does participation in associations with non-political goals, like sports or hobby clubs. Being close to the political sphere may imply that the organisation's goals are to be reached only with political assistance; it also enhances the likelihood of conversations in the organisations being about political matters. These conversations may themselves foster political participation because substance matters, i.e. not just talking, but talking politics triggers political participation (Knoke 1990: 1054ff.; MacClurg 2003: 454f.; Kwak *et al.* 2004: 648). Unfortunately, although there is a question about the frequency of political discussion in ESS1, this is not to be found in ESS3. Content is important, and so is source. Therefore, effects may be expected to be positively related to the closeness to a conversation partner. This is why having friends in these organisations may foster political participation.

On the basis of factor analysis, the voluntary organisations are classified in five categories, with some being considered as close to the political area (economic and humanitarian organisations) and others being only remotely connected with politics (hobby organisations) (Gabriel 2004: 327). Religious organisations are to be found in between. Though Verba *et al.* (1995: 18, 383) state that, in the United States, churches reduce participation biases caused by other factors[18] – possibly by a direct and indirect 'spill-over' (Petersen 1992: 124) from church participation to political participation – there are remarkable differences between US and European churches.

First, there are dominant denominations in Europe: the Catholic Church in France and the Protestant and Catholic Churches in Germany. In corporatist states, Bowler *et al.* (2003: 1116) assume that 'membership in church groups may involve ties to the wider political structure'. On the other hand, the stronger hierar-

---

16. It may be argued that, due to the expansion of governmental activities in the post-war decades, the boundary between the political and the non-political sphere is blurred; participation in these organisations may, in that case, be considered political (van Deth 2003: 181).

17. People may become politicised in trade unions, or acquire civic skills by working voluntarily in them (Norris 2002: 169).

18. Brady *et al.* (1995: 276) state that church skills, unlike organisational and job skills, are only weakly determined by the level of formal education.

chical structure of the churches, especially that of the Catholic Church (Brady *et al.* 1995: 278), may be detrimental to participation.

Secondly, as Europeans do not attend church as often as Americans (Verba *et al.* 1995: 19), total effects on the frequency of political participation may be limited. Furthermore, concerning direct politicisation, it should be noted that US churchgoer participation often focuses on abortion, an issue far less salient in France and Germany.

Informal social interaction

Taking part in activities, ranging from meetings with friends to helping within organisations or outside is important in terms people being asked and motivated because 'informal conversations between network partners expose people to political information from the surrounding social environment' (MacClurg 2003: 450). As with the interaction within formal groups, source, as well as substance, may matter (MacClurg 2003: 454ff.; Kwak *et al.* 2004: 648). It can be assumed that participation in voluntary work fosters motivation by widening the spectrum of an individual's concerns, enhancing civic skills and increasing the likelihood of being asked to participate politically.

Family

Another aspect of possible network effects is familial integration (Kenny 1993: 234ff.; Gabriel and Völkl 2005: 567). While spousal[19] effects are believed to be equalising and generally tend to be positive between partners, transitions in marital status seem to have negative effects over a number of years (Stoker and Jennings 1995: 423ff.). For example, having children may limit the time available for political participation (Lane 1964: 210) or be a distraction from politics. On the other hand, there may be positive effects, e.g. involvement in parental groups may entail or lead to some forms of political participation.

The workplace

For people who do not have a job, their 'domestic isolation' (Schlozman *et al.* 1999: 30) means they will neither be involved in political discussions at their workplace, nor be the target of requests for participation there (Rosenstone and Hansen 1996: 81).

Employment status, i.e. whether somebody is employed or self-employed, may also be relevant. Independent business owners 'tend to be key figures in civic and political affairs' (Humphries 2001: 682) because, given to their central position in the social network, they are more often asked to join social and political activities (Humphries 2001: 691).

---

19. Stoker and Jennings (1995: 422) compared couples who were married with those not yet married, so that the effects of having a partner were kept constant.

Furthermore, at least in the case of men, Schlozman *et al.* (1999: 49) found there was a positive effect on political participation as a consequence of supervising others. A person's position within the workplace may affect the opportunity for acquiring civic skills and being asked to participate politically. Besides the communication skills gained by managing employees, it is quite plausible that, as with the self-employed, they are more likely to be asked to join in political action.

Finally, Sobel (1993: 344ff.) suggests an eventual 'self-selection bias among those with participatory predispositions' in the case of workplace participation. This may be the case with other voluntary associations, too. When cross-sectional data is used, the possibility that 'the correlation between organisational membership and political participation is spurious' (Armingeon 2007: 361) cannot be ruled out. Social and political participation may be unconnected and simply result from the same factors.

Nonetheless, despite everything that has been said about the probable positive effects of formal and informal social involvement, detrimental effects can occur. After all, participation in voluntary associations and the workforce reduces the amount of time remaining for political participation (Schlozman *et al.* 1999: 30ff.; van Deth 2001: 198); the same holds true for informal social integration. Furthermore, although the social environment and peer pressure may foster participation, it may also hinder it, if a person belongs to cross-cutting networks (Mutz 2002: 841ff.).

Social trust

Some forms of political participation are collective activities. Demonstrations, as well as parties or action groups, are often sufficiently big as to be essentially made up of unknown persons. Membership fees and data given for petitions may be misused. Therefore, social trust can be crucial when deciding whether to participate in such activities (Kwak *et al.* 2004: 645), although this can also work the other way round (Claiborn and Martin 2000: 270). This means that, just as participation can be fostered by trust, trust can be enhanced by participation.

As expected, organisations closer to the political arena, like economic or humanitarian organisations, foster their activists' political participation far more compared to organisations that are only remotely related to politics (see Table 3.5). However, influences stemming from informal helping activities are stronger than those from formal organisations. Among the work-related factors, supervising stands out as most important for political participation. Familial integration, however, is relatively unimportant for political participation in both countries.

Political attitudes

The factor that could most obviously motivate citizens to participate politically is political attitude. With regard to the effects of political trust on political participation, positive as well as negative effects are plausible. Low trust may lead to apathy and then on to lower participation. However, it is just as plausible that it may enrage and motivate people to do something about the causes of their distrust (Norris 2002: 30) and that 'high trust' leads to participatory constraint (Warren 1999: 4). However, Norris (1999: 263) detected negative effects of mistrust on party-related forms and positive effects on petitions and demonstrations.

Likewise, the effects of policy satisfaction may be positive (Dalton 2006: 51), but it is also possible that dissatisfied citizens participate to 'find redress of grievances' (Di Palma 1970: 44). This also applies to satisfaction with the way democracy works. Since trust and satisfaction are highly correlated, they have, accordingly, been combined before being entered into the analysis.

Ideology may matter too (Dalton 2006: 51). The extension of the participatory repertoire by demonstrations or petitions may have taken place more on the left of

Table 3.5: Determinants: microenvironment

	France				Germany			
	ESS1		ESS3		ESS1		ESS3	
	B	Beta	B	Beta	B	Beta	B	Beta
Hobby org.	.24	.12[a]	.08	.04[n]	.09	.05[c]	-.07	-.04[n]
Econ. org.	.81	.16[a]	.71	.16[a]	.43	.12[a]	.43	.12[a]
Human org.	.64	.16[a]	.50	.13[a]	.70	.17[a]	.21	.07[a]
Religious org.	.03	.01[n]	.04	.01[n]	.02	.01[n]	.03	.01[n]
Other org.	.41	.09[a]	.06	.01[n]	.05	.01[n]	.09	.03[n]
Helping	n.a.	n.a.	.17	.25[a]	n.a.	n.a.	.15	.24[a]
Integration	.17	.13[a]	.07	.05[c]	.12	.10[a]	.06	.05[b]
Family	.00	.00[n]	-.04	-.03[n]	.04	.03[n]	-.00	-.03[n]
Paid work	.10	.05[n]	.14	.07[a]	.07	.04[c]	.06	.03[c]
Supervising	.18	.09[a]	.08	.04[n]	.15	.08[a]	.23	.12[a]
Self-employed	.11	.03[n]	-.04	-.01[n]	.14	.04[c]	.08	.03[n]
Social trust	.00	.00[n]	.02	.03[n]	.02	.04[a]	.01	.02[n]
Social int.	.17	.13[a]	.07	.05[c]	.12	.10[a]	.06	.05[b]
Constant	.10[n]		-.20[n]		.07[n]		-.37[a]	
R^2 adj.	.14		.16		.09		.14	
N	1,334		1,801		2,599		2,533	

Significance: [a] ≤ 0.001; [b] ≤ 0.01; [c] ≤ 0.05; [n] = not significant at the 5%-level.
Source: European Social Survey 1 and 3; author's calculations.

the political spectrum, while conservatives may generally prefer Schumpeterian (1984: 295 [first published 1942]) restraint between elections, showing dislike for these ways of expressing demands. Further, 'activists tend to be ideologues and ideologues activists' (Nagel 1987: 57), i.e. self-ascribed extremism on the left or right may correlate with activism, its cause and effect (Nagel 1987: 57; Lüdemann 2001: 53; Bowler *et al.* 2003: 1119).

Causality between political efficacy and political participation (Van Deth 1997: 305ff.; Lüdemann 2001: 48) may run from the perception of one's own abilities (internal efficacy) or system responsiveness (external efficacy) to political participation. On the other hand, both kinds of efficacy may be affected by political participation, even being negative if activists become disappointed (Nagel 1987: 13ff).[20]

The positive effects of political interest on participation (Putnam 2000: 35) are not as obvious as one might consider. Dalton (2006: 58) explains the 'paradox' of an assumed simultaneous increase of political interest and a decline in political participation in the last few decades, arguing that the concept of political participation is considered too narrowly, and that more direct and less formalised actions are disregarded. Van Deth (2000: 116ff.) offers an alternative explanation, pointing out that it is misleading to equate interest with salience. While people engage in things they consider interesting, this interest may be caused by the same factors that make people less dependent on politics, in particular, education and skills. All of this may have led to the emergence of a new group, the '*Zuschauer*' (spectators) who consider 'politics as interesting, but relatively irrelevant' (van Deth 2000: 127). Furthermore, the positive effects of political interest on participation at the micro level on the one hand, and rising educational sophistication, associated with rising political interest at the macro level on the other hand, would only be contradictory if political interest were the sole predictor of political participation, which is certainly not the case.

Another point is that political interest can be endogenous, i.e. not only causing participation, but also caused by it (Brady *et al.* 1995: 280). Concerning salience, surveys show that politics are of minor relevance compared to other life spheres (Rosenstone and Hansen 1996: 37; van Deth 2000: 121; Gabriel and Völkl 2005: 573). Unfortunately, the impact of the importance of politics for participation cannot be examined here because the relevant question was asked only in ESS1, and not in ESS3.

Not surprisingly, the existence and strength of party identification may be positively bound up with party-related participation (Rosenstone and Hansen 1996: 155), although partisanship may not only lead to participation, but also result from it (Finkel and Opp 1991: 366).

---

20. In a US Panel, Finkel (1985: 903ff.) discovered reciprocal effects between campaigning participation and external efficacy, but only effects between internal efficacy and campaigning, not vice versa.

Another aspect of political attitudes is that a sense of civic duty may motivate people to participate (Gabriel and Völkl 2005: 567).

Lastly, a politicised feeling of belonging to a discriminated group is another reason for participating (Miller *et al.* 1981: 494ff; van Deth 1997: 306). However, the total impact on political participation could be extremely limited if only a small number of people feel systematically underprivileged (Miller *et al.* 1981: 508).

Table 3.6 confirms the expected effects. Only a few variables remain insignificant. Compared to other life spheres, political attitudes contribute to the strongest reduction of unexplained variance. The strong influences from left to right self-placement may result from the fact that the analysis includes demonstrations, a form of participation mostly favoured by the political left. Remarkably, French participants seem to be primarily ideologically motivated, while in Germany the effects of party identification predominate.

The strongest predictor is political interest, suggesting that – at least when it is uncontrolled for education and income – people engage in what they find interesting, and vice versa. The perception that good citizens participate politically motivates the citizens of both countries to participate.

Table 3.6: Determinants: political attitudes

	France				Germany			
	ESS1		ESS3		ESS1		ESS3	
	B	Beta	B	Beta	B	Beta	B	Beta
PI	.05	.07[b]	.06	.09[a]	.10	.15[a]	.15	.23[a]
Left–Right	-.08	-.19[a]	-.08	-.20[a]	-.07	-.13[a]	-.04	-.08[a]
Extreme	.12	.06[c]	.11	.05[c]	.23	.10[a]	.21	.09[a]
Pol. sat. + trust	-.00	-.01[n]	-.02	-.03[n]	-.01	-.02[n]	-.00	-.01[a]
Pol. interest	.22	.20[a]	.27	.26[a]	.16	.14[a]	.17	.16[a]
Int. efficacy	.09	.09[a]	.10	.09[a]	.03	.03[n]	.12	.11[a]
Discrimination	.22	.07[b]	.24	.08[a]	.19	.04[c]	.10	.02[n]
Part-norm	.05	.11[a]	n.a.	n.a.	.06	.15[a]	n.a.	n.a.
Constant	.08[n]		.03[n]		-.08[n]		-.44[a]	
R² adj.	.18		.19		.16		.16	
N	1,348		1,801		2,587		2,419	

Significance: [a] ≤ 0.001; [b] ≤ 0.01; [c] ≤ 0.05; [n] = not significant at the 5%-level.
n.a. = not available in this wave of ESS.
Source: European Social Survey 1 and 3; author's calculations.

Media use

In modern large-scale democracies such as France and Germany, citizens gain political information and experience via the mass media rather than from their social surroundings. All the same, media use consumes a remarkable amount of time in the daily lives of citizens; time that cannot be used for social or political activities. Therefore, the use of different types of media may affect citizens' participatory behaviour.

As both Holtz-Bacha (1989: 249) and Norris (1996: 478) have differentiated between information and entertainment TV and discovered effects working in opposite directions,[21] it is reasonable to analyse the two factors separately.

In what concerns political information – garnered from information TV and newspaper reading – two different effects on political participation are plausible. According to the media malaise hypothesis, by emphasising politics' negative side, the news media discourages viewers from participation in politics. On the other hand, Norris (2002: 29) considers it proven that people become motivated to participate as a result of TV news, newspapers and internet information.

In the case of entertainment TV, only negative effects[22] are plausible. According to the 'time-displacement' hypothesis (Besley 2006: 43), watching it lessens the time people have to spend other things (Kwak *et al.* 2004: 647). Indirect negative influences may either result from attitudes triggered by entertainment television, like social distrust or reduced civic participation (Besley 2006: 42), which in turn may lower political participation.

Prior (2005: 577ff.) distinguishes between the 'low-choice environment' of the post-war decades and today's 'high-choice environment'. He asserts that, in the past, as people only had a small number of channels to choose from, they watched the news simply because there was nothing else on, thereby learning about politics by default rather than by interest. If participation is induced by information, then a limited choice of channels indirectly motivated such viewers to participate. While low choice has been an equaliser (Lane 1964: 221), today's high-choice environment, characterised by a huge number of TV programmes, may tend to divide media consumers according to their initial interest in politics. Those interested amass as much political information as they want and become motivated to participate. Those not interested in politics, no longer being forced by low choice to watch the news, learn less about politics than in the past, and therefore participate even less.

If it is to become 'the mass medium of the twenty-first century' (Tolbert and

---

21. Holtz-Bacha's (1989: 241) analysis is restricted to forms of political participation regarded as conventional at the time, like voting, visiting political events, party work, etc. Her results remain stable, even when taking political alienation into account (1989:249). Norris (1996: 478) analysed voting, campaign activities and protest; media effects on the latter were not, however, significant.

22. Putnam (2000: 283) attributes a quarter of America's decline in civic engagement to TV, without differentiating between information and entertainment TV. He asserts that the differences in frequency of civic engagement between the 'long civic generation' and their successors are, at least partly, due to the former's primary socialisation without TV (Putnam 1995: 677).

MacNeal 2003: 175), the internet's effects on political participation could be of increasing relevance. Its use may affect the dependent variable in two ways. First, the internet may be used to garner information and to network for offline participation. Secondly, some of the activities reported like signing petitions, contacting officials or undertaking party work may have been exercised online. Even joining political parties online is on the rise (Wiesendahl 2006: 78). In both cases, one could assume that lower information costs lead to higher accessibility of information and, therefore, higher political participation (Bimber 2001: 54). It is not clear whether those already over-represented in political participation are more capable of and willing to use the internet to participate (reinforcement hypothesis). It may, however, be the case that internet use equalises biases in favour of under-represented societal groups (the expansionist argument) by allowing 'those from lower status groups to feel more empowered in an online environment' (Krueger 2002: 481) and by lowering information and communication costs, so that class biases in information access are reduced (Stanley and Weare 2004: 506ff.). While both hypotheses are compatible, agreeing with their predictions that internet use fosters political participation, but differing over the question as to which societal groups it will affect most, Tolbert and MacNeal (2003: 184) suggest that, in the long run, the internet could lower political participation. As with entertainment TV today, its use could reduce the amount of time left for political activity or help spread apathy.

Participatory differences 'between the information rich and poor' in a society may be considered problematic if the distribution of internet access is uneven among various societal groups (Norris 2001: 4ff.).

Table 3.7 reveals strongly negative effects as regards entertainment TV, and strongly positive ones from internet use. The effects of media use are essentially similar in both countries. These results are uncontrolled for background variables; it remains to be seen how effects change when they are taken into account.

Table 3.7: Determinants: media use

	France				Germany			
	ESS1		ESS3		ESS1		ESS3	
	B	Beta	B	Beta	B	Beta	B	Beta
Information	.07	.07[c]	.08	.07[a]	.10	.09[a]	.09	.09[a]
Entertainment	-.05	-.09[a]	-.06	-.12[a]	-.09	-.17[a]	-.06	-.12[a]
Internet use	.10	.22[a]	.06	.21[a]	.06	.17[a]	.05	.15[a]
Constant		.58[a]		.52[a]		.53[a]		.40[a]
R^2 adj.		.07		.08		.08		.05
N		1,467		1,974		2,906		2,884

Significance: [a] ≤ 0.001; [b] ≤ 0.01; [c] ≤ 0.05; [n.] = not significant at the 5%-level.
Source: European Social Survey 1 and 3; author's calculations.

Values

Values – defined as 'trans-situational goals, varying in importance, that serve as guiding principles in the life of a person or a group' – have their origins in people's 'temperaments, personalities, socialisation experiences, unique life experiences, surrounding culture, and so on' (Prince-Gibson and Schwartz 1998: 49), i.e. everywhere, all the time. That being the case, they may also be induced by political participation experiences. However, values are basic personality traits, while political participation is sporadic at best so, if there is a correlation to be observed, it is safe to suggest that participation is far more influenced by values than the other way round.

According to Schwartz (1992: 13ff.), there are up to ten value types to be found, depending on the particular country concerned.[23] These ten types can be viewed as part of 'four higher order value types that form two basic, bipolar, conceptual dimensions' (Schwartz 1992: 43) (see Table 3.8).

Table 3.8: Ten value types and four higher order value types

Openness to change	Stimulation	Hedonism	Achievement	Self-enhancement
	Self-direction		Power	
Self-transcendence	Universalism		Security	Conservation
	Benevolence	Conformity	Tradition	

Source: Author's presentation on the basis of Schwartz 1992: 45.

Value types located in diametrically opposite corners, such as 'achievement' and 'benevolence', conflict with each other. The same applies to higher order value types, like 'openness to change' and 'conservation' or 'self-transcendence' and 'self-enhancement' (Davidov *et al.* 2008: 423ff.). People holding values from any one higher value order type are likely to oppose values from the opposite one. While the importance of different values and, correspondingly, different higher order value type varies cross-culturally, their underlying structure, their compatibility and incompatibility, is universal (Davidov *et al.* 2008: 425). Since these dimensions and Inglehart's survival/self-expression dimension are partly analogical (Besley 2006: 45), values on the left side of Table 3.8 may be described as 'post-materialist', and those on the right side as 'materialist'.

It is possible that effects resulting from the higher order value type 'openness to change' work in opposite directions. People holding self-direction values may want to influence matters that affect them. However, the items included in the index mostly represent values belonging to stimulation and hedonism.[24] In

---

23. In a non-representative German sample of 377 students with a mean age of twenty-two, Schwartz (1992: 25) discovered all ten value types.
24. The item representing self-direction (making own decisions and being free) had to be omitted. If anything, it should have been incorporated as part of self-transcendence.

Schwartz's graph (1992: 45), hedonism can belong to 'self-enhancement' as well as 'openness to change'. Factor analysis (not shown) suggests that in France and Germany it belongs to the latter. The representation of the value type hedonism means that if participation is exciting and pleasurable, respondents holding 'openness to change' values will be motivated to participate. However, if participation is boring and burdensome, people seeking fun and excitement may refrain from these activities.

Concerning 'conservation', it is to be expected that a preference for 'hierarchical leadership' (Besley 2006: 46) should lessen the motivation for political participation. This may apply primarily to less formalised forms of participation, although, because of the hierarchical structure of political parties, there should not be a contradiction between participation in such parties and conservation. It is to be expected that those eager to follow rules, and favouring strong government, will be less willing to challenge the political system for two reasons. First, because they think that a good citizen accepts the elites' decisions. Secondly, because 'conservation' contains statements expressing conflict avoidance,[25] which inhibits conflict-laden forms of political participation (Ulbig and Funk 1999:266ff.).

It may be that that those seeking wealth and power ('self-enhancement') are more willing to participate in politics provided it serves only their own goals, i.e. if there is the prospect that their endeavours will not be wasted on some public good that others will get for free (Besley 2006: 46). While it may be irrational for them to contribute to the public good by attending demonstrations or paying membership fees, people often contact politicians or public officials to serve their 'narrowly defined interests'[26] (Putnam 2000: 454). Furthermore, people striving for admiration may find some forms of political participation helpful in this respect (Lane 1964: 129).

In contrast to openness to change and self-enhancement, 'self-transcendence' values are altruistic (loyalty, helpfulness). Respondents appreciating equality, respect and tolerance, and who care for others' well-being, may participate for the sake of other people's interest. Therefore, it follows that self-transcendence values should foster political participation.

In both countries (see Table 3.9), conservation values have strong negative effects on political participation: those who appreciate security, strong government and obedience tend to abstain from political participation, which is as expected. The opposite applies in the case of self-transcendence values such as equality, understanding, loyalty and helpfulness. Since 'self-enhancement' values are insignificant in both countries and both ESS 1 and 3, the most remarkable differences

---

25. Ulbig and Funk (1999: 277) state that conflict avoidance reinforces already existing participation biases because those already under-represented, i.e. low-status people (and women, Verba *et al.* 1999: 1062) are more likely to shy away from conflicts.

26. In an American study, among several kinds of political and communal activities, contacting proved to be the one mostly motivated by material benefits and one of the least motivated by civic or policy gratifications (Schlozman *et al.* 1995: 16).

in strength of influence for these two higher order values types are the positive effects of 'openness to change' values in France. Here, in both ESS 1 and 3, those preferring fun, adventure and enjoyment participate significantly more in politics. As mentioned above, because of the high numbers of petitioners and demonstrators, these activities predominate in the analysis. The correlation, however, may be spurious if some French groups prefer both 'openness to change' values and demonstrations. It is not impossible that this applies to young French people and not to young Germans. Another possible explanation is that French demonstrations attract those seeking fun and adventure.

Table 3.9: Determinants: values

	France				Germany			
	ESS1		ESS3		ESS1		ESS3	
	B	Beta	B	Beta	B	Beta	B	Beta
Openness	.08	.09[b]	.06	.07[b]	.01	.01[n.]	-.02	-.02[n.]
Conservation	-.25	-.27[a]	-.17	-.19[a]	-.16	-.17[a]	-.12	-.13[a]
Self-enhancement	-.04	-.04[n.]	-.01	-.01[n.]	.01	.02[n.]	.03	.03[n.]
Self-transcendence.	.28	.23[a]	.25	.20[a]	.23	.18[a]	.27	.21[a]
Constant		.25[n.]		.01[n.]		.12[n.]		-.26[n.]
R² adj.		.10		.06		.05		.05
N		1,282		1,924		2,721		2,754

Significance: [a] ≤ 0.001; [b] ≤ 0.01; [c] ≤ 0.05; [n.] = not significant at the 5%-level.
Source: European Social Survey 1 and 3; author's calculations.

Genuine country effects

To detect genuine country effects on the single dependent variables included in the index, logistic regression analyses have been conducted, with the countries as dummy variables, and France being coded '0', and Germany '1'. This means that if Exp(B)[27] is above 1, there is a positive effect for Germany (and a negative one for France) on the probability of political participation.

As can be seen in Table 3.10, all kinds of participation, except that of political

---

27. Roughly put, the Exp(B) minus 1 value expresses the change of probability in the dependent variable if the independent variable applies, other things being equal, without forgetting that the range in the coding of the independent variable has to be taken into account.

work, have statistical significance. Essentially, party membership is positively affected by Germany, whereas residing in France positively affects the probability of respondents attending demonstrations, signing petitions or contacting politicians and public officials.

Table 3.10: Country effects

Type of participation	Pseudo R^2 Nagelkerke	Exp(B)	N	N activists
Party membership	.013	2.0[a]	4,890	163
Political work	.000	1.10[n]	4,896	180
Contacting	.003	0.79[c]	4,892	657
Petition	.007	0.74[a]	4,890	1,471
Demonstration	.044	0.38[a]	4,898	532

Significance: [a] ≤ 0.001; [b] ≤ 0.01; [c] ≤ 0.05; [n] = not significant at the 5%-level.
Coding: 0 = France; 1 = Germany.
Source: European Social Survey 2006; author's calculations.

An integrated explanatory model of conventional political participation

Since the effects of the variables on conventional political participation shown in the different parts of the section above (see earlier section 'Explaining conventional political participation') are uncontrolled for factors contained in the other subsections, an integrated model will be analysed. For the sake of parsimony concerning explanatory variables, those independent variables that were not significant at the 5 per cent level in the preceding analyses have been excluded from the integrated model.

The remarkable reduction of the number of cases, compared to Table 3.3, has been due to the high number of refusals for questions concerning household income and, to a lesser extent, self-placement on the left to right political spectrum. Since it is conceivable that those refusing to answer these questions are more often to be found at the extremes (perhaps the main reason for their refusal), the missing values were not replaced by mean values.

Not surprisingly, with an explained variance of between 20 per cent and 30 per cent, the integrated model offers a better explanation than all those models restricted to one set of factors alone. However, it should be noted that this level of explained variance results from the inclusion of twenty-six explanatory variables or indexes.

As the relevant explanatory factors are generally somewhat similar for both France and Germany, country specifics will only be mentioned in cases where the differences are considerable.

In Table 3.11, for the sake of clarity, only those factors that are significant, and whose Betas are higher than .10 in one of the four possible cases, will be shown. However, it should be noted that 16 other variables and indexes were included in the regression, so that the effects have been controlled for various other factors.

Socio-economic characteristics

The first striking result is the limited direct relevance of the socio-economic characteristics, which is the reason for their absence in Table 3.11. Age had to be excluded because of its insignificance in the first analysis. Gender becomes insignificant in the whole model[28] and is therefore not shown. This implies that it is not gender *per se*, and some 'masculine taste for politics' (Verba *et al.* 1997: 1053) not measured in other variables that explain male over-representation, but factors related to gender included in the whole model. All of this equally applies to education and household income. Nevertheless, the position in the funnel of causality of these factors, and their initial significance, suggests that they could be at the starting point of indirect effects.

This means that class biases do not occur directly, but indirectly because, for example, people with higher education and higher incomes tend to be politically more interested. This is not too serious, since many factors influenced by social status are questions of motivation. Lower-class people may have a lower likelihood of being politically interested or a higher one of watching entertainment TV, but there is nothing stopping them from acting otherwise.

The microenvironment

The microenvironment a person lives in offers a stark contrast to the socio-economic characteristics. Activities in voluntary associations which depend on political actors to achieve their objectives lead their activists towards politics. This applies to trade unions and business, professional or farmers' organisations, subsumed under the term 'economic organisations'. Additionally, political participation stems from activism in human rights, peace, environmental and animal rights organisations ('humanitarian organisations'). Though this result is not surprising, these results may imply causality where there is none. Somebody who has, for example, attended demonstrations or signed petitions organised by trade unions or animal groups, correctly replies in the affirmative to questions about demonstrations and petitions (which are phrased without the label 'political'), and does likewise when answering questions concerning participation in these groups. Since the effects in France are stronger than in Germany, French organisations may be considered as more important for citizen mobilisation.

Participation in hobby organisations, however, has no effect upon political par-

---

28. This result is in line with Verba *et al.* (1997: 1053): 'Only when differences in political interest, information and efficacy are taken into account do gender differences in participation disappear'.

Table 3.11: The strongest determinants

	France				Germany			
	ESS1		ESS3		ESS1		ESS3	
	B	Beta	B	Beta	B	Beta	B	Beta
Microenvironment								
Econ. org.	.56	.12[a]	.56	.12[a]	.33	.09[a]	.29	.08[a]
Hum. org	.28	.07[b]	.32	.08[a]	.38	.10[a]	.16	.06[c]
Helping	n.a.	n.a.	.14	.20[a]	n.a.	n.a.	.12	.19[a]
Political attitudes								
PI	.05	.07[c]	.07	.11[a]	.10	.16[a]	.11	.17[a]
Left-Right	-.06	-.16[a]	-.06	-.15[a]	-.04	-.08[a]	-.03	-.05[c]
Extreme	.11	.05[n.]	.11	.05[c]	.27	.12[a]	.25	.10[a]
Pol. interest	.13	.12[a]	.18	.17[a]	.07	.06[c]	.11	.10[a]
Part-norm	.05	.12[a]	n.a.	n.a.	.04	.11[a]	n.a	n.a.
Values								
Cons	-.11	-.11[a]	-.05	-.05[c]	-.04	-.04[n.]	-.10	-.10[a]
Self-trans.	.14	.11[a]	.13	.10[a]	.08	.06[c]	.09	.06[b]
Constant	-.46		-.44[n.]		-.43[n.]		-1.08[a]	
R²adj.	.29		.30		.21		.25	
N	1,073		1,516		1,924		1,753	

Significance: [a] ≤ 0.001; [b] ≤ 0.01; [c] ≤ 0.05; [n.] = not significant at the 5%-level; n.a. = not available in this round of ESS.
Not shown: Gender, Education, Income, Hobby org., Other org., Integration, Paid work, Supervising, Self-employed, Social trust, Internal efficacy, Discrimination, Information, Entertainment, Internet use, Openness to change.
Source: European Social Survey 1 and 3; author's calculation.

ticipation. This is true also in what concerns religious groups, which confirms the participatory irrelevance of European churches when compared to their US counterparts. Work-related factors are also negligible, thus confirming Ayala's (2000: 111) insight that experiences in less voluntary circumstances have far weaker effects than those made in voluntary ones. The sole exceptions are for France in 2003, where participation in hobby organisations and the task of supervising other employees' work was positively related to political participation.

The strongest predictor is the 'helping' index. People who help others are likely to be politically active. Another, weaker factor (consequently not shown) is societal integration. Meeting others and taking part in social activities leads to political participation, perhaps because the chances of being asked are higher or, as MacClurg (2003: 454ff.) suggests, people hear about political issues from those around them. The unavailability of the 'helping' index in ESS 1 reveals the similarity of both indexes: once 'helping' is included, the explanatory power and significance of 'integration' decrease considerably. This similarity may also explain the insignificance of social trust. Trust is correlated to integration and helping; only by leaving both these variables aside can the significance of trust be demonstrated.

The irrelevance of work-related factors is reassuring. Since many conflicts arise over the distribution of goods – like welfare services and taxes – and since interests have their roots in a person's position in the economic sphere, the absence of biases and therefore over- and under-representation of interests is a good sign. Considering the strong effects stemming from participation in economic organisations, and the plausible assumption that people in work are overrepresented in them, the following appears to be the case: employees or employers are overrepresented and make their voices heard louder than those – students, pensioners and the unemployed – who are not in work.

Furthermore, the strong likelihood of both helping and socially-integrated people being political activists indicates that simply focusing on formal organisations offers an incomplete picture. From a theoretical point of view, the assumption that both, what is termed humanitarian organisations here, as well as helping activities, are open to everyone, shows that biases caused by these factors can be attributed to 'don't want' rather than to 'can't'.

Political attitudes

Since some of the political activities combined in the participation index are party related (party membership, party work, or even contacting), the strong effects of party identification on political participation in Germany are not surprising. Presumably, this is derived from the higher motivation attributed to party identifiers. However, this causality may be reversed, i.e., party identification may be strengthened by political activities for the party. Contrary to the effects of party identification, locating oneself on the left side of the political spectrum is far more important in France than in Germany.[29] This may be partly due to the high proportion of petitioners and demonstrators among France's activists. However, being on

---

29. French respondents place themselves more on the right side (4.83) than Germans (4.51). However, in both countries, about 30 per cent place themselves at point 5, the central point of the spectrum.

the left or right fringe of the political spectrum is more important in Germany.[30] Political interest, however, is more important in France, although this is a result that cannot be fully evaluated because, on the one hand, nobody is prevented from being politically interested, while on the other hand, political interest is strongly affected by socio-economic status, which people are not totally free to choose.

As regards internal efficacy, this is, in most cases, insignificant and, consequently, not shown. In what concerns political equality, this may be interpreted positively: people do not abstain from participation due to lack of self-confidence, participation is not dominated by sophomoric people. While participatory norms – in this case, the belief that a good citizen is characterised by political activity – are strong and highly significant predictors in both countries, political satisfaction and trust are of minor importance and are, therefore, not shown. As for the feeling of being discriminated against,[31] it is largely irrelevant.

As to the question of which groups' voices are louder, the over-representation of left people and of extreme people is a negative sign resulting, in the case of the latter, in an unbalanced expression of extreme demands to the disadvantage of more moderate and balanced views.

When it comes to biases between societal groups, it is clear from the outset that nothing stops a person being politically interested, feeling efficacious or believing that a good citizen is characterised by political participation. However, as mentioned in the section above (see 'Socio-economic characteristics'), certain interpersonal differences are to be found as a result of the particular socio-economic background. Political disinterest or low efficacy, for example, may result from low education or income; lack of motivation may be caused by lack of ability – what Hooghe (2001:172) termed the 'sour grapes phenomenon': in order to avoid frustration, what is unattainable is proclaimed worthless. Alternatively, two-way causality may plausibly limit the gravity of biases. Political participation may cause political interest, efficacy and the belief that participants are good citizens.

Media use

As all three variables used here are either insignificant, or have only negligible effects, none of them are shown in Table 3.11. In contradiction to the results obtained by Norris (1996: 476; 2002: 29), neither newspaper reading nor watching news and programmes about public affairs significantly foster political participa-

---

30. There are 15 per cent of extremes in Germany and 27 per cent in France. The numbers may tell the whole story: the French political system is more polarised, but the fact of being extreme is not as important for political participation as it is in Germany. Another interpretation could be that German respondents are far more reluctant to place themselves on the left or right fringe of the political spectrum. This means that those calling themselves extreme in Germany are really on the fringe, whereas the high number of French extremes may signal that in France the social desirability of being in the political centre is lower. Interestingly, self-proclaimed German left radicals outnumber their right counterparts in a ratio of 2.1:1, whereas in France it is merely 1.2:1

31. Roughly 10 per cent of French and 5 per cent of German respondents feel discriminated against.

tion. Significance and explanatory power, to be seen in the small model media variables, disappear when other factors are taken into account. However, watching other things on TV does have slightly adverse effects on political participation in both countries. This may be due to a time displacement effect or a 'mean world effect' (Putnam 1995: 679), a negative outlook on the world, prompted by TV, and leading to reluctance to participate. The persistence of TV's negative effects when social trust is taken into account points to a time displacement interpretation. However, this correlation may be spurious, if watching entertainment TV and being politically passive results from the same independent variable, general passivity. Another eventuality, suggested by Putnam (1995: 679) referring to Neil Postman, is that TV induces passivity. A fifth possibility, besides time displacement, mean world effect, spurious correlation and entertainment TV fostering passivity, is that causality exists, but in the reverse direction. While Gabriel (1999: 111) plausibly argues that political participation may result not just from the consumption of informative media content, but also vice versa, it is at least conceivable that those avoiding politics also avoid political media content (and turn to entertainment TV, cf. Holtz-Bacha 1989: 250).[32]

Compared to entertainment TV, the contrasting effects of internet use effects are stronger. At least so far, this media has not become the new entertainment TV, obstructing participation via the mechanisms mentioned above. This persistent significance of internet use to be found in the model, especially in France, suggests that internet use has a genuine, albeit minor, effect on political participation, even when controlled for education, income and other factors believed to be systematically related to both internet use and political participation.

As for possible biases, and using Norris's (2001a: 4) terms 'digital divide' and 'social divide' sub-phenomena, both of which constitute information gaps within countries, these translate into 'democratic divides', i.e. differences in using the internet for political participation. However, in ESS3, this is only true of France. Thus, even when applying controls for other factors such as education, income or political interest, being online enhances the likelihood of participation; watching entertainment TV lowers it. Though biases due to entertainment TV are voluntary, this applies only partly to the use of internet. Some people might not be able to access it due to lack of ability or financial problems, but where this is the case any violation of the democratic principle of equality is not deliberate.

---

32. Another point mentioned by Gabriel (1999:111) is that a crucial condition for causality from x to y is that of x occurring earlier than y; but ESS3 questions are about political participation in the last 12 months and TV consumption today; that is to say, in the wrong temporal order.

Values

After the exclusion of the insignificant higher order 'self-enhancement' value type from the analysis, it is to be observed that 'self-transcendence' has, as expected, positive effects on political participation, especially in France. Respondents who think it is important to treat people equally, be creative, understanding, loyal, helpful and protective of the environment were in both countries, and in both ESS waves, more likely to have participated politically than others. The opposite is true for 'conservation'. People preferring safe surroundings, strong government, obedience and the respect of traditions are less likely to participate, perhaps due to a Schumpeterian (1984 [1942]: 295) understanding of citizens' appropriate role in politics. In the whole model, 'openness to change', still significant in France in the section containing only the 'value' variable, is insignificant in all four cases and is not, therefore, shown in Table 3.11.

Although the over- and under-representation of political demands from people holding 'openness to change' values may be considered voluntary, its political relevance should be noted. The participatory abstention of people favouring strong government and security and other related goals on the one hand, and the above-average participatory level of people demanding the protection of the environment and related political goals on the other hand, may result – if the democratic principle of governmental responsiveness is fulfilled – in a distribution of governmental priorities and resources that match citizen preferences in a merely suboptimal way. 'Under these conditions, politics serves primarily the needs of active, resourceful groups' (Gabriel 2000: 101; author's translation).

Conclusion

First and foremost, differences between France and Germany are to be found as regards the frequencies of their different forms of political participation, but less so in what concerns its determinants.

Differences between the two countries concerning the frequency of political participation lie primarily in French people's stronger reliance on the newer forms, such as petitions and demonstrations, and Germans' greater activity in party-related forms. Compared to their European neighbours, however, the citizens of both countries display the characteristic traits of modern democratic societies with their below-average frequency of party-related forms and their above-average petitioning and demonstrations.

For the determinant analyses, the five forms of political participation – party membership, political work, contacting, petitions and demonstrations – had to be indexed.

Five life spheres, with relevant factors generating the necessary resources, motivation, and the chances of being asked for political participation were examined, to find out their impact upon the likelihood of participation. The first step of the regression analysis is presented in the specific sections dealing with these five life spheres; in the second step, the significant variables have been combined into a complete explanatory model.

The first step had two main advantages: the comparison of the explanatory power between various life spheres and the identification of the unnecessary variables. In this comparison, it became obvious that the life sphere offering the best (and most trivial) explanation of political participation is what has been termed 'political attitudes'. Another important sphere is a person's social life, especially activities outside of the family and workplace. Of less significance (but with fewer variables, too) are socio-economic characteristics, media use and values.

The second step reveals the whole model's explanatory power and the effects of the individual variables, controlled for the variables of other life spheres. The explained variance lies between 20 per cent and 30 per cent, which means that many factors are not examined or are not examinable.[33] Besides the direct insignificance of socio-economic characteristics, certain interesting patterns appear: participation in organisations with goals related to politics, helping others inside and outside of organisations, and informal meetings with friends are the primary social factors behind political participation. The political factors relevant here are party identification, political interest, participatory norms and left and/or extreme political leanings. Concerning media consumption, it is not news and information that seem to matter, but entertainment TV. It either diminishes political participation, by time displacement, a 'mean world effect' (Putnam 1995: 679) or passivity effects, or results from the same factors as political passivity. The metamorphosis of the internet into the new entertainment TV has not yet taken place. Lastly, people favouring security and strong government – 'materialists' in Inglehart's terms – are significantly under-represented among political activists. Those, however, who favour equality, understanding, helpfulness, loyalty and environmentalism – 'post-materialists' – are more likely to participate politically.

Concerning the implications for the realisation of the democratic principle of governmental responsiveness, the citizens of both countries do not seem to be reluctant when it comes to voicing their demands, albeit in different ways. Further, it should be noted that governmental responsiveness may result not just from citizens' participation, but also from the political elites' anticipation of this participation: according to the 'law of anticipated reactions', the former try to be responsive to citizens' as yet unarticulated demands to 'keep them from becoming active' (Almond and Verba 1989: 353). This is because far greater than citizens' actual participation is their 'reserve of influence' (Almond and Verba 1989: 347), to be seen, for example, in the citizens' great readiness to participate, if need be.[34]

---

33. Other possibly relevant factors at the micro level are extroversion, activity (not being a 'couch potato', Kwak et al. 2004: 646), health (Jankowski and Strate 1995: 92), being friends with a party official (Smith and Zipp 1983: 975), campaign attention (Norris 2002: 29) or language skills (Verba et al. 1993: 456ff; 1995: 304). On the macro level, aggregate-level commuting (Putnam 2000: 213; Kwak et al. 2004: 688) and the social composition of the neighbourhood (Huckfeldt et al. 1993: 370) may be relevant; as regards city size, its positive effects on petitions and demonstration could be demonstrated (Bowler et al. 2003: 1125), plausibly this are opportunity effects. Equally, institutional settings may be relevant.

34. In Gabriel's analysis (1999: 122ff.), a wide discrepancy is to be observed between citizens' actual

In particular, French politicians, when considering whether they should take unpopular decisions, can be expected to bear in mind their citizens' readiness to take to the streets.

The fulfilment of the other principle, 'equal consideration of the interests of each citizen' (Verba *et al.* 1995: 1) is furthered by their equal use of voice. However, explained variances of only 20 per cent to 30 per cent, despite taking many independent variables into account, reveal an important finding. Even someone combining several relevant characteristics – a politically interested, efficacious-minded, extreme-left trade-unionist, for example, strongly identifying with a (presumably socialist) political party, thinking that participation makes a good citizen and so on – is not much more likely to participate politically than others. Furthermore, taking into account that a person's position concerning many relevant factors is a matter of choice rather than ability, this bias in voice seem to be merely a minor violation of the democratic principle of political equality.

---

participation and their readiness. This gap is their threat potential; for example, the gap between 17 per cent actual demonstrators (or, even less, if one counts only those who demonstrated in the recent past) and 61 per cent potential ones in Western Germany in 1996.

Appendix

Dependent variables

'During the last 12 months, have you done any of the following?
Have you:
- (a) contacted a politician, government or local government official
- (b) worked in a political party or action group
- (c) signed a petition
- (d) taken part in a lawful public demonstration'

'Are you a member of any political party?'

Independent variables

Socio-economic characteristics:
Gender coded by Interviewer:
Age (1) 15–31 (5) 66–96; *Education* France (0) no primary (6) second stage of tertiary, Germany (1) primary (6) second stage of tertiary; *Household income* total net income from all sources (1) less than €150 €/month [year: €1,800] (12) more than €10,000/month [year: €120,000].

Microenvironment:
Participants in *hobby organisations*:
Respondents who in the last 12 months participated in:
- (a) a sports clubs or clubs for outdoor activities; or
- (b) an organisation for cultural or hobby activities; or
- (c) a social club, club for the young, the retired/elderly, women, or friendly societies.

Economic organisations–
- (a) a trade union; or
- (b) a business, professional, or farmers' organisation.

Humanitarian organisations
- (a) an organisation for humanitarian aid, human rights, minorities, or immigrants
- (b) an organisation for environmental protection, peace or animal rights.

Religious organisations
- (a) a religious or church organisation.

Other organisations
- (a) any other voluntary organisation such as the one I've just mentioned.

Helping:
>6-point additive index consisting of activities in the past 12 months:
>(a) How often did you help with or attend activities organised in your local area?
>(b) Not counting anything you do for your family, in your work, or within voluntary organisations, how often did you actively provide help for other people?
>(c) How often did you get involved in work for voluntary or charitable organisations?

These 3 items are included in the ESS3-Rotating module 'Personal & Social Well-Being' and are consequently not available in ESS1.

Integration:
>5-point additive index consisting of:
>(a) How often do you meet socially with friends, relatives or work colleagues?
>(b) Compared to other people of your age, how often would you say you take part in social activities?

Social trust:
>10-point additive index consisting of:
>(a) Generally speaking, would you say that most people can be trusted, or that you can't be too careful in dealing with people?
>(b) Do you think that most people would try to take advantage of you if they got the chance, or would they try to be fair?
>(c) Would you say that most of the time people try to be helpful or that they are mostly looking out for themselves?

Married:
>Are you or have you ever been married? 'Married' is part of the ESS3-Rotating module 'The timing of life' and consequently is not available in ESS1. The variable used stems from question F58 in ESS1 about marital status. Respondents coded as 'married' are or have been married, including the 1 per cent of French respondents who are in a PACS, i.e. a *'pacte civil de solidarité'* (civil partnership).

Children:
>Have you ever given birth to/fathered a child?

Paid work:
>Are you currently in paid work of any kind?

Children is part of the ESS3-Rotating module 'The timing of life' and consequently is not included in ESS1.

Supervising:
> In your main job, do/did you have any responsibility for supervising the work of other employees?
> *Self-employed*: In your main job are/were you an employee of/self-employed/ working for your own family's business?

Political Attitudes:
Party identification:
> 5-point scale
> (a) Is there a particular political party you feel closer to than all the other parties?
> (b) How close do you feel to this party? Respondents negating the first question were coded on the lowest point of the scale.

Left-Right Placement: In politics, people sometimes talk of 'left' and 'right'. Where would you place yourself on this scale, where 0 means the left and 10 means the right?

Extremism: Respondents who place themselves between 0 and 2 or 8 and 10 on the left-right scale.

Political satisfaction:
> 11-point additive index
> (a) Now, thinking about the [country] government, how satisfied are you with the way it is doing its job?
> (b) How satisfied are you with the way democracy works in [country]?

Political trust:
> 10-point additive index consisting of trust in:
> (a) parliament
> (b) politicians
> (c) parties.
> In the case of donations (ESS1):
> (a) parliament
> (b) politicians.

Political interest:
> 4-point scale. How interested would you say you are in politics:
> (1) Not at all interested
> (4) Very interested.

Internal efficacy:
> 5-point index consisting of:
> (a) How difficult or easy do you find it to make your mind up about political issues?

(b) How often does politics seem so complicated that you can't really understand what is going on?

Discriminated group:
Would you describe yourself as being a member of a group that is discriminated against in this country?

Media use:
Information:
8-point index consisting of:
  (a) TV news
  (b) newspaper
  (c) newspaper news.

Entertainment:
8-point scale TV consumption excluding TV news.

Internet use:
0 no access 7 every day.

Values:
The Schwartz scale in the ESS contains 21 questions. While there is a suggestion from Schwartz as to which items belong to one of the 10 values [http://ess.nsd.uib.no/files/2003/ESS1CodingHumanValueScale.doc; Davidov 2008: 427f.], and to which higher order value types they belong in turn (Table 3.8), this is not practical for several reasons. First, hedonism is not clearly ascribable to a higher order value type. Second, the classification did not include France. Third, it is 15 years old. Just as values can change so, too, can the structure. Lastly, as Schwartz (1992: 19) used a non-random sample, it is necessary to thoroughly examine the structure to be found. A factor analysis [Schwartz advises against using an exploratory factor analysis, because it cannot reveal the 'quasi-circumplex' of the relation among the values. However, factor analysis is conducted not to discover the relation among the values, but to ascribe the value items to their higher order value types.], proving that it is possible to create 4 indexes with 17 variables, each representing one higher order value type of the indexes. For the sake of comparability between the two countries, 4 values loaded on different higher order value types in France and Germany were omitted. This person is (6) very much like me (1) not like me at all.

Openness to change:
It is important:
  (a) to seek fun and pleasure
  (b) to seek adventures and have an exciting life
  (c) to have a good time.

Conservation:

It is important:
- (a) to live in secure and safe surroundings
- (b) that government is strong and ensures safety
- (c) to do what is told and follow rules
- (d) behave properly
- (e) to follow traditions and customs.

Self-enhancement:

It is important:
- (a) to be rich, have money and expensive things
- (b) to show abilities and be admired
- (c) to be successful and that people recognise one's achievements.

Self-transcendence:

It is important
- (a) to think new ideas and being creative
- (b) that people treated equally and have equal opportunities
- (c) understand different people
- (d) be loyal to friends and devote to people close
- (e) to help people and care for others well-being
- (f) to care for nature and environment.

Omitted items:
- (a) to try new and different things in life [France: *Self-Transcendence*, Germany: *Openness to change*]
- (b) to be humble and modest, not draw attention [France: *Self-Transcendence*, Germany: *Conservation*]
- (c) to make own decisions and be free [France: Too low factor loading on *Self-Transcendence*, Germany: *Self-Transcendence*]
- (d) to get respect from others [France: *Conservation*, Germany: *Self-Enhancement*]. Method: Factor Analysis, Oblimin Rotation.

According to Davidov *et al.* (2008: 440), who tested the Schwartz scale's validity with data from ESS1 and ESS2, 'people in Europe appear to understand the meaning given to the values by their indicators in a similar manner'.

References

Almond, G. A. and Verba, S. (1989) *The Civic Culture: Political attitudes and democracy in five nations*, London: Sage Publications.

Armingeon, K. (2007) 'Political participation and associational involvement' in J. W. van Deth, J. R. Montero and A. Westholm (eds) *Citizenship and Involvement in European Democracies: A comparative analysis*, London; New York: Routledge.

Ayala, L. J. (2000) 'Trained for democracy: The differing effects of voluntary and involuntary organizations on political participation', *Political Research Quarterly*, 53(1): 99–115.

Barnes, S. and Kaase, M. (eds) (1979) *Political Action: Mass participation in five western democracies,* Beverly Hills; London: Sage Publications.

Besley, J. C. (2006) 'The role of entertainment television and its interactions with individual values in explaining political participation', *The International Journal of Press/Politics*, 11(2): 41–63.

Bimber, B. (2001) 'Information and political engagement in America: The search for effects of information technology at the individual level', *Political Research Quarterly*, 54(1): 53–67.

Bowler, S., Donovan, T. and Hanneman, R. (2003) 'Art for democracy's sake? Group membership and political engagement in Europe', *Journal of Politics*, 65 (4): 1111–29.

Brady, H., Verba, S. and Schlozman, K. L. (1995) 'Beyond SES: A resource model of political participation', *American Political Science Review*, 89(2): 271–294.

Claiborn, M. P. and Martin, P. S. (2000) 'Trusting and joining? An empirical test of the reciprocal nature of social capital', *Political Behavior*, 22(4): 267–291.

Dahl, R. A. (1994) 'A democratic dilemma: System effectiveness versus citizen participation', *Political Science Quarterly*, 109 (1): 23–34.

Dalton, R. J. (2006) *Citizen Politics: Public opinion and political parties in advanced industrial democracies,* 4th edn., Washington D.C.: CQ Press.

Dalton, R. J. and Wattenberg, M. P. (2000) 'Unthinkable democracy: Political change in advanced industrial democracies' in R. J. Dalton and M. P. Wattenberg (eds) *Parties Without Partisans: Political change in advanced industrialized societies,* Cambridge: Cambridge University Press.

Davidov, E., Schmidt, P. and Schwartz, S. H. (2008) 'Bringing values back in: The adequacy of the European Social Survey to measure values in 20 countries', *Public Opinion Quarterly*, 72(3): 420–45.

Di Palma, G. (1970) *Apathy and Participation: Mass politics in western societies,* New York: The Free Press.

Finkel, S. E. (1985) 'Reciprocal effects of participation and political efficacy: A panel analysis', *American Journal of Political Science*, 29(4): 891–913.

Finkel, S. E. and Opp, K.-D. (1991) 'Party identification and participation in collective political action', *Journal of Politics*, 53: 339–371.

Fuchs, D. (1991) 'The normalization of the unconventional: New forms of political action and new social movements' in G. Meyer and F. Ryszka (eds)

Political Participation and Democracy in Poland and West Germany [*Politische Partizipation in Polen und Westdeutschland*], Warsaw: Ośrodek Badań Społecznych.

Fuchs, D. and Klingemann, H. -D. (1995) 'Citizens and the state: A relationship transformed' in H. -D. Klingemann and D. Fuchs (eds) *Citizens and the State: Beliefs in government*, Oxford: Oxford University Press.

Gabriel, O. W. (1990) 'Politischer Protest und politische Unterstützung: Entsteht eine neue subkultur des protestes in Westeuropa?', *Politische Bildung*, 23(3): 34–52.

— (1995) 'Politischer Protest und politische Unterstützung in den neuen Bundesländern' in H. Bertram (ed.) *Ostdeutschland im Wandel: Lebensverhältnisse – politische einstellungen*, Opladen: Leske and Budrich.

— (1999) 'Massenmedien: Katalysatoren politischen Interesses und politischer Partizipation' in G. Roters, W. Klingler and M. Gerhards (eds) *Information und Informationsrezeption*, Baden-Baden: Nomos.

— (2000) 'Partizipation, Interessenvermittlung und politische Gleichheit' in H. -D. Klingemann and F. Neidhardt (eds) *Zur Zukunft der Demokratie: Herausforderungen im zeitalter der globalisierung*, Berlin: Sigma Verlag.

— (2004) 'Politische Partizipation' in J. W. van Deth (ed.) *Deutschland in Europa: Ergebnisse des European Social Survey 2002–2003*, Wiesbaden: VS Verlag für Sozialwissenschaften.

Gabriel, O. W. and Kunz, V. (1999) 'Politische Partizipation und soziales Engagement' in A. Khol, G. Ofner, G. Burkert-Dottolo and S. Karner (eds) *Österreichisches Jahrbuch für Politik*, Wien; München.

Gabriel, O. W., Kunz, V. and Roßteutscher, S. (2002) *Sozialkapital und Demokratie: Zivilgesellschaftliche ressourcen im vergleich*, Wien: WUV-Universitätsverlag.

Gabriel, O. W. and Völkl, K. (2005) 'Politische und Soziale Partizipation' in O. W. Gabriel and E. Holtmann (eds) *Handbuch Politisches System der Bundesrepublik Deutschland*, 3rd edn., München: Oldenbourg.

Holtz-Bacha, C. (1989) 'Verleidet uns das Fernsehen die Politik? Auf den Spuren der "Videomalaise"' in M. Kaase and W. Schulz (eds) *Massenkommunikation: Theorien, methoden, befunde*, Opladen: Westdeutscher Verlag.

Hooghe, M. (2001) '"Not for our kind of people": The sour grapes phenomenon as a causal mechanism for political passivity' in P. Dekker and E. M. Uslaner (eds) *Social Capital and Participation in Everyday Life*, London/ New York: Routledge.

Huckfeldt, R., Plutzer, E. and Sprague, J. (1993) 'Alternative contexts of political behavior: Churches, neighborhoods, and individuals', *Journal of Politics*, 55(2): 365–381.

Humphries, S. (2001) 'Who's afraid of the big, bad firm: The impact of economic scale on political participation', *American Journal of Political Science*, 45(3): 678–699.

Huntington, S. P. (1998) *The Clash of Civilizations and the Remaking of World Order*, London: Touchstone Books.

Jankowski, T. B. and Strate, J. M. (1995) 'Modes of participation over the adult

life span', *Political Behavior*, 17(1): 89–106.
Kaase, M. (1992) 'Vergleichende politische Partizipationsforschung' in D. Berg-Schlosser and F. Müller-Rommel (eds) *Vergleichende Politikwissenschaft: Ein einführendes studienhandbuch*, Opladen: Leske and Budrich.
Kenny, C. (1993) 'The microenvironment of political participation', *American Politics Research*, 21 (2): 223–238.
Klein, M. (2006) 'Partizipation in politischen Parteien: Eine empirische analyse des mobilisierungspotentials politischer parteien sowie der struktur innerparteilicher partizipation in Deutschland', *Politische Vierteljahresschrift*, 47(1): 35–61.
Knapp, A. (2002) 'France: Never a Golden Age' in P. Webb, D. Farrell and I. Holliday (eds) *Political Parties in Advanced Industrial Countries*, Oxford: Oxford University Press.
Knoke, D. (1990) 'Networks of political action: Toward theory construction', *Social Forces*, 68(4): 1041–1063.
Krueger, B. S. (2002) 'Assessing the potential of internet participation in the United States: A resource approach', *American Politics Research*, 30(5): 476–498.
Kwak, N., Shah, D. V. and Holbert, L. R. (2004) 'Connecting, trusting, and participating: The direct and interactive effects of social associations', *Political Research Quarterly*, 57(4): 643–652.
Lane, R. E. (1964) *Political Life: Why and how people get involved in politics*, New York: The Free Press.
Lijphart, A. (1997) 'Unequal participation: Democracy's unresolved dilemma', *American Political Science Review*, 91(1): 1–14.
Lüdemann, C. (2001) 'Politische Partizipation, Anreize und Ressourcen: Ein Test verschiedener Handlungsmodelle und Anschlusstheorien am ALLBUS 1998' in A. Koch, M. Wasmer and P. Schmidt (eds) *Politische Partizipation in der Bundesrepublik Deutschland: Empirische befunde und theoretische erklärungen*, Opladen.
MacClurg, S. (2003) 'Social networks and political participation: The role of social interaction in explaining political participation', *Political Research Quarterly*, 56(4): 449–464.
Mair, P. and van Biezen, I. (2001) 'Party membership in twenty European democracies, 1998–2000', *Party Politics*, 7(1): 5–21.
Marsh, A. (1990) *Political Action in Europe and the USA*, London: MacMillan.
Miller, A. H., Gurin, P., Gurin, G. and Malanchuk, O. (1981) 'Group consciousness and political participation', *American Journal of Political Science*, 25(3): 494–511.
Mutz, D. C. (2002) 'The consequences of cross-cutting networks for political participation', *American Journal of Political Science*, 46(4): 838–855.
Nagel, J. H. (1987) *Participation*, Englewood Cliffs, N.J.: Prentice Hall.
Norris, P. (1996) 'Does television erode social capital? A reply to Putnam', *PS Political Science and Politics*, 29(3): 474–480.
—— (1999) *Critical Citizens*, Cambridge: Cambridge University Press.
—— (2001a) 'Conclusions: The growth of critical citizens and its

consequences' in P. Norris (ed.) *Critical Citizens: Global support for democratic government,* Oxford: Oxford University Press.

— (2001b) *Digital Divide: Civic engagement, information poverty, and the internet worldwide,* Cambridge: Cambridge University Press.

— (2002) *The Democratic Phoenix: Reinventing political activism,* Cambridge: Cambridge University Press.

Norris, P. and Lovenduski, J. (1993) '"If only more candidates came forward": Supply-side explanations of candidate selection in Britain', *British Journal of Political Science,* 23(3): 373–408.

Petersen, S. A. (1992) 'Church participation and political participation: The spillover effect', *American Politics Research,* 20(1): 123–139.

Pison, G. (2008) 'La population de la France en 2007', *Population & Sociétés,* 443: 1–4.

Prince-Gibson, E. and Schwartz, S. H. (1998) 'Value priorities and gender', *Social Psychology Quarterly,* 61(1): 49–67.

Prior, M. (2005) 'News vs. entertainment: How increasing media choice widens gaps in political knowledge and turnout', *American Journal of Political Science,* 49(3): 577–592.

Putnam, R. (1995) 'Tuning in, tuning out: The strange disappearance of social capital in America', *PS Political Science and Politics,* 28(4): 664–683.

— (2000) *Bowling Alone: The collapse and revival of American community,* New York/London: Simon and Schuster.

Rosenstone, S. J. and Hansen, J. M. (1996) *Mobilization, Participation and Democracy in America,* New York: Longman.

Scarrow, S. E. (2000) 'Parties without members? Party organisation in a changing electoral environment' in R. J. Dalton and M. P. Wattenberg (eds) *Parties Without Partisans: Political Change in Advanced Industrialized Societies,* Cambridge: Cambridge University Press.

— (2007) 'Political activism and party members' in R. J. Dalton and H. -D. Klingemann (eds) *The Oxford Handbook of Political Behaviour,* Oxford: Oxford University Press.

Schlozman, K. L., Burns, N. and Verba, S. (1999) 'What happened at work today?': A multistage model of gender, employment, and political participation', *Journal of Politics,* 61(1): 29–53.

Schlozman, K. L., Verba, S. and Brady, H. (1995) 'Participation's not a paradox: The view from American activists', *British Journal of Political Science,* 25(1): 1–36.

Schumpeter, J. A. (1984) *Capitalism, Socialism and Democracy,* New York: Harper Perennial.

Schwartz, S. H. (1992) 'Universals in the content and structure of values: Theoretical advances and empirical tests in 20 countries', *Advances in Experimental Social Psychology,* 25: 1–65.

Smith, J. and Zipp, J. F. (1983) 'The party official next door: Some consequences of friendship for political involvement', *Journal of Politics,* 45(4): 958–78.

Sobel, R. (1993) 'From occupational involvement to political participation: An explanatory analysis', *Political Behavior,* 15(4): 339–353.

Stanley, J. W. and Weare, C. (2004) 'The effects of internet use on political participation: Evidence from an agency online discussion', *Administration & Society*, 36(5): 503–27.
Stoker, L. and Jennings, M. K. (1995) 'Life-cycle transitions and political participation: The case of marriage', *American Political Science Review*, 89(2): 175–85.
Tolbert, C. J. and MacNeal, R. S. (2003) 'Unraveling the effects of the internet on political participation?', *Political Research Quarterly*, 65(2): 175–85.
Ulbig, S. G. and Funk, C. L. (1999) 'Conflict avoidance and political participation', *Political Behavior*, 21(3): 265–82.
van Deth, J. W. (1997) 'Formen konventioneller politischer Partizipation: Ein neues Leben alter Dinosaurier?' in O. W. Gabriel (ed) *Politische Orientierungen und Verhaltensweisen im vereinigten Deutschland*, Opladen: Leske and Budrich.
— (2000) 'Das Leben, nicht die Politik ist wichtig' in O. Niedermayer and B. Westle (eds) *Demokratie und Partizipation: Festschrift für Max Kaase*, Wiesbaden: Westdeutscher Verlag.
— (2001) 'Soziale und politische Beteiligung: Alternativen, Ergänzungen oder Zwillinge?' in A. Koch, M. Wasmer and P. Schmidt (eds) *Politische Partizipation in der Bundesrepublik Deutschland: Empirische befunde und theoretische erklärungen,* Opladen: Leske and Budrich.
— (2003) 'Vergleichende politische Partizipationsforschung' in D. Berg-Schlosser and F. Müller-Rommel (eds) *Vergleichende Politikwissenschaft: Ein einführendes handbuch,* 7th edn., Opladen: Leske and Budrich.
— (2009) 'Politische Partizipation' in V. Kaina and A. Römmele (eds) *Politische Soziologie: Ein studienbuch,* Wiesbaden: VS Verlag für Sozialwissenschaften.
Verba, S., Burns, N. and Schlozman, K. L. (1997) 'Knowing and caring about politics: Gender and political engagement', *Journal of Politics*, 59(4): 1051–72.
Verba, S., Schlozman, K. L., Brady, H. and Nie, N. H. (1993) 'Race, ethnicity, and political resources: Participation in the United States', *British Journal of Political Science*, 23(4): 453–93.
Verba, S., Schlozman, K. L., and Brady, H. (1995) *Voice and Equality: Civic voluntarism in American politics*, Cambridge, Mass.: Harvard University Press.
Warren, M. E. (ed.) (1999) *Democracy and Trust,* Cambridge: Cambridge University Press.
Widfeldt, A. (1995) 'Party membership and party representativeness' in H.-D. Klingemann and D. Fuchs (eds) *Citizens and the State: Beliefs in government,* Oxford: Oxford University Press.
Wiesendahl, E. (2006) 'Partizipation in Parteien: Ein Auslaufmodell?' in B. Hoecker (ed.) *Politische Partizipation zwischen Konvention und Protest,* Opladen: Verlag Barbara Budrich.
Zuckerman, A. S, and West, D. M. (1985) 'The political bases of citizen contacting: A cross-national analysis', *The American Political Science Review*, 79(1): 117–131.

chapter four | local electoral participation
Angelika Vetter and Vincent Hoffmann-Martinot

The research question

Ever since the new millennium, questions of democratic quality and public administration efficiency have been at the very heart of France and Germany's public agendas. In addressing these questions, both countries' local authorities constitute important actors – although to different degrees (Hoffmann-Martinot 2006; Kersting and Vetter 2003; Pierre 1990; Hesse and Sharpe 1991; Stoker 1991; Sharpe 1970). Our focus in this chapter is on citizen participation, a major dimension of the democratic quality of local government.[1] Not only is citizen participation seen as a democratic value in itself, but it is also an essential element in increasing the quality of local democracy by relating political decisions to citizens' preferences. In order to achieve such responsiveness, citizens' active participation in the local decision-making processes is crucial. In Germany, many new ideas are currently being tried out in order to increase citizen participation in local politics (e.g. referendums, round tables, future conferences). The same holds true for France, although to a far lesser extent (Vetter 2006 for Germany; Hoffmann-Martinot 2006 for France). With regard to local citizen participation, for both countries voting for the local councils and mayors remain the most common expression of political activity at the local level. Therefore, in this chapter, we focus on local electoral participation. Do we find any differences or similarities in local electoral turnout between France and Germany, and if so, how can they be explained?

Comparing the two countries with regard to local turnout, their local government and local politics differ in many respects (see Chapter Five). They stem from different traditions: Napoleonic for one and Germanic for the other; they are rooted in different central-local relationships; they differ in terms of local authority size, local electoral systems, as well as in ways power is wielded by the mayors and local councils (see for examples Vetter 2007; Loughlin 2001; Hesse and Sharpe 1991). In line with these differences, we expected local turnout to differ substantially as well. However, the first, and certainly the biggest, surprise came right at the beginning of our analysis: the local turnout in both France and Germany was similar (see section below 'Local turnout in France and Germany'). Therefore, the question became: why is local turnout in France and Germany so similar, even though their local elections are held in quite different contexts?

Traditionally, when explaining electoral turnout, the focus is on individual

---

1. By 'local' we refer to both countries' municipal level, including different-sized villages and towns, but excluding regional, departmental or inter-municipal structures.

characteristics affecting the likelihood of individuals being politically active: resources (socio-economic status), political socialisation (political interest and norms), and integration into mobilising networks (van Deth 2003; Verba et al. 1995; Brady et al. 1995; Verba et al. 1978). However, in this chapter we do not deal with such individual characteristics; instead, we examine the contextual differences of local elections in the two countries and their relationship with local turnout. From past research we know that such macro characteristics as the prevailing social structure, the political institutions, and aspects related to electoral campaigns – the number and strength of political parties, issues, candidates, or the degree of political competition – also affect turnout probability (see Figure. 4.1). In the following sections we look more closely at five such contextual differences that might affect local turnout in France and in Germany:

1. geo-political fragmentation, i.e. the size of local units;
2. the importance of the institutions involved;
3. the political salience of sub-national elections with regard to national politics;
4. the voting systems applied; and
5. differences in the discretion of local government and politics.[2]

These five factors are generally used to explain differences in turnout. In this chapter, however, the challenge is to explain why local turnout in France and Germany does not differ as much as we might expect even though the elections take place in quite different socio-structural, institutional, and political settings.

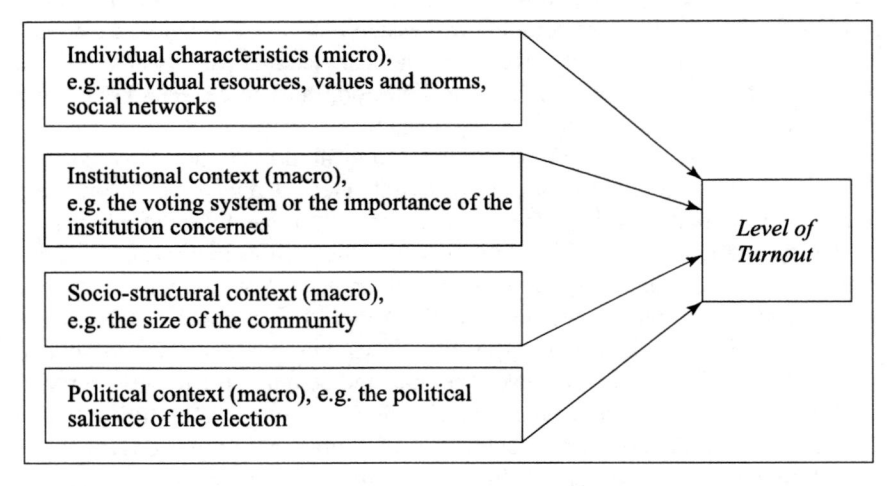

```
┌─────────────────────────────────────────┐
│ Individual characteristics (micro),     │
│ e.g. individual resources, values and   │
│ norms, social networks                  │
└─────────────────────────────────────────┘
┌─────────────────────────────────────────┐
│ Institutional context (macro),          │         ┌──────────┐
│ e.g. the voting system or the importance│────────▶│ Level of │
│ of the institution concerned            │         │ Turnout  │
└─────────────────────────────────────────┘         └──────────┘
┌─────────────────────────────────────────┐
│ Socio-structural context (macro),       │
│ e.g. the size of the community          │
└─────────────────────────────────────────┘
┌─────────────────────────────────────────┐
│ Political context (macro), e.g. the     │
│ political salience of the election      │
└─────────────────────────────────────────┘
```

Source: Author's presentation

Figure 4.1: Explanatory factors affecting turnout

---

2. For more details about the theoretical relationships, see the following sections.

local electoral participation | 115

Examining many variables in a comparison involving only two countries (i.e. a very small N) does not allow for highly-sophisticated empirical hypothesis testing. Accordingly, we use statistical techniques to explain differences in local turnout only when controlling for municipal size effects; the other explanatory factors are dealt with descriptively in our two-N case study, using results from the existing literature. Before dealing with the explanation of local electoral behaviour in France and Germany, the section below 'Local turnout in France and Germany', provides a detailed description of local turnout in both countries. We look at aggregated data of local turnout at the national (and state) levels, as well as at two large samples of towns and villages from both countries, which provide a more detailed picture.

Local turnout in France and Germany

Starting with the descriptive part of our analysis, we first consider data collected for two large samples: 4,431 municipalities in Germany and 6,784 in France between 1999 and 2002 (see Table 4.1).[3] The local elections analysed for Germany were held between January 1999 and March 2002, with the local elections for six out of eleven states being held on the same day as the elections for the European Parliament (June 13, 1999). In the other states, the local elections were held on different days and in different years. Average local turnout in Germany measured from our municipal samples was 65.5 per cent (West Germany 66.1 per cent; East Germany 63.5 per cent). With 36.7 per cent, turnout was lowest in the city of Burg in Saxony-Anhalt and highest in Trockenborn-Wolfersdorf (Thuringia), with 98.1 per cent. The figures show strong variations in mean turnout between the German states, with local turnout scoring lowest in Saxony-Anhalt (50 per cent) and highest in Rhineland-Palatinate (72 per cent); all this supports our assumption that contextual factors affect turnout.

Municipal council elections are held throughout France on the same day. Local electoral data for France refers to the first ballot of the municipal election in March 2001. Average local turnout here was 74.4 per cent, about nine percent-

---

3. The 4,431 municipalities in Germany belong to eighty German metropolitan regions (for the definition of this term, see Walter-Rogg 2005). The municipalities are located in eleven different states. The three city-states – Berlin, Hamburg, and Bremen – were excluded from the sample because of their different status as both state and city. Municipalities from Schleswig-Holstein had to be excluded as there is no data available. Data is also lacking for Brandenburg, as here local and national elections were held the same day in 1998, thereby strongly distorting local turnout. The German municipal sample covers 36 per cent of all 12,428 German municipalities in 2004. The data was delivered by the states' statistical offices. Local turnout refers to the percentage of voters/all eligible voters in a municipality. We would like to thank the DFG Foundation for their financial contribution to the work involved in collecting the German data used in this chapter. Electoral data for France comes from 6,784 communes belonging to the forty-two French metropolitan regions with over 200,000 inhabitants (only Lomme, a suburb of Lille is missing, as Lomme was merged with Lille in 2000; for more details on the French data, see Hoffmann-Martinot 2005). Turnout for municipal elections is measured by the percentage of voters/registered citizens.

age points higher than in Germany. Similarly, a regression analysis, including a French/German dummy variable, shows a mean difference in local turnout between French and German municipalities of 8.9 percentage points.

Table 4.1: Local turnout in France and Germany 1999–2002

State	Elections held on	Local electoral turnout				
		Mean	N	Std. Dev.	Min.	Max.
Lower Saxony	09.09.2001	63.4	456	7.6	39.5	85.4
Northrhine-W.	12.09.1999	59.9	301	6.2	44.2	75.8
Hesse	18.03.2001	56.7	238	6.3	40.0	77.3
Rhineland-P.	13.06.1999	72.0	1,133	8.2	43.7	94.3
Baden-Württ.	24.01.1999	58.8	576	6.4	37.2	79.3
Bavaria	03.03.2002	70.0	706	7.8	47.7	89.9
Saarland	13.06.1999	64.5	52	8.3	46.7	81.2
Mecklenbg.-W.	13.06.1999	59.3	140	9.7	37.8	84.9
Saxony	13.06.1999	60.5	225	7.1	42.2	81.3
Saxony-Anhalt	13.06.1999	50.0	309	10.2	36.7	89.9
Thuringia	13.06.1999	71.4	295	10.3	44.5	98.1
Germany West	–	66.1	3,462	9.5	37.2	94.3
Germany East	–	63.5	969	10.9	36.7	98.1
Germany	–	65.5	4,431	9.7	36.7	98.1
France	11.03.2001	74.4	6,784	9.8	41.0	100.0

Notes: Local elections were held on the same day as elections for the European Parliament.
Eta for comparison France/Germany = 0.41; Eta² = 0.7
Sources: authors' data, collected from the state Statistical Offices in Germany and the French Ministry of Internal Affairs.

When studying changes in local turnout since the beginning of the 1950s, we used aggregated electoral data from the French Ministry of Internal Affairs and the Germany's state Statistical Offices (see Figure 4.2). From the early 1950s until the 1980s, average local turnout rates in both countries varied between 75 and 80 per cent and remained rather stable. Since the end of the 1980s, however, local turnout in both countries has declined. In Germany, turnout rates are about 52 per cent in West Germany and 46 per cent in East Germany. Summarising these results, German local electoral participation dropped in 20 years by about 20 percentage points. Turnout rates in East Germany are generally lower than in West Germany, but the trend holds for both parts of the country. The figures for France display a similar picture. Mean local turnout had ranged between 75 and 80 per cent since 1947, before it entered a phase of regular diminution: from 78.4 per cent in 1983, it decreased to 72.8 per cent in 1989, then to 69.4 per cent in 1995, and only 62.2 per cent in 2001. In 2007, about 65 per cent of French registered voters cast their ballots in the local elections, which were interpreted by the media as an election against the President of the Republic, Nicolas Sarkozy. With about 15 percentage points, the decline in France was reasonably comparable to that in Germany.[4]

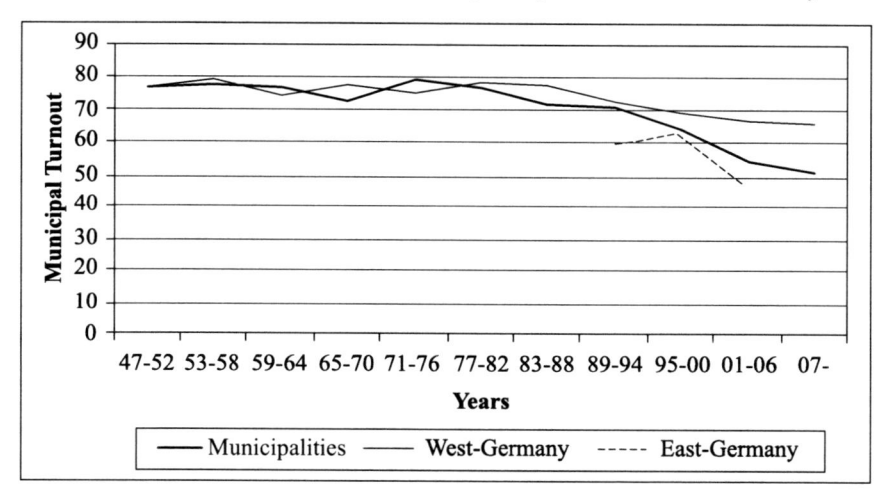

Figure 4.2: Local electoral turnout in France and Germany 1950-2007

Notes: Local turnout figures for Germany are average values calculated from several local elections in the different states that took place in one parliamentary term. The number of elections per parliamentary term varies between four and fifteen. For more details on the different local elections in Germany, see the Appendix.
Sources: authors' data, collected from the state Statistical Offices in Germany and the French Ministry of Internal Affairs.

This declining trend in local turnout fits into a common picture, usually attributed to modernisation processes in Western societies (Steinbrecher *et al.* 2007). In most countries, traditional cleavages have lost their mobilising capacity and no

---

4. Table 4.1, which gives the data for a sample of French and German municipalities, shows higher turnout rates than the data in Figure 4.2. This effect is mainly due to the fact that the turnout rates are calculated differently. In Table 4.1, average turnout rates are calculated from turnout levels per municipality. In Figure 4.2, average turnout rates are calculated for Germany by the number of actual voters to the number of all eligible voters and for France by the number of actual voters to all registered voters.

longer stimulate people any more to cast their votes. In turn, social group norms – for example, the duty to vote, or feelings of party identification – began to erode. Such other modernisation processes as secularisation, individualisation, and increasing societal mobility, have also negatively affected voters' desire to go to the polls. 'In light of these theories, declining, or at least unstable turnout, is a consequence of social change within a society' (Steinbrecher *et al.* 2007: 5).

According to official statistical data, local electoral participation in France today is about 8 per cent higher than in West Germany, and about 16 per cent higher than in East Germany. This result runs counter to our initial assumption: we expected local turnout in Germany to be higher than in France, as local government in Germany is said to have a long tradition of local self-government, while the opposite holds for France (Hesse and Sharpe 1991; Page 1991; Vetter 2007: 94ff.). At first glance, reality proves this assumption to be invalid. On closer examination, however, a second problem emerges: the official turnout figures are based on different measurements, themselves affected by different mechanisms of voter registration. In Germany, turnout is measured by the number of actual voters to all eligible voters. In France, turnout is measured by the number of actual voters to all registered voters, and registration is not automatic, as it is in Germany. There is no official information available about the number of non-registered citizens in France. Estimations by one of the authors, based on different surveys, indicate about 10 per cent of non-registered citizens in local as well as in national elections. With the number of registered voters in France being definitely lower than the number of all eligible voters, turnout in France is 'artificially' increased when compared turnout in Germany. A re-estimation of the French results now leads to a 10 per cent reduction in the overall local turnout figures for France! And there is a second effect distorting the comparison of local turnout figures between France and Germany. Estimations show that of all automatically-registered voters in Germany, between 2 to 5 per cent are either 'double-listed', have died but are still listed, or are wrongly counted as eligible voters for other reasons (Kleinhenz 1995: 73ff.). These citizens 'artificially' increase the number of eligible voters and, hence, the 'denominator' in the German way of calculating turnout. Consequently, official data for local turnout in Germany is lower than it should be, given the real number of all eligible voters.

Once these points are taken into account and the turnout figures compared, there is scarcely any real difference between the two countries. Previous results showing local turnout in France as higher than that of Germany now become invalid, leading us to reformulate our research question: Why is there hardly any difference in local turnout between France and Germany, even though their local elections are held in quite different socio-structural, institutional, and political contexts?

Explaining the similarities in local turnout between France and Germany

There are two possible answers to our reformulated research question, the first being that contextual differences between the two countries do not affect local turnout. However, as past research shows, context does matter, so such an answer is unconvincing. Therefore, we assume that the effects of local turnout context are to be found behind a more complex pattern, and that mobilising and de-mobilising effects are simultaneously at work. Figure 4.3 shows five factors that we assume to be at work when voters in France and Germany are mobilised or demobilised to cast their ballots in local elections. Whereas the first three factors should lead to higher local turnout in France, the last two should theoretically lead to higher local turnout in Germany. In sum, their effects could counterbalance each other, leading to the phenomenon of similarity shown above.

	France	Germany
Size of municipality	+	−
Importance of the institution	+	−
Political salience of local council elections	+	−
Applied voting systems	−	+
Local discretion	−	+

Figure 4.3: Hypotheses on turnout effects from different contexts

Municipal size and local turnout

Research on the relationship between the size of a community and citizen participation is extensive.[5] In a prominent publication on the topic, Dahl and Tufte (1974: 13ff.) summarise ambivalent assumptions about the influence of community size on political involvement. On the one hand, they expect participation in smaller units to be strong, because:

> smaller democracies provide *more opportunity for citizens to participate effectively* in decisions [...] smaller democracies are likely to be more nearly *homogeneous* with respect to beliefs, values, and goals [...] smaller democracies make it easier for a citizen to perceive a relation between his own self-interest or *understanding* of the good and a public or general interest, the interests of others, or general conceptions of the good [...] smaller democracies make possible greater speed and accuracy of *communication* among all members of the system [...] smaller democracies provide more opportunities for all citizens to gain *knowledge* needed for decisions by direct observation and experience.

---

5. Nevertheless, the question as to why size is related to turnout has still not been answered satisfactorily. There are several competing theories, such as rational choice explanations and modernisation hypotheses.

But, on the other hand, participation and involvement might also be stronger in larger political communities, with the interest in and the understanding of politics being perhaps more developed than in smaller democracies, as:

> larger democracies provide opportunities for citizens to participate, at least by voting in elections, in the decisions of a political system large enough to *control all or most of the major aspects of their situation* that can be controlled [...] larger democracies provide more opportunity for *divergence of views* on individual, group, and general interests and goals [...] larger democracies reduce the likelihood that a single interest of one segment of the members will dominate the whole system [...] larger democracies provide greater opportunities for individuals to develop skills, hence to develop skills needed for rational solutions to problems.

While Dahl and Tufte do not find any clear-cut relationship between size and electoral participation (1973: 61ff.), many other authors do report a negative relationship, with participation in smaller municipalities being stronger than in bigger cities. This mobilising effect in smaller communities is often explained by a stronger homogeneity, a higher capacity for social and political integration, a closer relationship between the voters and their elected representatives, and a greater reduction of participation barriers (Verba *et al.* 1978; Blais and Carty 1990; Rallings and Thrasher 1997; Blais and Dobrzynska 1998; Oliver 2000, 2001; Frandsen 2002).

In Germany, the local level is made up of either county-subordinated or county-free municipalities. After reunification in 1990, the number of municipalities in the whole of Germany was about 16,070. In 2003, only 13,157 of them remained, following territorial reforms in East Germany.[6] But East and West Germany still show enormous discrepancies in the number and size of their municipalities: on average, whilst an East German municipality has 2,700 inhabitants, a West German one has 8,100.[7]

France, compared to Germany, is a far more fragmented nation. An international comparison based on indicators measuring the geo-political fragmentation of metropolitan areas shows that, with its 36,570 communes (January 2006)[8], France is even more fragmented than either Switzerland or the United States (Hoffmann-Martinot and Sellers 2005). Some 58 per cent of all French municipalities count fewer than 500 inhabitants, and the average demographic size of a French municipality – 1,640 inhabitants – is even smaller than in East Germany.

---

6. The number of municipalities in East Germany has been reduced by more than 38 per cent (from 7,564 in 1990 to 4,642 in 2003), while the number of municipalities in West Germany remains almost the same. In West Germany, amalgamation took place in the early 1970s, when the number of municipalities was reduced by more than 60 per cent (see Council of Europe 1995: 16).
7. These average numbers mask large variations between the different West German states.
8. This number increases to 36,784 if we also take into account French overseas territories.

If, as past research has shown, size is negatively related to turnout, local turnout in France should consequently be much higher than in Germany, given the differences in municipal fragmentation between the two countries.

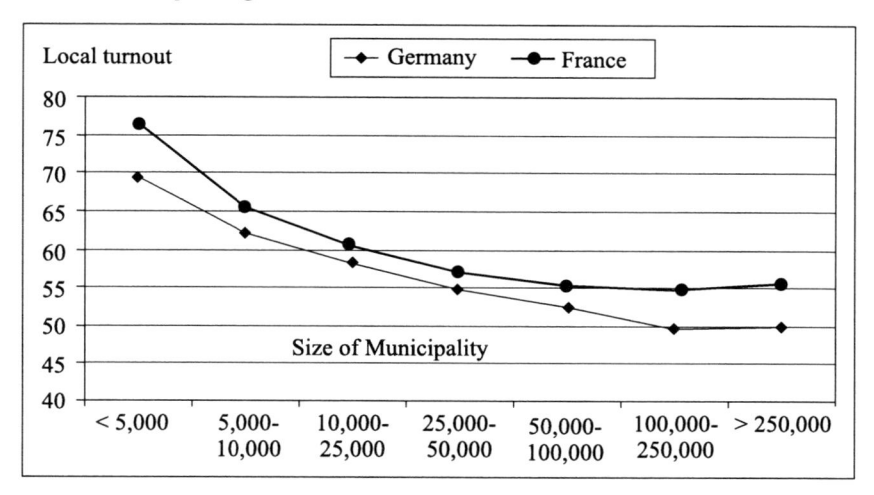

	< 5,000	5,000-10,000	10,000-25,000	25,000-50,000	50,000-100,000	100,000-250,000	> 250,000
France	N = 5,778	N = 481	N = 317	N = 130	N = 42	N = 29	N = 7
Germany	N = 2,844	N = 623	N = 621	N = 228	N = 76	N = 50	N = 24

Source: Authors' data, collected from the state Statistical Offices in Germany and the French Ministry of Internal Affairs.

Figure 4.4: Municipal size and local turnout in France and Germany

Figure 4.4 clearly shows a negative size effect on local turnout for both countries as expected: the larger a municipality, the lower is its local turnout. Although these negative effects are similar in France and in Germany, the effects of size on turnout are not linear. The decrease in turnout is most obvious for municipalities with fewer than 50,000 inhabitants, but this is far less true for larger municipalities. In order to estimate size effect strength, we performed a regression analysis with a transformed size variable. By using the natural logarithm of size (ln), we adjusted our estimation model to the non-linearity of the relationship.

The strong effect of municipal size on local turnout now becomes obvious with the difference in geo-political fragmentation of the two countries explaining about half of the variance in local turnout (see Table 4.2). In the first regression model, only a country dummy variable is included, showing a mean difference in local turnout between France and Germany of 8.9 per cent. This difference is – as we have shown – mainly due to differences in the measurement of turnout. When we include the logged size variable, the standardised coefficients show that size is a really important factor in explaining turnout. From this we conclude that, given the French/German differences in geo-political fragmentation and the strong, negative size effect in both countries, municipal fragmentation is a factor that should definitely result in local turnout being higher in France than in Germany.

Table 4.2: Municipal size and local turnout in France and Germany

	Local turnout	Local turnout
	74.4***	103.9***
France/Germany	−8.9 (−.42)***	−4.5 (−.21)***
Size (ln)	–	−4.3 (−.64)***
R²	.17***	.54***
N	10,944	10,944

Source: Author's data, collected from the state Statistical Offices in Germany and the French Ministry of Internal Affairs. Pooled analyses for France and Germany are weighted to a sample size of 5,500 cases each. In brackets: beta-coefficients.

The importance of the institution

According to the existing literature, another mobilising factor involved in casting a ballot in an election is the importance of the institution (Reif and Schmitt 1980; Reif 1984). The importance of the institution, related to its power to affect political decisions, is reflected by voters calculating how much there is at stake when their ballot has to be cast. Referring to European Parliament elections for example, Franklin (2002: 153) states:

> An election that does not decide the disposition of executive power [...] can be expected to prove less important (and therefore less likely to motivate voter turnout) [...] If executive power is at stake, then we would expect that more people will turn out.

Looking at French and German local council elections from this point of view, we argue that French local council elections should be of much greater importance to French voters than German local council elections to German voters; in France there is much more at stake when citizens vote for their local councils, as local council elections are equally mayoral elections. The institutional differences between France and Germany are explained in greater detail below.

The internal organisation and power distribution of French local authorities display two main characteristics. First, communes, departments, and regions share a uniform statute. This means that, unlike what happens in most Western countries, the same organisational model is enforced throughout the whole territory, with only a few special cases being excluded (overseas departments and territories; Corsica, Alsace and Moselle; Paris, Lyon and Marseille). Secondly, and of primary importance, most competences lie with the relevant executive, i.e. the mayor (commune). The mayor's power has very few institutional limits:

> In most municipalities evidence persistently shows that the mayor, far from being a peer, becomes the boss of his colleagues. He makes his supporters dependent from him far more than he depends from them. Power inside the municipal polity polarises around him.
>
> (Thoenig 2006: 48)

The all-powerful role of the mayor and, since the decentralisation laws, that of the presidents of general and regional councils, echoes the influential position at national level of the President of the Republic. There is no real separation of powers, as the mayor wears at least three hats: executive of the municipality (head of its administration); chairperson of the local assembly; and representative of the state for the functions exercised by the commune on behalf of the state. The political regime of French local authorities can readily be compared to that of a typically presidential one, even though it is still up to the municipal assembly to choose the new mayor. Local council elections in France should, therefore, be of high salience to voters as they are both council and mayoral elections.

In Germany, on the contrary, local council elections offer less salience for voters. Before reunification, there were four different forms of local government system. In some, the councils were given the power to select the mayors and the chief executive officers, while in others the mayors were directly elected by the citizens, and the councils were far less powerful (Gunlicks 1986: 73ff.; Knemeyer 1999). In Bavaria and Baden-Württemberg (*South German Council* form), the council was weakest: the mayor was directly elected for eight years and the council members had no control over the local executive. The mayor, who was also head of both the council and the administration, became the most powerful actor in the local political arena. Local council elections in such cases obviously had less salience for the voters as they did not involve any selection or control of the mayoral position. In Rhineland-Palatinate, in the Saarland, and in parts of Schleswig-Holstein (*Strong Mayor* form), council members appointed the formally strong mayor for a term of ten years. Not only did he chair council committees and meetings and control the agenda, but he was also the chief administrative officer, as well as the legal and ceremonial head of town. Local council elections here, similar to those in France, were also mayoral elections, with a much higher salience than in Bavaria and Baden-Württemberg. In Hesse and, in part, in Schleswig-Holstein (*Magistrat* form), the council was a strong collective body in its own right. Headed by a chairperson – not the mayor – elected from its own members, this chairperson set the agenda, chaired council meetings and served as the legal and ceremonial head of the municipality. The council also elected a collegial organ – the *Magistrat*, consisting of the mayor and several deputies – as its executive organ, responsible for routine administration. Theoretically, local council elections here should have had even more salience than under the *Strong Mayor* form.

Finally, in Northrhine-Westfalia and Lower Saxony (*North German Council* form), the council was most powerful vis-à-vis the executive. First, the council elected the mayor as the chairman of the council and the ceremonial head of town. Second, the chief administration officer was also elected by the councillors. Local council elections in this institutional setting, therefore, should have had most salience. In the 1990s, all state governments in East and West Germany implemented far-reaching institutional reforms for local government (Vetter 2006, 2009a). Today, the mayors, directly elected in all states, all chair both the local councils and the local administration. Local councils have, accordingly, lost their power. Consequently, ever since the beginning of the 1990s, local council elections are expected to be of less importance to voters as they are no longer of any relevance for the composition of the local executive office, i.e. the mayor, whose position has been strengthened throughout the length and breadth of Germany.

In summary, not only do local council elections in France play an important role as regards the selection of local council members, but voters also decide about their local executives (mayors), who are even more powerful than the 'strongest' mayors in Germany. French voters casting their ballots in local elections obviously have much more at stake than is the case for German voters. Theoretically, this higher salience of French local council elections should – as for municipal size – result in local turnout in France being higher than in Germany (see Table 4.2).

The 'political' salience of local elections for national politics

A third factor that should promote higher local turnout in France than in Germany is the political salience of local elections within the national political context. All local elections in France are held on the same day, and these local elections are interpreted by many political actors and the media as representing a mid-term contest for the president's party. With such intense national media reporting and party involvement, mobilisation in local elections in France should, therefore, be stronger than in Germany.

In Germany, only a certain number of states hold their local elections on the same day (when they coincide with elections for the European Parliament: see Table 4.1). In general, however, there is no horizontal simultaneity of local elections: they are organised by each state on different days and in different years. What is more, local elections in Germany are of no consequence for the distribution of power at either state or national level. The situation is different, however, in the case of state elections, where outcomes may alter the majority status of the political parties (coalitions) in the second national chamber, the *Bundesrat*. This lack of simultaneity and the absence of a local chamber at the national level lead, first, to non-existent/low media coverage of local elections on national TV channels, which, in turn, implies a low mobilisation of voters. Secondly, national parties are less interested in local elections and only partly fulfil their mobilising function. On average, only 45.5 per cent of all local votes go to parties that are present at the national level (see Table 4.3). While national parties in Northrhine-Westfalia and Saarland, for example, receive on average more than 90 per cent of all local votes, they only obtain about 25 per cent in Rhineland-Palatinat, and about 40 per cent in Bavaria, Saxony-Anhalt and Thuringia. As all other votes go to local parties (citizens' lists), combinations of local lists, or to independent candidates, party mobilisation is quite low in most German local elections.

The data available do not allow us to empirically test our argument of a higher 'political salience' of local elections in France. But a close study of the differences in turnout between municipal and first-order elections (the French presidential election and the election for the German *Bundestag*) in both countries could support our assumption: from the 1950s until 1990, local turnout in Germany

Table 4.3: Votes for national parties, free lists, list combinations and independent candidates in German local elections

State	Local votes as percentage				Number of municipalities
	National parties	Free lists	List combinations	Independent candidates	
Baden-Württemberg	45.0	47.9	–	7.0	1,110
Bavaria	40.0	45.6	14.2	0.1	2,058
Hesse	81.8	17.0	–	0.2	426
Lower Saxony	78.7	20.9	–	0.5	1,023
Northrhine-Westf.	90.2	9.6	–	0.1	396
Rhineland-P.	24.6	17.9	0.0	57.5	2,306
Saarland	93.4	6.6	0.0	–	52
Brandenburg	44.1	45.0	–	10.2	421
Mecklenburg-W.	43.3	43.6	–	13.0	873
Saxony	60.5	39.4	–	–	518
Saxony-Anhalt	37.9	41.0	–	21.1	1,121
Thuringia	39.2	56.3	2.5	1.5	998
Total mean	45.5	35.5	2.9	16.1	11,302
Mean West Germany	46.8	30.0	4.0	19.2	7,371
Mean East Germany	43.1	45.7	0.7	10.4	3,931

Source: Reiser et al. 2008

tended to be about ten percentage points lower than national turnout (see Figure 4.5). Since the beginning of the 1990s, however, this gap has constantly widened. Today, on average the turnout gap between federal and local elections in Germany is about 28 per cent. This turnout gap indicates that mobilisation in local elections today is far lower than in national elections, which might be caused by voters feeling local elections to be far less important than national elections.

In France, the gap as regards turnout between local and presidential elections is, on average, only 10 per cent. The smaller mobilisation gap between French local and national elections – compared to the equivalent German gap – might well be due to a higher political salience of local elections. The local elections in France are held simultaneously and benefit from the stronger interest shown in them by both the national media and the national political parties, which should, in turn, influence turnout positively.

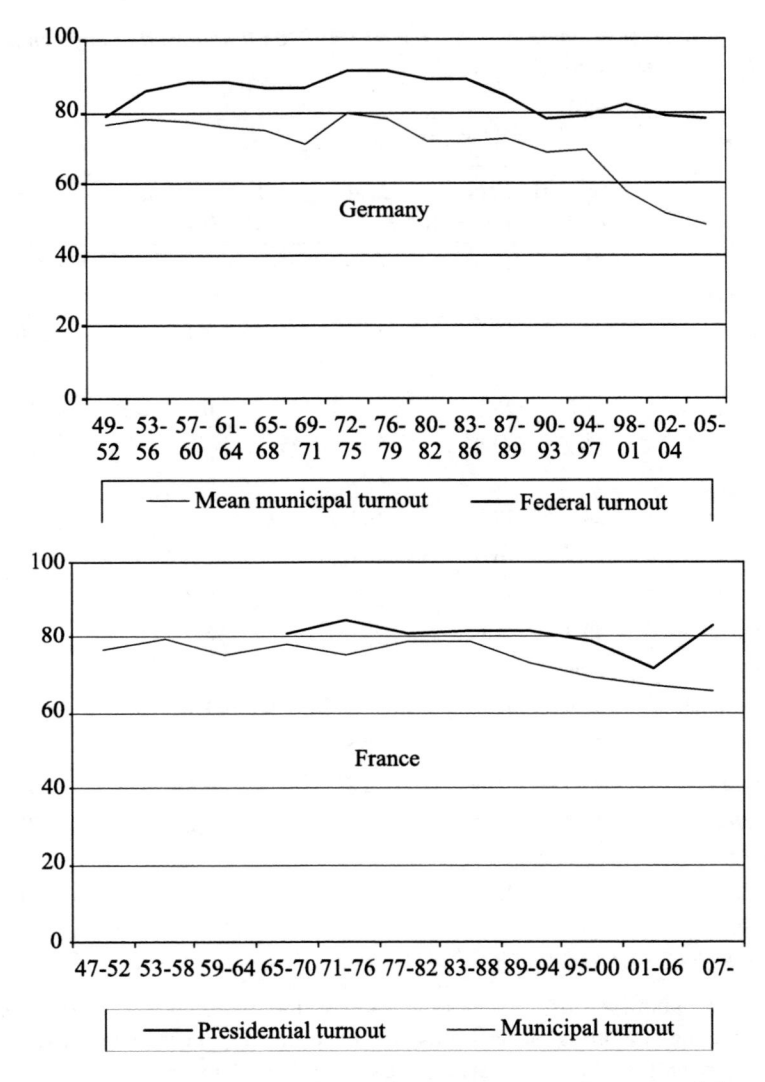

Figure 4.5: Local and National Electoral Participation in France and Germany

Notes: Local turnout figures for Germany are average values calculated from several local elections in different states, all taking place in one parliamentary term. The number of elections per parliamentary term varies between 9 and 15. For more information, see the Appendix.
Sources: for Germany: official electoral results from the state Statistical Election Offices; authors' calculation of averages; for France: Ministry of Internal Affairs.

Local voting systems and their mobilising capacity

The sections above have dealt with context factors that should promote higher local turnout in France than in Germany, and we now turn to two aspects that should work the other way round – the local electoral systems and local discretion – thereby fostering higher turnout in Germany than in France. There is a wide range of literature dealing with the effects of voting systems on electoral participation (Blais and Carty 1990; Powell 1992; Lijphart 1994; Blais and Dobrzynska 1998; Perea 2002; van der Kolk 2007) and most of it investigates the effects of majority voting and proportional representation. The general conclusion is that proportional representation (PR) systems have a higher capacity to mobilise citizens to cast their vote.

Local elections in France and in Germany strongly differ with regard to the particular voting system applied, which, in turn, should positively affect German, rather than French, local electoral mobilisation. In Germany, although local voting systems vary from state to state, they are all proportional in nature. Additionally, they offer citizens different possibilities in preference voting and ticket splitting (*kumulieren* and *panaschieren*). During the reforms of the 1990s, most local voting systems were modified in order to give citizens more say about which candidates they wanted to have a seat in the local councils. Today, closed lists for local elections exist only in Northrhine-Westfalia and in Saarland. In all other states, the citizens have at least three votes to be cumulated and split between different lists. In some states, even, citizens have as many votes as there are seats in the local council (up to 60 votes). Nevertheless, even the closed list systems in Germany are strongly proportional in character.

In the French local 'presidential' regime, on the contrary, the executive power is based on a sufficiently large majority of municipal councillors, whose formation is favoured by the use of a majoritarian electoral system with two ballots. Majority rule, suppressed under the Fourth Republic in communes of over 9,000 inhabitants, was gradually reintroduced by ordinances in 1959 and by laws in 1964 and 1976. This legislation prevented lists with less than 12.5 per cent of votes being presented for the second ballot. On November 19, 1982, Parliament adopted a law establishing a mixed system for the larger municipalities. Since the municipal elections of 1983, and while the majority system with two ballots and open lists has been maintained in communes of fewer than 3,500 inhabitants (93 per cent of all French communes), the electoral rules have been modified in the bigger communes, where the lists of candidates are fixed. At the first ballot, the list with an absolute majority of votes obtains half of the seats, the other seats being distributed according to the PR rule between all the lists, including the majoritarian one, but excluding those with less than 5 per cent of the votes (mechanism of the highest average). If no list obtains the absolute majority, a second ballot is held for those lists having received at least 10 per cent of the votes. The list with an absolute or relative majority of votes then obtains half the seats, the rest being distributed as previously indicated. Usually described as a 'mixed system', the French local voting system has, nevertheless, a rather strong majoritarian component, due to the use of the highest average device and the 10 per cent barrier. In fact, the winning list can rely on a solid majority in the council: more than three-quarters of the seats if it is already successful at the first ballot and more than two-thirds when it is elected at the second ballot with just one third of the votes.

From these differences in the different local voting systems applied in Germany and France, and from the effects of the voting systems on turnout reported in the literature we conclude that, in Germany, local turnout should be higher than in France, thereby counterbalancing the effects of geo-political fragmentation, the importance of the institution, and the political salience of the local council elections.

Local discretion and local turnout

Finally, we relate local turnout to the discretion of local government and local politics in both countries. Why do we do this? In 1835, Tocqueville (1985: 59) argued that local autonomy was the main reason for the Americans' attachment to their townships and their participation in local politics:

> The inhabitant of New England is attached to his township not so much because he was born there but as because he sees in that township a free and strong corporation that he is part of and that is worth his trouble to seek to direct.

In 1965, Almond and Verba compared the political culture of five nations and concluded that differences in feelings of local political competence arise from different degrees in the countries' local autonomy (p.145). Similarly, Dahl and Tufte (1974: 13ff.), as well as Vetter (2007), found that the more political decisions citizens can control theoretically (i.e. the higher the degree of local discretion), the higher their interest and, hence, the likelihood of their participating in local politics.

If we are to relate local turnout in France and Germany to these findings, we have to look at the degree of local discretion exercised in each country. By 'local discretion' we refer to 'the ability of actors within local government to make decisions about the type and level of services it delivers within the formal statutory and administrative framework for local service delivery, and about how that service is provided and financed' (Page and Goldsmith 1987: 5). Once again, we find remarkable differences between the two countries. Until the beginning of the 1990s, numerous studies on local government in Europe attributed a low degree of discretion to French local government, while local government in Germany was said to enjoy a high degree of autonomy and/or discretion (Hesse and Sharpe 1991). The French local government system stems from a 'Napoleonic' tradition, enjoying only a limited functional role within the national political system, but a far stronger political role. Traditionally, its local governments depended on the central authority exercising formal supervision via a prefect and allowing only limited autonomy. In the early 1980s, this situation began to change. There was, at first, a remarkable shift of competences from central state agencies to local authorities in 1982. This movement towards a stronger decentralisation within the 'one and indivisible' nation was strengthened, in 2003, by a second wave of reform. However, because of the still highly-fragmented system of local government in France and its low administrative capacity, decentralisation incentives were mainly directed towards the regions and the departments, while municipalities and villages were left, more or less, to one side (Hoffmann-Martinot 2003; Borraz 2004; Wollmann 2008). It is still the strong representation of local politicians in the national political arena,[9] and not an increase in municipal discretion that helps to safeguard local politics from being neglected by Paris. Local government in Germany, in contrast, is said to belong to a group of local government systems with a long tradition of 'self-government' like the local governments of Norway, Sweden, Denmark, Austria, Switzerland, and the Netherlands.

> Local government [in these countries] [...] enjoys both a strong constitutional status and relatively high degree of policy-making autonomy and financial independence. It also seems to have absorbed a larger share of 'personal', client-oriented welfare state functions...
>
> (Hesse and Sharpe 1991: 607).

During the past two decades, financial constraints and political decisions, especially with regard to social policy, have narrowed the scope of action for German local governments (Vetter 2009b). Nevertheless, we still expect the tradition of strong local self-government in Germany to be present in the political culture and citizens' minds, thereby fostering higher German local turnout than municipal turnout in France.

Summary

France and Germany – although both are at the very heart of Europe – differ in many respects. Therefore, when comparing local turnout in these two countries, we also expected local turnout to vary strongly as well. On closer examination, however, we encountered a big surprise: local turnout in both countries scarcely differs, despite the rather different geo-political, institutional and political contexts in which their citizens participate at the local level. Although official turnout data shows a turnout gap between the two countries of about 10 percentage points (with local turnout in France being higher than in Germany), this gap is mainly due to different registration procedures and different ways of defining (measuring) the turnout rate. In Germany, turnout is measured as the percentage of actual voters to all *eligible* voter*s, with registration being automatic.* In France, turnout is measured as the percentage of actual voters to all *registered* voter*s, with voter registration not being automatic.* Adjusted for this difference, local turnout in both countries is more or less the same. The aim of this chapter, therefore, is to explain not the difference, but the unexpected phenomenon of similarity in local turnout in both countries.

---

9. This representation is strengthened by the 'cumul de mandats' of the mayors exercising both a local and a national mandate.

While most literature on voting behaviour refers to individual characteristics for explanation, we have chosen to focus on the socio-structural, institutional, and political contexts and their effects on local turnout, as both countries vary greatly with regard to these aspects. By comparing just two cases we did not intend to test existing hypotheses used when explaining turnout levels in both counties. We tried, instead, to use the existing knowledge on context effects to delve deeper and enhance our understanding of the similarity phenomenon.

One first possible answer to our question might have been that the different local election contexts in France and Germany do not affect turnout. The existing literature, however, confirms that contexts do shape individual behaviour. We therefore concluded that there must be different effects at work counterbalancing each other and finally resulting in similar behaviour at the aggregate level. We concentrated on five such contextual differences considered in the literature to affect turnout. The data collected for more than 11,000 municipalities and villages in both countries allowed us to set out a number of points.

1. The difference in *geo-political fragmentation* should result in a major difference in aggregated local turnout between the two countries. Local turnout is always higher in smaller rather than larger municipalities, with the strongest effects in local communities with fewer than 50,000 inhabitants. As France is far more fragmented than Germany, the geo-political structure of both countries should definitely account for higher local turnout in France than in Germany.

2. We expected French local council elections to have a higher *institutional importance* for voters than for Germans voting in their local elections. Local council elections in France are simultaneously both council and mayoral elections, which should result in a stronger mobilisation of voters in their local ballots.

3. We attributed far stronger *political salience for national politics* to local elections in France: they are held on the same day; they are considered as a referendum on national government; and, as the media attention they are accorded is much stronger than in Germany, this should result in citizens being more highly mobilised to vote.

However, there are also two other institutional aspects that should work the other way round, thereby counterbalancing the effects just described above. First, local voting systems differ strongly. Whereas a majoritarian system is applied in France, the local voting systems in Germany all follow the PR-rule, which should increase turnout there. Secondly, we pointed to the traditionally strong differences in local discretion between France and Germany, which again should account for higher local turnout in Germany.

The rather unexpected phenomenon of similar local turnout in two countries as different as France and Germany leads us to conclude that some of these effects are probably at work, counterbalancing each other, thereby leading to the result described.

Looking closely at local turnout in two countries and trying to explain the surprising phenomenon of similar behaviour in rather different contextual settings seemed of special importance to us. We have tried to provide a deeper understanding of local electoral behaviour, one which goes even beyond the two countries studied here. Local election turnout is also in decline in many other European countries (van der Kolk 2009). The question as to whether reforms of the contexts of elections can foster turnout is therefore a relevant question in other countries, especially with regard to the future of local democracy and the ongoing disentanglement between citizens and politics in an increasingly globalised world.

Appendix

Table 4.4: Local and national electoral turnout percentage in Germany by states, 1949–2006

Years	49-52	53-56	57-60	61-64	65-68	69-71	72-75	76-79	80-82	83-86	87-89	90-93	94-97	98-01	02-04	05-06	Diff. 87-06
Fed. Election	78.5	86.0	87.8	87.7	86.8	86.7	91.1	90.7	88.6	89.1	84.3	77.8	79.0	82.2	79.1	77.7	-0,1
West Germany																	
Bavaria	81.9	79.9	79.2	–	77.5	–	76.1	78.3	–	74.7	–	75.0	67.3	–	63.2	59.6	-15,4
Baden-Württ.	67.7	69.2	68.9	66.3	66.2	65.6	67.3	–	62.6	61.8	61.4	–	66.7	53.0	52.0	–	-9,4
Hesse	76.8	78.0	80.1	79.3	76.9	–	81.4	78.9	76.3	75.8	78.0	71.3	66.0	52.9	–	45.8	-32,2
Lower Saxony	78.7	77.2	77.4	74.8	77.0	–	82.7	91.4	76.2	72.1	–	68.3	64.5	56.2	–	51,8	-16,5
Northrhine-West.	76.0	76.9	–	76.2	–	68.6	86.4	69.9	–	65.8	65.6	–	81.7	55.0	54.5	–	-11,1
Rhineland-P.	79.3	79.6	79.7	81.4	–	76.2	81.1	78.4	–	76.3	77.2	–	74.1	62.9	57.6	–	-19,6
Schleswig-H.	76.5	74.5	76.1	71.2	68.7	72.3	79.2	78.3	73.8	68.7	–	69.4	70.5	62.8	54.4	49.5	-19,9
Saarland	–	87.	79.1	81.8	81.8	–	83.9	81.3	–	78.6	79.1	–	73.9	59.3	56.3	–	-22,8
East Germany																	
Brandenburg												59.7	–	77.9	46.0	–	-13,7
Mecklenburg-W.												–	65.7	50.5	44.9	–	-20,8
Saxony												–	70.1	53.8	46.1	–	-24,0
Saxony-Anhalt												–	66.2	49.6	42.1	–	-24,1
Thuringia												–	72.3	58.1	50.6	–	-21,7
Mean	76.7	77.9	77.2	75.9	74.7	70.7	79.8	77.4	72.2	71.7	72.3	68.7	69.9	57.7	51.6	51.6	-19,3
Mean West	76.7	77.9	77.2	75.9	74.7	70.7	79.8	77.4	72.2	71.7	72.3	71.0	70.6	57.4	56.3	51.6	-18,4
Mean East	–	–	–	–	–	–	–	–	–	–	–	59.7	68.6	58.0	45.9	–	-20,9

Source: authors' data, collected from the state Statistical Offices.
Note: '–' local elections were not held in this parliamentary term.

References

Almond, G. A. and Verba, S. (1965) *The Civic Culture: Political attitudes and democracy in five nations*, Boston: Little, Brown and Company.
Blais, A. and Carty, R. K. (1990) 'Does proportional representation foster voter turnout?', *European Journal of Political Research*, 18: 167–181.
Blais, A. and Dobrzynska, A. (1998) 'Turnout in electoral democracies', *European Journal of Political Research*, 33: 239–261.
Borraz, O. (2004) 'Les territoires oubliés de la décentralisation' in G. Marcou and H. Wollmann (eds) *Annuaire 2004 des Collectivités Locales*, Paris: CNRS.
Brady, H., Verba, S. and Schlozman, K. L. (1995) 'Beyond SES: A resource model of political participation', *American Political Science Review*, 89(2): 271–294.
Council of Europe (1995) *The Size of Municipalities, Efficiency and Citizen Participation*, Local and Regional Authorities in Europe, 56, Strasbourg Cedex: Council of Europe Press.
Dahl, R. A. and Tufte, E. R. (1974) *Size and Democracy: The politics of the smaller European democracies*, Stanford: Stanford University Press.
Frandsen, A. G. (2002) 'Size and electoral participation in local elections', *Environment and Planning C: Government and Policy*, 20: 853–869.
Franklin, M. N. (2002) 'The dynamics of electoral participation' in L. LeDuc, R. G. Niemi and P. Norris (eds) *Comparing Democracies 2: New challenges in the study of elections and voting*, London: Sage Publications.
Gunlicks, A. B. (1986) *Local Government in the German Federal System*, Durham: Duke University Press.
Hesse, J. J. and Sharpe, L. J. (1991) 'Local government in international perspective: Some comparative observations' in J. J. Hesse and L. J. Sharpe (eds) *Local Government and Urban Affairs in International Perspective: Analyses of twenty western industrialised countries*, Baden-Baden: Nomos.
Hoffmann-Martinot, V. (2003) 'The French Republic, one yet divisible?' in N. Kersting and A. Vetter (eds) *Reforming Local Government in Europe: Closing the gap between democracy and efficiency*, Opladen: Leske and Budrich.
—— (2005) 'Towards an Americanization of French political areas' in V. Hoffmann-Martinot and J. Sellers (eds) *Metropolitanization and Political Change*, Wiesbaden: VS Verlag für Sozialwissenschaften.
—— (2006) 'Reform and modernization of urban government in France' in V. Hoffmann-Martinot and H. Wollmann (eds) *State and Local Government Reforms in France and Germany*, Wiesbaden: VS Verlag für Sozialwissenschaften.
Hoffmann-Martinot, V. and Sellers, J. (2005) 'Conclusion: The metropolitanization and political change' in V. Hoffmann-Martinot and J. Sellers (eds) *Metropolitanization and Political Change*, Wiesbaden: VS Verlag für Sozialwissenschaften.

Hoffmann-Martinot, V. and Wollmann, H. (eds) (2006) *State and Local Government Reforms in France and Germany*, Wiesbaden: VS Verlag für Sozialwissenschaften.

Kersting, N. and Vetter, A. (eds) (2003) *Reforming Local Government in Europe: Closing the gap between democracy and efficiency*, Opladen: Leske and Budrich.

Kleinhenz, T. (1995) *Die Nichtwähler: Ursachen der sinkenden Wahlbeteiligung*, Opladen: Westdeutscher Verlag.

Knemeyer, F. -L. (1999) 'Gemeindeverfassungen' in H. Wollmann and R. Roth (eds) *Kommunalpolitik: Politisches Handeln in den Gemeinden*, Opladen: Leske and Budrich.

Lijphart, A. (1994) 'Democracies: Forms, performance, and constitutional engineering', *European Journal of Political Research*, 25: 1–17.

Loughlin, J. (2001) *Subnational Democracy in the European Union*, Oxford: Oxford University Press.

Oliver, J. E. (2000) 'City size and civic involvement in metropolitan America', *American Journal of Political Science*, 94(2): 361–373.

— (2001) *Democracy in Suburbia*, Princeton, N.J.: Princeton University Press.

Page, E. C. (1991) *Localism and Centralism in Europe: The political and legal bases of local self-government*, New York: Oxford University Press.

Page, E. C. and Goldsmith, M. J. (1987) 'Centre and locality: Functions, access and discretion' in E. C. Page and M. J. Goldsmith (eds) *Central and Local Government Relations: A comparative analysis of west European unitary states*, London: Sage Publications.

Perea, E. A. (2002) 'Individual characteristics, institutional incentives and electoral abstention in Western Europe', *European Journal of Political Research*, 41: 643–674.

Pierre, J. (1990) 'Assessing local autonomy' in D. S. King and J. Pierre (eds) *Challenges to Local Government*, London: Sage Publications.

Powell, G. B. (1992) 'Contemporary democracies: Participation, stability and violence' in A. Lijphart (ed.) *Parliamentary versus Presidential Government*, New York: Oxford University Press.

Rallings, C. and Thrasher, M. (1997) *Local Elections in Britain*, London: Routledge.

Reif, K. (1984) 'National Electoral Cycles and European Elections 1979 and 1984', *Electoral Studies*, 3: 244–255.

Reif, K. and Schmitt, H. (1980) 'Nine second-order national elections: A conceptual framework for the analysis of European results', *European Journal of Political Research*, 8: 3–44.

Reiser, M., Rademacher, C. and Jaeck, T. (2008) 'Präsenz und Erfolg kommunaler Wählergemeinschaften im Bundesländervergleich' in A. Vetter (ed.) *Erfolgsbedingungen lokaler Bürgerbeteiligung*, Wiesbaden: VS Verlag für Sozialwissenschaften.

Sharpe, L. J. (1970) 'Theories and values of local government', *Political Studies*, 18(2): 153–174.

Steinbrecher, M., Huber, S. and Rattinger, H. (2007) *Turnout in Germany: Citizen participation in state, federal, and European elections since 1979*, Baden-Baden: Nomos.
Stoker, G. (1991) 'Introduction: Trends in European Local Government' in R. Batley and G. Stoker (eds) *Local Government in Europe: Trends and developments*, Houndmills: MacMillan.
Thoenig, J. -C. (2006) 'Modernizing sub-national government in France: National creativity and systematic stability' in V. Hoffmann-Martinot and H. Wollmann (eds) *State and Local Government Reforms in France and Germany*, Wiesbaden: VS Verlag für Sozialwissenschaften.
Tocqueville, A. de (1985) *Über die Demokratie in Amerika*, Stuttgart: Reclam.
van der Kolk, H. (2007) 'Local electoral systems in Western Europe', *Local Government Studies*, 33(2): 159–180.
— (2009) 'Does turnout decline?', paper presented at the 5th ECPR General Conference, Potsdam, September 2009.
van Deth, J. W. (2003) 'Vergleichende politische Partizipationsforschung' in D. Berg-Schlosser and F. Müller-Rommel (eds) *Vergleichende Politikwissenschaft: Ein einführendes handbuch*, 7th edn., Opladen: Leske and Budrich.
Verba, S., Nie, N. H. and Kim, J. -O. (1978) *Participation and Political Equality: A seven-nation comparision*, Cambridge: Cambridge University Press.
Verba, S., Schlozman, K. L. and Brady, H. (1995) *Voice and Equality: Civic voluntarism in American politics*, Cambridge, Massachussets; London: Harvard University Press.
Vetter, A. (2006) 'Modernizing German local government: Bringing people back in?' in V. Hoffmann-Martinot and H. Wollmann (eds) *State and Local Government Reforms in France and Germany*, Wiesbaden: VS Verlag für Sozialwissenschaften.
— (2007) *Local Politics: A resource for democracy in Western Europe? Local Autonomy, Local Integrative Capacity, and Citizens' Attitudes Toward Politics*, Lanham, MD: Lexington.
— (2009a) 'Changes in German local autonomy 1985–2005' in M. J. Goldsmith and E. C. Page (eds) *Local Autonomy in Europe*, London: Routledge.
— (2009b) 'Citizens versus parties: Explaining institutional change in German local government 1989-2008', *Local Government Studies*, 35(1): 125–142.
Walter-Rogg, M. (2005) 'Metropolitan areas and political impact in Germany' in V. Hoffmann-Martinot and J. Sellers (eds) *Metropolitanization and Political Change*, Wiesbaden: VS Verlag für Sozialwissenschaften.
Wollmann, H. (2008) 'Reformen dezentral-lokaler Organisationsstrukturen zwischen Territorialität und Funktionalität: England, Schweden, Frankreich und Deutschland im Vergleich' in H. Heinelt and A. Vetter (eds) *Lokale Politikforschung Heute*, Wiesbaden: VS Verlag für Sozialwissenschaften.

chapter five | local democracy – a comparison of mayoral perceptions

Björn Egner and Eric Kerrouche

Introduction

Although the importance of the local level in the political systems of Western democracies has never been seriously contested, research specifically aimed at that level has not really been in vogue. Recently, however, with standard political science research questions being extended to the local level, a number of interesting methodological and conceptual insights have come to light. Not surprisingly, most contributions stem from *policy analysis*. In this case, the local level often appears either in discussions on policy implementation, or at a generic level for research interest concerning policy fields institutionally connected to the local level: planning, housing, waste disposal, water supply, infrastructure, economic development, culture policies, etc. (Lorrain 2003; Négrier and Jourda 2007). Certain researchers have tried to transfer knowledge about *politics* from the national or sub-national level to the local one, in attempts to explain the results of local council elections (Egner and Stoiber 2008) or the building literature on local *polity* – namely, the different local government systems and their impact on politics and policies (Hesse and Sharpe 1991; Mouritzen and Svara 2002). Yet other contributions have tried to establish a global synthesis of the global trends that characterise the local level (Caulfield and Larsen 2002; Denters and Rose 2005). The development of this field of research is particularly interesting, since it comes at a time when local governments are being contested in many ways, both as regards their output- and input-legitimacy (Kersting and Vetter 2003b).

In this literature, the democratic dimension of local government plays an essential role. Indeed, modernising local democracy by increasing citizen involvement has been a *leitmotiv* of all political parties and governments since the beginning of the 1990s. Such a development stems from the fact that territorial democracy, the main feature of which is aimed at ensuring a greater proximity of citizens vis-à-vis political leaders, is submitted to an overall increase in dissatisfaction and criticism concerning its fundamentals and modalities (Hoffmann-Martinot 1999). One of the trivial expressions of this internal crisis is a tendency towards a decline in electoral turnout (Goldsmith 2003). What is at stake is both a reconsideration of all communication channels with the local community, as well as an appeal to consider new forms of coalitions between council parties (Bäck 2003); there is also a growing local democracy (Denters and Rose 2005). In other words, under the umbrella label of 'participatory democracy' or 'deliberative democracy', the main idea is to involve citizens in the political decision-making process and 'educate' them to become active, responsible members of the community (Kersting and Vetter 2003a).

Nevertheless, most of the studies focused on participation restrict themselves to specific dimensions (e.g. the attitude of citizens towards local participation or the tools of local democracy). A 'decentred' approach, taking leaders' perceptions of local democracy into account, is rarely available; the present contribution will try to bridge this gap in respect of France and Germany. Using a survey carried out by an international team,[1] this chapter envisages local democracy from a special point of view: that of French and German mayors. Mayors are crucial for local participation. They remain essential actors at a local level in the two countries. Being elected directly (Germany) or quasi-directly (France) by their respective citizens, they have a special connection with the commune inhabitants. As key actors for local politics and policies, mayors can encourage participatory policy making or else ensure the implementation of policy outputs produced in participatory arenas; they may also, however, try to block and/or avoid participation. Moreover, there is a growing expectation that political leaders will extend further contact with their public via participatory strategies; indeed, certain aspects of local government reforms in Europe testify to this determination to strengthen local democracy (Kersting and Vetter 2003b). In this sense, the role of political leadership extends to the coordination of different forms of democracy (Haus and Sweeting 2006).

The need for such research is particularly relevant as regards the comparison of elites. If the diverse tendencies of citizens from different countries have been the subject of major international surveys, this has certainly not been extended to the case of elites. Comparison of elites – local elites in particular – remains a domain that political scientists have, with a few recent exceptions, most often tended to neglect. This is even more so with regard to Franco-German comparisons. Therefore, it would seem interesting to discover how mayors themselves perceive participation. Such an approach differs from what is currently to be found in the scientific literature: for the most part, several municipalities in one country are studied (Le Bart 2003), or else a few municipalities in more than one country are compared (Bäck 2005; Heinelt and Egner 2005). The purpose of this chapter is to take this a step further by comparing several municipalities in two countries. In France and Germany, in fact, very little is known about how mayors perceive the

---

1. The survey on mayors was conducted in 2003 and 2004. It is based on a questionnaire sent out to all mayors of towns of over 10,000 inhabitants in Norway, Sweden, Denmark, England, Ireland, France, Belgium, the Netherlands, Germany, Poland, the Czech Republic, Austria, Switzerland, Hungary, Portugal, Spain, Italy and Greece. The collection of data in France was carried out by Eric Kerrouche and in Germany by Björn Egner, Michael Haus and Hubert Heinelt. French responses attained an absolute number of 188 and 637 in the case of German responses (i.e. a response rate of 21 per cent and 41 per cent respectively). The responses of the German mayors show an 'over-representation' of mayors from towns with up to 50,000 inhabitants. The response rate by regions (Länder) shows no remarkable disparities – with the exceptions of Bavaria (where it was higher) and Lower Saxony (where it was lower). The responses of the French mayors show a slight under-representation of towns with more than 30,000 inhabitants. (cf. Bäck *et al.* 2006).

democratic dimension. What do they think about local democracy? How do they believe it works? How do they evaluate the new tools that allow them to interact with citizens? Is there a difference between German and French mayors, or do they hold similar views about what is going on in 'their' municipality? As pointed out in the research questions, we want to address the participatory dimension of local democracy; we will not, however, address the phenomena of local governance arrangements from the mayors' point of view, since this topic has already been investigated (Heinelt *et al.* 2006).

There are three main methodological constraints that need to be borne in mind when interpreting the results of this survey:

1. It is only from an international comparative perspective that the roles of mayors in the French and German local government system are similar: they have a strong position in relation to the council and are formally responsible for the municipal administration and its management. Only from such a general perspective are both countries subsumable under the 'strong mayor form' of local government systems (Mouritzen and Svara 2002).

2. Choosing mayors as the respondents of a large-N analysis means conducting an 'elite study', which does not therefore provide a complete picture of how the inhabitants see local democracy. Nevertheless, analysing mayors' opinions can provide interesting insights. The mayors of both countries are, in many respects, the most powerful actors in 'their' municipality. Most of the time, they also have the best overview of what is going on in 'their' city. At the same time, as the most visible actors in the municipality, they also constitute 'living symbols' for their city.

3. The data used does not cover all municipalities, but only those of a certain size (10,000 or more inhabitants). This implies that the results are not representative of all municipalities in both countries, and this is especially true in what concerns France.[2]

This chapter is structured as follows: it begins with a very brief description of the institutional framework of local democracy, focusing on the mayor's role therein (2); then the different ways in which German and French mayors perceive participation is compared (3). The last section is devoted to conclusions concerning the research questions and their connections with other findings in this respect (4).

The institutional framework for local democracy

Since the tools of local democracy are described in another chapter (see Chapter Four), the purpose of this section is to briefly describe the situation of the two local systems so that the contextual, as well as situational, differences of the French and German mayors are clearly brought out.

---

2. The total number of cases from all countries was N = 2,711. Since we use only the cases from Germany (N = 636) and France (N = 188) for this contribution, we have 824 cases to compare: this corresponds to almost one third of all questionnaires returned.

Vertical relations and territorial fragmentation

German municipalities are often described as 'Janus-faced': although they implement policies set up at the Länder and federal level (*Auftragsverwaltung*), municipalities are also free to develop their own policies in accordance with the 'principle of self-administration' guaranteed in the constitution (art.28 GG (Basic German Law)). This dual responsibility has forged the veritable strength of German municipalities regarding public investment and public employment.[3] Today, there are 12,685 municipalities in Germany (Bogumil and Holtkamp 2006). This number seems quite low in comparison with France when the total population of each country is taken into account. However, the wave of territorial reforms conducted in West Germany in the late 1960s and 1970s, when municipality numbers were slashed from over 24,000 to 8,400 – mainly by merging municipalities (Laux 1999) – should not be forgotten even if, in practice, the intensity of territorial reforms varied greatly between the western Länder (Egner 2007). At the same time, the number of German Democratic Republic municipalities was also reduced from over 10,000 to 7,600. Despite this, over 77 per cent of German municipalities have fewer than 5,000 inhabitants. In contrast, Germany's 81 big cities (defined as municipalities with more than 100,000 inhabitants) account for more than 25 million residents, some 31 per cent of the national population.

As for France, the current map of all its communes has its roots in the Revolution. For more than two centuries, the different French regimes have been unable to cut down the number of municipalities. The figure has only been whittled down from 38,500 in 1800 to its present-day 36,682; 31,632 of these have fewer than 2,000 inhabitants and represent only 24.3 per cent of the French population; a mere 951, representing 49.9 per cent of the population, have more than 10,000 inhabitants. The fragmentation of the French communes remains a constant, in spite of the development of inter-municipality (Kerrouche 2008). Nonetheless, despite this problem of fragmentation, the competences accorded to all communes are considerable.[4] The principal statutes dealing with French decentralisation have not radically changed this general state of affairs. The commune, the basic local territorial unit, besides serving as an administrative constituency for the state, also possesses a wide range of powers that stem from the notion of local public interest. As for other aspects, the provisions of the Acts of January and July 1983, dealing with the allocation of jurisdiction between the different authorities, conferred, for each of the major areas of activity, a specific jurisdictional domain for each administrative

---

3. For example, one third of all employees of the German public administration (excluding agencies, military, federal bank, railways, etc.) are located at the local level. Municipal employees accounted for 1.28 million, on 30th June 2005. (*Source:* Statistisches Bundesamt)

4. All the French communes have the same political structures and prerogatives, despite huge differences in terms of population. Nevertheless, it is worth mentioning that the three major cities do have their own special status, with the two Acts of 31st December 1980, known as the PLM Acts – for Paris, Lyon and Marseille – establishing a special system of internal deconcentration at the level of the *arrondissement*, an administrative subdivision of the *commune*.

level, be it *commune* (municipality), *département* (province) or *région* (region).[5] It should be recalled, however, that the two Acts of 1983 did not do away with earlier laws organising commune intervention in more traditional matters. Equally, other more recent laws have been introduced to detail or extend commune jurisdiction. Moreover, and notwithstanding the statutory definition of commune jurisdiction, a *commune* can still act to complement the action of another administrative authority, such as a county council. From the comparative point of view, there are two main differences between German and French municipalities regarding the relationship between the local and the state level. First, as already noted, territorial fragmentation is far more prevalent in France than in Germany. The second difference is, however, far more striking: the German *Städte* und *Gemeinden* are much more powerful than French communes (Heinelt and Hlepas 2006) in terms both of tasks and autonomy. German municipalities are responsible for the implementation of social policy, have financial autonomy and benefit from a remarkable share of overall public spending with regard to gross domestic product (GDP), whereas French communes are rather weak in this respect.

Local government systems, participation and the place of mayors

In Germany, after World War II, the victorious allies quickly installed the *Länder*, with their respective governments, and enforced the setting up of democratic levels of government. In the Western occupied zones, the 'municipal codes introduced reflected the different political systems of the allies and thus their different notions about the 'best' political systems' (Knemeyer 1999). In the French zone, a strong mayoral system, based on the role of the French mayor, was installed. In the British zone, the 'city manager model', copying key aspects of the English local government system, was introduced. In the US zone, the *Länder* reintroduced major aspects of their earlier democratic system: Hesse reverted to the *Magistrat* system, with a collective body leading the administration, while the southern states reinstalled their old 'local system of presidentialism' (Wollmann 1999). In the Sowjet zone, the era of local-level democratic government soon came to an end: in 1952, the German Democratic Republic decided to incorporate municipalities into its 'democratic centralism' system. Shortly after the re-unification of the two German states in 1990, a wave of reforms began. Only in Baden-Württemberg and Bavaria did the municipal codes remain stable; in all the other *Länder*, state parliaments passed laws to change key elements of the local institutional set-up. The most important modification was the introduction of directly elected mayors in all states, as well as the replacement of the 'dual-head' system by a city manager in both of the big northern states – Lower Saxony and North-Rhine Westphalia (Kost 2005). Four essential mayoral functions reveal that German mayors are ma-

---

5. It must be borne in mind that the current reform bill, whilst leaving the commune untouched, will have an impact on both *département* and *region*, see http://www.senat.fr/leg/pjl09-060.pdf.

jor *political* and *administrative* actors at the local level[6]:

1. The mayor is the head of the municipal administration and hence monitors everyday tasks in the town hall.
2. The mayor supervises the other executive officers, each of whom manages a specific department of the municipal administration.
3. The mayor assumes the role of legal adviser to the municipality – he thus has to veto unlawful council decisions or even decisions violating 'common welfare'.
4. The mayor is the legal representative of the municipality.

As for the council, it exercises three vital competences:

1. it approves the municipal budget and is responsible for other major decisions, e.g. the land utilisation plan;
2. it controls the administration (the mayor and the executive officers) by implementing policies; and
3. it keeps additional control over the administration by electing the executive officers.

Despite certain convergences in local institutional set-ups in the various *Länder*, there is still a remarkable divergence in the balance of power between these two local major players, namely the directly elected mayor and the council (Buss 2002; Holtkamp 2005). This is especially true for mayoral institutional attributes, such as the term of office, which may range from five to eight years, depending on the *Land*.

It has often been argued that the institutional diversity resulting from the convergence process generates significant variations in the policy-making styles of mayors and councillors in each *Land* (Bogumil and Holtkamp 2005; Haus *et al.* 2005). Institutional diversity also produces effects on mayors' perceptions of a number of topics (Egner and Heinelt 2005), especially as regards questions concerning the relation between politics and administration. It has also been shown that the shift of institutional settings towards a strong mayor system in most of the *Länder* is relevant not only in theoretical, but also in practical terms. Indeed, as mayors see it, the greater the institutional changes are, the greater is the shift of power from councils to them (Egner 2007). The local level can also be considered as a starting point for political careers (Egner 2007). Additionally, *local referenda* were introduced in all *Länder* (see Chapter Four).

In France, the commune possesses a very definite mark of originality: in its efforts to establish a perfectly interlocking network for the whole of its national territory, the state has made the commune an administrative constituency. The state, however, does not delegate any representative, preferring instead to make

---

6. The mayor is not assigned all four functions in every *Land*; there are various configurations (see Egner 2007: 76ff).

use of the mayor, who thus wears two hats: that of a local agent and that of an agent for the state. As state agent he serves as the lowest-level representative of decentralised government. The mayor is subject, as such, to the hierarchical power of the *Procureur* (Attorney General) or to that of the *préfet* (prefect). This explains certain of the mayor's administrative responsibilities, such as officially publishing and applying laws and by-laws in the commune, organising elections, issuing certificates, and applying public safety measures. It also explains his judicial activities as a registrar, celebrating civil marriages, and keeping various registers concerning the population; he is, too, a magistrate. But all these functions are somewhat minor when compared with his other responsibilities. Not only does the mayor serve as an agent of the state, but he also has a number of other important administrative obligations. In particular, he is charged with carrying out the decisions of the municipal council, which supervises his actions. His missions include representing the commune, negotiating and signing contracts, preparing the budget, as well as managing commune assets. The mayor also exercises other attributions delegated to him by the municipal council and, at least in theory, is answerable to it for his actions. These delegated attributions, which embrace a wide range of domains, such as allocating commune property, taking out loans, creating classes in schools, and handling lawsuits, for example, can be revoked at any time.

The mayor is, likewise, invested with his own specific authority regarding the assignments and management of commune staff. He also has authority over the local police force, and must ensure public law and order, as well as public safety, security and health. But, over and beyond all such competences, the importance of the mayor stems from a long, historical and institutional evolution. For a long time, the mayor used to be appointed to his post; the law of 5th April 1884, which introduced his direct election by the local council, has gradually allowed a new type of political practice to be established. The relevant texts of law do, it is true, indicate that it is for the local council to elect its mayor; in fact, however, it is the mayor who co-opts the council. When the mayor draws up his electoral list, he thereby establishes his authority over the municipal council, rather than having to depend on the council to designate him. The fact that he is not elected by universal suffrage does not prevent him playing the leading role on the local political stage, easily keeping control – as party or majority coalition leader – over the local assembly.

The mixed electoral system introduced in 1983, for communes with more than 3,500 inhabitants, certainly helps in this respect. In essence, the election remains one that favours the majority, due to the rule of the greatest average, and to the eliminatory barrier of a 10 per cent minimum requirement. The list of those in the lead benefits from a guaranteed majority: more than three-quarters of the seats, if the list is first-past-the-post after the first round; or more than two-thirds, if the list is elected after the second round, even should only one third of the votes be cast. We must remember, too, that the period of six years, for which the mayor and his list are elected, represents a rather long time. Moreover, the distinction between a deliberative assembly that decides and an executive organ has practically lapsed, since it is the executive that now holds all the power. Equally, the institution of a collegial organ and of a division of tasks (deputy majors, vice-presidents) is often not what prevails, since the mayor keeps those elected on his list on a very tight rein. As (Hoffmann-Martinot 1999) remarks: if local councillors are entirely free to express their grievances and to speak on behalf of various requests and projects, it is for the mayor to govern alone or by delegation, helped by his collaborators – in the biggest communes – and by deputy mayors subordinate to him, and the mayor does so in almost perfect immunity. After all, there is no question of forsaking the mayor or overthrowing him by a vote of no confidence, as is the case in other legislations.

Within the specific terms of this territorial equation, the mayor remains the benchmark for elected representatives, a local figure that must always be taken into account. As regards the relationship between council and mayor in France, several empirical findings confirm that the importance of the mayor as representative of the citizenry is increasingly shifting towards an 'urban presidentialism' (Hoffmann-Martinot 2006). In many respects, the mayor constitutes the cornerstone of French territorial organisation. Because of his central position within French local government, the mayor is also a powerful manager and a community leader.

The French and the German situations are substantially different as far as the institutional insertion and prerogatives of mayors are concerned. Nevertheless, as already noted, the two local governments do share a certain number of features. That is why some scholars like Wollmann (2008) consider that both countries may be classified in the same subgroup of local government, namely the continental European group. This is premised on the 'dualistic competence model' (a local council with an executive counterpart), the 'dual task model' (local authorities fulfil their task, but can be put in charge of carrying out public tasks assigned by the state) and the 'integrationist model' (in the conduct of delegated tasks, local authorities are subject to an overview by the state, which, typically, goes beyond a pure legal review). Equally, if France and Germany are not classified in the same subgroup of local government in a recent typology (Bäck *et al.* 2006), this is essentially because of the difference concerning relations with local administrations: German mayors have full responsibility. In both countries, however, mayors are the political representatives of their local communities and, in part because of the way they are elected, have direct contact with citizens. This is why it seems relevant to compare the attitudes of French and German mayors towards the democratic dimension of local government. This comparison is especially important because local democracy represents a substantial facet of leadership. Therefore, it is necessary to gain a deeper insight into the attitudes of local political leaders vis-à-vis the different notions of democracy and then study how such attitudes may have consequences on the way they govern.

Mayoral perceptions of local democracy

In the following section, the basic mayoral perceptions of local democracy are compared. Since all variables from the questionnaire were designed using a Likert scale, non-parametric tests (T-tests) will be conducted to determine whether varia-

Table 5.1: Statements on the functioning of local democracy

Statement	mean		Diff.	p	eta
	Germany	France	Δ		
1) Political representatives should make what they think are the right decisions independently of the current views of local citizens/ groups.	3.09	3.29	.20	.024	.079
2) The results of local elections should be essentially decisive for determining municipal policies.	3.43	4.05	.63	.000	.271
3) Residents should have the opportunity to make their views known before important local decisions are made by elected representatives.	3.83	3.40	.43	.000	.202
4) Council decisions should reflect a majority opinion among residents.	3.55	3.40	.15	.059	.067
5) Residents should participate actively and directly in making important local decisions.	3.53	3.23	.30	.000	.134
6) Urban leaders should try to generate consensus and shared values among local citizens/ groups.	4.18	3.78	.40	.000	.208

Note: scale for all items: 1= little importance 5= very important
Source: see footnote 1

tions in the perceptions of mayors in the two countries are significant.[7] After a brief discussion of differences between the attitudes of German and French mayors towards representative and participatory democracy, a number of regressions were conducted to control for personal effects. Gender, age, educational level, party membership, size of municipality and experience as an elected official are used as controls.

---

7. We also give arithmetic means for all the items in order to give an approximate overview of existing variances. We know that calculating arithmetic means and standard deviations for the ordinal variables used here are methodologically problematic. We believe, however, that arithmetic means and standard deviations are useful for interpretation, provided they do not serve as the basis for subsequent calculations.

Representative and participatory democracy

When studying mayoral attitudes towards local democracy, it is – first and foremost – necessary to examine whether there are variations between German and French mayors concerning the functioning of local democracy, especially as regards differentiation between *representative* and *participatory* democracy (for a discussion of the concept, see Haus and Sweeting 2006). On the one hand, representative democracy is traditionally regarded as the essence of democracy. Local elections, i.e. the selection of councillors and mayors, remain the starting point for local democracy. On the other hand, calls for participatory democracy, which were popular in the 1960s and 1970s, have since re-emerged. Although many different procedures are often considered as participatory, democracy is said to have taken a 'deliberative turn' at both the national and local level. In order to illustrate this tendency, we chose the same methodology as Haus and Sweeting (2006). The mayors' scores for six statements available in the questionnaire were measured as displayed in Table 5.1. Those six questions constitute a good proxy of the two democratic dimensions at stake. Each of the first five statements shows a progression in what concerns a reduction in council sovereignty and an increase in direct citizen influence. The sixth statement is more focused on the question of whether local leaders have a more consensual or antagonistic picture of local democracy.

The results clearly indicate different conceptions of the functioning of local democracy. First, German mayors emphasise active, direct citizen participation more strongly than their French colleagues, whilst also stressing the importance of being attentive to public opinion. German mayors expect political leaders to be 'consensus generators', thereby providing an interesting insight into their own role perceptions. French mayors, however, stress the meaningfulness of local election outcomes more strongly than German mayors. All these results are in line with the opposition between participatory and representative democracy expressed above. German mayors put more emphasis on the former, while French mayors are more oriented towards the latter.

French mayors prioritise effectiveness to the detriment of transparency towards citizens, citizens who all too often are evinced from local matters. In France there is assimilation between the commune and democracy at the local level (Aubelle 1999). Local democracy is a self-evident concept, whose alleged superiority is due to the morphological conditions of proximity that make the etymological ideal of democracy possible (Paoletti 1997). Yet – and this is consubstantial with representative democracy – the only real moment when 'locally' governed citizens exercise their sovereignty is at election time. In the commune, perhaps even more so than in the case of other ballots, everything happens as though 'the elections ought to embrace and exhaust all the democratic virtues, as if the public domain could not construct and renew itself legitimately other than through the elective process' (Caillosse 1999). The corollary of this logic is that it allows elected representatives to systematically disqualify other modalities of democracy as being prejudicial to the representative model: representatives cannot transfer their own incumbent powers (Le Bart 2003). This vision is, moreover, confirmed by the population:

in France the commune remains the archetype of localism and the mayor is still considered in public opinion surveys as the political figure inhabitants feel closest to, or appreciate the most (Thoenig 2006). In Germany, the mayoral predisposition for participatory elements can be explained by the role of the local referendum, which – over and beyond electoral mechanisms – remains an essential procedure for citizens (see Chapter Six). Mayor and council may try to pre-emptively include citizens in the political process before a decision is taken by the elected bodies, in order to prevent citizens from requesting referendums about disputed policies and thus formally interfering in politics. Another self-evident explanation for the conceptions of German mayors might be the fact that, unlike their French counterparts, many of them do not belong to any party. However, statistical analysis of German mayors shows that as party membership as a whole has no effect on mayoral attitude towards participatory or representative democracy, it is therefore independent of the sphere of party politics (Egner 2007: 260ff).

Having shown these country variations, we then conducted regression models on four statements that indicated significant inter-country variations (see Tables 5.2). The goal was to test whether country differences were still present when personal attributes and city size were taken into account. The question about the determinant of the electoral result demonstrates that a significant country effect is still effective (with adj. R^2=.072).

Table 5.2: Basic regression for the importance of election results

Variable	B	beta	T	p
(Constant)	4.055		72.772	.000
Germany dummy	−.625	−.271	−7.983	.000

Note: countries with equal weight.
Source: see footnote 1

Table 5.3: Regression for the importance of election results including controls

Variable	B	Beta	T	p
(Constant)	1.136		.106	.916
Germany dummy	−.598	−.257	−6.650	.000
Female	.240	.053	1.469	.142
Age	.001	.008	.174	.862
Educational level	.005	.065	1.686	.092
Party membership	.218	.074	1.997	.046
Experience as elected official	.001	.009	.214	.830
Size of municipality	.000	.008	.215	.830

Note: countries with equal weight.
Source: see footnote 1

Control variables were then added to see whether the country dummy was still significant.

As can be seen from the Table 5.3, the model is slightly improved (with adj. $R^2=.087$), with the striking determinant for the mayors' attitude still being nationality. Only one control variable is also significant, although it is very close to the threshold (with p=.046), and that is party membership. Not surprisingly, mayors who are themselves members of a party stress the importance of the election result for local decisions. Of course they do: mayors who are members of a party are players in *party politics* at the local level; they are embedded in a local branch of a party and most often enjoy a council majority (or that, at least, is the case in a ruling coalition). It is their party that holds a reasonable share of council mandates, thereby explaining why these mayors favour the election results to be decisive for local level decisions.

The second regression model (see Table 5.4) deals with the statement 'Urban leaders should try to generate consensus and shared values among local citizens/ groups'. In the basic regression, (with adj. $R^2= .042$), the country dummy is again significant:

Table 5.4: Basic regression for the importance of generating consensus

Variable	B	Beta	T	p
(Constant)	3.779		79.549	.000
Germany dummy	.400	.208	6.009	.000

Note: countries with equal weight.
Source: see footnote 1

Table 5.5: Basic regression for the importance of generating consensus with controls

Variable	B	Beta	T	p
(Constant)	22.202		2.469	.014
Germany dummy	.399	.208	5.286	.000
Female	.085	.023	.623	.533
Age	−.013	−.118	−2.629	.009
Educational level	.001	.012	.305	.761
Party membership	.068	.028	.736	.462
Experience as elected official	−.009	−.087	−2.022	.044
Size of municipality	.000	.006	.167	.867

Note: countries with equal weight.
Source: see footnote 1

When a more sophisticated model is tested (see Table 5.5), the degree of explanation shows a slight increase (with adj. $R^2 = .053$).

As can be seen, two personal attributes are connected with the importance of generating consensus. First, the importance of consensus generation declines significantly with age, but the overall unstandardised effect seems relatively low: a variation of one point in a five-point-scale would be generated by a variance of 77 years. The other determinant is the length of experience as an elected official: the longer mayors are in public office, the lower the importance of consensus generation. It is especially interesting that both age and seniority exert influence in the same direction. This means that not only do experienced mayors rate consensus lower than newcomers do, but life experience itself becomes a driving force. This situation is also an expression of the 'professionalisation' process of mayors, which is comparable with that of other elected representatives (Wood and Young 1997). The career of an elected representative evolves over time and if, at the very beginning, direct contact with people is considered an essential factor, this tends to change as time goes by, and mayors start focusing on other aspects of their roles (public policies, projects, etc.).

The third basic model (with adj. $R^2 = .039$) also shows a significant country effect (see Table 5.6).

Table 5.6: Basic regression for the importance of residents making their views known

Variable	B	Beta	T	p
(Constant)	3.404		65.438	.000
Germany dummy	.427	.202	5.841	.000

Note: countries with equal weight.
Source: see footnote 1

Table 5.7: Basic regression for the importance of residents making their views known with controls

Variable	B	Beta	T	p
(Constant)	18.883		1.894	.059
Germany dummy	.466	.221	5.604	.000
Female	.386	.096	2.598	.010
Age	−.007	−.058	−1.277	.202
Educational level	.002	.022	.570	.569
Party membership	−.183	−.069	−1.817	.070
Experience as elected official	−.008	.069	−1.576	.116
Size of municipality	.001	.036	.970	.332

Note: countries with equal weight.
Source: see footnote 1

If control variables are added to the model (see Table 5.7), the quality increases slightly (adj. $R^2 = .051$), and gender can be identified as an additional significant determinant.

In addition to the country-specific effect, female mayors significantly favour the idea that residents should be given the chance of making their views known before decisions are taken, thereby confirming the intuitive idea that female elected representatives practice politics differently (Lépinard 2004). But these results have to be treated with caution since the number of female mayors in both countries is generally low – 11.2 per cent in France and only 3.9 per cent in Germany[8] – which means that the basis for the analysis is a very low number of cases (actually, there are N = 45 female mayors in the French-German database).

Let us now look at the last statement on participation, the question about citizen's active and direct participation (see Table 5.8). The model is quite poor (with adj. $R^2 = .017$), but even in this model the country effect can be identified.

Table 5.8: Basic regression for the importance of active and direct participation

Variable	B	Beta	T	p
(Constant)	3.230		57.570	.000
Germany dummy	.304	.13	3.851	.000

Note: countries with equal weight.
Source: see footnote 1

Table 5.9: Basic regression for the importance of active and direct participation with controls

Variable	B	Beta	T	p
(Constant)	40.505		3.808	.000
Germany dummy	.310	.138	3.459	.001
Female	.096	.022	.598	.550
Age	-.010	-.079	-1.744	.082
Educational level	-.002	-.029	-.735	.463
Party membership	-.140	-.049	-1.295	.196
Experience as elected official	-.018	-.153	-3.504	.000
Size of municipality	.000	-.034	-.902	.367

Note: countries with equal weight.
Source: see footnote 1

---

8. In international comparisons, there are only two countries with a smaller proportion of female mayors, namely Portugal and Greece (Steyvers and Reynaert 2006: 50).

When adding the control variables, the model slightly improves (adj. $R^2=.033$) but country still makes a remarkable difference (see Table 5.9).

Again, seniority (measured in years in public office) plays a negative role in what concerns active and direct participation. This corresponds to the findings mentioned above about leaders as 'consensus generators'.

Generally speaking, such control variables as size of the municipality and the personal attributes of the mayor, have only limited impact on explanations of the four variables under scrutiny. In case of any difference, even if control variables are added to the regression models, country effect is always present.

When confronted with two statements regarding (1) the *role of political parties* as participation arena – which points to representative democracy – and (2) *local referendums*, a major aspect of participatory democracy, German and French mayors again turn out to be somewhat different (see Table 5.10).

Table 5.10: Statements on the role of parties and local referendums

Statement	means		Diff.	p	eta
	Germany	France			
Political parties are the most suitable arena for citizen participation	3.48	3.11	.37	.000	.185
Local referenda lead to high quality public debate	2.99	2.94	.05	.374	.031

Note: scale for all items: 1 = strongly disagree; 5 = strongly agree
Source: see footnote 1

As regards local referendums, mayors in both countries tend to be 'two-faced', with the average mayor situating himself practically in the middle of the five-point scale. The result is not very surprising for France and, indeed, the history of local referendums is complicated. The authorities – especially local elected representatives, with the *cumul des mandats* at the National Assembly – have always tried to reduce local referendums to simple consultations in order to avoid the contestation of representative system principles (Premat 2006).

Nonetheless, when analysing mayoral statements about the role of parties as a citizen participation arena, German mayors are slightly (but significantly) more likely to agree. This is so, even if 82.4 per cent of French mayors tend to belong to a party, as opposed to 79.4 per cent of their German counterparts – an apparent paradox with no really convincing explanation. When looking at a possible intra-German variance, it can be found that the role of parties as arenas for citizen participation and local referenda does not significantly differ between mayors from East and West. The basic regression model for the role of parties (with adj. $R^2 = .033$) shows systematic variances between the two countries (see Table 5.11).

After adding the control variables (see Table 5.12), the quality of the model increases considerably (adj. $R^2=.136$). The country dummy is still significant, although three additional determinants do appear.

The most important additional variable is party membership, which seems intuitively consequential: mayors who are members of a party, of course, think that parties are the right arena for participation. This point is especially essential, since this is an indirect acknowledgement by mayors of the importance of the party arena which, it must not be forgotten, is also a selection arena (Norris and Lovenduski 1993). Equally, the size of the municipality is crucial: mayors in the big cities tend to rate the role of parties higher. This correlation is also perfectly understandable, since party politicisation of the political process increases with city size (Egner 2007). The third significant effect is due to seniority; although this is negatively connected to the role of parties as suitable participation arenas, the effect is rather weak.

Table 5.11: Basic regression for the role of parties

Variable	B	Beta	T	p
(Constant)	3.112		64.398	.000
Germany dummy	.367	.185	5.371	.000

Note: countries with equal weight.
Source: see footnote 1

Table 5.12: Regression for the role of parties with controls

Variable	B	Beta	T	p
(Constant)	20.137		2.278	.023
Germany dummy	.348	.175	4.656	.000
Female	-.248	-.065	-1.841	.066
Age	-.005	-.044	-1.015	.311
Educational level	.001	.007	.191	.848
Party membership	.732	.291	8.106	.000
Experience as elected official	-.009	-.082	-1.972	.049
Size of municipality	.002	.103	2.940	.003

Note: countries with equal weight.
Source: see footnote 1

Tools of local democracy

Since the representative aspect is more predominant in the French case, it seems relevant to consider the eventual consequences of this attitude as regards which particular communication channels with people are prioritised. To assess this particular aspect, all of the related set of answers given by mayors concerning typical local democracy tools was used.[9]

---

9. The question was formulated as follows: there are many ways of communicating with local

Table 5.13: Tools of communication with local people

Statement	mean Germany	mean France	Difference	p	eta
Information on citizens' position gathered by the councillors	1.18	1.78	.60	.000	.477
Neighbourhood panels or forums	1.42	1.87	.45	.000	.410
Referenda	1.37	0.88	.49	.000	.364
Formalised complaints or suggestions	1.39	1.75	.36	.000	.301
Forums via the internet	0.84	0.59	.25	.000	.206
Self-organised citizen initiatives	1.20	1.42	.22	.000	.178
Petitions	1.16	1.37	.21	.000	.159
Information on citizens' position gathered by the local parties	1.02	0.82	.20	.000	.154
Citizens' letters via the internet	1.50	1.30	.20	.000	.152
Information on citizens' position gathered by people working in local administration	1.37	1.55	.18	.000	.139
Focus groups	1.00	0.83	.17	.000	.138
Citizens' letters in the local press	1.21	1.04	.17	.001	.118
Satisfaction surveys	1.13	1.22	.09	.052	.069
Personal meetings in the town hall	1.93	1.90	.03	.122	.054
Public meetings and debates	1.72	1.75	.03	.395	.030

Note: scale for all items: 0 = not effective; 1 = only effective in special circumstances; 2 = effective
Source: see footnote 1

Table 5.13 allows us to distinguish again between German and French mayors, and confirms, from a different perspective, the tendency that has already been isolated. Certain statements are bound up with the mayor's role as local leader (personal meetings in the Town-Hall, public meetings and debates). They are understandably credited with high scores. Others statements tend to show a real dichotomy between our population samples. Generally speaking, German may-

---

people and for people to let local politicians know what they think. To be informed about what citizens think, how useful are, in your opinion, the following sources and instruments? 3 scores were available: 0: not effective; 1: only effective in special circumstances; and 2: effective.

ors are more open to new methods of democratic communication (internet, focus groups) and, as already noted above, are more willing to use direct democracy possibilities (referendum).

As for French mayors, they generally prefer more formalised tools of communication (complaints, petitions, self-organised citizen initiatives) and are wary of direct democracy (referendums). They also rely more on the information collected by local councillors or by people working in the local administration, thereby confirming a tendency to centre on the mayor and his political and administrative 'team' (Kerrouche 2005), even if some new tools are emerging (panels, forums and surveys).

In the basic regressions, the country dummy is not significant in three out of fifteen items.[10] When control variables are added (see Table 5.14), the results do not differ greatly. The country separator is significant in fourteen out of fifteen models concerning the tools for acquiring information about what people think. This underlines what was pointed out before, namely that French and German mayors are very different with regard to the particular information channels they find appropriate to know what citizens think. Interestingly, only three of the other variables cause effects in some models: gender and age (as experienced also in other models), and party membership.

Summary and conclusions

This chapter focused on establishing a comparison between French and German mayors and it now becomes important to determine the reasons for the variations brought to light. This is all the more essential as we were unable to find a significant difference when using variables other that of country as an independent variable. Generally speaking, traditional SES variables like age, gender, education, seniority, or context factors such as municipality size, show significant variations in relatively few models. In other words, if some discrepancies are to be found taking into account all these aspects, they essentially make sense within each country; it is, however, mayoral nationality that remains the key factor. Such a result is not surprising: European mayors are a fairly homogeneous elite group (Steyvers and Reynaert 2006). This is why we consider that the variations isolated in this chapter essentially depend on mayoral nationality.

To illustrate this point, we used logistic regressions to predict the nationality of mayors according to the independent variables already used. Almost all the results support this interpretation. The example in Table 5.15 illustrates this.

Even if the level of prediction differs from one country to the other, the two items – 'taking into account the views of residents' and 'generating consensus' – are more connected with German mayors. The representative dimension (v151) is more of a French feature.

It is quite difficult to explain all these variations in mayoral attitudes. Nevertheless, we favoured the idea that the impact of the institutional pattern, and

---

10. Satisfaction surveys, public meetings and debates, personal meetings in the Town-Hall

local democracy – a comparison of mayoral perceptions | 155

particularly the way the mayor is chosen, has a huge effect on everyday mayoral practice. With regard to France, Thoenig (2006) has demonstrated the atypical place occupied by the French mayor; chosen by the local council from among its members, he also heads the same council and ensures the legal execution of the decisions legitimised by the council. The separation of powers, in particular between the legislative and executive branches, is totally blurred locally, and the opposi-

Table 5.14: Overview of regressions for tools of communication with local people with controls

Statement	adj. R^2	Germany	Female	Age	Educational level	Party membership	Experience	Size
Citizens' letters via the internet	.064	+	–			+		
Citizens' letters in the local press	.010	+						–
Formalised complaints or suggestions	.109	–		–				
Petitions	.020	–		–				–
Information on citizens' positions gathered by the councillors	.216	–		+		+		
Information on citizens' positions gathered by people working in local administration	.028	–	+					
Information on citizens' positions gathered by the local parties	.026	+				+		
Public meetings and debates	.003					–		
Satisfaction surveys	.002	–						
Neighbourhood panels or forums	.175	–						
Forums via the internet	.068	+	+					
Focus groups	.021	+	+					
Self-organised citizen initiatives	.037	–	+					
Referendums	.166	+			–	–		
Personal meetings in the town hall	.003	+	+					
No. of significant effects		14	5	5	0	5	2	0

Note: countries with equal weight.

Table 5.15: Regression on the statements about the functioning of local democracy

Model summary

Step	−2 Log likelihood	Cox & Snell R Square	Nagelkerke R Square
1	1010.102[a]	.139	.190

a. Estimation terminated at iteration number 4 because parameter estimates changed by less than .001.

Classification table[a]

			Predicted		
			1 = Germany, 0 = France		Percentage correct
	Observed		France	Germany	
Step 1	1 = Germany, 0 = France	France	138	175	44.1
		Germany	75	486	86.7
	Overall percentage				71.4

a. The cut value is .500

Variables in the equation

			B	S.E.	Wald	df	Sig.	Exp(B)
Step 1[a]	v147	Residents should have the opportunity to make their views known before important local decisions are made by elected representatives.	.275	.073	14.209	1	.000	1.316
	v150	Urban leaders should try to generate consensus and shared values among local citizens/groups.	.545	.086	39.769	1	.000	1.725
	v151	The results of local elections should be essentially decisive for determining municipal policies.	−.605	.076	62.887	1	.000	.546
		Constant	−.316	.447	.501	1	.479	.729

a. Variable(s) entered on step 1: v147, v150, v151.
Source: see footnote 1

tion excluded. This stems from the fact that the mayors themselves constitute the council before the election. One must question the impact of legitimacy given by the election – particularly high in France – and the fact that most French mayors are in the situation of a *cumul des mandats* (Costa and Kerrouche 2007). As for Germany, since its mayors are elected directly, they can be recalled by the people (Wollmann 2008). Mayors can also use referendums to successfully defend their agenda against a 'hostile majority' in the council – at least, they could threaten the council with this option (even if this seldom happens). Whereas the election in France is more of a symbolic consecration, in Germany, the democratic dimension is of a much more practical nature.

Finally, this chapter confirms, but via another perspective, our previous findings. If governance implies the interdependence of many actors (Kooiman 2003) and if the democratic dimension remains at the core of this concept (Kjær 2004), German mayors are, generally speaking, more open-minded and prepared to govern their communes by governance than are their French colleagues, because they are more in favour of a consensual and deliberative understanding of democracy. French mayors tend to favour government-oriented policy making based on majoritarian decisions and representative democracy.

References

Aubelle, V. (1999) 'Le sens de la démocratie locale' in CURAPP (ed.) *La Démocratie Locale, Représentation, Participation et Espace Public*, Paris: Presses Universitaires de France.

Bäck, H. (2003) *Explaining Coalitions: Evidence and lessons from studying coalition formation in Swedish local government*, Uppsala: Uppsala University Press.

— (2005) *Urban Political Decentralization: Six Scandinavian cities*, Wiesbaden: VS Verlag für Sozialwissenschaften.

Bäck, H., Heinelt, H. and Magnier, A. (eds) (2006) *The European Mayor: Political leaders in the changing context of local democracy*, Wiesbaden: VS Verlag für Sozialwissenschaften.

Bogumil, J. and Holtkamp, L. (2005) 'Die Machtposition der Bürgermeister im Vergleich zwischen Baden-Württemberg und NRW' in J. Bogumil and H. Heinelt (eds) *Bürgermeister in Deutschland: Politikwissenschaftliche studien zu direkt gewählten bürgermeistern*, Wiesbaden: VS Verlag für Sozialwissenschaften.

— (2006) *Kommunalpolitik und Kommunalverwaltung: Eine policyorientierte einführung*, Wiesbaden: VS Verlag für Sozialwissenschaften.

Buss, A. (2002) *Das Machtgefüge in der heutigen Kommunalverfassung: Zur machtverteilung zwischen vertretungskörperschaft und hauptverwaltungsorgan bei urwahl der Bürgermeister*, Baden-Baden: Nomos.

Caillosse, J. (1999) 'Éléments pour un bilan juridique de la démocratie locale en France' in CURAPP (ed.) *La Démocratie Locale, Représentation,*

Participation et Espace Public, Paris: Presses Universitaires de France.
Caulfield, J. and Larsen, H. O. (2002) *Local Government at the Millennium*, Opladen: Leske and Budrich.
Costa, O. and Kerrouche, E. (2007) *Qui Sont les Députés Français: Enquête sur des élites inconnues*, Paris: Presses de la Fondation Nationale des Sciences Politiques.
Denters, S. A. H. and Rose, L. E. (2005) (eds) *Comparing Local Governance: Trends and developments*, London: Palgrave Macmillan.
Egner, B. (2007) *Einstellungen Deutscher Bürgermeister: Lokale eliten zwischen institutionen und kontext*, Baden-Baden: Nomos.
Egner, B. and Heinelt, H. (2005) 'Sozialprofil und Handlungsorientierung von Bürgermeistern in Deutschland' in J. Bogumil and H. Heinelt (eds) *Bürgermeister in Deutschland: Politikwissenschaftliche studien zu direkt gewählten Bürgermeistern*, Wiesbaden: VS Verlag für Sozialwissenschaften.
Goldsmith, M. J. (2003) 'Renouveau démocratique et participation locale' in V. Hoffmann-Martinot and C. Sorbets (eds) *Démocraties Locales en Changement*, Paris: Éditions Pedone.
Haus, M., Heinelt, H., Egner, B. and König, C. (2005) *Partizipation und Führung in der Lokalen Politik*, Baden-Baden: Nomos.
Haus, M. and Sweeting, D. (2006) 'Mayors, citizens and local democracy' in H. Bäck, H. Heinelt and A. Magnier (eds) *The European Mayor: Political leaders in the changing context of local democracy*, Wiesbaden: VS Verlag für Sozialwissenschaften.
Heinelt, H. and Egner, B. (2005) 'Sozialprofil und Handlungsorientierung von Bürgermeistern in Deutschland' in J. Bogumil and H. Heinelt (eds) *Bürgermeister in Deutschland: Politikwissenschaftliche studien zu direkt gewählten Bürgermeistern*, Wiesbaden: VS Verlag für Sozialwissenschaften.
Heinelt, H. and Hlepas, N. -K. (2006) 'Typologies of local government systems' in H. Bäck, H. Heinelt and A. Magnier (eds) *The European Mayor: Political leaders in the changing context of local democracy*, Wiesbaden: VS Verlag für Sozialwissenschaften.
Heinelt, H., Kerrouche, E. and Egner, B. (2006) 'From government to governance at the local level: Some considerations based on data surveys with mayors and chief executive officers' in V. Hoffmann-Martinot and H. Wollmann (eds) *State and Local Government Reforms in France and Germany*, Wiesbaden: VS Verlag für Sozialwissenschaften.
Hesse, J. J. and Sharpe, L. J. (1991) 'Local government in international perspective: Some comparative observations' in J. J. Hesse and L. J. Sharpe (eds) *Local Government and Urban Affairs in International Perspective: Analyses of twenty western industrialised countries*, Baden-Baden: Nomos.
Hoffmann-Martinot, V. (1999) 'Les grandes villes françaises: Une démocratie en souffrance' in O. W. Gabriel and V. Hoffmann-Martinot (eds)

Démocraties Urbaines:L'état de la démocratie dans les grandes villes de 12 pays industrialisés, Paris: L'Hartmattan.

— (2006) 'Reform and modernization of urban government in France' in V. Hoffmann-Martinot and H. Wollmann (eds) *State and Local Government Reforms in France and Germany*, Wiesbaden: VS Verlag für Sozialwissenschaften.

Holtkamp, L. (2005) 'Reform der Kommunalverfassungen in den alten Bundesländern: Eine Ursachenanalyse' in J. Bogumil and H. Heinelt (eds) *Bürgermeister in Deutschland: Politikwissenschaftliche studien zu direkt gewählten Bürgermeistern*, Wiesbaden: VS Verlag für Sozialwissenschaften.

Kerrouche, E. (2005) 'The powerful French mayor: myth and reality' in R. Berg and N. Rao (eds) *Transforming Local Political Leadership*, Basingstoke: Palgrave Macmillan.

— (2008) *L'Intercommunalité en France*, Paris: Montchrestien: Lextenso éditions.

Kersting, N. and Vetter, A. (2003a) 'Democracy versus efficiency? Comparing local government reforms across Europe' in N. Kersting and A. Vetter (eds) *Reforming Local Government in Europe: Closing the gap between democracy and efficiency*, Opladen: Leske and Budrich.

— (eds) (2003b) *Reforming Local Government in Europe: Closing the gap between democracy and efficiency*, Opladen: Leske and Budrich.

Kjær, A. M. (2004) *Governance*, Malden: MA: Polity Press.

Knemeyer, F. -L. (1999) 'Gemeindeverfassungen' in H. Wollmann and R. Roth (eds) *Kommunalpolitik: Politisches handeln in den gemeinden*, Opladen: Leske and Budrich.

Kooiman, J. (2003) *Governing as Governance*, London: Sage Publications.

Kost, A. (2005) 'Der Siegeszug der Süddeutschen Ratsverfassung: Ein überblick über die verschiedenen kommunalpolitischen strukturen in den bundesländern', *Das Parlament*, 55 (1/2).

Laux, E. (1999) 'Erfahrungen und Perspektiven der kommunalen Gebiets- und Funktionalreformen' in H. Wollmann and R. Roth (eds) *Kommunalpolitik: Politisches handeln in den gemeinden*, Opladen: Leske and Budrich.

Le Bart, C. (2003) *Les Maires: Sociologie d'un Rôle*, Villeneuve d'Ascq: Presses Universitaires du Septentrion.

Lépinard, E. (2004) 'Les femmes vecteur de changement en politique locale: Réalités et illusions d'un discours consacré' in S. Denèfle (ed.) *Femmes et Villes*, Tours: Presses Universitaires François Rabelais.

Lorrain, D. (2003) 'Gouverner "dur-mou": Neuf très grandes métropoles', *Revue Française d'Administration Publique*, 107: 447–54.

Mouritzen, P. E. and Svara, J. H. (2002) *Leadership at the Apex: Politicians and administrators in western local governments*, Pittsburgh: University of Pittsburgh Press.

Négrier, E. and Jourda, M. -T. (2007) *Les Nouveaux Territoires des Festivals*, Paris: Éditions M. de Maule.

Norris, P. and Lovenduski, J. (1993) '"If only more candidates came forward": Supply-side explanations of candidate selection in Britain', *British Journal of Political Science*, 23(3): 373–408.

Paoletti, M. (1997) *La Démocratie Locale et le Référendum: Analyse de la démocratie locale à travers la genèse institutionnelle du référendum*, Paris: L'Hartmattan.

Premat, C. (2006) 'Autonomy as a balance of freedom and equality', *International Social Science Journal*, 58(190): 681–95.

Stoiber, M. and Egner, B. (2008) 'Ein übertragbarer Amtsinhaber-Bonus bei Kommunalwahlen: Eine vergleichende Analyse in drei Bundesländeren', *Zeitschrift für Vergleichende Politikwissenschaft*, 2(2): 287-314.

Steyvers, K. and Reynaert, H. (2006) 'From the few are chosen the few: On the social background of the European mayor' in H. Bäck, H. Heinelt and A. Magnier (eds) *The European Mayor: Political leaders in the changing context of local democracy*, Wiesbaden: VS Verlag für Sozialwissenschaften.

Thoenig, J. -C. (2006) 'Modernizing sub-national government in France: National creativity and systematic stability' in V. Hoffmann-Martinot and H. Wollmann (eds) *State and Local Government Reforms in France and Germany*, Wiesbaden: VS Verlag für Sozialwissenschaften.

Wollmann, H. (1999) 'Kommunalpolitik: Zu neuen (direkt-)demokratischen Ufern?' in H. Wollmann and R. Roth (eds) *Kommunalpolitik: Politisches handeln in den gemeinden*, Opladen: Leske and Budrich.

— (2008) 'Reforming local leadership and local democracy: The cases of England, Sweden, Germany and France in comparative perspective', *Local Government Studies*, 34(2): 279–298.

Wood, D. M. and Young, G. (1997) 'Comparing constituency activity by junior legislators in Great Britain and Ireland', *Legislative Studies Quarterly*, 22(2): 217–232.

chapter six | initiatives and referendums
Christophe Premat

Introduction

Ever since the 1980s, there has been a participatory revolution (Kaase 1982) thanks to the inclusion in the legislation of post-industrial countries of direct democratic procedures – seen as a way of reducing the gap between citizens and politicians in a representative system. In fact, by putting subjects that are of particular concern to local populations on to the agendas of politicians', direct democratic procedures, such as initiatives and referendums, complement representative government and compel it to be more responsive. Focusing on such instruments allows us to describe both the implementation of participatory elements and the transformation of representative government. Jörgen Westerståhl distinguished four types of political participation:

1. electoral participation;
2. direct participation through initiatives, referendums, district councils and local assemblies;
3. indirect participation via political parties and organisations; and
4. potential participation based on knowledge of and interest in political matters.

(Westerståhl 1981: 438)

In this chapter, we analyse direct participation in France and Germany and its effects on each country's political system. In other words, the institutional setting of initiatives and referendums and the influence of referendum practices on political decisions will be the main research indicators used in measuring the shift towards a more participatory democracy.

The goal of a referendum is to ascertain whether people reject or approve a particular political decision; this means that the higher the turnout, the more significant the result, reflecting as it does the will of a majority of voters. Initiatives and referendums, as modern instruments of direct democracy, differ from earlier instruments such as communal assemblies, which were based on face-to-face relations. In a referendum democracy, people do not decide in one and the same physical place (Sartori 1993: 84); instead, face-to-face relations (Fishkin 1995: 5) are abandoned for a series of individual choices. When we move from national to local referendum, we do not find the same characteristics. As the population size is much smaller, such a referendum aims at creating a local public space in which people can react, or initiate political decisions that affect their environment. This is why the literature (Bacqué *et al.* 2005: 23) often associates these referendums with participatory democracy. Giovanni Sartori, however, points out the difficulty of obtaining clear signals for public policies associated with referendums; these instruments do not deliver a straightforward answer to referendum issues because their pros and cons tend to neutralise each other (Sartori 1993: 84). In this chapter, we assume that two factors have to be taken into account in determining the success of referendums: turnout and the distinction between winners and losers. A referendum is more likely to influence the choice of public policies if these two criteria are met.

We analyse the political implications of referendums by comparing two representative systems that do not consider local referendums in the same way. For a federal state, like Germany, with unitary tendencies (French Interior Ministry 2003: 7), referendums are strictly defined by specific legislation in all the *Länder*. This is not the case for a unitary state, like France, with its decentralised tendencies and somewhat ambivalent legislation in this domain. Admittedly, ever since the early 1990s, both countries – because of reunification in Germany and the decentralisation process in France – have reinforced the use of semi-direct democratic procedures (Hoffmann-Martinot 2005: 234–35). At the same time, however, the use of national referendums in each country is diametrically opposed. In Germany, federal referendums are proscribed by the Basic Law (Luthardt1994: 107) to avoid the misused plebiscites of the Third Reich; in France, however, national referendums are seen as another way of expressing national sovereignty (article 3 of the 1958 Constitution).

The aim of this chapter is to analyse the effects of local referendums on political systems. What are the legal provisions in France and Germany, and what is the common practice there? Furthermore, if national referendum practice has been the subject of comparative studies (LeDuc 2003), this is much less true of local referendum practise. The institutional perspective in this respect is central, focusing as it does on the way the legal conditions are understood and experienced by the referendum initiators. First, we study how frequent local referendums are in both countries. In Germany, various requirements play a decisive role in the actions of initiators: the need for a high quorum of signatures limits the development of local referendums. In France, the legislation maintains a double orientation with, on the one hand, consultative referendums and, while on the other hand, binding referendums requiring a 50 per cent approval quorum. After an analysis of local referendums in each country, we examine the referendum *praxis* in Baden-Württemberg and France, using a data set examining personal attitudes that show consultative referendums have political effects, and that binding referendums can be subject to severe legislative constraints.

A subjective variable – 'satisfaction from the initiators' point of view' – has also been introduced, in order to measure the likelihood of initiators winning the popular vote. How can we explain the success of popular initiative referendums? We examine whether certain types of referendum topics create social conflict. We also take into consideration the relationship between referendum topics and citizens' values. In summary, comparing direct democratic participation at the local level in France and Germany makes it possible to describe the emergence of local public spaces.

Direct democratic procedures in Germany and France

Direct democratic procedures can be classified into three main categories: communal assemblies, popular initiatives and local referendums. Table 6.1 shows all three types, with popular initiatives and referendums – affecting as they do the political system – being the most common.

Table 6.1: Types of direct democratic procedures

Instrument	Concept	Characteristics	Location	Agenda
Communal assembly	Meeting of all citizens at a particular date	Replaces the local representative system	Forty-six communes of Schleswig-Holstein, several communes of Brandenburg	Regular assembly (once a year)
Popular initiative	Quorum of signatures	Consultative and binding initiatives	Binding popular initiatives in Germany, consultative popular initiative in France	Reactive initiatives aimed at abrogating a local decision (German Länder); initiatives for public policy projects
Local referendum	Vote on a question of local interest outside elections	Consultative and binding referendums	Binding referendums in Germany; consultative and binding referendums in France	In France, no local referendums six months before or six months after the municipal elections

Source: author's synthesis.

The *communal assembly*, the oldest instrument of direct democracy, is still to be found in some small German municipalities, where the inhabitants meet regularly to decide on the main local policies. It is this type of direct democratic procedure that is employed in the forty-six communes of Schleswig-Holstein and Brandenburg (Karr 2003: 119). In France, in the 1970s, the idea of a self-organised society was promoted by some left-wing mayors (from the Unified Socialist Party): one example of this concerned the municipality of Coupvray (1,300 inhabitants) in Seine-et-Marne (Wargny 1978: 41). The main characteristic of direct democracy is the fact that people stand in a face-to-face relationship (Fishkin 1995: 4). In Germany, in order to perpetuate the old direct democratic tradition, several communes instituted a *Bürgerversammlung*, a local assembly; although not a direct democratic instrument, it does constitute a participatory tool somewhat akin to the French district councils that have been compulsory for cities of over 80,000 inhabitants, ever since the law of 27th February 2002. The city of Nuremberg's *Bürgerversammlung,* for instance, involves a regular meeting with the mayor, who goes round every one of the twenty-two districts to explain certain local policies to the inhabitants. 'Theoretically, this assembly takes place once a year but, in practice, it is held every two years. Out of the 30,000 inhabitants of a district who could, in theory, attend a meeting, there are only 300 and 400 participants.'[1] This instrument is intended for districts that do not have any local council representative.

In France, the central state has always been opposed to the institutionalisation of direct democratic instruments. The case of Alsace-Lorraine is particularly striking in this regard. When the region was annexed by Germany, the government authorised the local assembly system for small communes (Herrenschmidt 1936). Later, however, when the region was handed back to France, the French Government chose not to pursue this principle of self-administration (Kesselman 1972: 65). In Germany, the tradition of local democracy is rooted in the construction of the federal state and in the autonomy of the *Länder*; in France, however, the republican tradition is embodied in a strictly representative system.

The *popular initiative*, the second instrument of direct democracy, involves a demand for a referendum – a *Bürgerbegehren* – on a specific issue. In Germany, this can be used to react against a decision of the local council within a certain time limit, or to put forward a local policy proposal. However, whereas such popular initiatives are binding in Germany, they are only consultative in France. In Germany, a popular initiative can be rejected by the local authorities if there are procedural flaws. Alternatively, it can be accepted directly by the local authority, which forgoes the need to organise a local referendum.

A *local referendum*, the third instrument of direct democracy, originates either from a popular initiative or a request of the local council. In France, most local referendums are organised by mayors, since the popular initiative does not have any binding effects. Generally speaking, if we leave aside the case of local assemblies, the most direct procedure affecting representative government is the popular initiative referendum. Popular initiative referendums serve as indicators of the demands of civil society – in France, there are very few such referendums; in Germany, they are firmly rooted in the local political system.

---

1. Semi-directive interview conducted by us on 30th May 2005 in Nuremberg with Mr Frommer, who is in charge of the communal administration of the city.

Table 6.2: The institutional set-up for local referendums and popular initiatives in Germany (quorum and deadlines)

Date of the introduction of direct democratic procedures	Popular initiative: quorum of signatures (entry quorum)	Time allowance for corrective initiatives	Approval quorum
Baden-Württemberg (1956)	5–10%	6 weeks	25%*
Bavaria (1995)	3–10%	No delay	10–20%
Brandenburg (1993)	10%	6 weeks	25%
The City of Bremen (1994)	10%	3 months	25%
Bremerhaven (1996)	10%	6 weeks	30%
Hamburg (1998)	2–3%	6 months	No quorum
Hessen (1993)	10%	6 weeks	25%
Mecklenburg-West Pomerania (1994)	2.5–10%	6 weeks	25%
Lower Saxony (1996)	10%	3–6 months	25%
North Rhine-Westphalia (1994)	3–10%	6 weeks–3 months	20%
Rhineland-Palatinate (1994)	6–15%	2 months	30%
Saarland (1997)	5-15%	2 months	30%
Saxony (1993)	15%	2 months	25%
Saxony-Anhalt (1993)	6–15%	6 weeks	30%
Schleswig-Holstein (1990)	10%	4 weeks	20%
Thuringia (1993)	13–17%	1 month	20–25%

Source: author's synthesis.

One marked difference between the two countries is that, in Germany, a minimum approval rate is required (Wollmann 2002: 182). This means that a local decision can be held after a referendum if, and only if, those who voted in favour of it represent a significant proportion of the electors. The higher the turnout, the more likely it is that success can be guaranteed, although a high turnout is not

---

* In June 2005, the quorum was reduced from 30 per cent to 25 per cent, and the deadline for reactive initiatives was extended to six weeks.

an automatic condition of success. Table 6.2 illustrates all the legal requirements concerning direct democratic procedures in Germany. The question of a quorum, with its different phases, is very important: there is the initial quorum of signatures needed to validate popular initiatives, as well as the approval rate – the final quorum for a local referendum. For reactive initiatives, a time-limit has been determined in all the *Länder*, except for Bavaria; in that particular *Land*, a political decision can be reversed by a referendum originating from a popular initiative. Only a certain number of topics can be considered in every *Land* and it is essential that the form of the initiative (validity of signatures) is taken into account when the initiative is examined. Some *Länder* have a progressive quorum, depending on the size of the city. Having to collect signatures and attain a quorum of 10 per cent in a city of 200,000 inhabitants or in a village of 500 inhabitants obviously does not represent the same amount of work. Depending on institutional conditions, the legislation of Hamburg, Bavaria or North Rhine-Westphalia is less restrictive for the development of popular initiatives than that of Thuringia, Saxony or Saarland. The average quorum of signatures is 10 per cent in every *Land*, but the authorised subjects of such initiatives differ from one *Land* to the other. The deadline for reactive initiatives is quite long in Hamburg and Lower Saxony, allowing initiators to organise themselves to contest a local decision. However, we need to analyse the combination of all three institutional requirements: the period of time allowed for reactive initiatives, the quorum of signatures for popular initiatives, and the quorum for the approval rate. The approval rate for Saarland, Rhineland-Palatinate, Saxony-Anhalt and Bremerhaven is very high, whereas for Bavaria and Hamburg it is low. In the case of Saarland, a popular initiative, which must be launched against a local decision within two months, stands very little chance of being converted into a successful local referendum.

In East Germany, semi-direct democratic procedures were introduced in the *Länder* very early on, only a few years after the organisation of free elections. This shows that direct democracy does not simply constitute a consolidation phase (Whitehead 2006: 3) of representative government, but also represents the deepening of a transitory process. Both popular initiatives and local referendums were institutionalised before – or at the same time as – the direct election of mayors. In the cases of Saxony, Thuringia and Saxony-Anhalt, direct democratic mechanisms there were introduced one year before the direct election of mayors. In Brandenburg, local referendums, popular initiatives and the direct election of mayors were all institutionalised in 1993, whereas in Mecklenburg-West Pomerania, direct democratic procedures were introduced in 1994, five years before the direct election of mayors. All these initiatives and referendums were designed to extend political participation at the local level.

In France, the Law of 1st August 2003 institutionalised binding referendums, provided the turnout exceeds 50 per cent. The history of local referendums reveals that the authorities always try to reduce a referendum to a simple consultation in order to avoid the principles of the representative system being contested. Although there is a right of petition in France, we cannot really speak of popular initiatives because local authorities are not compelled to hold local referendums.

Law N° 92-125 of 6th February 1992 introduced the ambiguous notion of 'local consultations' in its definition of territorial administration. As for popular consultative initiatives, these were recognised for the first time by Law N° 95-115 of 4th August 1995: one fifth of the electorate can require the communal authorities to hold local referendums. This possibility was extended in Law N° 99-533 of 1999 to inter-municipal bodies and then to departments and regions. In Law N° 71-588 of 16th July 1971, binding local referendums were introduced exclusively for the specific subject of commune mergers: a merger is declared either after a local referendum or after a decision by the different local councils concerned. From 1975 until 1992, we recorded 270 communal consultations, less than a fifth of them being binding referendums about the merger or separation of communes.[2] The legislation is less detailed than in Germany, which means that there is no rigorous entry or exit price for direct democratic procedures. With the second Act of Decentralisation of 2003,[3] French communes were given two options: organise either a local consultation or a binding referendum.

The development of direct democratic procedures is related to the financial capacity of local governments; this means that citizens have first to identify these capacities in order to formulate the appropriate demand. The adequate use of direct democratic procedures depends on the clarity of the political system for its citizens. Whereas in Germany the instruments of direct democracy are only decisional, French legislation has added the possibility of binding referendums to that of consultations. Popular initiatives are purely consultative and have a similar status to petitions. An analysis is required of how institutionalisation compels both actors and local governments to adapt to the rules. Two criteria, in particular, are decisive in institutionalising local referendums in both countries: turnout and approval rate.

The practice of local referendums in France and Germany

If we compare the number of local referendums in both countries between 1975 and 2005, there were 667 in France against 1,788 in Germany, i.e. there were 2.7 times more local referendums in Germany than in France, even though there Germany has far fewer communes (14,865 communes). Optimal development of the practice in France between 1992 and 2005 could, in theory, have led to as many as 183,895 communal referendums. Between 1992 and 1995, each commune could have organised one consultation, two between 1995 and 2001, and two between 2001 and 2005. Instead, only 375 referendums in total were held in France between 1992 and 2005. We calculated optimal practice by taking the restrictions of the legislation into account (the possibility of organising a consultation at least one year before or after a local election, and the impossibility of organising two consultations on the same issue within the same period). Optimal practice is, how-

---

2. Marion Paoletti (1996: 475–479) noted 202 communal consultations; we complemented her research with an additional sixty-eight consultations.
3. The first Act of Decentralisation refers to the series of laws passed in 1982 and 1983.

ever, merely indicative, as every referendum depends on specific opportunities for it to become active. Furthermore, a referendum complements the representative system by invoking a subject that the authorities have not themselves raised. A local referendum can never be a regular tool of public action: ideal practice simply indicates a maximum limit for the practice within a particular legal framework.

In Germany, popular initiatives and local referendums are compulsory in certain strictly-defined conditions. We have not adopted a procedural point of view (Castoriadis 1996: 221–41) with regard to direct democratic mechanisms, but have chosen instead an institutionalist perspective (Apter 1991: 493) that shows the effects of institutions on the practice of local referendums. The various institutions impose specific constraints on the actors organising the procedures; within a few years, however, once the actors have mastered the particular institutional logic at work, they are better armed to launch popular initiatives. All these institutions are the product of participatory demand; they influence participatory culture in the country by a feed-back process. In France, because the decentralisation process makes it difficult to distinguish between the competencies of all the local entities (Hoffmann-Martinot 2005: 337), local representatives are reluctant to introduce such procedures that they consider threaten the general interest. We conducted an interview with a local member of the *Conseil Général* of Gironde about the characteristics of participatory democracy:

> I am in favour of participatory democracy; I am against referenda. A representative is elected in order to take decisions, otherwise he is not useful. Referenda mean that local representatives are deprived of their role. Why not organise referenda via the *préfets*? We would no longer need any local representatives anymore. A local referendum is a bad thing; it is not adapted to the complexity of problems.[4]

Such a reaction reveals how local representatives in France fear this instrument and how they find it difficult to associate local referendums with participatory democracy. The plebiscitary aspect involved explains the strong reaction against this instrument (Denquin 1976). According to a survey of 2,711 European mayors of communes of more than 10,000 inhabitants, 26 per cent of the French mayors agreed with the fact that local referendums lead to high quality public debate, against 29 per cent of the German mayors. However, whereas 43 per cent of the German mayors considered referendums as effective tools of communication, only 16 per cent of the French mayors did so. Local referendums in France are seen as constraints on the decisions of local representatives, and not as a deliberative process. We also find this suspicious attitude among theorists, like Benjamin Barber, who favour participatory democracy: 'Referendum and initiative processes divorced from innovative programs for public talk and deliberation fall easy victims to plebiscitary abuses and to the manipulation by money and elites of popular prejudice' (Barber 1984: 263). In Germany, the expression 'plebiscitary mechanisms' (März 2003: 54) is used to qualify the introduction of direct

---

4. Interview made in Bordeaux on 2nd February 2005.

democratic procedures (Fijalkowski 2002: 306). In fact, there are two kinds of plebiscites in Germany: the *Real-Plebiszit* and the *Personal-Plebiszit*. The former refers to popular votes (*Bürgerinitiativen, Bürgerbegehren, Bürgerentscheide, Bürgerbefragungen*), whereas the latter refers to elections and recalls (Weixner 2002: 82). In Germany, the plebiscite is an umbrella term for referendums and elections with a personal perspective, whereas, in France, there is a debate about the difficulty of distinguishing referendums from plebiscites (Bacot 1994: 132). Table 6.3 illustrates the ongoing development of German legislation, as well as the requisites for popular initiatives and local referendums.

The legislation in both Bavaria and Hamburg strongly favours direct democracy as their respective quorum is not high. Half of the local referendums were held in Bavaria although, since a recent reform (März 2003: 56) introduced the possibility of petition (*Bürgerantrag*), the number of popular initiatives and local referendums is decreasing. Certain popular initiatives did not need to be transformed into local referendums because the authorities acted promptly and simply solved the problem. Although the number of popular initiatives is high in North Rhine-Westphalia and in Hessen, many initiatives there failed and were not transformed into referendums (see Table 6.4).

If we consider the survey of European mayors, approximately 86 per cent of German mayors and French mayors think that it is important for them to help citizens resolve complaints. In France, 49 per cent consider petitions to be an effective communication tool, against only 30 per cent in Germany[5]; French mayors are in favour of such instruments as they feel themselves free to decide on the object of the petition. In France, the local referendum interferes with the preparation of a decision; it resembles a survey, which is why turnout is so crucial. When mayors want either to provide a local service or plan something important, they can act with more legitimacy after a local referendum.

Table 6.4 shows that, even in *Länder* that have legislation favouring local referendums (Bavaria), local initiatives are not as regular as local elections, except in certain communes with a deeply-rooted tradition of direct democracy. Table 6.4 ranks *Länder* in terms of local initiative frequency compared to the number of communes: although Saarland, for example, shows a high frequency, its legislation is very restrictive about the development of direct democratic tools. The other comment is that popular initiative referendums are quite numerous, which means that local referendums reflect the direct demands of civil society in less than 50 per cent of cases. Baden-Württemberg has the greatest proportion of popular initiative referendums, though its legislation is quite restrictive. But the number of its popular initiative referendums is low when set against the number of its communes. In Bavaria, the proportion of popular initiative referendums is more significant, with 653 popular initiative referendums within a ten-year period.

---

5. Database SSD 0822 'The European mayor: political leaders in the changing context of local democracy', Henry Bäck, School of Public Administration, Göteborg University.

Table 6.3: Number of popular initiatives and local referendums in Germany

Date of the introduction of direct democratic procedures	Number of local popular initiatives	Number of local referendums*	Average frequency of popular initiatives per year since their introduction
Baden-Württemberg (1956)	(1956–2006): 397**	199	9.9
Bavaria (1995)	(1995–2006): 1,338	884	121.6
Brandenburg (1993)	(1993–2006): 189	130	14.5
The city of Bremen (1994)	(1994–2006): 2	1	0.2
Bremerhaven (1996)	–	–	–
Hamburg (1998)	(1998–2006): 48	7	6
Hessen (1993)	(1993–2006): 259	92	19.9
Mecklenburg-West Pomerania (1994)	(1993–2006): 88	31	6.8
Lower Saxony (1996)	(1996–2006): 129	34	12.9
North Rhine-Westphalia (1994)	(1994–2006): 474	122	39.5
Rhineland-Palatinate (1994)	(1994–2006): 124	47	10.3
Saarland (1997)	(1997–2006): 10	0	3.3
Saxony (1993)	(1993–2006): 214	101	16.5
Saxony-Anhalt (1993)	(1990–2006): 216	142	13.5
Schleswig-Holstein (1990)	(1990-2006): 243	119	15.2
Thuringia (1993)	(1993-2006): 73	19	5.6

* Some of the results for each *Land* are incomplete.
** According to research made with Fabian Reidinger (*Mehr Demokratie*), we recorded 384 popular initiatives between 1975 and 2006, and 13 popular initiatives in the 1960s.
Source: author's synthesis.

Table 6.4: Frequency of popular initiatives in the German Länder (1956–2005)

Land (*)	Period	Number of communes	Number of communal referendum demands: N	Frequency per year (Every year in X communes): N (1/X)		Popular initiative referendums
Bavaria (1)	1995–2005	2,100	1,457	145.7 (1/14)	653	45%
North Rhine Westphalia (1)	1994–2004	406	300	30 (1/14)	98	33%
Baden-Württemberg (8)	1956–2005	1,110	296	6 (1/185)	153	52%
Schleswig-Holstein (6)	1990–2002	1,126	202	16.8 (1/67)	86	43%
Hessen (3)	1993–2002	434	150	16.7 (1/26)	67	45%
Saxony (5)	1993–2002	778	130	14.4 (1/54)	65	50%
Low-Saxony (7)	1996–2005	1,029	105	11.7 (1/88)	38	36%
Rhineland Palatinate (11)	1994–2004	2,306	75	7.5 (1/308)	31	41%
Thuringia (10)	1993–2004	1,051	46	4.2 (1/250)	20	43%
Brandenburg (9)	1993–2001	1,092	36	4.5 (1/243)	6	17%
Mecklenburg West-Vorpomerania (12)	1994–2005	1,069	36	3 (1/356)	8	22%
Saarland (4)	1997–2000	52	9	1.1 (1/47)	–	–
Saxony-Anhalt (13)	1993–2000	1,272	4	0.3 (0/1272)	2	50%
Total		1,3835	2,846	261.9 (–)	1227	43%

*Classification of Länder as regards the frequency of initiatives.
Source: data collected and presented by Oscar Gabriel and Melanie Walter-Rogg.

It is important to identify the proportion of popular initiatives in communes, to ascertain whether size has an influence on the number of signatures collected. Table 6.5 examines in greater detail the relationship between the frequency of local initiatives and the size of the communes in Baden-Württemberg.

Table 6.5: Frequency of local popular initiatives in Baden-Württemberg (1996–2006)

Frequency of initiatives Size of the commune	Number of communes	Number of local referendums	Number of referendums per year	Referendum every X years for each commune	Percentage of non-valid popular initiatives
Up to 1,999 inhabitants	88	12	1.2	157 years	30%
2,000 to 4,999	401	19	1.9	211 years	145.8%
5,000 to 9,999	270	16	1.6	169 years	50%
10,000 to 19,999	152	11	1.1	138 years	29.7%
20,000 to 49,999	78	18	1.8	43 years	52.5%
50,000 to 99,999	13	7	0.7	19 years	39%
Over 100,000	9	8	0.8	11 years	46%
Total	1,111	91	9.1	122 years	40%

Source: report made with Fabian Reidinger* on direct democratic procedures in the Land of Baden-Württemberg.
* Website: http://www.mitentscheiden.de/fileadmin/pdfarchiv/LV_Baden-Wue/2006-bawue-be-bilanz.pdf (accessed 16th February 2008).

Contrary to expectation, popular initiatives do not take place frequently in small communes. The bigger the commune, the more likely it is that the local authorities will have to face a popular initiative. Nevertheless, for communes of more than 100,000 inhabitants, 46 per cent of popular initiatives are rejected. The optimal relation between the size of the commune and the frequency of accepted popular initiatives can be found for those communes with between 20,000 and 50,000 inhabitants (only 30 per cent of popular initiatives are rejected in this category, for a frequency of one local initiative every 28 years for each commune). Furthermore, 17.8 per cent of all popular initiatives in Baden-Württemberg were launched for this last category of communes. Dahl and Tufte wondered whether an optimal size of commune exists in which the antagonistic couple, local democracy/ efficiency of public policies, was at work (1974: 135). We see that in communes with 20,000 to 49,999 inhabitants, even though social demand is quite high, not all those initiatives are converted into local referendums. The probability of having a local referendum in those peculiar communes averaged one in every 43 years, and only 22.2 per cent of those referendums were valid; in other words, there is no systematic correlation between commune size and the effects of direct democracy. However, if we compare the data from Tables 6.4 and 6.5 for Baden-Württemberg, we notice that, over a ten-year period, the probability of having a local referendum increased because the approval rate was lowered from 30 per cent to 25 per cent in June 2005. In France, between 1995 and 2004, 62 per cent of the communes that held a referendum had fewer than 5,000 inhabitants whereas 27.2 per cent of them had more than 10,000 inhabitants (30.8 per cent of the communes that organised a referendum had fewer than 1,000 inhabitants).

If we take into account the number of local consultations between 1992 and 2006 in communes with more than 5,000 inhabitants (103 consultations), only thirteen communes were not integrated into an inter-municipal structure: 36 per cent of them belonged to a *communauté d'agglomération*.[6] The mayors organising local consultations reinforce their legitimacy, especially when their commune is not the most influential one in the inter-municipal structure. Most of these communes are located near Paris (27 per cent) and the mayors who organise such procedures concurrently hold another elective function (in 79 per cent of cases). In fact, these mayors are familiar with local politics and try to increase the presence of their commune in the inter-municipal structure to obtain more resources for the development of local policies.[7]

In France, the parliamentary discussion of law N° 2003-705 of 1st August 2003 concerned turnout. There was an allusion to the German situation, albeit with a certain degree of misunderstanding, when the deputies proposed to fix a 40 per cent turnout:

> M. Jean-Pierre Blazy[8] [...] found it necessary to determine a quorum and considered the choice of the Senate was too restrictive. He recalled that, in Germany, this kind of consultation depended on a participation quorum of all the electors [and not voters] of between 25 per cent and 30 per cent.[9]

---

6. Investigation made, with Julien Dewoghélaëre, on 1,881 French communes of more than 5,000 inhabitants at the Institute of Political Studies of Bordeaux, between March and December 2006.
7. In Germany, 12,121 communes, or 82 per cent have fewer than 5,000 inhabitants whereas, in France, 95 per cent of the communes have fewer than 5,000 inhabitants; 49 per cent of German, and 92.8 per cent of French communes have fewer than 1,000 inhabitants. Most popular initiatives take place in communes of under 20,000 inhabitants: 2,787 popular initiatives were located in those communes.
8. Jean-Pierre Blazy is a socialist representative and mayor of the city of Gonesse.
9. Alain Gest, Report n°956 made at the National Assembly for the Constitutional Commission, 18th June 2003, http://www.assemblee-nationale.fr.

In fact, the requisite quorum referred to was the approval rate, which does not exist in France. The Senate, the lobby of local representatives, rejected the proposal of a 40 per cent turnout and increased it to 50 per cent. The phenomenon of *cumul des mandats* explains that deputies and senators want to control the process of decentralisation in their own way: 90.8 per cent of the deputies and 80.7 per cent of senators have, in fact, another local function (Sadran 2004: 77). They do not want to confront counter-powers emerging at the local level, as they see themselves as the key persons in the local democratic process. Local democracy, in the republican imagination, means the extension of elections to all levels: participatory instruments are employed only if they do not lead to decisions that bind local representatives.

In France, according to statistics from the Interior Ministry, 60.6 per cent of the local consultations held since 1992 have had a turnout of more than 50 per cent. According to our own research, between 1995 and July 2004, the average turnout was 53.8 per cent and the average approval rate was 40 per cent. If we compare these figures with those of Baden-Württemberg for the same period, we obtain the results presented in Table 6.6.

Table 6.6: Local referendums in Baden-Württemberg (1995–2004)

Period	Number of local referendums	Incomplete and missing data	Average turnout	Average approval rate	Number of failures (invalid referendums)	Percentage of failures due to legislation
1995–2004	84	4	52.5%	34.3%	32	38.1%

Source: research made with Fabian Reidinger (May 2006).

In Baden-Württemberg, there was an average turnout of 52.5 per cent between 1995 and 2004, with an average approval rate of 34.3 per cent. More than one third of the local referendums failed as they did not meet legislative requirements. In June 2005,[10] the approval quorum was reduced to 25 per cent and the parliamentary negotiations over this 5 per cent difference were quite heated. When we look at the data we see that, between 1995 and 2004, only thirteen referendums out of eighty-four[11] would have failed on the basis of the 2005 legislation. In France, the authorities refused to enter into a discussion about a minimum quorum. If we had applied the 50 per cent French criterion established by the Law of 2003 to the situ-

---

10. We attended the parliamentary discussion about this quorum on 1st June 2005. The CDU was against the reduction of the approval rate from 30 per cent to 25 per cent, and one MP warned that too many popular initiatives could threaten local politics.
11. Four local referendums were not taken into account in the Interior Ministry list. Our personal list revealed that a lot of popular initiatives were not registered in the official statistics.

ation in Germany, then 44 per cent of them would have been invalid. If the initiators of referendums in Baden-Württemberg want to succeed, they have to obtain a high turnout in order to reach the required approval rate. Table 6.7 shows the influence of the institutional constraint on the development of local referendums in Baden-Württemberg between 1956 and 1987.

Table 6.7: Communal referendums in Baden-Württemberg between 1956 and 1987

Communal referendums	1956–75	%	1976–87	%	Total	%
Number of referendums	118	100	53	100	171	100
Local council's initiative	93	79	14	26	107	63
Popular initiative	25	21	39	73.6	64	37
Satisfaction of initiators' point of view	9	7.6	23	43.4	32	18.7
Failure of referendums because of turnout/approval rate	30	25	14	26	44	25

Source: archives of *Mehr Demokratie* in Stuttgart (May 2006).

It is the requirement of a 30 per cent approval rate rather than that of a 50 per cent turnout that encourages the practice of popular initiatives. If, between 1956 and 1975, 21 per cent of popular initiative referendums were held, this percentage rose to 37 per cent between 1976 and 1987. Satisfaction from the initiators' point of view also increased from 7.6 per cent to 18.7 per cent between the two periods, when both local council and popular initiatives were taken into account. At the same time, the approval rate constitutes a stronger hurdle for the validation of the result: 25 per cent of local referendums that failed because they did not obtain the 30 per cent approval rate is a higher figure than the 14 per cent of failures due to turnout. The approval rate helps to avoid the paradox of Sartori (1993), which can be presented in the following terms: the referendum tends to freeze the positions of the winners and losers. In fact, it is very difficult to say who wins and who loses when a referendum is held because the 'majority' lacks clarity. In France, turnout is even more important than the result itself.

In France, official statistics disregard many referendums and ignore the fact that many communes do not transmit the results of local votes. For instance, we interviewed the vice-mayor of Cadaujac, a commune near Bordeaux, who told us that 'a local referendum was organised in Cadaujac on the status of military service, after the reform proposal of [former president] Chirac, with a public debate explaining what the military service would become. The turnout was 3 per cent.'[12]

---

12. Our interview with the vice-mayor of Cadaujac dates back to 16th January 2006, and was made

The result was so low that the commune did not communicate the result and destroyed the documents concerning this failure. The vice-mayor told us that many communes had unsuccessfully attempted to vote on this question.

The legislation is more restrictive in France as regards local referendum topics, which is why many are not valid. During the period 1995 to 2004, this was the case for one local referendum out of five. Almost all these referendums were merely consultative, except those concerning the merger of communes: forty-six referendums, a total of 21.6 per cent of all the referendums for the same period, concerned this topic. The average turnout for a local referendum and consultation is 53.9 per cent, the average approval rate 40.2 per cent. In Germany, the popular initiative (*Bürgerbegehren*) and the initiative of the local authorities (*Ratsbegehren*) are distinguished; in France, the expression of 'local initiative referendum' (*référendum d'initiative locale*) is ambiguous, as popular initiatives do not have a decisional value.

The success of popular initiatives: winners and losers

Direct democracy is involved whenever a specific demand emanates from outside the standard political setting. Democratic decision-making implies that citizens weigh up the pros and cons and choose the option they prefer (Weale 1999: 67). In other words, the popular initiative is a reliable indicator of direct democratic procedures. In Germany, popular initiatives are more developed than in France. There is a civic culture (Guggenberger and Kempf 1984) in Germany, which enhances the use of popular initiatives whereas, in France, local representatives control those procedures in order to avoid opposition to their power. Between 1995 and 2004, in France, ten referendums out of 213, or 4.2 per cent, stemmed from a popular initiative, which is seen as a simple right of petition. Many popular initiatives were, in fact, not successful. There is a petition culture in France, but the authorities are reluctant to institutionalise popular initiatives. That is why popular initiatives are not really defined in the law of 2003: 10 per cent of the electors of a district, a department or a region, can request a referendum. The local authority must examine and deliberate on the demand, but cannot be compelled to organise a vote. The popular initiative constitutes a form of petition that requires the organisation of a referendum. Henri Roussillon pointed out that, in a first draft of the Law on the Modification of Communal Borders (July 1971), a minimum quorum of 20 per cent was envisaged, but the possibility of having a binding popular initiative was not maintained in the final draft (Roussillon 1972: 195).

In Germany, we observe that the double filters imposed on popular initiatives and on approval rates limit the development of popular initiative referendums. In Baden-Württemberg, between 1995 and 2004, 119 popular initiatives were launched; only fifty-five passed the first obstacle and, in the end, fifty-two local referendums were organised. If we examine the detail, forty popular initiatives

---

in Bordeaux.

passed the second obstacle, but only twenty-five fully corresponded to initiators' wishes.[13] It is necessary to distinguish between the objective success of the result (hurdles passed) and the subjective success (aims of the initiators) in order to assess, from the very beginning of the process, the likelihood of a popular initiative being successful.

The first obstacle (5–10 per cent quorum) is the most difficult because, once an initiative enters the political system, it has, approximately, a 45 per cent chance to satisfy the initiators' wishes. Between 1995 and 1998, such popular initiatives did not really satisfy their initiators: we recorded fifty-six popular initiatives, twenty-three of which led on to local referendums, with fifteen overcoming the second obstacle and only eight satisfying their initiatives. Out of these eight popular initiative referendums, four were supported by different political parties and only four by the initiators. We can conclude that, at that particular period, only 13.8 per cent of all popular initiatives were likely to satisfy their initiators, which shows that direct democracy does not mean immediate democracy (Rosanvallon 2004: 66). Direct democratic procedures require time and an effective organisation of all the actors concerned. If we compare the data to that of some other *Länder*, we obtain the results indicated in the Table 6.8.

Table 6.8: Local referendums in the old Länder

	Successful local referendums	Majority not reached	Failure because of the approval rate	Turnout
Baden-Württemberg	34%	32%	35%	62%
Hessen	55%	27%	18%	54%
Lower Saxony	57%	21%	21%	–
North Rhine-Westphalia	34%	3%	63%	26%
Rhineland-Palatinate	48%	28%	24%	–
Schleswig-Holstein	47%	34%	19%	–

Source: Holtkamp *et al.* 2006: 151.

Between 1999 and 2004, the results were much better in the Land of Baden-Württemberg: 61 popular initiatives were launched and twenty-seven led to local referendums; twenty-five overcame the second hurdle, and 17 satisfied the initiators' point of view. From 1999 to 2004, there was a 27.9 per cent probability of popular initiatives proving successful. There were more initiatives during

---

13. Database made with Fabian Reidinger (May 2006).

that period both because of the generalisation of local referendums in most of the *Länder*, and a better grasp of the procedure required. The approval quorum is also crucial for popular initiatives because, between 1995 and 2004, 62.5 per cent of the initiatives which were finally accepted were likely to satisfy their initiators' point of view. Nevertheless, mobilisation does not automatically evolve in the way its initiators might expect: popular initiatives do not necessarily become converted into local referendums. Even in Bavaria, where the legislation favours direct democratic mechanisms, the destiny of popular initiatives is quite uncertain.

In Bavaria, out of 1,747 popular initiatives, 884 (50.8 per cent),[14] led to the organisation of a local referendum; this means that one popular initiative out of two is likely to lead to a local referendum. The more knowledge people have of direct democratic mechanisms, the more efficient they are at preparing popular initiatives. Some popular initiatives were initially rejected before being accepted the second time round. Failure helps initiators to reinforce their initiative so that it stands a better chance of winning. Initiators' experience is an important variable in the success of a popular initiative as the question has to be reworked. For instance, in 1992, a popular initiative about the construction of a community hall was launched in Murrhardt. It was rejected because the question posed was ambiguous; in 1993, the same initiative was submitted and a local referendum was held on March 1993. It failed because it did not meet the quorum of signatures, although the result satisfied the initiators' point of view. In a local referendum process, the initiators try to define a question that can be understood by everyone. How can citizens ensure that a problem is formulated as an issue concerning local public policy (Meyer 1986)?[15] A more specific question sometimes suffices to create stronger mobilisation. Table 6.9 presents mobilisation intensity in the case of such reworked initiatives.

We defined a mobilisation index in order to measure the relationship between the distribution of arguments and the mobilisation of electors. First, we calculated the difference $D(x)$ between the pros and cons. Secondly, we created a distribution index $P(x)$ in which $P(x) = 1-D(x)$.[16] A well-balanced cleavage implies that the difference between pros and cons is weak. In fact, the referendum situation is well-balanced between 'Yes' voters and 'No' voters when the coefficient approaches 1 (1 means that there are 50 per cent of 'No' voters, and 50 per cent of 'Yes' voters). If the coefficient decreases, then the voters prefer one option rather than the other one (0 means that 100 per cent of the electors voted ,'Yes' or 'No'). In other words, a weak coefficient reveals a consensus among the local population because voters make a clear choice about a concrete question. The mobilisation index $I(x)$ is calculated by multiplying $P(x)$ with the turnout $T(x)$. The mobilisation index

---

14. Database from the University of Marburg (accessed 14th March 2007).
15. We apply the concept of 'problematology', as defined by Michel Meyer, to the problem of translating demand into local public policy.
16. For both $D(x)$ and $T(x)$, 50 per cent is 0.5. The mobilisation index was made with the help of Professor Oscar W. Gabriel.

initiatives and referendums | 179

Table 6.9: Reworked popular initiative referendums in Baden-Württemberg (1975–2006)

Name of the commune (number of inhabitants)	Date of local referendum	Turnout (%)	Approval rate (%)	Difference between 'Yes' and 'No' (%)	Mobilisation index
Ehingen (24, 046)	1979	63.4	36.1	13.6	0.55
Fridingen an der Donau (2,864)	1980	82.7	45	9	0.75
Adelsheim (4,239)	1983	49	35.2	43.6	0.28
Kirchheim am Ries (1,644)	1985	69.4	43.3	24.8	0.52
Trochtelfingen (5,277)	1985	59.9	35.9	19.8	0.48
Bad Peterstal-Griesbach (3,216)	1986	76.8	44.2	15.2	0.65
Sulzburg (2,585)	1995	83.3	59.9	43.8	0.47
Nufringen (4,488)	1996	68.9	52.1	51.3	0.33
Gondelsheim (3,190)	1997	67.9	35.1	3.5	0.74
Eppingen (19,422)	1998	48.5	31.2	28.4	0.35
Albstadt-Ebingen (48,155)	1999	39.1	28.5	46.1	0.21
Durlangen (2,960)	1999	63.7	37.6	18	0.52
Pforzheim (119,325)	2006	21.9	16.8	53.4	0.12
Schluchsee (2,670)	2006	56.5	32.1	13.4	0.49
Average (17,000)	–	60.8	38.1	27.4	0.44

Source: database on local direct democracy in Baden-Württemberg.

depends on the relationship between turnout and the distribution of arguments. If the value of the index is 1, mobilisation is complete and the arguments in the local population are well-balanced; when it is 0, mobilisation is weak and the arguments are not well-balanced, as only those in favour the electors vote.

Between 1975 and 2006, we recorded 384 popular initiatives and 214 local referendums in Baden-Württemberg. The average turnout for those referendums was 53.2 per cent and 34.6 per cent for the average approval rate. When we examine the cases where popular initiatives were reworked, the average turnout was 60.8 per cent and the average approval rate 38.1 per cent, which means that a reformulated popular initiative has a better turnout. A reworked popular initiative has more chance of being successful because of the experience of its initiators. This indicates a deepened understanding of the rules, which helps to clarify the question. At the same time, the mobilisation index, which measures the intensity of mobilisation, is relatively high (0.44); in fact, citizens are more divided in the case of a reworked popular initiative, where the pros and cons are more balanced and citizens are more involved than they were initially.

Some German communes, unlike those in France, have a real tradition of direct democratic tools: until 2006, the city of Murrhardt held five popular initiatives in fifteen years, the cities of Freiburg, Radolfzell and Konstanz, each held four initiatives, and Ludwigsburg and Leonberg held three. Some communes had to organise several referendums in order to work out a solution. In the city of Schönau, two were held in 1991 and 1997 on the replacement of the electricity supplier by a renewable energy company (Dijkstra and Graichen 2000). In both cases, there was no consensus on the vote. The first popular initiative in 1991 was supported by local environmentalists and the Social-Democrats (SPD), whereas the second initiative in 1996 was supported by the Conservatives (CDU). This example shows how the local referendum can be used in the political game of a commune without creating a strong consensus for a solution. In this particular case, Sartori's prediction is verified: the frequency of local referendums on the same topic does not mean that a local consensus is created within a short lapse of time. The positions become more well-balanced, and the conflict more visible, but the referendum does not manage to produce a consensus among the population.

In France, some communes did hold several referendums because their mayors had a participative ideology (Wolf and Osselin 1979) and were convinced of the benefits. Mons-en-Baroeul (near Lille) has held three since the end of the 1970s, but none of them stemmed from a popular initiative. The new right of petition might encourage the use of popular initiatives, but insofar as they are not binding, those instruments are not really efficient. The rules are controlled by the mayors who prevent citizens, as well as local councils, from organising those procedures. The game is not accepted, which also explains why French legislation in this domain is still somewhat unachieved. In Germany, however, the citizens and political groups have had their say. In France, a local referendum is an epiphenomenon evolving in the margins of participatory democracy whereas, in Germany, direct democratic tools reveal a growing empowerment of citizens.

A new participatory culture?

If local referendums differ from participatory tools, they are part of an emerging participatory culture in both countries. They express the transformation of citizens' values (Taniguchi 2006: 216). Citizens want to have a greater say on questions concerning their environment. The priorities of public policies are not only economic problems, but also those concerned with the quality of life (van Deth and Scarbrough 1995: 9). In addition to this, the ways in which citizens become involved in politics have changed, and plebiscitary mechanisms can be seen as expressing this new way of doing politics. Oscar W. Gabriel (2003: 120) distinguishes four types of political participation in Germany:

- protest actions (petitions, demonstrations, popular initiatives and referendums);
- participation with a specific goal (evaluation of all legal procedures, meeting with politicians);
- participation in political parties; and
- civil disobedience.

As regards petitions, we can usefully examine the European Social Survey data, which includes a sub-category indicating whether the respondent had signed a petition in the last twelve months.[17]

We observe that 33.6 per cent of East German respondents took part in a protest action, versus 26.8 per cent for West Germans. Those *Länder* with a low approval quorum, like Bavaria and Hamburg, have good scores, as their respondents are more likely to sign a petition within the context of a popular initiative. At the same time, citizens living in regions with restrictive legislation concerning direct democratic procedures use this instrument in order to attract the authorities' attention (Bremen). In France, the proportion of respondents who signed a petition in the last twelve months is 32.4 per cent,[18] which is similar to the situation in Germany. In France, petitions are strongly linked to demonstrations and pressure on the central power whereas, in Germany, they are related to direct democracy. It is, thus, necessary to analyse the relationship between the mobilisation of citizens and typical referendum topics in France as presented in Table 6.10.

Table 6.10 shows that referendums focusing on the topics of communal life and local borders (merger of communes or adhesion to another local structure) have the highest turnout, which means citizens become more involved in questions of local identity. Questions of local borders and invalid consultations have high approval rates. For referendums concerning local borders, the future of the commune is at stake whereas, for invalid referendums, the people are organised and quite convinced of the result. In fact, invalid consultations send a signal to the

---

17. Source: R. Jowell and the Central Co-ordinating Team, *European Social Survey 2004/2005: Technical Report*, London: Centre for Comparative Social Surveys, City University (2005). NB Number of respondents: 5,779.
18. There were 3,301 French respondents in the survey.

Table 6.10: Topics, turnout and approval rates of French local referendums (1992–2004)

Topics	Number of referendums between 1992 and 2004	Average turnout (%)	Average approval rate (%)	Difference Yes/No (%)	Mobilisation index
Urban planning (transport)	56	50.2	35.6	46.3	0.27
Public infrastructures (schools, swimming pools)	39	52.1	39.8	49.1	0.26
Communal life (name of the commune, cultural aspects)	26	58.2	38.9	40.1	0.35
Consultations refused by the central state	22	53.4	44.6	70.4	0.16
Local borders	51	60.4	47.5	52.5	0.29
Total (complete data)	194	54.5	40.5	48.5	0.28

Source: author's research.

state as regards projects (highways, for instance) that have an impact on the local environment. There is a consensus of the local population supporting the position of local representatives; often those representatives draw the attention of the central state to a particular problem. These local referendums also show that communal competencies are limited in France. In almost every local referendum, the difference between 'Yes' and 'No' voters is quite high, which clearly indicates that initiators do not organise a local referendum if they are not sure of winning. In Germany, the official classification of topics is more detailed, as not all *Länder* include topics that can eventually trigger a local referendum.

If we define an indicator that distinguishes classical topics of local politics (transport, economic projects, local by-laws and regulation, local borders) from new topics (social public policies, public infrastructures and environmental issues), then 1,901 popular initiatives concerned new political topics (46 per cent) (see Table 6.11). Popular initiatives and local referendums reflect the growing importance of environmental issues and problems of local standards of living. We can assume that there is an evolution in local demands for public policies inspired by post-materialist values (Inglehart 1977: 70) – values that concern the way of life, protection of the local environment, social and cultural policies. Volker Kunz *et al.* have shown the development in German citizens' values: a new political culture, with priority given to education, culture and a more environmentally-centred

Table 6.11: Popular initiative topics in Germany (1975–2007)

Classification of topics	Number of initiatives	Proportion
Waste disposal policies	219	5.2%
Territorial reforms	540	12.8%
Taxes	125	3%
Status of administrative staff	58	1.4%
Cultural projects	180	4.3%
Urban planning	8	0.2%
Transport	647	15.3%
Economic activities	597	14.1%
Cell phone antennas	25	0.6%
Housing	133	3.1%
Public infrastructures	842	19.9%
Social infrastructures	502	11.8%
Particular cases	214	5.1%
Sundry cases	136	3.2%
Total	4,226	100%

Source: www.forschungsstelle-direkte-demokratie.de/ (accessed 14th March 2007).

way of life (Kunz et al. 1993: 214). This is why economic projects are no longer at the head of referendum topics. In some old *Länder*, like Baden-Württemberg, new topics have come to the fore (Table 6.12).

When we compare the old topics of local politics with the new ones, we find the following results: the turnout for classic topics is almost the same as for new topics; approval rates for old and new topics are also very similar, as is the case for 'Yes' and 'No' voting. Out of 210 local referendums held in Baden-Württemberg between 1975 and 2006, 128 concerned new topics and 82 classic topics. The cleavages are stronger for old-styled problems than for the new ones, which corresponds to the development of citizens' values. Some old topics give rise to social conflicts, with citizens reacting against the environmental impact of an economic project. This is why, even for old-type topics, we can observe a transformation in the attitudes of citizens. They are ready to become involved in order to improve the offer of public policies that suit their quality of life.

Table 6.12: Topics, turnout and approval rates of local referendums in Baden-Württemberg (1975–2006)

Topics	Number of referendums between 1975 and 2006	Average turnout (%)	Average approval rate (%)	Mobilisation coefficient	Cleavage
Economic projects	18	59.1	37	0.44	++
Local by-laws and regulations	8	48	27.5	0.39	+
Social public policies	21	50.7	28.2	0.35	+/–
Particular cases	4	37.7	28.7	0.18	–
Transport	48	51.3	33.5	0.35	+
Public infrastructures (water, garbage problems, etc.)	37	55.4	39.3	0.32	+/–
Housing	4	46	31.5	0.28	–
Cultural projects	66	53.6	33.7	0.39	+
Local borders	4	75	50.9	0.48	++
Total	210	53.3	34.7	0.37	

Notes: ++ Strong cleavage; + cleavage; +/– weak cleavage; – No cleavage.
Source: author's research.

Referendum questions of the new type occur more frequently in communes that have between 5,000 and 30,000 inhabitants: 61 per cent of all cases. In France, the question of quality of life arises in invalid referendums when mayors want to prevent the construction of a highway. The Nimby ('not in my backyard') effect is more obvious in France, as the local populations want to maintain a certain local way of life. The Nimby phenomenon signifies that the inhabitants of a small community are willing to react against any kind of project that would modify their local environment (Bobbio 2003: 195). In our database of popular initiatives in Baden-Württemberg, we recorded forty-seven popular initiatives between 1975 and 2006 reacting against local council decisions, and deprived of any counter proposal. The topic of those initiatives concerned the local environment, which is why we can regard them as Nimby initiatives: their initiators simply disapprove of certain policies (e.g. creation of a waste recycling area). In France, local representatives use referendums to refuse a national policy that threatens the local lifestyle. In the department of Ille-et-Villaine, the small commune of Cornillé had to fight against an incinerator plan. The mayor of this commune decided to organise a local referendum in order to send out a strong signal. For him, the referendum was the only way the inhabitants could express their point of view.

> When we were informed for the first time by the Préfecture, we had the impression that everything was already decided and that we could not say anything. What about the health risks? The future of the commune? Our questions went without an answer [...] until we decided to hold this referendum at the end of November [2002]. The following day, a public meeting in Vitré was announced.[19]

A local referendum can be the expression of a local complaint and the ultimate possibility for local populations to maintain their lifestyle. In a way, the Nimby effect could also be considered as an expression of post-materialist values: local populations are ready to pursue every possibility in order to preserve a certain standard of living.

Conclusion

A comparison of local participation in referendums in France and Germany shows a different grasp of the process. In France, the local referendum is a participative instrument with a somewhat ambiguous status. If the last Act of Decentralisation recognises decisional value referendums, the required turnout of 50 per cent limits their development. The coexistence of consultative and decisional referendums in the law makes the outlines of the procedure unclear. In Germany, the local referendum is now part and parcel of the various *Länder* and their local democratic systems. However, the wide range of criteria involved indicates that it is very hard to obtain a popular decision in the sense of the initiators' wishes. The entry and exit price requires a high turnout and long-term mobilisation if the initiators want to succeed. In France, local consultation does not include any deadline and any conditions for the result, except as regards turnout. In summary, the approval rate is a minimal risk, which avoids the neutral tendency of referendums when the pros and cons are well-balanced. Direct democracy does not suppose an ambiguous consensus (Kesselman 1972), but is an occasion for organised minorities to take part in different public debates. Consequently, those procedures are adapted to a complex society in which opposed interests can confront each other: direct democracy generates regulation in local politics. A new form of participatory culture has come into being, with local populations showing great sensitivity about environmental and social issues. Nevertheless, if people become concerned about the topics and want to define public policies that suit their local environment, local referendums do not always produce a strong consensus; rather, they express mobilisations of local protest.

---

19. 'L'incinérateur qui embrase Cornillé', Libération, 21st and 22nd December 2002.

References

Apter, D. E. (1991) 'Un regard neuf sur l'institutionnalisme', *Revue Internationale des Sciences Sociales*, 129: 493–513.
Bacot, P. (1994) *Dictionnaire du Vote, Élections et Délibérations*, Lyon: Presses Universitaires de Lyon.
Bacqué, M.-H., Rey, H. and Sintomer, Y. (eds) (2005) *Gestion de Proximité et Démocratie Participative: Une perspective comparative*, Paris: Éditions La Découverte.
Barber, B. (1984) *Strong Democracy: Politics for a new age*, Berkeley: University of California Press.
Bobbio, N. (2003) 'Approches dialogiques de la localisation d'équipements indésirables' in V. Hoffmann-Martinot and C. Sorbets (eds) *Démocraties Locales en Changement*, Paris: Éditions Pedone.
Castoriadis, C. (1996) 'La démocratie comme procédure et comme régime' in C. Castoriadis (ed.) *La Montée de l'Insignifiance*, Les Carrefours du Labyrinthe IV, Paris: Seuil.
Dahl, R. A. and Tufte, E. R. (1974) *Size and Democracy: The politics of the smaller European democracies*, Stanford: Stanford University Press.
Denquin, J.-M. (1976) *Référendum et Plébiscite*, Paris: Éditions LGDJ.
Dijkstra, B. R. and Graichen, P. R. (2000) S*howdown in Schönau: A contest case study*, Discussion paper series, Heidelberg: University of Heidelberg, Department of Economics.
Fijalkowski, J. (2002) 'Zum Problem direkt-demokratischer Beteiligung' in D. Fuchs, E. Roller and B. Weßels (eds) *Bürger und Demokratie in Ost und West*, Wiesbaden: Westdeutscher Verlag.
Fishkin, J. (1995) *The Voice of the People: Public opinion and democracy*, New Haven: Yale University Press.
French Interior Ministry 'Les régions entre l'état et les collectivités locales: Etude comparative de cinq états européens à autonomies régionales ou constitution fédérale (Allemagne, Belgique, Espagne, Italie, Royaume-Uni)', Grale Report, Paris, January 2003.
Gabriel, O. W. (2003) 'Le peuple législateur: Analyse empirique des initiatives populaires et des référendums municipaux' in V. Hoffmann-Martinot and C. Sorbets (eds) *Démocraties Locales en Changement*, Paris: Éditions Pedone.
Gabriel, O. W. and Walter-Rogg, M. (2006) 'Bürgerbegehren und Bürgerentscheide: Folgen für den kommunalpolitischen Entscheidungsprozess', *Deutsche Zeitschrift für Kommunalwissenschaften*, 45(2): 39–56.
Guggenberger, B. and Kempf, U. (1984) *Bürgerinitiativen und Repräsentatives System*, Darmstadt: Westdeutscher Verlag.
Herrenschmidt, J.s-D. (1936) *Le Problème des Petites Communes en France*, Paris: Ph.D.
Hoffmann-Martinot, V. (2005) 'Zentralisierung und Dezentralisierung' in A. Kimmel and H. Uterwedde (eds) *Länderbericht Frankreich: Geschichte,*

politik, wirtschaft, gesellschaft, Schriftenreihe 462, Bonn: Bundeszentrale für Politische Bildung.
Holtkamp, L., Bogumil, J. and Kißler, L. (2006) *Kooperative Demokratie: Das politische Potenzial von Bürgerengagement,* Frankfurt/Main: Campus Verlag.
Inglehart, R. (1977) *The Silent Revolution: Changing values and political styles among western publics,* Princeton, N.J.: Princeton University Press.
Kaase, M. (1982) 'Partizipatorische Revolution? Ende der Parteien' in J. Raschke (ed.) *Bürger und Parteien: Ansichten und analysen einer schwierigen beziehung,* Opladen: Westdeutscher Verlag.
Karr, P. (2003*) Institutionen direkter Demokratie in den Gemeinden Deutschlands und der Schweiz: Eine rechtsvergleichende untersuchung,* Baden-Baden: Nomos.
Kesselman, M. (1972) *Le Consensus Ambigu: Étude sur le gouvernement local,* Paris: Cujas.
Kunz, V., Gabriel, O. W. and Brettschneider, F. (1993) 'Wertorientierungen, Ideologien und Policy-Präferenzen in der Bundesrepublik Deutschland' in O. W. Gabriel and K. G. Troitzsch (eds) *Wahlen in Zeiten des Umbruchs,* Frankfurt/Main: Peter Lang.
LeDuc, L. (2003) *The Politics of Direct Democracy: Referendums in global perspective,* Toronto: Broadview Press.
Luthardt, W. (1994) *Direkte Demokratie: Ein Vergleich in Westeuropa,* Baden-Baden: Nomos.
März, P. (2003) 'Kommunalpolitik in Bayern' in A. Kost and H. -G. Wehling (eds) *Kommunalpolitik in den Deutschen Ländern,* Wiesbaden: Westdeutscher Verlag.
Meyer, M. (1986) *De la Problématologie, Philosophie, Science et Langage,* Bruxelles: Mardaga.
Paoletti, M. (1996) *Analyse de la Démocratie Locale à Travers la Genèse Institutionnelle du Référendum,* Bordeaux: Ph.D.
Rosanvallon, P. (2004) *Le Modèle Politique Français: la société civile contre le Jacobinisme de 1789 à nos jours,* Paris: Seuil.
Roussillon, H. (1972) *Les Structures Territoriales des Communes: Réformes et perspectives d'avenir,* Paris: Éditions LGDJ.
Sadran, P. (2004) 'Les enjeux de la réforme, démocratie locale: les enjeux de "l'acte II"', *Cahiers Français,* (318): 73–79.
Sartori, G. (1993) *Democrazia Cosa é,* Milano: Rizzoli.
Taniguchi, M. (2006) 'A time machine: new evidence of post-materialist value change', *International Political Science Review,* 27(4): 405–425.
van Deth, J. W. and Scarbrough, E. (eds) (1995) *The Impact of Values,* Oxford: Oxford University Press.
Wargny, C. (1978) *Mairies Frappées d'Autogestion,* Paris: Éditions Syros.
Weale, A. (1999) *Democracy,* New York: Saint Martin's Press.
Weixner, B. M. (2002) *Direkte Demokratie in den Bundesländern,* Opladen: Leske and Budrich.

Westerståhl, J. (1981) 'Participation and Representation' in P. Torsvik (ed.) *Mobilization Center-Periphery Structures and Nation-Building*, Bergen: Universitetsforlaget.
Whitehead, L. (2006) 'Closely fought elections and the institutionalization of democracy', *Taiwan Journal of Democracy*, 2(1): 1–11.
Wolf, M. and Osselin, J. (1979) *Les Ascenseurs de la ZUP: Contrôle populaire et autogestion municipale*, Paris: François Maspéro.
Wollmann, H. (2002) 'Kommunale Referenden in den ostdeutschen Kommunen – Regelung, Anwendungspraxis, Bestimmungsfaktoren' in T.Schiller, V. Mittendorf (eds) *Direkte Demokratie, Forschung und Perspektiven*, Wiesbaden: Westdeutscher Verlag.

chapter seven | social participation
Silke I. Keil

Introduction

In a book that highlights various facets and manifestations of political participation in France and Germany, it might, initially, seem surprising and require explanation that this chapter should be concerned with *social* participation.

First, it should be obvious that participation research concerns both political *and* social participation. From the very outset, however, participation research was concerned almost exclusively with the political aspect, in the sense of activities that refer to purely political objects. Recently, however, the field of participation research has gone beyond political participation in this narrow sense. Now, thanks to the increasing popularity of the concept of 'social capital', first introduced into political science debate by Coleman (1988), and then brought to the fore by Robert D. Putnam (1993, 2000), interest in social participation research has grown. Although, in the early days, social participation was regarded as a driving force of political participation, it was not until civic engagement was rediscovered as an important resource for democracy that it gained significance of its own in the domain of political science research. Social participation, so the argument goes, not only stimulates political participation, it also adds to the integration of modern societies, to the effectiveness of the economy, state and society, as well as to a better quality of democracy (Gabriel *et al.* 2002). Social participation is discussed in this book both because of its outstanding relevance for the generation and explanation of political participation, and the importance accorded to it in what concerns democracy. It should be mentioned at this point, however, that there is not just some one-way relationship between social and political participation; instead, an interdependence of effects has to be assumed (Zukin *et al.* 2006).

It is not only research, however, that has become increasingly aware of the importance of social participation for the quality of a democracy; the public, too, now sets great store by social participation in society. The inauguration of an International Year of Volunteers (IYV), as well as of a special day devoted to Volunteers, indicates the official esteem in which social participation is held, both in what concerns everyday life within the community and as regards democracy. In 1997, the United Nations General Assembly proclaimed 2001 'International Year of Volunteers', and December 5th was chosen as the day on which it would be celebrated worldwide. Ever since, this 'Day of Volunteers' (IVD) – '*Tag des Ehrenamts*' in Germany, '*Journée mondiale du bénévolat*' in France – has been commemorated by both nations. However, volunteers are not simply recognised at an official level, they are also celebrated in special TV shows and in press articles.

The (re-)discovery of social participation and voluntary associations as important issues can be observed in current debate and in scientific discussion. According to democratic theory, citizens' participation in political and social life is one of the most important characteristics of a democracy (Dahl 1971). The idea that 'citizen participation is at the heart of democracy' (Verba *et al.* 1995: 1) is deeply rooted in political thinking. Tocqueville had already emphasised the decisive role of associations for a lively democracy and, when concluding his analysis of democracy in the United States, he stressed that the key to the vitality of American democracy was to be found in the diversity of its social participation. More recently, Robert D. Putnam (1993, 2000), taking up and developing the ideas of Tocqueville, introduced social capital theory into the scientific debate; this theory soon became very popular and increased researchers' interest in social participation. As for Almond and Verba, the well-known founding fathers of research on political culture, not only did they present some ideas and empirical data on this topic, but also demonstrated that people who are behaviourally engaged in the voluntary sector tend to show greater trust in other people and also consider themselves as more active and influential players in the political game than the average citizen (Almond and Verba 1989: 211).

Similarly, but using an alternative theoretical approach, Robert D. Putnam assumes that an active civic life and such central characteristics as interpersonal trust and reciprocity norms all have a positive impact on democracy (Putnam 1993: 91–116, 2000: 31–47). Numerous empirical studies concerned with the impact of individual social participation and civic attitudes on democracy confirm Putnam's macro-level findings. There seems to be no doubt regarding the role of social activity as a crucial determinant for the vitality of a democracy (see, for example: Verba and Nie 1972; Verba *et al.* 1978; Verba *et al.* 1995; Parry *et al.* 1992; Pattie *et al.* 2004; van Deth 1996; 2001).

Social participation seems, then, to be a positive component of a pluralist democracy. But what sort of social participation are we talking about, exactly? Research confirms that it is not just the existence *per se* of social participation that is important, but that its influence is stronger or weaker according to its intensity. It is obvious and empirically proven that it makes a difference whether people are merely passive, paying party-members or whether they are actively involved in party organisation – either during election campaigns or via their continuous voluntary engagement. It would be hard to explain how mere membership – which does not entail any active participation – could lead to acquiring political skills and learning co-operative norms and forms of behaviour. More probably, participation in organisational life works as a mechanism for social learning (Dekker and van den Broek 2006).

Against this background of the importance of social participation in general and the intensity of social participation in particular, this chapter will further examine the determinants of social participation. Only if we know what factors promote social participation, can the general conditions for social participation be improved. Unfortunately, there are no specific empirical results allowing a Franco-German comparison to be made. This chapter is therefore concerned with French-German similarities and differences and addresses the following questions:

- To what extent is the German and French population involved in social activities?
- What stimulates people to become involved in social activities?
- What stimulates the degree of intensity of French and German social engagement?

In the next section, I will delineate the concept of social participation and present the main hypotheses. Subsequently, some data on the distribution of social participation in Germany and France will be presented. Afterwards I will examine the factors of explanation in terms of different types of social engagement. In the concluding section, I will summarise and discuss the findings in the light of current debate.

The concept of social participation

What is social participation? Unlike the term 'political participation', the concept of social participation is defined more broadly; it also comprises actions that do not have a political goal. However, the notions of social participation or civic engagement are often vague with, in many cases, political participation not being clearly distinguished. Thus, the umbrella term of 'civic engagement' subsumes social and political participation into one concept. Gabriel *et al.* (2002: 39; and see van Deth 1996: 389) propose the following definition: 'all actions voluntarily undertaken by citizens in associations'. When using this definition, we should bear in mind that only the social engagement undertaken in or via voluntary organisations is included. Although these voluntary actions are likely to make up the core of civic engagement in modern societies, there are other forms of social participation, carried out by individuals or informal groups, and these forms are not comprised within this definition. I want to stress this point, although it is not dealt with specifically in this chapter. Social participation, therefore, comprises membership and active participation, as well as such things as accepting offices in voluntary organisations, voluntary engagement and providing social help for others (Schwarz 1996: 169ff.). But the empirical analyses that follow 'only' concern associations. In most cases, however, social participation could be defined as: 'activities, carried out with others, that take place either in formal organisations (voluntary organisations and associations, respectively) or informal groups (action groups/citizen initiatives, neighbourhoods, friends, colleagues, project groups)'.

As noted above, this chapter focuses on social participation in voluntary associations because of the great importance of this particular category. This gives rise to the following question: why is social engagement in voluntary associations so important? According to social capital theory, participation in organisations increases interest in public issues and affairs; this, in turn, affects political participation. Equally, the networks generated via increased social contacts within these organisations can, in turn, stimulate political activity. Olsen goes much further than this, seeing a direct connection without the need of any form of transfer: the generation of certain skills, information and mechanisms of social interaction are all requisites for effective political participation (Olsen 1982). Social capital exerts a positive effect, thanks to the experiences and interactions that take place within voluntary associations (Armingeon 2007: 366). It has already been determined that social capital can circulate through active participation in particular, but participation can vary enormously, going from nominal membership or simple inclusion in a mailing list, on the one hand, to full-scale activism, on the other hand (Morales and Geurts 2007: 142). For a differentiated consideration of voluntary engagement in associations, it is therefore necessary to distinguish between different forms of participation. Morales and Geurts (2007: 143) suggest distinguishing between passive and active participation: this chapter follows their suggestion and differentiates accordingly.[1]

As already mentioned, social and political participation are closely related. What does this correlation look like, or – to use the words of van Deth (2001) – is it a matter of 'completions, alternatives or twins'? In modern societies, it is not always easy to differentiate between political and social participation. The dividing line between the political and social sphere has become more and more blurred because of the state's increasing involvement in all types of social spheres. The rediscovery of civic engagement in political science has also contributed to this blurred demarcation between private and public sphere. Similarly, in terms of political and social involvement, it is not always possible to pin down whether an action is based on political motives, serves political purposes, or addresses political issues (Putnam 2000; Norris 2002).

In terms of social and political participation there are, basically, two competing hypotheses. The first hypothesis is based on the assumption that the two forms of participation are in competition, with social participation being regarded as an alternative to political participation. Participation in associations leads to social peace, but also to political demobilisation. The advocates of a negative or missing correlation between the two forms of participation make a simple assumption: as social engagement is time-consuming, citizens with an average amount of spare time are unable to assume extensive political engagement (van Deth 2001: 198).

The second, and far more common approach, advances the thesis that political participation can be learned through social participation and that, as active participation in associations leads to the acquisition of democratic skills, it is, consequently, an essential requisite for political participation. Once this learning process has been achieved, there is no longer any need for an interaction between political and social participation (van Deth 2001).

However, this chapter is not concerned with the question of any eventual interaction between the two forms of participation, but is aimed rather at pointing out that a lot of research has already examined the relationship between social

---

1. The available database, the European Social Survey, admits this kind of classification; it also allows the question – What leads people to act passively or actively in organisations? – to be answered. The different degrees of engagement retrieved from the database ranged from simple membership to active participation in the various organisations concerned.

and political participation. This chapter, in fact, focuses on the question of social participation in itself, not least because of its importance for political participation.

Before giving an overview of the distribution of social participation in Germany and France, the research strategy adopted to test the relevant hypotheses will first be presented. Based on the explanations given above, we would like to develop the following hypotheses:

- The selection and influence of social participation determinants vary with regard to activity intensity.
- With regard to the intensity of social participation, it can be expected that active social participation would be explained better by norms, networks and socio-economic determinants than by passive participation.

Social participation in France and Germany: an explanatory model and research strategy

Why do some people decide to become involved socially while others do not? This is the question at the core of research on participation from its earliest beginnings. It is among the most important challenges of empirical research and will be discussed in what follows. Furthermore, this chapter does not restrict itself to the determinants of social participation in general, but focuses on the matter of which particular determinants are responsible for active and which for passive participation.

In the literature, three strategies are used in attempting to explain social participation (the following explanations in this paragraph are essentially based on Gabriel and Völkl 2004).

1. a strategy acts on the assumption that correlations exist (Milbrath and Goel 1977, inter alia);
2. concerns with low- and middle-range theories (Inglehart 1979, 1983, inter alia);
3. reference to theories that lay claim to general validity (Downs 1957 and Ajzen and Fishbein 1980, inter alia).

As regards empirical research, the approach that has proven to be the most efficient serves as the basis for our analysis: these middle-range explanatory approaches were developed by a group of researchers around Sidney Verba (Nie *et al.* 1969a, 1969b; Verba and Nie 1972; Verba *et al.* 1978; Verba *et al.* 1995).

The model developed by Verba, Nie and Kim (1978) explains forms of participation by using a combination of socio-economic and political factors. Socio-economic factors are summarised in the model of socio-economic resources, with material resources being measured by income, and immaterial resources by level of education. Like other researchers (Nie *et al.* 1969a; Milbrath and Goel 1977; Marsh and Kaase 1979; Parry *et al.* 1992, inter alia), Verba, Nie and Kim assumed a positive correlation between the level of socio-economic resources and the extent of social participation. During the 1990s, the Verba/Schlozman/Brady research group developed an innovative contribution (Verba *et al.* 1995). According to these authors, participation will probably take place if the following conditions prevail:

- the active persons concerned possess the requisite resources (time, money, knowledge, competencies);
- they show some motivation to become involved in social activities due to their primary or secondary socialisation; and
- they are encouraged or asked to participate by their social environment, associations or political elites.

The stronger the appeal of these factors, then the greater is the likelihood of their social engagement.

Since the explanatory model has been presented in detail in the introductory chapter, there is no need for further elaboration here (see Chapter One). As far as theoretical models are concerned, it should be mentioned that there is another important theoretical approach used in explaining social participation. In the ongoing debate about the future of civic engagement in modern democracies, one particular approach – strongly resembling the 'civic-voluntarism-model' of Verba, Schlozman and Brady (1995) – was to attract great interest. In several works, Robert D. Putnam (1993, 2000) called attention to the productive role of social capital for the efficiency of modern societies and states. He referred to social capital as the interaction of social networks, interpersonal trust, and the support of values that relate to the community. According to Putnam, the interaction of these factors promotes social engagement. Thus, people who trust in their social environment and support values and norms that relate to society are very active participants in voluntary associations (van Deth 1996, 2001; Gabriel *et al.* 2002; Enquete-Kommission Bürgerschaftliches Engagement 2002). Except for socio-economic resources, the concept of social capital contains the same variables as the explanatory model developed by Verba, Schlozman and Brady. The determinants included in the following multivariate analyses were chosen in accordance with the comments of these authors.

The empirical analysis will show how the individual factors – *resources, motives and networks* – have been weighted in terms of their explanatory power. Logistic regression analyses have been made to find out which determinants influence different intensities of participation in associations. The dependent variable is formed by two different characteristics of social participation: basic membership on the one hand, and active participatory involvement on the other (this includes intermittent engagement *and* regular honorary work, but excludes donating money).[2] The independent variables are derived from the Verba/Schlozman/Brady model and follow – as already mentioned – the logic of the social capital approach. The *resources complex* is included via the *education* and *professional*

---

2. However, we should bear in mind that factors other than formal social activity may be important for the vitality of a democracy, e.g. informal social participation.

prestige variables. Additionally, *gender* and *age* are taken into account as ascribed variables. *Motivations* – the second important explanatory set, according to Verba/Schlozman/Brady – is operationalised via the *political interest* and *internal efficacy* variables. Unfortunately, the ESS dataset does not allow all the variables relevant for the *motives complex*[3] to be included. To include *networks* adequately, the *integration in family index* has been created. In addition, *frequency of church attendance* is meaningful in this respect, as well as *interpersonal trust*, which is also important according to Putnam's social capital theory.

Engagement in social life: France and Germany

The widespread development of social engagement in democratic societies has been investigated by several empirical studies (Almond and Verba 1989; Verba *et al.* 1978; Verba *et al.* 1995; Norris 2002; van Deth 2004; Zukin *et al.* 2006). These studies, however, do not contain any explicitly systematic comparison of France and Germany. Instead, results for both countries are generally – but not exclusively – presented within the framework of European studies (Curtis *et al.* 1992; Zimmer and Priller 2007; Gabriel and Völkl 2008). The European Social Survey, carried out in 2002 and 2006, serves as a valuable source for a differentiated, comparative analysis of the intensity of membership in social organisations in France and Germany.[4] However, before addressing the question of how German and French citizens make use of their respective participation opportunities, there is one prior question: what are the different kinds of participation option available?

In both France and Germany, close networks of voluntary associations are to be found. As Tables 7.1 and 7.2 make clear, the number of associations and, consequently the opportunities for social engagement, are impressive in both countries. Before this array of associations is dissected, it should be mentioned that associations in France far outnumber those in Germany. France, with nearly twice the number of associations, owes its dominance in this domain to its territorial organisation: France is divided into 33,000 municipalities, German has only 15,000. As voluntary organisations are locally based this, in turn, has an impact on their numbers (Tchernonog 2007: 42). Moreover, the legal framework, particularly Law 1901, which mainly governs the constitution of associations in France, is the origin of the high number. In contrast to the German law, Law 1901 imposes fewer formal requirements for the formation of *associations* and this facilitates the creation of associations and results in higher numbers (Burhoff 2002; La Documentation Française 2002).

---

3. The concept of external efficacy was not present throughout, and neither was the aspect of voting as a civic duty, which is relevant as a participation norm indicator.

4. Although several Eurobarometers and World Values Surveys provide data for France and Germany, the database of the ESS is of much higher quality (Kohler 2008).

Table 7.1: Registered associations in Germany: 2001, 2003, 2005 (entries in absolute numbers)

	2001	2003	2005	Difference (2001–2005)	Percentage change
Sports clubs	215,439	222,897	226,120	+10,681	+4.96%
Leisure clubs	95,044	100,732	109,026	+13,982	+14.71%
Welfare and charitable associations	72,530	74,726	76,757	+4,227	+5.83%
Culture clubs	61,983	63,907	68,680	+6,697	+10.80%
Associations in Occupations/ Economics/ Politics	51,581	55,847	56,479	+4,898	+9.50%
Interest Groups	42,510	48,613	49,225	+6,715	+15.80%
Environmental and Nature Organisations	5,614	7,637	7,990	+2,376	+42.32%
Total	544,701	574,359	594,277	+49,576	+9.10%

Source: http://www.registeronline.de/vereinsstatistik/.

For Germany, figures for almost 600 local association registers were compiled for the first time in 2001. According to these figures, there are more than half a million registered associations all over Germany. When other forms of voluntary organisations are added, the resulting figures are even more impressive. The 2001 figures were first updated in autumn 2003, and then in 2005, at which time, 594,277 associations were registered in Germany. When compared to those of 2001, association numbers had increased by 49,576 or 9 per cent. Relatively speaking, the highest growth rates can be observed in the fields of leisure and culture, as well as among interest groups. If we consider the low base level in 2001, then the increase of about 42 per cent in the number of environmental and nature associations is also impressive. Charitable association numbers, however, increased only slightly, and the same goes for sports clubs, for which an increase of 'merely' 5 per cent can be observed. Nonetheless with over 226,120 associations, they rank first as far as absolute numbers are concerned.

With more than one million associations in France, the range of social participation opportunities is extremely broad; the sports, leisure, and cultural domains alone concern well over half a million associations, and involvement in interest groups is also very high.[5] A comparison of the figures of 1999 with those of 2005 reveals impressive growth rates in almost all categories over a period of six years. A particularly high increase – some 50 per cent and more – can be observed for the fields of welfare and occupation/economics/politics. Only leisure clubs show single digit growth; in the case of occupational, educational and professional integration clubs, there is a slight decrease.

Table 7.2: Registered associations in France: 1999, 2005 (entries in absolute numbers)

	1999	2005	Difference	Percentage change
Sports clubs	195,500	264,700	+69,200	+35.40%
Culture clubs	157,000	204,800	+47,800	+30.45%
Leisure clubs	180,000	196,100	+16,100	+8.94%
Interest groups (literally translated: 'representation of rights and interests')	145,000	170,700	+25,700	+17.72%
Associations in the social sector and healthcare associations	92,200	123,800	+31,600	+34.27%
Associations in the economic and educational sectors (education, training, etc.)	53,500	44,800	-8,700	-16.26%
Welfare and charitable associations (literally translated: 'charitable and humanitarian associations')	26,800	40,800	+14,000	+52.24%
Associations in occupations/ economics/politics (representation of economic interests)	23,500	40,600	+17,100	+72.77%
Others	6,500	13,700	+7,200	+110.77%
Total	880,000	1,100,000	+220,000	+25.00%

Source: http://www.jeunessesports.gouv.fr/IMG/pdf/Chiffres_Cles_vie_associative_2007.pdf.

---

5. Translated literally: 'representation of rights and interests'.

The increase in voluntary associations in both countries is remarkable when set against the debate about decreasing social participation among the population. The fact that engagement among the population is decreasing cannot, therefore, be attributed to a lack of social participation; quite the contrary, in fact. On the supply side,[6] increased efforts are made to broaden the range of social participation options and to encourage the population to participate. Association numbers in France and Germany are not the same, and nor are the categories they cover. Although sports clubs occupy the first rank in both France and Germany, there are considerably more culture clubs in France than in Germany. At 204,000, these clubs rank second in France, but only take fourth place in Germany. Absolute numbers make this difference even clearer: there are slightly fewer than 70,000 culture clubs in Germany. There is also a huge difference between Germany and France with regard to interest groups. Whereas in France their numbers are almost as high as those concerning leisure clubs (170,700), their numbers are relatively low in Germany (49,225). Even a cursory examination of the range covering different fields of activity in 2005 shows huge differences between France and Germany. But, when trends become the focus of attention, it soon becomes apparent that, in France, associations have grown on a much larger scale, with an overall increase of 25 per cent; compare this to a growth rate of only 9 per cent in Germany. However, I should qualify this statement by mentioning that the points in time used for comparison differ. Whereas in France the trend is evaluated for the period between 1999 and 2005, it is only possible to make a statement about the German trend from 2001 onwards – growth rates for the period between 1999 and 2001 may have been higher than was subsequently the case.

Nonetheless, in spite of all these differences, Tables 7.1 and 7.2 show quite clearly that both countries do provide numerous opportunities for participation. This leads on to another question: to what extent do French and German citizens take advantage of their opportunities to become involved in social activities?

Figure 7.1 highlights two aspects very clearly: in France, the population's commitment to passive or active participation in social activities is somewhat evenly divided and between 2002/03 and 2006/07 there are signs of a slight increase for both forms of participation, while, in Germany, the picture is very different (Gensicke *et al.* 2008); here the passive participation level exceeds the active one by 20 per cent, a considerable difference. What is more, both active and passive participation levels tend towards the negative; German membership figures, in particular, show a decline from 70 to 56 per cent.

It can be seen that, in 2002/03, the levels of both passive and active engagement in France resembled the level of active engagement in Germany. Thereafter, passive and active engagement in France increased, with both types being higher

---

6. As mentioned above, only the formal types of social engagement undertaken in or via voluntary organisations are taken into account here. In order to know the exact number of engagement opportunities, these numbers have to be completed by all the existing informal forms of social engagement, which, for the moment, are difficult to discern.

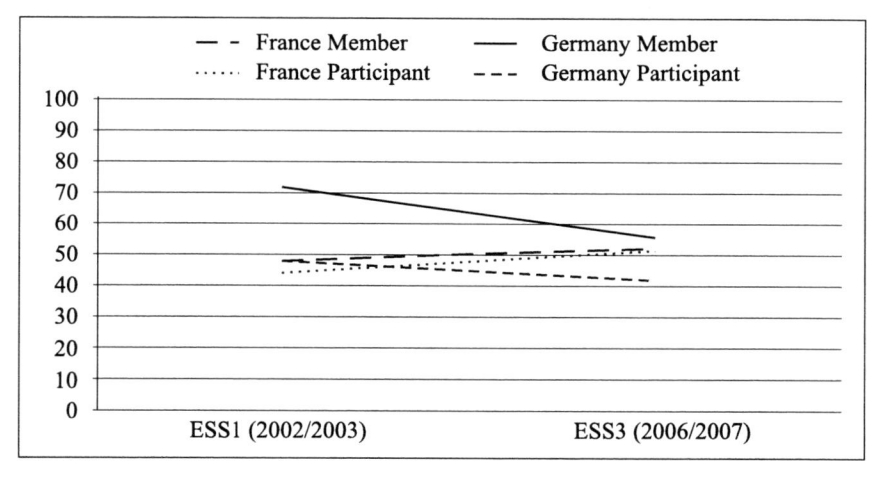

```
          — -  France Member           ——— Germany Member
          ····· France Participant     - - - Germany Participant
    100
     90
     80
     70
     60
     50
     40
     30
     20
     10
      0
          ESS1 (2002/2003)              ESS3 (2006/2007)
```

Figure 7.1: Social Participation in France and Germany, 2002/03, 2006/07
Source: European Social Survey 2002/03 and 2006/07.

than active participation in Germany. But the basic membership in Germany exceeds its equivalent in France.

How should we interpret these results in terms of our initial question? This chapter offers a description of social engagement in France and Germany, attempting to analyse and explain why people are socially active. Clearly, there are differences between France and Germany in what concerns social engagement. Whether these differences in behaviour consequently mean that behaviour can be explained differently is analysed below.

Explanatory factors for the differing intensity of social engagement

Determinants in France and Germany

As already shown, social engagement in voluntary associations is often considered as an essential requisite of democracy. It is supposed that co-operating with their fellow citizens leads people to learn the values, norms, skills and attitudes required of good citizenship for a functioning democracy. Social engagement also encourages people to participate politically. As already shown, it certainly makes a difference to the vitality of a democracy, whether its citizens are engaged actively or passively. Thus, it is important to study the determinants of social engagement in order to find possible useful starting points for persuading citizens to participate and to stabilise and/or improve the democracies of Germany and France.

Although numerous studies consider the importance of social participation in general, empirical analyses of the various sorts and degrees of social participation determinants are rare. What follows is an analysis of the particular determinants that are responsible for the intensity of social participation.

Logistic regression analysis is an appropriate method to analyse the determinants of active and passive engagement because the dependent variable is available as a dummy variable. Before the determinants in the two countries are examined, a first step is to analyse whether – and if so, to what extent – a specific country effect can be observed. In order to study the influence exercised by each country on the type and extent of its social engagement, a country dummy variable is first generated, with the value '1' being assigned to Germany and the value '0' to France. The first model, therefore, does not restrict itself to the variables used by Verba, Schlozman and Brady; a country dummy variable is also taken into account. When the regression analysis incorporates a country dummy variable, it becomes clear that there are country effects (see Table 7.3).[7] The fact that respondents live in Germany exerts a positive influence on the probability that people there will become members of an organisation; the fact that respondents live in France exerts a positive influence on the probability that people will be actively involved in social activities.

Table 7.3: Country effects

Intensity of participation	Pseudo Nagelkerke R^2	Exp(B)	N
Member	.023	0.82[a]	9324
Participant	.003	1.71[a]	9324

Notes: a $\leq$ 0.001; b $\leq$ 0.01; c $\leq$ 0.05; n.s. = not significant; coding: 0 = France; 1 = Germany
Source: European Social Survey 2002/03 and 2006/07; author's calculations.

Apart from the country effect, how well can the theoretical model explain membership and active social engagement in France and Germany? First of all, the Pseudo Nagelkerkes R^2 column in Tables 7.4 and 7.5 – which indicates the extent of a model's explanatory power – shows in this case that the Verba/Schlozman/Brady-model has no convincing explanatory power for either country. In France, the explanatory power as regards both forms of social participation is 9 per cent. In Germany, the model can bind a variance of 11 per cent when explaining membership, and a variance of 7 per cent when explaining social engagement. It would seem that other indicators, not incorporated in the model, are involved.

For France, not only does the model prove less explanatory than is the case for Germany, but fewer coefficients also prove to be significant. Whereas the analysis of membership (Table 7.4) shows that all chosen indicators are significant in Germany, this is the case for only five out of nine variables in France. In what concerns the results for active social engagement (Table 7.5), the discrepancy is even greater. Admittedly, two of the variables shown for Germany prove to be non-significant, but for France there are six such non-significant variables.

---

7. As far as the interpretation of Exp (B) is concerned, there is a positive effect for Germany when the value is greater than 1.

Table 7.4: Determinants of membership in France and Germany, 2002/03–2006/07 (in Exp (B))

	France	Germany
Education level	2.99[a]	2.78[a]
Age	1.00[n.s.]	.99[a]
Gender	.80[a]	.70[a]
Professional prestige	1.01[a]	1.02[a]
Political interest	1.07[n.s.]	.68[a]
Internal efficacy	1.41[n.s.]	2.22[a]
Interpersonal trust	1.60[c]	1.96[a]
Frequency of church attendance	3.42[c]	5.46[a]
Integration into family	1.06[n.s.]	1.19[a]
Constant	.40[n.s.]	.20[a]
Nagelkerkes R^2	.09	.11
N	3,088	5,020

Notes: level of significance: a = p ≤ 0.001; b = p ≤ 0.01; c = p ≤ 0.05; n.s. = not significant; F = France; G = Germany
Source: pooled ESS data sets 2002/03–2006/07; author's calculations.

Table 7.5: Determinants of active social participation in France and Germany, 2002/03–2006/07 (in Exp(B))

	France	Germany
Education level	4.19[a]	1.98[a]
Age	1.00[n.s.]	.99[a]
Gender	.90[n.s.]	.93[n.s.]
Professional prestige	1.00[n.s.]	1.01[a]
Political interest	.86[n.s.]	.87[n.s.]
Internal efficacy	1.05[n.s.]	1.58[a]
Interpersonal trust	1.00[63c]	2.40[a]
Frequency of church attendance	3.63[a]	5.40[a]
Integration into family	.98[n.s.]	1.07[c]
Constant	.31[a]	.22[a]
Nagelkerkes R^2	.09	.07
N	3,088	5,020

Notes: level of significance: a = p ≤ 0.001; b = p ≤ 0.01; c = p ≤ 0.05; n.s. = not significant; F = France; G = Germany.
Source: pooled ESS data sets 2002/03–2006/07; author's calculations.

What determinants are important for a cross-national explanation of social participation? With regard to membership, the following factors are to be considered: *gender, occupational prestige, education, church attendance* and *trust in other persons*. This means that, in terms of the triple-factor theoretical model of Verba, Schlozman and Brady – *resources, motives and networks* – only the *resources* and *networks* components are important in France. As for Germany, all three factors are relevant. As far as the extent of the effects is concerned, church attendance and education turn out to be the major determinants in both countries. This means that the probability of becoming a member of an organisation increases with longer education and frequent church attendance. In addition, in Germany it plays a significant role as to whether or not respondents regard themselves as competent.

A similar picture emerges as regards the question of people becoming actively involved in social activities. Again, only resources and network indicators are important in France whereas, in Germany, the motive of internal efficacy is also a decisive factor for becoming involved in social activities. As far as the extent of the effects is concerned, it is mainly education and church attendance that exert a positive influence in France. Education, however, does not play such a preponderant role in Germany; it seems, instead, to be more important for people to both trust in others and attend church frequently.

It seems, then, that the indicators based on the theoretical model of Verba, Schlozman and Brady, only explain membership in organisations and active social engagement to a certain extent. In both countries, network variables and resource variables influence social participation although, in the case of Germany, additional motives are involved.

Determinants in Eastern Germany

Germany has been reunited for more than 20 years; the question then arises as to whether a separate analysis in terms of new and old federal states is necessary. We know from research on political culture and participation that differences regarding the attitudes of the population persist in configurations. The different party systems in Eastern and Western Germany already indicate a number of regional particularities. As for social participation, it is plausible to assume that there are also differences in that respect. Accordingly, the analyses were repeated, but this time separately, for both new and old federal states (although these have not been presented in table form). This was to test empirically whether there are differences between Eastern and Western Germany as regards the explanation of membership and active social participation.

As far as the explanatory power of the entire model is concerned, no differences are to be found. The models for the explanation of membership can bind a moderate 11 per cent variance in both societies; those for the explanation of active engagement can only bind a variance of 8 per cent in each case. However, there are differences with regard to the levels of significance and effect sizes. In Eastern Germany, only two indicators prove to be significant as regards membership. Church attendance exerts an outstanding influence, and the probability of becoming a member of an organisation is something that increases as political interest grows. In Western Germany, in addition to the similarly outstanding influence of church attendance, education, political interest, family integration, occupation and age variables all play a role. When we turn to active engagement, the particularities of Eastern Germany are even more striking. Only church attendance exerts a significant positive influence: all other variables prove non-significant.

The separate analyses of old and new federal states clearly show that the theoretically relevant determinants are less significant in Eastern Germany than in Western Germany. When comparing the indicator effects of East Germany, West Germany and France, it seems that the variables are most appropriate in West Germany and then in France, with East Germany in final position.

Conclusion

Irrespective of the different points of view concerning the necessary extent of civic engagement, participation and democracy are intrinsically bound up. Once it has been agreed that participation and democracy go hand in hand, the questions arises: how is it that social participation is so similar in France and Germany? In both countries, people have a broad range of opportunities at their disposal for taking part in shaping social circumstances. Ever since the early nineteenth century, a diversified system of voluntary organisations – encompassing social and professional associations, citizens' initiatives and political parties – has developed. The close network of voluntary organisations adds to the integration of people in society and helps to communicate values, norms and behaviour (Putnam 2000). Good conditions exist to improve the quality of democracy and the efficiency of society by stimulating social engagement (Gabriel *et al.* 2002; Norris 2002). Although both France and Germany can lay claim to numerous organisations, the number in France is huge, far exceeding German ones. As for active participation, there are considerable differences between German and French respondents. Members and participants are practically identical in France, while there is a huge difference in Germany, with a large number of members, but few active participants. Furthermore, differing trends are to be observed in the two countries. In France, both forms of social participation show signs of a slight increase. In Germany, however, the opposite is true: there is a strong decline in members as well as a downward trend for actively involved people.

Logistic regression analyses were conducted to establish whether these differences in behaviour also result in differences regarding the explanation of social engagement. In the process, the following question comes to the fore: what encourages people to become socially involved? This question deserves to be treated in a differentiated form, distinguishing between mere members as opposed to active participants. As we know from social capital theory, active engagement exerts a particularly positive influence on democracy. This leads on to the following question: which specific determinants are responsible for active and which for passive engagement?

It has already been explicated that the question of determinants has not yet been analysed in a comparison of France and Germany. Empirical findings about the determining factors of social participation of activists as opposed to passive individuals are not yet available.

The analyses described here indicate that there are both differences and similarities between France and Germany in terms of social engagement. The theoretical model developed by Verba/Schlozman/Brady, which forms the basis of the analysis, has only moderate explanatory power as regards the two countries. All three components – *resources, motives* and *networks* – exert a significant influence on social participation in Germany. In contrast, the indicators chosen for the operationalisation of *motives* play no role in France. *Education* and *church attendance*, however, can be identified as major determinants in both countries.

Overall, a broad repertoire of participation options, used by the respective populations to a greater or lesser extent, has developed in Germany and France since the end of the Second World War. Whether the existing level of participation is considered sufficient depends, ultimately, on the criteria used. The normative theory of democracy provides no clear conceptions of how active the population has to be to meet democratic requirements. Seen against an international comparative and historic perspective, German and French civic participation levels are not problematic. It is important, however, that those who want to participate have the opportunity to do so. Democracy not only implies the right to social participation, but also the freedom not to make use of this right – whether on a temporary or more permanent basis.

References

Ajzen, I. and Fishbein, M. (1980) *Understanding Attitudes and Predicting Social Behavior,* Englewood Cliffs, N.J.: Prentice Hall.

Almond, G. A. and Verba, S. (1989) *The Civic Culture: Political attitudes and democracy in five nations,* London: Sage Publications.

Armingeon, K. (2007) 'Political participation and associational involvement' in J. W. van Deth, J. R. Montero and A. Westholm (eds) *Citizenship and Involvement in European Democracies: A comparative analysis,* London/New York: Routledge.

Burhoff, D. (2002) Vereinsrecht. Ein Leitfaden für Vereine und ihre Mitglieder, Herne/Berlin: Verlag Neue Wirtschafts-Briefe.

Coleman, J. (1988) 'Social capital in the creation of human capital', *American Journal of Sociology,* 94, Supplement: 95–100.

Curtis, J. E., Grabb, E. G. and Baer, D. E. (1992) 'Voluntary association membership in fifteen countries: A comparative analysis', *American Sociological Review,* 57(2): 139–152.

Dahl, R. A. (1971) *Polyarchy: Participation and opposition,* New Haven/London: Yale University Press.

Dekker, P. and van den Broek, A. (2006) 'Is volunteering going down?' in P. Ester, M. Braun and P. Mohler (eds) *Globalization, Value Change and Generations: A cross-national and intergenerational perspective,* Leiden: Brill.

Downs, A. (1957) *An Economic Theory of Democracy*, New York: Wiley.
Enquete-Kommission (2002) Zukunft des Bürgerschaftlichen Engagements' Deutscher Bundestag (ed.) *Bürgerschaftliches Engagement und Zivilgesellschaft*, Opladen: Leske and Budrich.
Gabriel, O. W., Kunz, V., Roßteutscher, S. and van Deth, J. W. (2002) *Sozialkapital und Demokratie: Zivilgesellschaftliche ressourcen im vergleich*, Wien: WUV-Universitätsverlag.
Gabriel, O. W. and Völkl, K. (2004) 'Auf der Suche nach dem Nichtwähler neuen Typs: Eine analyse aus anlass der bundestagswahl 2002' in F. Brettschneider, J. W. van Deth and E. Roller (eds) *Die Bundestagswahl 2002: Analysen der Wahlergebnisse und des Wahlkampfes*, Wiesbaden: Westdeutscher Verlag.
— (2008) 'Politische und soziale Partizipation' in O. W. Gabriel and S. Kropp (eds) *Die EU-Staaten im Vergleich*, 3rd edn., Wiesbaden: VS Verlag für Sozialwissenschaften.
Gensicke, T., Picot, S. and Geiss, S. (2008) *Freiwilliges Engagement in Deutschland 1999–2004: Ergebnisse der repräsentativen trenderhebung zu ehrenamt, freiwilligenarbeit und bürgerschaftlichem engagement*, Wiesbaden: VS Verlag für Sozialwissenschaften.
Inglehart, R. (1979) 'Political action: The impact of values, cognitive level, and social background' in S. Barnes and M. Kaase (eds) *Political Action: Mass participation in five western democracies*, Beverly Hills; London: Sage Publications.
— (1983) 'Changing paradigms in comparative political behavior' in A. W. Finifter (ed.) *Political Science: The state of the discipline*, Washington D.C.: American Political Science Association.
Kohler, U. (2008) 'Assessing the quality of European surveys: Towards an open method of coordination for survey data' in J. Alber, T. Fahey and C. Saraceno (eds) *Handbook of Quality of Life in the Enlarged European Union*, London: Routledge.
La Documentation Française (2002) *Centenaire de la loi du 1er juillet 1901 sur la liberté d'association*. Online. Available http://www.ladocumentationfrancaise.fr/dossiers/centenaire-loi-associations/index.shtml (Accessed 13th June 2011).
Marsh, A. and Kaase, M. (1979) 'Background of political action' in S. Barnes and M. Kaase (eds) *Political Action: Mass participation in five western democracies*, Beverly Hills; London: Sage Publications.
Milbrath, L. W. and Goel, M. L. (1977) *Political Participation: How and why do people get involved in politics?*, 2nd edn., Chicago: Rand McNally College Pub. Co.
Morales, L. and Geurts, P. (2007) 'Associational involvement' in J. W. van Deth, J. R. Montero and A. Westholm (eds) *Citizenship and Involvement in European Democracies: A comparative analysis*, London/New York: Routledge.

Nie, N. H., Powell, G. B. and Prewitt, K. (1969a) 'Social structure and political participation: developmental relationships', Part I, *American Political Science Review*, 63(1): 361–376.
— (1969b) 'Social structure and political participation: developmental relationships', Part II, *American Political Science Review*, 63(1): 808–832.
Norris, P. (2002) *The Democratic Phoenix: Reinventing political activism*, Cambridge: Cambridge University Press.
Olsen, M. E. (1982) *Participatory Pluralism: Political participation and influence in the United States and Sweden*, Chicago: Nelson-Hall.
Parry, G., Moyser, G. and Day, N. (1992) *Political Participation and Democracy in Britain*, Cambridge: Cambridge University Press.
Pattie, C., Seyd, P. and Whiteley, P. (2004) *Citizenship in Britain: Values, participation and democracy*, Cambridge: Cambridge University Press.
Putnam, R. (1993) *Making Democracy Work: Civic traditions in modern Italy*, Princeton: Princeton University Press.
— (2000) *Bowling Alone: The collapse and revival of American community*, New York: Simon and Schuster.
Schwarz, N. (1996) 'Ehrenamtliche Tätigkeiten und soziale Hilfeleistungen' in K. Blanke, M. Ehling and N. Schwarz (eds) *Zeit im Blickfeld: Ergebnisse Einer Repräsentativen Zeitbudgeterhebung*, Stuttgart/Berlin; Köln: Kohlhammer.
Tchernonog V. (2007) *Le paysage associatif français: Mesures et évolutions*, Paris: Dalloz.
Tocqueville, A. de (2000) *Democracy in America*, ed. H. C. Mansfield and D. Winthrop, Chicago: University of Chicago Press.
van Deth, J. W. (1996) 'Voluntary associations and political participation' in J. W. Falter and O. W. Gabriel (eds) *Wahlen und Politische Einstellungen in Westlichen Demokratien*, Frankfurt/Main: Lang.
— (2001) 'Soziale und politische Beteiligung: Alternativen, Ergänzungen oder Zwillinge?' in A. Koch, M. Wasmer and P. Schmidt (eds) *Politische Partizipation in der Bundesrepublik Deutschland: Empirische befunde und theoretische erklärungen*, Opladen: Leske and Budrich.
— (2004) 'Soziale Partizipation' in J.W. van Deth (ed.) *Deutschland in Europa: Ergebnisse des European Social Survey 2002–2003*, Wiesbaden: VS Verlag für Sozialwissenschaften.
Verba, S. and Nie, N. H. (1972) *Participation in America: Political democracy and social equality*, New York: Harper and Row.
Verba, S., Nie, N. H. and Kim, J. -O. (1978) *Participation and Political Equality: A seven-nation comparision*, Cambridge: Cambridge University Press.
Verba, S., Schlozman, K. L. and Brady, H. (1995) *Voice and Equality: Civic voluntarism in American politics*, Cambridge, Mass./London: Harvard University Press.

Zimmer, A. and Priller, E. (2007) *Gemeinnützige Organisationen im Gesellschaftlichen Wandel*, Wiesbaden: VS Verlag für Sozialwissenschaften.

Zukin, C., Keeter, S., Adolina, M., Jenkins, K. and Carpini, M. X. (2006) *A New Civic Engagement? Political participation, civic life and the changing American citizen*, Oxford: Oxford University Press.

chapter eight | turnout in parliamentary elections
Kerstin Völkl

Introduction

Voter turnout, the most widespread form of political participation, is – together with other forms of civic participation – a central component of behaviour research. According to Verba and Nie (1972), who distinguish between different forms of political participation (see Chapter One, Table 1.1 of this volume), voter turnout is characterised by the following qualitative features:

- it requires little individual initiative;
- its scope of outcome refers, respectively, to all members of the nation or political collective; and
- conflict arising from voter participation is considered to be relatively extensive.

It is thanks to this specific mode of interaction – voter turnout – that citizens are able to put pressure on their elite.

As far as voter turnout and participation are concerned, there are two points to be considered: first, the way universal franchise was institutionalised during the democratisation of modern nations and the organisation of the voting process and, secondly, the extent to which the electorate makes use of this participatory right (Dalton 2001: 35ff.; Nohlen 2004; Topf 1995).

In many Western democracies, since the 1980s, a change in voting behaviour has taken place: its core characteristics are the dissolution of traditional party attachments, increasing voter volatility and a disposition to abstain from voting (Dalton and Rohrschneider 1990; Franklin *et al.* 1992). This development runs counter to structural changes in Western society: the general educational level has risen since the beginning of the 1970s, access to political information has improved, and interest in politics has, at least, not declined (Mackie and Franklin 1992). Despite such significant improvements in preconditions, the proportion of non-voters in both France and Germany has been higher than ever before since the beginning of the 1990s. This marked abstention has received increased attention from researchers into political behaviour in both countries.

If the decrease in voter turnout has not been triggered by changes in the social structure, its underlying causes could be rooted in changes in the political orientations of the population and, more especially, in growing dissatisfaction with the political system, its institutions and the actors involved (Arzheimer 2002; Maier 2000). Since vote abstention stems from a variety of motives – which may vary from one election to the next – empirical research has to pose the classical question of electoral sociology that arises with each new election: 'How and why do people participate in politics?' In this contribution we will consider the motives that explain why French citizens abstain more often than Germans from going to the polls.

This chapter about non-voter patterns in Germany and France is divided into four parts.

1. An examination of parliamentary election participation in both countries from a long-term perspective, including a detailed presentation of each country's different suffrage regulations.
2. An attempt to explain vote abstention and the empirical testing problems involved.
3. The empirical analysis concerning parliamentary election vote abstention in the two countries.
4. A discussion of the consequences of vote abstention.

Data and approach

Two datasets are used in this study, with either aggregate or individual data being used, according to the type of analysis undertaken (see Chapter One, Figure 1.1). The analysis of the long-term turnout development of both countries is based on aggregate data from official electoral statistics. However, since this database does not allow the conditions of either voter turnout or vote abstention to be studied in depth, the pooled European Social Survey (ESS) cross-sectional dataset – which includes the results of representative surveys from the years 2002/2003, 2004/2005 and 2006/2007 – has been used instead. This particular dataset contains 14,000 cases, with 8,705 respondents from Germany (5,573 citizens from the former Federal Republic and 3,132 from the former East Germany) and 5,295 respondents from France. The analyses have been adjusted so that each survey period has the same weight, with both Germany and France being accorded the same weight when those countries are the subject of comparison. As East Germans are over-represented in all three survey periods compared with their West German counterparts, analyses based on the pooled dataset are weighted accordingly. Thus the number of respondents in Eastern and Western Germany corresponds to the real population distribution, thereby ensuring that any corresponding biases are eliminated.

There are both technical and substantial reasons for using a pooled dataset. The technical aspect concerns the effect of social desirability in questions about voter turnout. Even with large sample sizes, the tendency to report individual voting in line with presumed social norms produces only a small absolute number of non-voters, thereby setting narrow boundaries for multivariate analyses. By pooling three surveys, this problem can be mitigated, even if the disadvantageous distribution characteristics of the data remain. As for the substantial reasons, the use of a pooled dataset corresponds to the aim of testing the general determinants of vote abstention. The differences in constellations that occur from one election to the next are not particularly relevant for this analysis (Gabriel and Völkl 2004: 223).

Electoral law and voter turnout in France and Germany

The electoral law

Like all forms of political participation, going to the polls takes place in a certain institutional context, with characteristics that can either encourage or discourage turnout (Lijphart 1999; Norris 2004). Among the most well-known institutional determinants of voter turnout are electoral legislation and the technical definitions of the election process. Even though this chapter does not attempt to determine the effects of different institutional regulation in France and Germany, it is essential to offer a brief overview, as the two electoral systems show fundamental differences (see Chapter One). While a majority voting system is used to elect the *Assemblée Nationale députés* (National Assembly members) in the French semi-presidential[1] system, proportional representation is used in the parliamentary system of the Federal Republic to elect members of the *Bundestag* (Jesse 2008). The regulations of electoral laws in both countries are described in more detail below.

Electoral law regulations in France

Ever since 4th October 1958,[2] when the Constitution of the Fifth French Republic came into effect, the French have elected their *députés* (members) in accordance with the *scrutin majoritaire uninominal à deux tours* (the two-round Romanic majority voting system) for a legislative period of five years. One successful candidate from each constituency takes up a seat in the *Assemblée Nationale*. Winning a constituency requires obtaining the absolute majority of the votes cast; if no candidate attains an absolute majority in the first round, a run-off poll for those

---

1. The term 'semi-presidentialism' was coined by Maurice Duverger (1980). According to Lijphart (1999), however, the regime is not an independent one. In fact, the position of the president depends on the extent of the majority in the *Assemblée Nationale*. If the presidential party also has a parliamentary majority, the governmental system assumes presidential characteristics. If the parliamentary majority does not conform to the presidential party's political leanings, the governmental system resembles a parliamentary one.

2. The new constitution – introduced while a serious crisis for French domestic affairs, the Algerian War (1954–1962), was being waged – clearly bears the stamp of de Gaulle. The executive was strengthened substantially, especially by an increase in presidential powers at the expense of parliament. From a purely formal point of view, the *Assemblée Nationale députés* have the supreme legislative authority but, when there is a clear majority, their parliamentary functions are reduced. As a result of all these new measures, de Gaulle thought that the crisis – caused, in part, by the instability of the Fourth Republic and its frequently changing government and government majorities – (Grote 1995: 44ff.; Lüsebrink 2003: 136; Schild 2006: 68; Weisenfeld 1997: 130) could be resolved.

candidates who received at least 12.5 per cent of the first-round votes is then held one week later. Whereas the first-round requires an absolute majority vote, a simple majority suffices to win the constituency in the second round (*Code Électoral*; Grote 1995: 68ff.; Jesse 2008: 307; Müller-Brandeck-Bocquet and Moreau 2000: 85ff.; Nohlen 2004: 289; Schild 2006: 92ff.).[3]

Even the simple act of participating in the parliamentary elections is beset with greater hurdles for the French than for the Germans. The French have to register by a certain due date before they can go to the polls. This means that they have to enter their names on an electoral list in the constituency in which they either have their permanent residence or else have resided for at least the last six months (Appleton 2000: 207ff.). This regulation was mitigated in 1997 by a new law (*Code Électoral* L11-1), as between two and five million French citizens entitled to vote were not on the lists (*Code Électoral* L9 ff.; *Association Cidem, civisme et démocratie*).[4] The above-mentioned law states that every person reaching the age of eighteen will automatically be added to the lists. However, the problem of people having to register every time they relocate remains. This, as well as lack of motivation, is one of the major obstacles to voter turnout (Pierce 1995: 113).

The French, unlike the Germans, cannot vote by mail. Special provisions apply in the case of French citizens who reside abroad: they can register as *Français de l'étranger* at the embassy and then can cast their vote there on the day of the election. Citizens not living in France can thus vote for what is known as the *Assemblée des Français à l'étranger*, which is supposed to represent their interests and which delegates members to sundry institutions. Voting by mail is only possible for someone previously registered as a *Français de l'étranger*, who can then vote by mail for the *Assemblée des Français à l'étranger*; this is termed a *vote par correspondence*. An alternative for French citizens either not residing in France or unable to vote in the constituency, for which they are registered, is the principle of *vote par procuration*. This means that someone else living in the same municipality can be authorised to vote in lieu of the absentee. This authorisation has to be filled out at the embassy or some other official institution (such as the *gendarmerie* or the *Commisariat de Police*) and is then valid for a particular length of time (*Code Électoral* L9ff.; Ministère de l'Intérieur).

Another institutional regulation that can influence voting participation in France is the one that allows the president to dissolve the *Assemblée Nationale* and reorder another election. Although the prime minister has the right to be heard, the ultimate decision lies with the president alone. However, each dissolution

---

3. It was only the *Assemblée Nationale* election of March 1986 that was held on the basis of a proportional representation vote. The then left government thought it could keep the foreseeable loss of votes within a certain limit. The cohabitation government under Jacques Chirac, however, passed a resolution in July 1986 to revert to the Romanic majority voting system, which has been in effect ever since (Müller-Brandeck-Bocquet and Moreau 2000: 85; Schild 2006: 93).

4. For methodological reasons, estimating the total number of unregistered citizens is very difficult. Several studies on this subject assume that at least one out of every ten potential citizens entitled to vote is not registered (Appleton 2000: 208).

has to be justified by article 16 of the Constitution, which concerns the *exercice des pouvoirs exceptionnels*. Equally, a subsequent dissolution of the *Assemblée Nationale* in less than a year after the reordered election is not authorised (Grote 1995: 259ff.). The president's *de facto* right to dissolve this assembly has already led to the regular 5-year-cycle for *Assemblée Nationale* elections being shortened several times. In all, five of the twelve legislative elections held under the Fifth Republic took place ahead of time, because the President had reordered elections (Müller-Brandeck-Bocquet and Moreau 2000: 53ff.; Schild 2006: 75, 78). In the year 2000, a so-called *Quinquennat* (a five-year incumbency) was implemented to avoid cohabitation, as this often triggered the president's decision to dissolve parliament for tactical reasons.[5] This regulation was amended by the Law of 24th April 2001, which stipulates that the presidential elections have to be held before the parliamentary ones.

Electoral law regulations in Germany

German citizens generally elect their representatives for the *Bundestag* every four years in accordance with what is known as a 'personalised system of proportional representation'. Every voter has two votes. With their first vote – the personalised aspect, so to speak – citizens vote for a candidate in a constituency; the candidate who obtains a simple majority of the votes wins the constituency. In this way, the first half of the mandate of the *Bundestag* is allocated, the other half being decided on by proportional representation; then, with their second vote, citizens either vote for a party or an electoral list. This second vote is crucial to the composition of the *Bundestag* because the distribution of seats to the parties in the *Bundestag* depends on the ballots cast nationwide. Unlike what has frequently been alleged, this is no 'mixed system' consisting of proportional representation and first-past-the-post voting. The 'mixed system' form only applies if half of the *Bundestag* representatives are elected by a list and the other half is elected directly (Jesse 2008: 308; Korte 1999: 41ff.).

As regards technical election aspects, going to the polls is much easier for German citizens. 'Officially, all persons eligible to vote who are registered with the registration authorities on the thirty-fifth day before the election (qualifying date) must be entered in the voters' register' (*BWO* § 16 para. 1). The eligible German voters automatically receive a notification from the election authority. For those that cannot go to the polls on election day, the notification is accompanied by a postcard that can be returned to request absentee ballot documents. Requesting such documents is now possible online. The municipalities also accept oral ballot paper applications: 'Postal ballots can be handed in as standard letters to the German Federal Mail free of charge, if they are in the official voting envelope' (*BWG* § 36 para. 4), with postal charges being paid for by the federal state.

---

5. In a referendum, a vast majority of French citizens voted for a shortening of the president's incumbency from seven to five years, thus aligning it with the incumbencies of the *Assemblée Nationale deputés* (Hehn 2000; Schild 2006: 82).

Calling early an election for reasons of political stability requires a complicated procedure in which several constitutional bodies must participate. Parliament cannot dissolve itself; only the federal president can take this decision. According to article 68 of the Basic Law of Germany, the president may dissolve the *Bundestag* within 21 days, but this requires a proposal emanating from the German federal chancellor after the majority of the representatives have denied him their confidence (vote of confidence). The president, however, is not bound to accept the suggestion of the chancellor. Furthermore, the *Bundestag* can make use of what is known as a 'constructive vote of no confidence'. In this case the majority of the members of the *Bundestag* have to vote out the incumbent chancellor and, at the same time, elect a new one, which means that it is no longer necessary to dissolve the *Bundestag*. The federal president, however, has to accept the removal of the federal chancellor and agree to the appointment of the newly-elected one (Hesse and Ellwein 2004; Korte 1999; Rudzio 2006).

Similarities and effects of the electoral law regulations

Notwithstanding all the differences to be found in the electoral law and in the technical design of the French and German parliamentary election process, they share at least one point in common: eighteen is the minimum voting age. Further, both countries have avoided constitutional entrenchment of the electoral system; amending the electoral law is therefore easier than it would have been if the election mode had been determined by their respective constitutions (Jesse 2008: 306ff.).

How significant the different regulations ultimately are for voter turnout is difficult to assess. From a theoretical perspective, the assumption that electoral systems affect voter turnout could be perfectly plausible. For example, it is assumed that the existence of compulsory voting, the expression of competition within the party system and elections, and the threshold level of representation for small parties, all influence voter turnout level (Freitag 1996; Perea 2002).[6]

In practice, however, no clear trend is to be found. There are some countries in which a modification of the voting system has led to striking changes in voter turnout (e.g. Switzerland). Conversely, in other countries, no changes are observed after an alteration to the voting system (e.g. Germany 1912–1919, France; see Nohlen 2004: 377). However, since the impact of the institutional context on voter turnout is not the particular focus of this contribution, further reading may be found in: Blais 2006; Blais and Dobrzynska 1998; Jackman 1987; Lijphart 1997; International IDEA 1997; and Nohlen 2004.

Although contextual factors may provide some evidence of whether certain institutional arrangements encourage or restrain voter participation, they cannot

---

6. Hypotheses: more people vote in countries where voting is compulsory than in countries where this is not the case; democracies with big governments or government coalitions (measured by the proportion of votes) have a lower turnout than democracies with fairly 'small' government majorities (Freitag 1996: 111); the lower the small party representation threshold, the higher the turnout (Perea 2002).

indicate the specific causes of why individuals stay away from the ballot box (Powell 1980, 1986). This view is reinforced by the fact that, although the institutional arrangements in France and Germany have hardly changed throughout the period under consideration here, a decrease in parliamentary election participation in both countries has nevertheless been observed, as indicated in the following section.

The development of voter turnout in France and Germany

A direct comparison of voter turnout in France and Germany shows that the French are generally less involved in parliamentary elections than the Germans (see Figure 8.1). Participation in all elections to the *Assemblée Nationale* since the beginning of the Fifth Republic has averaged 74.1 per cent, which is 10.5 per cent less than average voter turnout in the Federal Republic from 1949 to 2005. Overall, the development of parliamentary election participation in France between 1958 and 2007 was somewhat irregular, i.e. characterised by a greater turnout decrease/increase from one election to the next compared with Germany. The highest parliamentary election turnout level was reached in both countries during the 1970s. In Germany, in 1972, 91.1 per cent of citizens participated in the election to the German *Bundestag*. In France, in 1978, 83.3 per cent of citizens cast their votes in the election to the *Assemblée Nationale*. The lowest level of participation in a parliamentary election was also reached in both countries in the recent election – in France in 2007 and in Germany in 2005 – and, with a 22.9 per cent decline

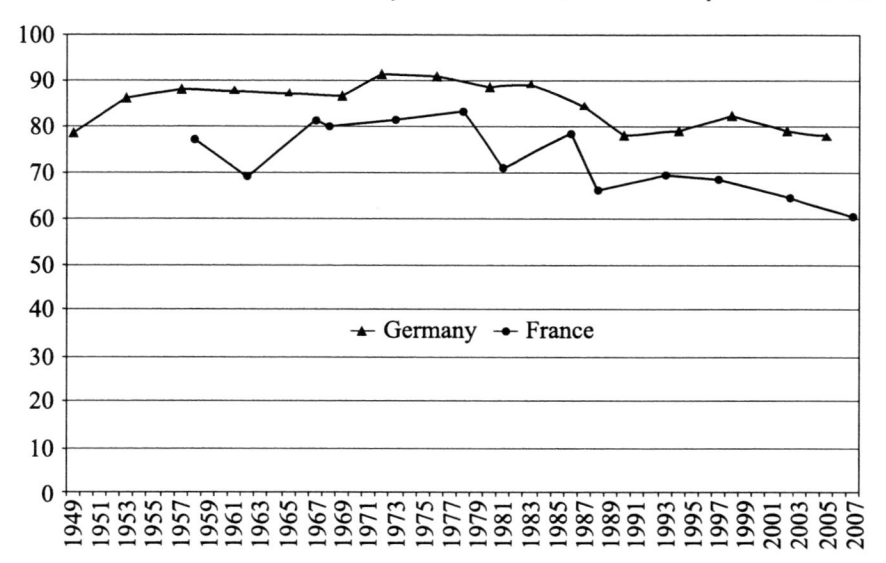

Figure 8.1: Voter turnout percentages in French and German parliamentary elections (1949–2007)

Source: Cevipof, http://www.bundeswahlleiter.de.

relative to its maximum level, the decline in France is particularly dramatic. In the parliamentary election of 2005, practically as many citizens participated as in the 1990 election, which was notable as the first election held in reunified Germany. All in all, German citizens are more active than their French counterparts when it comes to going to the polls.

However, these statements need to be qualified for both France and for Germany when any European comparisons are made. Certainly, there has been a significant decline in voter turnout since 2000, but as regards participation in parliamentary elections, this decline varies in each specific country (Filzmaier 2007). France ranks nineteenth out of the twenty-seven countries of the European Union as regards its participation level in parliamentary elections since 2000; Eastern European countries – Poland, Lithuania, Estonia, for example – have a significantly lower voter turnout.

As for Germany, compared with other European countries, its citizens participate very actively: average voter turnout in all parliamentary elections from 1949 to the last pre-Reunification election in the old West German *Länder* was 87 per cent, a very high level for countries not subject to compulsory voting (Leduc *et al.* 2002: 13ff.; Norris 2002: 35ff.; Franklin 2002). Only those countries with compulsory voting (e.g. Belgium, Luxembourg, Malta and Cyprus) show consistently high voter turnout, as would be expected.

Development in France

In an analysis of its voter turnout trend, France's institutional rules need to be considered. The possibility for the president to dissolve the *Assemblée Nationale* and precipitate new elections leads to close links between the presidential institutions and parliament. As a consequence, elections to the *Assemblée Nationale* cannot be understood without reference to the presidential elections, because it is these elections that primarily determine the political agenda in France. For this reason, the turnout figures of the presidential elections are given in Table 8.1 as a parliamentary election benchmark. The description of the long-term development of electoral participation in legislative elections is based on first-ballot participation rates. One element in support of this is that whereas the first ballot expresses the initial mobilisation of the voters, in the case of the second – ultimately legitimatising ballot – other relevant factors are involved. Generally speaking, one can assume that legislative elections in France will not attract the same interest as presidential elections and that, consequently, legislative elections will mobilise a lower proportion of the electorate (see Chapter Four).[7]

---

7. The presidential election of 1969 was the only one in which voter turnout fell below the level of the parliamentary elections. Although de Gaulle's right-wing camp had been greatly strengthened by the early *Assemblée Nationale* elections of June 1968 – which came in the wake of the students' uprising of May 1968 – de Gaulle himself, however, was soon dealt a deadly blow. In the referendum held on 27th April 1969, his proposals for regional reorganisation and for revision of the *Sénat* were defeated. As he had previously declared that he would resign in the wake of such

A good three-quarters of French citizens participated in the first election to the *Assemblée Nationale* in 1958. Following President de Gaulle's dissolution of that Assembly, new elections ahead of schedule took place four years later. Although the President obtained a more reliable majority in Parliament, voter turnout decreased by a significant 8.5 per cent, but in the next parliamentary election in 1967, turnout rose to 81.1 per cent. From the late 1960s until the late 1970s, France experienced a decade of high voter turnout in parliamentary elections, with participation rates attaining 80 per cent or more. In the 1967 election to parliament, de Gaulle's partisans only just gained the absolute majority. The spring of 1968, marked by student revolts and social unrest, was also taken advantage of by the Communist Party and trade unions. This ultimately led, after a series of resignation demands and abdication rumours, to the President dissolving parliament on May 30th 1968, justified on the basis of political instability and the threat of a communist coup (Weisenfeld 1997: 177ff.; Schild 2006: 78). Whereas voter turnout in the early elections of 1962 had undergone a marked decline, voter turnout in 1968 was stable at a high 80 per cent, a level that was maintained in the two legislative elections that followed in 1973 and 1978.

On May 22nd 1981, Mitterand, in order to avoid cohabitation, dissolved parliament in the wake of his election as president at the end of April 1981. The early elections that followed in June saw a sharp drop in voter participation, even though the Socialist Party won the absolute majority, as they had hoped. In the elections of 1986, held in accordance with the proportional representation system, significantly more people – 78.5 per cent – went to the polls. Starting in 1988, election participation rates fell to under 70 per cent. After his victory in the presidential election in April 1988, Mitterand once again dissolved parliament in order to obtain a favourable parliamentary majority. As in the years 1962 and 1981, this was obtained at the expense of voter turnout, which declined to 66.1 per cent.

In the 1993 election which – thanks to the victory of the RPR-UDF – led to a second cohabitation period in France, turnout was slightly better, standing at nearly 70 per cent. This period of cohabitation ended in 1995, when Chirac was elected president. In 1997, Chirac intended to avert impending election defeat in 1998 by dissolving the *Assemblée Nationale*, but this tactic was to be punished by the voters: the participation rate was low and Chirac was deprived of the parliamentary majority he had sought (Müller-Brandeck-Bocquet and Moreau 2000: 87; Schild 2006: 78ff.). The parliamentary election in June 2002, one month after Chirac's re-election, brought the hitherto lowest voter turnout: 64.4 per cent. In the 2007 parliamentary election, only 60.4 per cent of French voters went to the first ballot,

---

a referendum result, he did so before the definitive results were made known (Weisenfeld 1997: 189ff.; Schild 2006: 82). Voter turnout for Pompidou's election in June as the new president fell by seven percentage points to 77.6 per cent in the first round and to 68.9 per cent in the second. Since both candidates for the office of the president, Pompidou and Poher, belonged to the right-wing camp, and no candidate was nominated by the left wing, there was no traditional left-right competition in this election campaign. Moreover, both the Communist Party and the extreme-left parties had called on their supporters to abstain from voting (Appleton 2000: 214).

Table 8.1: Voter turnout percentages in parliamentary and presidential elections in France (1958–2007)

	1958	1962	1965	1967	1968	1969	1973	1974	1978	1981	1986	1988	1993	1995	1997	2002	2007
parl.	77.2	68.7	–	81.1	80.0	–	81.3	–	83.3	70.9	78.5	66.1	69.3	–	68.5	64.4	60.4
pres.	–	–	84.8	–	–	77.6	–	84.2	–	81.1	–	81.4	–	78.4	–	71.6	84.0

Notes: parl. = parliamentary election; pres. = presidential elections.
Source: Cevipof

Table 8.2: Voter turnout percentages in German Bundestag elections (1949–2005)

	1949	1953	1957	1961	1965	1969	1972	1976	1980	1983	1987	1990	1994	1998	2002	2005
G*	78.5	86.0	87.8	87.7	86.8	86.7	91.1	90.7	88.6	89.1	84.3	77.8	79.0	82.2	79.1	77.7

Notes: *1987 West Germany until 1987, 1990 Germany (G) as a whole from 1990 onwards.
Source: http://www.bundeswahlleiter.de.

the lowest participation rate at this time. Apparently, following a period of continuous election campaigns for the presidential elections, the parliamentary election campaign was of only little interest to the French. The expected victory of President Sarkozy's camp may also have played a role (*Stuttgarter Zeitung* 10th June 2007).

Looking at the elections to the *Assemblée Nationale* over time and taking the short-term fluctuations of the Fifth Republic into account, participation rates have been in steady decline since 1978.

Development in Germany

As far as German voter participation levels are concerned, two initial phases can be found in the history of the Federal Republic, starting from its foundation in 1949, after the Second World War, to Reunification in 1990. The first phase is from 1949 to 1976; the second begins in 1976. In the first federal elections, in 1949, turnout was 78.5 per cent, well below the 88.8 per cent attained in the last *Reichstag* election in 1933. Until the federal elections of 1972, the participation rate had risen from one election to the next. In 1972, 91.1 per cent of eligible voters participated in the *Bundestag* elections and four years later this rate was only marginally lower. Since then, the recorded decline in voter turnout has been variously interpreted; some observers see this as indicative of a crisis in party democracy (Wiesendahl 1998); others, however, see it as a sign of political normalisation after a period of over-politicisation (Roth 1992).

The first election to the *Bundestag* in reunified Germany in 1990 marked the start of a third phase in which turnout dropped back to its 1949 level, with just 78.6 per cent in Western Germany. Admittedly, the downward trend in the old states came to a halt at the following federal election. With a participation rate of 80.5 per cent, however, this was no recovery. In 1998, turnout increased again slightly but, in the next *Bundestag* election in 2002, it dropped back to the 1994 level. It was assumed that, because of the early *Bundestag* election of 18th September 2005, voter turnout would increase: dissolution of the *Bundestag* was a rare situation that should thus attract increased attention; these assumptions, however, were not to be confirmed. Instead, the participation rate was lower than in 2002; at 77.7 per cent, the 2005 figure represents the lowest turnout ever for a parliamentary election, whether in pre- or post-reunified Germany.

There are striking differences in the election participation of the old and new German states. The first free election of a national parliament in the post-war history of East Germany took place on 18th March 1990. At 93.4 per cent, voter turnout was the highest ever in Germany's election history. Since then, however, it has declined considerably and in the first all-German *Bundestag* election attained only 74.5 per cent. In the 1994 federal elections, it fell again by 1.9 per cent, but four years later the downward trend stopped. Then in the 2002 *Bundestag* election, a further decline of 7.2 per cent was recorded. As in the old West German states, participation rates in the 2002 *Bundestag* election resembled those measured in 1994. While participation figures in East Germany – unlike those in West Germany – increased slightly from 2002 to 2005, they are generally below the reported values for the old West German states. Overall, voter turnout in East Germany fell by 20 per cent between the election to the People's Chamber in March 1990 and the German Federal election of the same year, falling again slightly in the subsequent period. Compared to the West German population, the proportion of citizens who voted in the *Bundestag* elections has seen dramatic fluctuations in the last fifteen years. Obviously, the core civic role element – voting in elections – is significantly better institutionalised and more widely accepted in West Germany than it is in the new East German states (no tables have been shown).

Total German participation rates, despite long-term decline, are relatively high when compared with those of other democracies. However, the fact remains that not since the Federal Republic of Germany first came into being have so few citizens participated in *Bundestag* elections. Overall, this post-reunification trend can be interpreted as one of long-term low level stability.

Explanatory approaches for vote abstention at the individual level

In view of the special importance elections have in countries with a democratic constitution, the decline in voter turnout – both in Germany as well as in France – is an issue for two reasons. First, for the authorities, elections represent a mechanism that is critical in ensuring their legitimacy. By means of their votes, citizens transfer political power to a certain group which, for a set period of time, representatively makes decisions on behalf of the whole of society. Secondly, for many citizens, voting is their only way of being politically involved and thus able to exert a certain influence. As a result of their ballots, citizens can decide both on the formation of the government and on party influence so that the competing parties can enforce their political programmes in parliament (Arzheimer and Falter 2003; Caballero 2005).

The political importance of vote abstention in elections has long been the subject of controversy in the political sciences and the politically-interested public. As to the question of whether a low, or declining, voter turnout poses a problem for the stability and functioning of a democracy or whether it is a sign of democratic normality may be difficult to answer. As international comparisons show, some traditional democracies, like the United States or Switzerland, have very low participation rates, whereas in Denmark or Sweden, the participation rates are relatively high (Dalton 2001: 35–39; Franklin 2002: 150; Norris 2002: 53–54). No systematic correlation between the stability of a democracy and voter turnout level can be detected at an aggregate level.

Problems arise primarily in the following circumstances:

- when several population groups make very different use of their right to participate in electing their political leaders; and
- when this gives rise to different possibilities of implementing political demands; or
- when vote abstention indicates alienation from the political system and its institutions.

An empirical analysis of the respective determinants of voter turnout or vote abstention is required to ascertain which of the above is involved. Consequently, reliable statements about the effects on a democracy of increasing/decreasing voter turnout require an analysis of the causes of vote abstention (Kleinhenz 1995; Gabriel and Völkl 2004).

In studies from the 1970s, researchers had already come to the conclusion that the particular form and extent of citizens' political participation both vary in accordance with their social affiliations and political attitudes (Milbrath and Goel 1982; Verba et al. 1978). Verba, Schlozman and Brady (1995) developed a model integrating different theoretical approaches to explain why some people opt for an active political role and others for a passive one (see Chapter One). According to Gabriel, this is a medium-range theoretical approach that considers both environmental and personality factors. Verba, Schlozman and Brady (1995) distinguish three variable complexes: resources, motives and integration into mobilised networks. The more distinctive these three factors are, the more likely it is that political commitment will occur.

Since the explanatory model has already been presented in Chapter One, the following remarks will largely be limited to the variables available in the pooled ESS dataset to operationalise resources, motives and integration in networks.[8] In addition to 'income', a material resource, and 'education', an intellectual resource, such socio-demographic variables as 'use of political information spread by mass media'[9], 'occupational prestige'[10], 'age', and 'gender', are also included in the analysis. Additionally, the variable of 'belonging to an ethnic minority' will be taken into account as a possible explanatory factor. The reason for increased participation is, therefore, that resource-strong groups – on the basis of characteristics such as knowledge and reputation – have better contacts with the political leadership and possess certain political attitudes that have a positive effect on participation. Only when socio-economic resources are implemented in cognitive resources does this transformation lead to participation (Gabriel 2004: 322).

Unfortunately, the different aspects of supporting or inhibiting participation motives can only be researched from the ESS dataset within certain limits because certain questions had not been addressed in that study.[11] For the operationalisation of political attitudes, for example, the term of 'political interest' is used (Zaller

---

8. All indicators of resources, motives and networks are shown in single inverted commas.
9. This variable distinguishes between television viewers on the one hand and newspaper readers on the other hand – it cannot be ruled out that one or both of these exert different effects. For the use of political information as a resource indicator, see Schmitt-Beck and Schrott 1994 and Ohr et al. 2005.
10. This variable is used as a substitute for the subjective class membership, which lacking in the ESS dataset.
11. The concept of 'external efficacy' – which measures the openness of the political system from the citizen's point of view – has to be dispensed with in the absence of appropriate indicators as well as in the light of the analysis of Inglehart's affirmations that people with post-materialist value preferences are politically more active than those with materialistic or mixed value orientations.

1992). The effect on participation through 'recognition of democratic values and norms' (Sniderman 1975: 254ff.) is measured by the 'satisfaction with democracy' variable, which, however, applies less at the level of values and more at the level of performance of democratic attitudes. As the pooled ESS dataset contains no variable to empirically verify the 'theory of planned behaviour' of Ajzen and Fishbein (1980) – according to which endogenous values are necessary for the explanation of human behaviour – the concept of 'internal efficacy' is sometimes used as an approximation for subjective expectations, to determine the effectiveness of participation (Gabriel 2004: 325; Vetter 1997). As far as motivational determinants of political participation are concerned, other variables that cover the institutional integration of individuals are taken into account (Campbell *et al.* 1954, 1960); these include the 'strength of party identification' and 'confidence in institutions of the party or constitutional state'.

With regard to political participation, the networks to be found in the direct personal environment (family, school) and in voluntary organisations (Gabriel 2004: 326ff.; van Deth 2001) are especially significant. Since the pooled ESS dataset only contains the 'membership in trade unions and/or political parties' variable, the influence of social networks on political behaviour can only be reviewed to a limited extent.[12] Note that 'involvement in social organisations' was not surveyed at all. Family involvement is operationalised in references to existing 'partnership' and the 'number of persons in the household'. It is also possible to measure integration into religious networks in terms of 'frequency of church attendance', and to measure integration into the labour market under the heading 'employment'.[13] In addition, the ESS dataset includes variables that measure network of friends. These include 'frequency of participation in social activities' and 'meetings with third parties'; 'interpersonal trust' and the 'support of pro-social values and norms' ('income equality') are also explanatory factors in the analysis.

---

12. Although various indicators to operationalise the commitment of volunteers in the national modules of the first and third ESS-wave are available, these occasional surveys do not, unfortunately, allow any general statement to be made about the causes of vote abstention from 2002 to 2007, which is the goal of the present contribution.

13. It is assumed that unemployed persons, retirees and housewives are less politically active than employed persons.

Explanatory factors of vote abstention from an empirical perspective

The following section empirically tests explanatory approaches going back to Verba, Schlozman and Brady (1995); they considered the presence of various resources, motives and integration in social networks, and incorporated all into a complex analytical model. A latent question then arises: which approach could best serve as a comprehensive model? Apart from the threefold comprehensive model, a country-specific model could also be envisaged. This means that the individual determinants of the various approaches are relevant for vote abstention in France and Germany. It seems appropriate to consider all three approaches simultaneously because of the optimum comparability between the countries and because it enables the examination of possible interactions between the different approach variables. Additionally, an integrative explanatory approach seems apposite because the three sets of variables are complementary rather than mutually exclusive.

Logistic regression offers an appropriate analysis method, since the dependent variable – voter turnout in the last national election – is a dummy variable. The focus is on whether 'going to the polls' can be attributed to the same causes in France and Germany, or whether there are other explanatory factors involved. In Germany, there is an additional question: are the old and the new federal states similar or different as regards the reasons for voting? If we are able to detect differences, the next issue to analyse is whether West or East Germany resembles France relative to the factors that determine voter turnout.

Explanatory factors of voter turnout in France and Germany

Before interpreting the results of the cross-country analyses, attention was paid to the specific country effect in terms of voter turnout. For this purpose, a model was calculated in which, besides indicators for resources, motives and networks, a country dummy variable was introduced, with Germany coded as '1' and France as '0'. As the analysis shows (see Table 8.3, column 2), a significant difference exists between France and Germany with regard to the explanation of vote casting in elections, as the Germans are more likely than the French to go to the polls. Besides a country-specific effect, however, a close examination shows that there are other factors that play an explanatory role in the casting of votes in elections. Considered on a cross-country level, these include, in particular, 'age', 'political interest', 'existing party identification' as well as 'membership in a party'. The extent to which this applies to both France and Germany is described in greater detail in Table 8.3.

As measured by Nagelkerkes R^2, a reference for the overall explanatory power of the model, it seems that Verba, Schlozman and Brady offer the better explanation for German voter turnout (see Table 8.3, columns 3 and 4). While the model finds a 31 per cent variance for Germany, the explanatory power of 22 per cent is

Table 8.3: Determinants of vote abstention in France and Germany (2002/03–2004/05–2006/07 (in Exp(B))

		F + G	F	G
	Country dummy	1.44[a]	–	–
Resources	Education level	1.04	1.13	2.44[a]
	Income	1.21[b]	1.06	1.28[b]
	Age	4.34[a]	7.40[a]	2.02[a]
	Gender	.89[c]	.89	.80[b]
	Occupational prestige	1.37[a]	1.13	1.57[a]
	Pol. TV-consumption	.78[c]	.71[c]	.78
	Pol. newspaper reading	.91	1.00	.89
	Ethnic minority	.41[a]	.37[a]	.45[a]
Motives	Political interest	4.74[a]	3.50[a]	8.08[a]
	Internal efficacy	1.13	1.06	1.30
	Democracy satisfaction	1.23	.90	2.01[a]
	Existing party ID	3.82[a]	2.85[a]	6.53[a]
	Trust in party state	1.25	1.22	1.42
	Trust in constitutional state	1.66[b]	1.76[c]	1.56
Networks	Party membership	4.38[a]	4.22[b]	3.94[c]
	Labour union member	1.30[c]	1.31	1.27
	Interpersonal confidence	1.22	.78	1.63[c]
	Income equality	1.10	1.41[c]	.92
	Existing partnership	1.32[a]	1.38[b]	1.28[b]
	No. household members	1.01	1.00	1.04
	Freq. of social meetings	1.39[b]	1.38[c]	1.18
	Part. in social activities	1.63[a]	1.16	2.23[a]
	Freq. church attendance	1.47[a]	1.63[a]	1.28[c]
	Paid job	1.43[a]	1.49[b]	1.31[b]
	Unemployment	.83	.83	.92
	Retirement	1.38[b]	1.48[c]	1.44[c]
	Housewife	1.00	.88	1.08
Constant		.09[a]	.13[a]	.06[a]
Nagelkerkes R^2		.25	.22	.31
N		11,113	4,199	6,914

Notes: level of significance: a = $p \leq 0.001$; b = $p \leq 0.01$; c = $p \leq 0.05$; n.s. = not significant. F = France; G = Germany; Pol. = Political; No. = Number of; Freq. = Frequency; Part. = Participation.
Source: pooled ESS data sets 2002/03–2004/05–2006/07.

much lower for France. Apparently, other reasons, not taken into account in this model, are of special relevance for voter turnout in France.

A closer examination of the analysis results shows that there are some similarities in the explanation of French and German voter turnout. As cross-country regression analysis has already shown, 'age', 'political interest', 'existing party identification', as well as 'membership in a party', each exert a significant influence on voting in national elections in both countries; the extent of influence, however, varies with each country. In Germany, the two motivational determinants – 'political interest' and 'party identification' – represent the main explanatory factors; the likelihood of electoral participation rising with increased political interest and existing party identification. In France, this correlation also exists, but is far less marked than in Germany. In France, 'age' plays a dominant role in the decision to vote in national elections: the older people are, the more likely it is that they will go to the polls, whereas, in Germany, 'age' exerts a lesser influence. 'Membership of a party' has a relatively similar effect on voter turnout in both countries. Moreover, in both countries, people who 'live in a partnership', who 'participate in social meetings or activities' or who practise 'church attendance', as well as those with 'paid jobs' or 'retirees' are more likely to vote than others. In addition, those who belong to an 'ethnic minority' participate less frequently in elections in two countries, although this effect is somewhat more secondary. All in all, the collective explanation factors in France are fairly evenly divided between resources, motives and integration in social networks while, in Germany, motives predominate.

There are factors common to both countries, but there are also certain differences between Germany and France regarding an explanation for turnout. In addition to 'age', 'education', 'income' and 'professional prestige' are relevant to voting in Germany. Equally, a small but significant gender effect can be observed in Germany, with women being more likely to vote than men. In France, none of these factors exert any significant influence on electoral participation. Instead, a lower level of 'consumption of political TV' content has a more positive effect on voting than a high amount. Besides certain commonalities in Motives, there are also differences. Whereas 'satisfaction with democracy' has a positive effect on voter turnout in Germany, in France it is 'confidence in institutions of the constitutional state', such as the judiciary and the police, which has a positive effect. Apart from the common explanation factors, which have a similar influence in both countries, 'confidence in fellow citizens' increases the likelihood of Germans going to the polls, whereas 'support of pro-social values and norms' (measured by 'income equality') has a positive effect on voting in France.

All in all, the model of Verba, Schlozman and Brady (1995) explains German voter turnout better. 'Age', 'political interest' and 'existing party identification' as motivational indicators, and 'party membership' as a network indicator, are the main explanatory factors for going to the polls in both countries. However, on closer inspection, some differences between Germany and France do emerge.

While turnout in Germany is mainly attributed to motives, in France voter turnout is best explained by a threefold combination of all the components – resources, motives and networks.

Explanatory factors of voter turnout in East Germany

Separate analyses for West and East Germany show that the explanatory factors for voter turnout in West Germany are the same as those for the whole of Germany (no tables have been shown). In view of the weighted analyses for Germany as whole, in which West Germany is taken into account for 80 per cent and East Germany for 20 per cent, this is unsurprising. The essential difference between Germany as whole and West Germany is that the frequent consumption of political TV content now has a weak negative effect on election participation in West Germany – as is also the case in France. A clearer explanatory pattern of voting emerges for East German citizens. Whereas thirteen of the twenty-seven explanatory factors listed exercise a significant influence on French turnout, compared with seventeen on West German turnout, this figure falls to a mere five in East Germany. Although the number of explanatory factors is very low in East Germany, with a Nagelkerkes R^2 of .28, the explanatory power of the general model for East Germany lies between that of West Germany (.33) and France (.22).

Motivational determinants constitute the largest battalion of factors explaining why East Germans go to the polls, followed by network factors, with resources being almost irrelevant. With regard to motives, 'existing party identification' is a major explanatory factor – as is also the case in West Germany. 'Political interest', which plays the most important role in West Germany, also has a significant effect on voting in East Germany. The influence of 'trust in institutions of the constitutional state' in East Germany is comparable to France; the more citizens trust in the institutions of the constitutional state, the more likely they are to go to the polls. This correlation is even stronger in East Germany than in France, but it is not significant in West Germany. Furthermore, 'integration into social and religious networks' plays an important role. In East Germany, contrary to what pertains in West Germany and France, 'participating in social activities' and the 'frequency of social meetings' both represent the most significant factors for participation in national elections. Religious ties are also of importance as an explanatory factor for the behaviour of East German citizens. The weak influence of the 'frequency of church attendance' can be verified for France as well. In West Germany, on the other hand, no significant correlation exists.

Taking the separate analyses for East and West Germany into account, the summary outlined above should be revised insofar as far fewer explanatory factors influence voter turnout in East Germany than in West Germany or France. In addition to motives, 'social and religious integration into networks' also influences voter participation in East Germany. Nevertheless, the Verba, Schlozman and Brady (1995) model still offers a slightly better explanation of voter turnout in East Germany than it does for France, but a little less so as regards West Germany. It is remarkable to note that the probability of voter turnout in East Germany seems to be largely independent of resources.

Summary and conclusions

This contribution concerning the vote abstention pattern in France and Germany had two goals: first, to describe the different German and French institutional election arrangements and, based on those findings, describe voter turnout based on a long-term perspective; and, secondly, to explain vote abstention in Germany and France at an individual level.

The description of voter turnout in Germany shows German citizens participate very actively in parliamentary elections – even on the basis of a European and international comparison. This applies to East Germany as well, although the participation rates there are regularly below those to be found in West Germany. Voter turnout in France, compared to Germany as a whole, is lower and shows greater fluctuations. However, since the early 1990s, both countries have undergone a significant decline in voter turnout. In their last national parliamentary elections (2007 and 2005), France and Germany each experienced their lowest voter turnout ever.

Empirical analysis aimed at addressing the question of why some people participate in elections while others do not, has revealed certain similarities between Germany and France, as well as features that are specific to each country's population. Motives play a key role for in the explanation of election participation in both countries, with 'political interest' and 'party identification' proving particularly relevant. Another explanatory factor in France is 'age', a resource that influences voting turnout there. As regards integration into networks, this plays a relatively important role in both France and Germany, with 'party membership' being the most important network determinant in the two countries.

Finally, the question to be addressed is: to what extent are these results a cause for concern? The decline in voter turnout could reflect many kinds of dissatisfaction expressed by citizens (Feist 1994). It could, however, also be that declining voter turnout is a sign of normalisation within a political system. Its citizens, being satisfied with democracy, feel that they no longer need to participate in every election and – having become politically disinterested – numbers of them abstain from voting (Roth 1992). This may be what is occurring in both Germany and France. Although 'existing party identification' and/or 'membership in a party' exercise a positive influence on voting, these two criteria are not so much symptomatic of a crisis in a politically-disappointed society, but rather of a changing society, whose citizens are less willing to commit themselves, in a long-term perspective, to a political organisation. Even though the two criteria of 'satisfaction with democracy' and 'confidence in institutions of the constitutional state' influence the probability of going to the polls, they rank relatively low when compared to other factors. All in all, the great explanatory power of the motive 'political interest' in Germany and the resource 'age' in France, are, in fact, signs of normalisation.

Appendix

Operationalisation of the variables

Vote abstention:
Some people don't vote nowadays for one reason or another. Did you vote in the last [country] national* election in [month/year]? Yes (1), No (0).
* This refers to the last election of a country's primary legislative assembly.

Resources:
Education level:
What is the highest level of education you have achieved?

Income:
Using this card, if you add up the income from all sources, which letter describes your household's total net income?
If you don't know the exact figure, please give an estimate. Use the part of the card that you know best: weekly, monthly or annual income. Below average (0), average (0.5), above average (1).

Age (computed from year of birth):
And in what year were you born? 14–20 years (0), 21–24 years (0.11), 25–29 years (0.22), 30–34 years (0.33), 35–39 years (0.44), 40–44 years (0.56), 45–49 years (0.67), 50–59 years (0.78), 60–69 years (0.89), > 70 years (1).

Gender:
Female (0), Male (1).

Professional prestige:
What is/was the name or title of your main job?
Based on the code of occupation in reference to the ICSO-classification (according to Treiman) prestige values can be generated. The ISCO-classification empirically spans from 14.4 (low) to 78.9 (high). The variable was divided into quartiles.

Political television consumption:
And again on an average weekday, how much of your time watching television is spent watching news or programmes about politics and current affairs?
No time at all (0); Less than ½ hour (0.25); ½ hour to 1 hour (0.5); More than 1 hour, up to 1½ hours (0.75); More than 1½ hours, up to 2 hours; More than 2 hours, up to 2½ hours; More than 2½ hours, up to 3 hours; More than 3 hours (1).

Political newspaper consumption:
And how much of this time is spent reading about politics and current affairs?
No time at all (0), Less than ½ hour (0.25); computed mean value (0.5); ½ hour to 1 hour (0.75); More than 1 hour, up to 1½ hours (0.75); More than 1½ hours, up to

2 hours; More than 2 hours, up to 2½ hours; More than 2½ hours, up to 3 hours; More than 3 hours (1).

Ethnic Minority:
Do you belong to a minority ethnic group in [country]? Yes (1), No (0).
For these variables the mean value was substituted for the categories 'answer denied'/'don't know'/'no answer'.

Motives:
Political interest:
How interested would you say you are in politics – very interested (1), quite interested (0.67), not very interested (0.33) or not at all interested (0)?

Internal efficacy:
Index of two variables: How often does politics seem so complicated that you can't really understand what is going on? (scale inverted); How difficult or easy do you find it to make your mind up about political issues? Very incompetent (0), incompetent (0.25), neither incompetent nor competent (0.5); competent (0.75), very competent (1).

Satisfaction with democracy:
And, on the whole, how satisfied are you with the way democracy works in [country]? 11-point scale of 0-1; extremely dissatisfied (0), extremely satisfied (1).

Existing Party Identification:
Is there a particular political party you feel closer to than all the other parties? Yes (1), No (0).

Trust in institutions:
Please tell me on a score of 0–10 how much you personally trust each of the institutions I read out. 0 means you do not trust an institution at all, and 10 means you have complete trust.

Trust in institutions of the party state:
Index of two variables: [country]'s parliament, politicians. 11-point scale of 0–1; no trust at all (0), complete trust (1).

Trust in institutions of the constitutional state:
Index of two variables: the legal system, the police. 11-point scale of 0-1; no trust at all (0), complete trust (1).

Networks:
Member of party:
Are you a member of any political party?
Yes (1), No (0).

Member of trade union:
Are you or have you ever been a member of a trade union or similar organisation?
Yes (currently or previously) (1), No (0).

Interpersonal trust:
Index of three variables:
Generally speaking, would you say that most people can be trusted, or that you can't be too careful in dealing with people?
Please tell me on a score of 0 to 10, where 0 means you can't be too careful and 10 means that most people can be trusted.
Do you think that most people would try to take advantage of you if they got the chance, or would they try to be fair?;
Would you say that most of the time people try to be helpful or that they are mostly looking out for themselves?;
0 to 3 = low (1), 4 to 6 = middle (0), 7 to 10 = high (0)

Against equal income levels:
Please say to what extent you agree or disagree with each of the following statement:
The government should take measures to reduce differences in income levels.
Strongly disagree (0), disagree (0.25), neither agree nor disagree (0.5), agree (0.75), strongly agree (1).

Partnership:
What relationship is he/she to you? Lives with husband/wife/partner at household grid; Yes (1), No (0).

Number of household members:
Including yourself, how many people – including children – live here regularly as members of this household?
1 (0), 2 (0.25), 3 (0.5), 4 (0.75), 5–12 (1).

Frequency of social meetings:
How often do you meet socially with friends, relatives or work colleagues?
Never, less than once a month (0), once a month (0.2), several times a month (0.4), once a week (0.6), several times a week (0.8), every day (1).

Participation in social activities:
Compared to other people of your age, how often would you say you take part in social activities?
Much less than most (0), less than most (0.25), about the same (0.5), more than most (0.75), much more than most (1).

Frequency of church attendance:
Apart from special occasions such as weddings and funerals, about how often do you attend religious services nowadays?
Never (0), not very often (0.25), only on special holy days (0.5), at least once a month (0.75), once a week, more than once a week, every day (1).

Paid work, unemployed, retiree, housewife:
Which of these descriptions applies to what you have been doing fort the last 7 days?
Paid work (1), unemployed (actively/not actively looking for a job) (1), retired (1), doing housework, looking after children or other persons (1).

References

Ajzen, I. and Fishbein, M. (1980) *Understanding Attitudes and Predicting Social Behavior*, Englewood Cliffs, N.J.: Prentice Hall.
Appelton, A. M. (2000) 'The France doesn't vote: Nonconsumption in the electoral market' in M. S. Lewis-Beck (ed.) *How France Votes*, New York/London: Chatham House Publishers.
Arzheimer, K. (2002) *Politikverdrossenheit: Verwendung und Empirische Relevanz Eines Politikwissenschaftlichen Begriffs*, Wiesbaden: Westdeutscher Verlag.
Arzheimer, K. and Falter, J. W. (2003) 'Wahlen und Wahlforschung' in H. Münkler (ed.) *Politikwissenschaft: Ein Grundkurs*, Reinbek: Rowohlt.
Association Cidem (2006) *Civisme et Démocratie*. Online. Available http://democratie.cidem.org/documents/CP_inscriptions_2006.pdf (accessed 21 January 2007).
Blais, A. (2006) 'What affects voter turnout?', *Annual Review of Political Science*, 9: 111–25.
Blais, A. and Dobrzynska, A. (1998) 'Turnout in electoral democracies', *European Journal of Political Research*, 3: 239–61.
BWG (*Bundeswahlgesetz*). Online. Available http://www.bundeswahlleiter.de/de/bundestagswahlen/rechtsgrundlagen/bundeswahlgesetz.html (accessed 26 April 2011).
BWO (*Bundeswahlordnung*). Online. Available http://www.bundeswahlleiter.de/de/bundestagswahlen/downloads/rechtsgrundlagen/bundeswahlordnung.pdf (accessed 26 April 2011).
Caballero, C. (2005) 'Nichtwahl' in J. W. Falter and H. Schoen (eds) *Handbuch Wahlforschung: Ein einführendes Handbuch*, Wiesbaden: VS Verlag für Sozialwissenschaften.
Campbell, A., Converse, P. E., Miller, W. E. and Stokes, D. E. (1960) *The American Voter*, New York: Wiley.
Campbell, A., Gurin, G. and Miller, W. E. (1954) *The Voter Decides*, Evanston, Ill.: Row, Peterson and Company.
Code Électoral. Online. Available http://www.affaires-publiques.com/textof/codelect/codelectoral.html (accessed 26 April 2011).
Dalton, R. J. (2001) *Citizen Politics: Public opinion and political parties in the United States, Great Britain, West Germany, and France*, Chatham, N. J.: Chatham House Publishers.
Dalton, R. J. and Rohrschneider, R. (1990) 'Wählerwandel und die Abschwächung der Parteineigungen von 1972 bis 1987' in M. Kaase and H. -D. Klingemann (eds) *Wahlen und Wähler: Analysen aus Anlaß der Bundestagswahl 1987*, Opladen: Westdeutscher Verlag.
Duverger, M. (1980) 'A new political system model: Semi-presidential government', *European Journal of Political Research*, 8 (2): 165–87.
Feist, U. (1994) *Die Macht der Nichtwähler: Wie die Wähler den Volksparteien davonlaufen*, München: Droemer Knaur.

Filzmaier, P. (2007) 'Ein unaufhaltbarer Sinkflug? Wahlbeteiligung in Österreich und anderswo', *Informationen zur politischen Bildung*, 27: 45–51.
Franklin, M. N. (2002) 'The dynamics of electoral participation' in L. LeDuc, R. G. Niemi and P. Norris (eds) *Comparing Democracies 2: New Challenges in the Study of Elections and Voting*, London: Sage Publications.
Franklin, M. N., Macki, T. T. and Valen, H. (1992) 'Introduction' in M. N. Franklin, T. T. Macki and H. Valen (eds) *Electoral Change: Responses to Evolving Social and Attitudinal Structures in Western Countries*, Cambridge: Cambridge University Press.
Freitag, M. (1996). 'Wahlbeteiligungen in westlichen Demokratien: Eine Analyse zur Erklärung von Niveauunterschieden', *Schweizerische Zeitschrift für Politikwissenschaft*, 2(4): 101–34
Gabriel, O. W. (2004) 'Politische Partizipation' in J. W. van Deth (ed.) *Deutschland in Europa: Ergebnisse des European Social Survey 2002–2003*, Wiesbaden: VS Verlag für Sozialwissenschaften.
Gabriel, O. W. and Völkl, K. (2004) 'Auf der Suche nach dem Nichtwähler neuen Typs: Eine Analyse aus Anlass der Bundestagswahl 2000' in F. Brettschneider, J. W. van Deth and E. Roller (eds) *Die Bundestagswahl 2002: Analysen der Wahlergebnisse und des Wahlkampfes*, Wiesbaden: Westdeutscher Verlag.
Grote, R. (1995) *Das Regierungssystem der V. Französischen Republik*, Baden-Baden: Nomos.
Hehn, J. (2000) 'Das Referendum als Misstrauensvotum', *Die Welt*, 25 September 2000.
Hesse, J. J. and Ellwein, T. (2004) *Das Regierungssystem der Bundesrepublik Deutschland*, Berlin: De Gruyter.
International IDEA (ed.) (1997) *Voter Turnout from 1945 to 1997: A global report on political participation*, Stockholm: International Institute for Democracy and Electoral Assistance.
Jackman, R. (1987) 'Political institutions and voter turnout in the industrial democracies', *American Political Science Review*, 81: 405–23.
Jesse, E. (2008) 'Wahlsysteme und Wahlrecht' in O. W. Gabriel and S. Kropp (eds) *Die EU-Staaten im Vergleich*, 3rd edn., Wiesbaden: VS Verlag für Sozialwissenschaften.
Kleinhenz, T. (1995) *Die Nichtwähler: Ursachen der sinkenden Wahlbeteiligung in Deutschland*, Opladen: Westdeutscher Verlag.
Korte, K. -R. (1999) *Wahlen in der Bundesrepublik Deutschland*, Bonn: Bundeszentrale für Politische Bildung.
LeDuc, L., Niemi, R. G. and Norris, P. (2002) 'Introduction: Comparing democratic elections' in L. LeDuc, R. G. Niemi and P. Norris (eds) *Comparing Democracies 2: New challenges in the study of elections and voting*, London: Sage Publications.
Lijphart, A. (1997) 'Unequal participation: Democracy's unresolved dilemma', *American Political Science Review*, 91(1): 1–14.
—— (1999) *Patterns of Democracy: Government form and performance in*

thirty-six countries, New Haven: Yale University Press.
Lüsebrink, H. -J. (2003) *Einführung in die Landeskunde Frankreichs*, Stuttgart: Metzler.
Mackie, T. T. and Franklin, M. N. (1992) 'Electoral change and social change' in M. N. Franklin, T. T. Macki and H. Valen (eds) *Electoral Change: Responses to evolving social and attitudinal structures in Western countries*, Cambridge: Cambridge University Press.
Maier, J. (2000) *Politikverdrossenheit in der Bundesrepublik Deutschland: Dimensionen – Determinanten – Konsequenzen*, Opladen: Leske and Budrich.
Milbrath, L. W. and Goel, M. L. (1982) *Political Participation: How and why do people get involved in politics?*, Lanham: University Press of America.
Ministère de l'Intérieur *Les elections.* Online. Available/http://www.interieur.gouv.fr/sections/a_votre_service/elections (accessed 21 January 2007).
Müller-Brandeck-Bocquet, G. and Moreau, P. (2000) *Frankreich: Eine politische Landeskunde*, Opladen: Leske and Budrich.
Nohlen, D. (2004) *Wahlrecht und Parteiensystem: Zur Theorie der Wahlsysteme*, Opladen: Leske and Budrich.
Norris, P. (2002) *The Democratic Phoenix: Reinventing political activism*, Cambridge: Cambridge University Press.
— (2004) *Electoral Engineering: voting rules and political behaviour*, Cambridge: Cambridge University Press.
Ohr, D., Quandt, M. and Dülmer, H. (2005) 'Zur Funktion und Bedeutung der Parteibindung für den modernen Wähler' in J. W. Falter and O. W. Gabriel (eds) *Wahlen und Wähler: Analysen aus Anlass der Bundestagswahl*, Wiesbaden: VS Verlag für Sozialwissenschaften.
Perea, E. A. (2002) 'Electoral abstention in western Europe', *European Journal of Political Research*, 41: 643–73.
Pierce, R. (1995) *Choosing the Chief: Presidential elections in France and the United States*, Ann Arbor: University of Michigan Press.
Powell, G. B. (1980) 'Voting turnout in thirty democracies' in R. Rose (ed.) *Electoral Participation: A comparative analysis*, Beverley Hills/London: Sage Publications.
— (1986) 'American voter turnout in comparative perspective', *American Political Science Review*, 80: 17–43.
Roth, D. (1992) 'Sinkende Wahlbeteiligung: Eher Normalisierung als Krisensymptom' in K. Starzacher, K. Schacht, B. Friedrich and T. Leif (eds) *Protestwähler und Wahlverweigerer: Krise der Demokratie?*, Köln: Bund-Verlag.
Rudzio, W. (2006) *Das politische System der Bundesrepublik Deutschland*, 7th edn., Wiesbaden: VS Verlag für Sozialwissenschaften.
Schild, J. (2006) 'Politik' in J. Schild and H. Uterwedde (eds) *Frankreich: Politik, Wirtschaft, Gesellschaft*, 2nd edn., Wiesbaden: VS Verlag für Sozialwissenschaften.
Schmitt-Beck, R. and Schrott, P. R. (1994) 'Dealignment durch Massenmedien?

Zur These der Abschwächung von Parteibindungen als Folge der Medienexpansion' in H. -D. Klingemann and M. Kaase (eds) *Wahlen und Wähler: Analysen aus Anlaß der Bundestagswahl 1990*, Opladen: Westdeutscher Verlag.

Sniderman, P. M. (1975) *Personality and Democratic Politics*, Berkeley: University of California Press.

Stuttgarter Zeitung (10 June 2007) *Riesenerfolg für Sarkozy: Erdrutschartiger Erfolg des neuen Regierungsbündnisses*. Online. Available /http://www.stuttgarter-zeitung.de/stz/page/detail.php/1442789 (accessed 11 June 2007).

Topf, R. (1995) 'Electoral participation' in H. -D. Klingemann and D. Fuchs (eds) *Citizens and the State: Beliefs in government*, Oxford: Oxford University Press.

van Deth, J. W. (2001) 'Soziale und politische Beteiligung: Alternativen, Ergänzungen oder Zwillinge?' in A. Koch, M. Wasmer and P. Schmidt (eds) *Politische Partizipation in der Bundesrepublik Deutschland: Empirische Befunde und theoretische Erklärungen*, Opladen: Leske and Budrich.

Verba, S. and Nie, N. H. (1972) *Participation in America: Political democracy and social equality*, New York: Harper and Row.

Verba, S., Nie, N. H. and Kim, J. -O. (1978) *Participation and Political Equality: A seven-nation comparision*, Cambridge: Cambridge University Press.

Verba, S., Schlozman, K. L. and Brady, H. (1995) *Voice and Equality: Civic voluntarism in American politics*, Cambridge, Mass./London: Harvard University Press.

Vetter, A. (1997) *Political Efficacy: Reliabilität und Validität*, Wiesbaden: Deutscher Universitäts Verlag.

Weisenfeld, E. (1997) *Geschichte Frankreichs seit 1945: Von de Gaulle bis zur Gegenwart*, München: Beck.

Wiesendahl, E. (1998) 'Wie geht es weiter mit den Großparteien in Deutschland?', *Aus Politik und Zeitgeschichte* 48: 13–28.

Zaller, J. (1992) *The Nature and Origin of Mass Opinion*, Cambridge: Cambridge University Press.

chapter nine | political protest
Emmanuel Rivat and Matthias Stauer

Introduction

On 8th November 2008, an anti-nuclear demonstration in Gorleben, Germany, brought together some 15,000 people. Blockades and direct non-violent actions were widespread, and the event was dubbed the 'renaissance of the anti-nuclear movement' by the weekly newspaper, *Spiegel* (10th October 2009). Ever since the 1970s, this movement has constituted a strong protest force in France and Germany. Especially since 1996, French and German activists alike have been protesting against the transportation of radioactive waste and materials by Castor trains between the French reprocessing plant of La Hague to the waste storage facility of Gorleben, using the same tactics of non-violence, and often co-operating over the border for joint information or joint actions.[1] Initially, political protest and direct action would seem to be something that both France and Germany have in common. However, the political context has diverged since the 1970s. France has now become one of the spearheads for nuclear development and nuclear waste exports and, in 2000, Germany took the decision to phase out nuclear energy in 2020 – though this question is now back on the agenda. Obviously, French and German activists do have something in common, but since the political environment has changed and may modify protest conditions, the level of political protest may also change. To what extent then do France and Germany have similar or different levels and forms of protest behaviour?

Political protest actions do not emerge from a vacuum, but are deeply rooted in political values and traditions (Inglehart 1977). Whereas most citizens use such conventional forms of political participation as elections or community activities, political protest allows a much wider range of action repertoires, from demonstrations or petitions to more radical forms of direct action such as civil disobedience (Gamson 1990; Tilly 1986), all of these being often shaped by values and traditions.

Political protest actions are also strongly related to specific attributes of contemporary political systems: political protest is considered as political input for citizens who have neither access to or influence on the political system, and who aim at altering, stopping or initiating public policies by means that go beyond just conventional participation. As such, political protest contributes to the debate on the relations between democracy and political participation (Dahl 1971; Almond and Verba 1989; Ibarra 2003).

Political protest in France and Germany has been extensively studied. Whereas

---

1. Interviews with French activists.

France is often characterised by a high level of unconventional participation, relatively radical forms of protest and protest activities concentrated along traditional social conflict lines, Germany is characterised by a relatively low level of unconventional participation, moderate forms of political protest and protest activities concentrated on new social movements (Schild 2000; Dekker *et al.* 1997).

Although we can assume, from the literature, that the levels of political protest and civil disobedience could be higher in France than in Germany due to the general political context and nature of social movements, such patterns have mostly been studied from an objective, politically-structured perspective (Kriesi *et al.* 1995), without paying sufficient attention to collective perceptions of political structure.

This chapter aims, therefore, to throw more light on overlooked differences between France and Germany by highlighting, in particular, the influence of more specific determinants such as education, age, political interest, or the legitimacy of unconventional forms of protest. The research questions are then: what is the level of political protest in France and Germany? And, how can collective perceptions explain such differences?

We will use the World Value Survey (WVS), the European Social Survey (ESS) and the International Social Survey Programme (ISSP) data, all of which have proved invaluable for purposes of comparison (van Deth *et al.* 2007). The first major work focusing on political participation beyond electoral activities (Verba and Nie 1972) emphasised the link between socio-economic resources and political institutions. The actors concerned do not only embark on political protest in connection with such micro socio-economic features as income or political interest, but also in reaction to more general, country-specific political conditions. It seems, therefore, both justified and pertinent to interconnect the WVS, ESS and ISSP data, using two models of analysis: micro-individual and macro-institutional.

The literature presents two options. The Verba/Schlozman/Brady or 'civic voluntarism' (CV) model, which introduces three micro-variables – resources, motivation, and the existence of mobilising networks – to explore the level of political participation within a country (Verba *et al.* 1995). The 'Political Opportunity Structure' (POS) model has also proved to be a powerful tool for investigating the macro-political conditions of political protest between countries in terms of state structure (Dekker *et al.* 1997). These two models will be used to explain political protest comparing respectively:

- intra-country differences through an individual perspective; and
- inter-country differences through an institutional-context perspective.

A key feature of this chapter is that political opportunities are measured here through individual perceptions, and this approach may well possess more explanatory value than traditional considerations of objective opportunities.

This chapter proposes to assess the level of political protest and the level and legitimacy of illegal protest in France and Germany using a specific model to explain the data involved. After a review of recent literature, we examine protest levels in France and Germany. We then advance a subsequent theoretical explanation – making use of the Verba/Scholzman/Brady and the POS models – to provide a plausible explanation for the differences in protest behaviour in France and Germany. We believe that this theoretical background may well contribute to the development of hypotheses about the causes of country-specific differences and, more especially, as regards the main hypothesis: political protest and civil disobedience are more common in France than in Germany.

Analysing political protest

Definition, dimension of protest and methodology

Political protest is a special form of political participation. If political participation in general is defined as 'all voluntary activities by individual citizens intended to influence either directly or indirectly political choices at various levels of the political system' (Kaase and Marsh 1979: 42), how is the term 'political protest' to be demarcated? First, protest can be seen as the empowerment of all citizens who lack political resources and political access (Gamson 1990; Tilly 1986). Secondly, the consequences of protest on political choice or on a political regime depend to a large extent on the different objectives of political protests. These can be summarised as follows:

- 'target of influence', in order to alter political decisions and public policies;
- 'target of mobilisation', which deals with resources and energy for group constituency and activation of individual commitment; and
- 'target of benefits', when political protest has positive effects on actors outside the challenging group.

(Gamson 1975)

These objectives can overlap and create tensions over time. Issues of political participation can, indeed, lead to either conventional political protest or to more dramatic forms of political violence. In this respect, we must find a definition of political protest that associates political participation, political systems and values.

In their classic *Political Action* study, Samuel Barnes and Max Kaase (Barnes and Marsh 1979) divided political participation into conventional and unconventional participation, the latter being defined as 'behaviour that does not correspond to the norms of law and custom that regulate political participation under a particular regime' (Kaase and Marsh 1979: 41). As customs can change over time and between countries, this distinction proved to be too narrow and drew a lot of criticism (Schild 2000: 26). Instead of 'legitimacy', the criterion of 'regulation by laws or the constitution', first presented by Westle, introduces a more stable basis for cross-national comparison of political participation and political protest (Westle 1994: 14ff.). Regulated forms of political participation, explicitly mentioned in and organised by laws or the constitution are, by definition, institutionalised: the prototype of this is participating in elections. Non-regulated forms of participation are those, therefore, that are not legally defined. Whether they are perceived as legitimate or illegitimate, there remains an open question for empirical research. While re-analysing political action data, Westle (2003) identified three types of political protest: legal, non-institutionalised participation; illegal, non-violent participation; and political violence. Similar typologies were constructed by Uehlinger (1988: 125) and Fuchs (1995: 137).

Table 9.1: Typologies of political protest

	Typologies of political protest		
Barnes/Kaase	Unconventional participation		
Uehlinger	Problem-specific participation	Civil disobedience	Political violence
Fuchs	Demonstrative action	Confrontational action	Violent action
Westle	Legal, non-institutionalised participation	Illegal, non-violent participation	Use of force

Source: Matthias Stauer's presentation on the basis of Westle 2003; Uehlinger 1988; Fuchs 1995.

A careful study of relevant surveys reveals a wide range of participatory activities: signing petitions, attending (lawful or unlawful) demonstrations, contacting politicians, joining (legal or illegal) boycotts, joining (unofficial or official) strikes, occupying buildings or factories, working for political parties or political action groups and so forth. Van Deth noticed that even when the different forms of participation mentioned in several studies were classified in a loose, crude way, some seventy different activities could be observed (van Deth 2003: 175–7). One of these, civil disobedience, is an illegal form of political protest. At the same time, it shows some strong links of commitment to political participation and democracy, since civil disobedience asserts both the absence of human violence and the need to accept legal sanctions. (Arendt 1972).

To sum up, we can conclude that political protest, including civil disobedience, is a special form of political participation, characterised by non-regulation and multi-dimensionality. Accordingly, the two criteria to be used in subdividing political protest are 'legality', and the 'application of force'. But questions remain about the data and methodology.

Patterns of political protest between France and Germany have been traditionally approached through the use of Protest Event Analysis (PEA), a methodology based on the systematic analysis of media articles from different countries (Kriesi *et al.* 1995). Further refinement of the methodology has considered several other units of analysis, such as 'political discourse analysis' for the study of more discursive forms of protest, or 'political claim analysis', which aims at integrating the two first approaches (Koopmans and Rucht 2002; Guigni 2002). These methodologies have been strongly criticised on the grounds that they neglect certain flaws in the selection of media information and topics, and also overlook various informal or non-public forms of political participation such as lobbying activities (Filleule and Jimenez 2003). We consider that the World Value Survey (WVS) data can provide alternative data for these debates. Admittedly, by offering information about general collective perceptions, the WVS is less specific about special social movements, but it does propose determinants of political protest other than discourse, and the data is not biased by the media selection and construction of information.

The WVS provides interesting background information for investigating and comparing changes in values and political traditions (van Deth *et al.* 2007). Its dataset presents three advantages:

1. It deals with relevant variables, including the two dimensions of political protest previously presented, legal or illegal.
2. It is a good tool for grasping the variations of political participation in specific countries since it covers several countries for a period of ten years (1990–2000). France and Germany are part of the 1990 and 1999–2000 waves, while most surveys before 1990 refer only to West Germany, which would be inappropriate for our project.
3. The WVS survey contains more crucial items, especially illegal forms of political protest, than most other surveys.

Several different designs were indeed previously tested for our analysis: analysing time points, leaving some items out, including other items on social and political participation, using the European Social Survey (ESS) or International Social Survey Programme (ISSP) databases. But, systematically, we found the same result: a less congruent set of dimensions for France and Germany. It was the WVS that contained the best data for our analysis.

A few practical problems arose. A factor analysis of WVS might have validated the division of political protest into two dimensions, legal or illegal.[2] In the case of France, however, all items were presented as the underlying aspects of just one dimension, political protest, whereas Germany characterised two dimensions: legal protest and civil disobedience. Consequently, the dependent variable for the multivariate analysis should have contained all items, with one indicator for France and two indices for Germany. For the most part, this should not have posed a serious problem for theoretical explanation. But, in fact, there was a problem for the empirical analyses since the number of cases for Germany was too small to offer a solid model. We therefore chose a common indicator as our dependent variable.

The analysis matched our expectations for Germany: legal protest activities –

---

2. The typology above presents three dimensions, including political violence or violent action. The lack of suitable items in the WVS data for political violence does not pose a problem, however, for our analysis of political protest as a form of political participation, because it can justifiably be doubted that violent actions come under the heading of political participation (Gabriel and Völkl 2005: 529; Scaff 1975).

such as attending lawful demonstrations and signing petitions – constitute the first dimension of protest behaviour, while activities related to civil disobedience, like occupying buildings or factories, and joining unofficial strikes, constitute the second. We noticed, however, two problems with two indicators regarding the definition of political protest. First, joining boycotts concerns simultaneously the factor of legal protest activities and that of civil disobedience. Secondly, some scholars argue that signing petitions is not an unconventional activity, and therefore is not part of political protest, while others associate signing petitions with legal protest (Gabriel and Völkl 2005: 545 *et seq.*; Dekker *et al.* 1997: 223).

Some test runs of the analysis have shown that boycotts and petitions have something in common, both with other forms of illegal political protest and also of political protest.[3] Over and beyond this technical argument, one can assert that as boycotts are deliberate actions – going beyond legal means of protest – aimed at influencing both governments and market actors, they are, therefore, pertinent for politics (Micheletti 2003: 14; van Deth 2008).

Bearing this in mind, we confirmed that WVS provided the most suitable data for explaining co-variances between France and Germany.[4] Our WVS data is based on just one index of five features:

1. signing petitions;
2. attending lawful demonstration;
3. joining boycotts;
4. joining unofficial strikes; and
5. occupying buildings and factories.

The first two items serve as indicators for legal political protest activities; the latter ones are indicators for illegal activities of civil disobedience (see Table 9.2).

Level of protests

Using WVS data, this section investigates the level of political protest as well as the level and legitimacy of illegal protest, first in France, and then in Germany. Although France and Germany are very similar in many respects, their patterns of political participation are quite different. Certain scholars have successfully investigated patterns of civil disobedience in Germany (Rucht 2003), or in France (Hiez and Villalba 2008). Very few, however, have compared levels and patterns of political protest (Kitschelt 1986, Kriesi *et al.* 1995, Koopmans and Rucht 2002). These forms of political participation and political protest can be summarised as follows:

These data reveal two typical patterns of political participation. The first,

---

3. See Appendix: Table re Dimensions of Political Protest Participation (1999–2000).
4. The factor analysis was conducted using oblimin rotation, because we expected the dimensions of unconventional participation to be reciprocally correlated. The same type of analysis was also conducted for 1990.

represented by the Netherlands and less so by Germany, is characterised by low aggregate levels of protest and a relatively moderate nature. As regards the themes of protest, new social movements dominate the extra-parliamentary arena in these countries. The second pattern, represented most clearly by Spain and less so by France, displays higher or much higher levels of protest of a relatively radical nature, embodied primarily by social movements representing the 'old' cleavages labour-capital, centre-periphery and church-state. (Dekker et al. 1997: 235)

According to this diagnosis, France and Germany belong to different participatory types. They differ, first of all, concerning the *levels of political protest activities* and conventional political participation. Secondly, their *forms of protest behaviour* are used in different magnitudes. Thirdly, the activities are centred on different *issues*.

Some of these findings have been downplayed by more recent research including, *inter alia,* the underestimated importance of new social movements in France (Appelton 1999). Consequently, the first step is to validate these findings: are different levels of protest behaviour and civil disobedience observed in France and Germany? And do the French use more radical forms of protest more often than Germans do?

The WVS dataset, as presented above, is particularly significant for protest behaviour, via three types of answer: 'have done', 'might do', 'would never do', from 1990–2004, though figures are not available for illegal activities of civil disobedience in 2004.

According to our first hypothesis, the French are more prone to use civil disobedience than Germans. Indeed, the figures bring out this difference quite clearly. On average, 10.7 per cent of French respondents participated in unofficial strikes, 11.6 per cent joined in boycotts, and 8.0 per cent actually occupied buildings or factories. On average, and in contrast, about 1.9 per cent of German respondents participated in unofficial strikes, 8.4 per cent joined in boycotts, and 0.9 per cent occupied buildings or factories. It appears, then, that the level of illegal political protest – civil disobedience – is much higher in France than in Germany as regards unofficial strikes and occupying buildings. Our first hypothesis is confirmed.

As regards legal political protest activities, the difference is also quite striking. On average, 63.9 per cent of French respondents signed a petition and 40.5 per cent attended lawful demonstrations. In comparison, on average, 52.6 per cent of German respondents signed a petition, and 26.2 per cent attended lawful demonstrations. The level of these activities tends to be higher in France than in Germany. The gap between France and Germany is also on average quite similar for illegal and legal protest activities. On the whole, the figures for legal protests in Germany are quite high, but almost non-existent as regards civil disobedience. Our second hypothesis is confirmed.

Table 9.2: Percentage level of political protest (1990–2004)

		France				Germany			
		1990	1999/2000	2004	Mean	1990	1999/2000	2004	Mean
Signed a petition	Have done	51.4	67.1	73.1	63.9	57.3	47.4	53.0	52.6
	Might do	27.7	22.4	16.1	22.1	29.1	32.9	25.2	29.1
	Would never do	16.6	9.2	6.2	10.7	10.4	14.6	18.7	14.6
Attended a lawful demonstration	Have done	31.2	38.3	51.9	40.5	25.1	24.8	28.6	26.2
	Might do	30.9	33.5	22.6	29.0	38.2	38.0	31.8	36.0
	Would never do	33.2	25.4	19.4	26.0	30.2	30.7	36.6	32.5
Joined a boycott	Have done	11.3	11.9	–	11.6	8.1	8.7	–	8.4
	Might do	36.3	40.1	–	38.2	32.0	37.7	–	34.9
	Would never do	42.8	39.8	–	41.3	48.3	45.3	–	46.8
Joined an unofficial strike	Have done	9.4	12.0	–	10.7	2.1	1.6	–	1.9
	Might do	23.2	29.8	–	26.5	12.7	15.0	–	13.9
	Would never do	60.6	52.0	–	56.3	74.5	76.3	–	75.4
Occupied buildings or factories	Have done	7.2	8.7	–	8.0	1.0	0.8	–	0.9
	Might do	22.7	32.9	–	27.8	9.8	12.6	–	11.2
	Would never do	61.7	51.8	–	56.8	80.6	80.4	–	80.5
N		1,002	1,615	1,419		3,437	2,036	1,332	

Notes: From zero to 100 per cent: Don't know; Can't choose; No answer.
WVS: 'I am going to read out some different forms of political action that people can take, and I'd like you to tell me, for each one, whether you have actually done any of these things, whether you might do it or would never, under any circumstances, do it.'
ISSP: 'Here are some different forms of political and social action that people can take. Please indicate, for each one, whether you have done any of these things in the past year, whether you have done it in the more distant past, whether you have not done it but might do it or have not done it and would never, under any circumstances, do it.'
Source: World Values Survey 1990; World Values Survey 1999–2000, ISSP 2004; data weighted for Germany; Matthias Stauer's calculations.

According to our second hypothesis, civil disobedience is also considered as more legitimate in France than Germany. The data does not include an explicit measurement for legitimacy of political protest activities and, of course, this measurement would require specific questions about methodology. Nonetheless, it does offer an acceptable substitute. The response option 'would never do' allows us, in fact, to suggest the levels of legitimacy, since legitimacy depends to a large extent on the social construction of what is acceptable or not. In this respect, total opposition to an item can be interpreted as a basic refusal of this activity to attain one's political goals, treating such activity as illegitimate political behaviour. Therefore, it is quite justifiable to substitute an explicit measurement of legitimacy by means of this response option.

The figures, it should be stressed, are distributed in accordance with our assumptions: considerably more French respondents regard activities of civil obedience as possible future behaviour – on average, 41.3 per cent for boycotts, 56.3 per cent for joining unofficial strikes, and 56.8 per cent for occupying buildings or factories. In contrast, German respondents showed, on average, that 46.8 per cent would never take part in boycotts, 75.4 per cent would never join unofficial strikes, and 80.5 per cent would never occupy buildings or factories. The items on legal protest activities do not reveal any particularly significant result: on average, the number of people who would never sign a petition or attend a lawful demonstration is lower in France than in Germany, which implies that French people regard these activities as possible responses to political events.

The three options – 'have done', 'might do' and 'would never do' – are hence useful in illustrating another key aspect. 'Have done' and 'might do' display the level of potential protest.

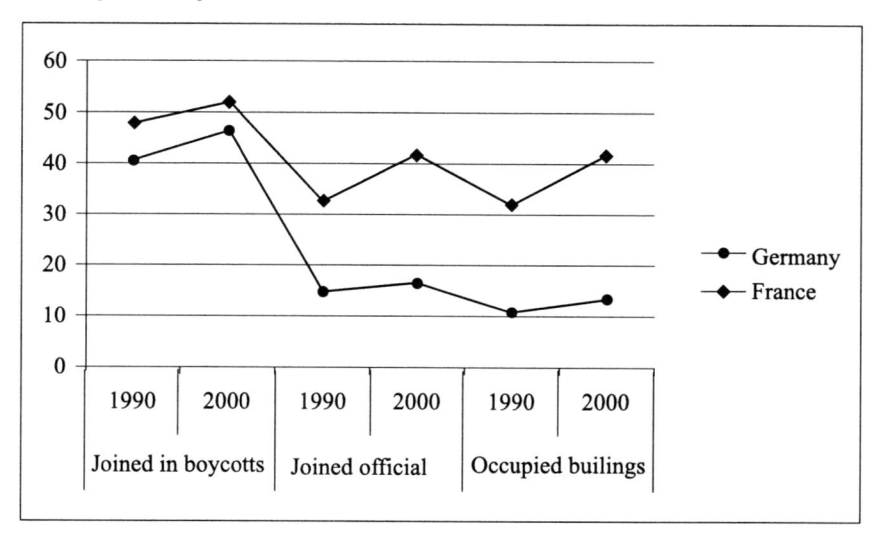

Figure 9.1: Potential of civil disobedience 1990–1999–2000

Notes: Values display the answers 'have done' + 'might do'.

Source: World Values Survey 1990; World Values Survey 1999–2000 presented 2000; data weighted for Germany; Matthias Stauer's calculations

Figure 9.1 offers an explicit view of this illegal protest potential in France and Germany. A person who 'might join' an unofficial strike clearly possesses the potential to do so in the future. Deliberately expressed behavioural dispositions serve best to predict individual behaviour (Marsh and Kaase 1979: 61 *et seq.*). It is quite obvious that the potential for civil disobedience and, hence, its predictable level for the future, is much higher in France than in Germany. The respective values for unofficial strikes and occupying buildings or factories are more than twice as high in France. The lesson is clear: France presents higher levels of illegal protest than Germany, not only as regards its behaviour, but also as regards its behavioural potential.

Level of protest and time restrictions

A second data source, the European Social Survey (ESS), allows further analysis of the levels of political protest and confirms the previous findings about France and Germany. One advantage of this dataset is simply that it contains the item 'voting in the last national election'. Furthermore, the ESS question is different from that shown in the WVS data: whereas the WVS question asks – without any time restrictions – whether a person had undertaken one sort of action, the ESS question asks whether a person had carried out one of the activities within the previous 12 months.

The level of protest may be estimated by the WVS, but the subjective stance of citizens can present a few flaws. Political protest, for example, is a highly situation-dependent form of behaviour (Schild 2000: 66). However, the ESS restriction concerning time might avoid an overestimation of protest behaviour that took place decades ago. Consequently, a bias regarding age, for example, can be avoided: without the time restriction, older people might indicate protest experience just because they had witnessed more situations giving rise to protests. These levels of protest are presented in Table 9.3.

Overall, the ESS data confirm the results of the WVS data: most protest activities are more common in France than in Germany – especially illegal protest activities, which are higher in France – albeit at a lower level in both countries. Participation in illegal protest activities, for example, is higher in France than in Germany – 2.3 per cent in France and 1.3 per cent in Germany – but these figures are, nevertheless, fairly low. Again, signing petitions is the most frequent form of popular protest activity. We can also point out that the prototype of conventional political participation – the vote – is more common in Germany.

It is clear that the ESS findings are interesting on two accounts: they downplay the importance of civil disobedience compared with conventional channels of participation as elections and confirm that the phenomenon is not widespread either in France or Germany. They also show the most popular forms of political protest. Signing a petition is, by far, the most frequent form of popular protest activity in both France and Germany. Boycotts of certain products are also very significant, compared to attending a demonstration, or contacting a politician, government or local government official, which was less expected.

Table 9.3: Levels of political protest as per cent (2002–2007)

	France			Germany		
	2002–3	2004–5	2006–7	2002–3	2004–5	2006–7
Voting in the last national election	64.8	68.1	67.1	77.8	72.0	72.8
... contacted a politician, government or local government official	16.8	15.0	15.1	13.0	11.3	12.4
... worked in a political party or action group	4.5	4.3	3.4	3.8	3.4	3.9
... worn or displayed a campaign *badge*/sticker	11.2	12.1	12.0	5.6	4.2	4.5
... signed a petition	33.7	31.3	33.1	31.3	32.4	28.2
... taken part in a lawful public demonstration	16.9	12.3	14.8	11.4	9.3	7.3
... boycotted certain products	25.8	29.3	26.5	24.6	20.7	22.2
... donated money to a political organisation or group	3.3	–	–	9.3	–	–
... participated in illegal protest activities	2.3	–	–	1.3	–	–
N	1,503	1,805	1,984	2,919	2,870	2,916

Notes: Wording of question:

[1] 'There are different ways of trying to improve things in [country] or help prevent things from going wrong. During the last 12 months, have you done any of the following? Have you ....

[2] 'Some people don't vote nowadays for one reason or another.

Did you vote in the last [country] national election in [month/year]?'

Source: European Social Survey; Matthias Stauer's calculations.

The ESS provides a good tool for comparing data with WVS and for drawing general conclusions At this point, we affirm that civil disobedience is much more common in France and more people there regard these activities as legitimate action alternatives. To put it concretely: more radical political activities are observable in France than in Germany, and those activities are regarded as legitimate by a greater proportion of the French population than in Germany.

Nonetheless, these observable patterns do not in themselves explain the reasons for these differences. The underlying research question of this article therefore remains: how can the different patterns of participation and political protest be explained? Bearing in mind these empirical results, the question itself can be broken down into two sub-questions: Why do French people use more radical forms of participation than Germans? Why do more Germans regard civil disobedience as illegitimate behaviour?

To start to tackle these questions, the following section begins with a model designed by Verba, Schlozman and Brady (1995) that explains political participation. Afterwards, the CV model is complemented by one focusing upon citizens' perceptions of the political system, based on the concept of political opportunity structure (Kitschelt 1986, Kriesi *et al.* 1995). The first model is designed to explain intra-country differences from a micro perspective; the POS model explains inter-country differences from a macro perspective.

Explaining political protest

This section examines the various determinants of political protest and how they can be tested. What are the most important and relevant variables? To what extent do the explanations have different impacts in France and Germany? Some theoretical models can help us understand these patterns. One of the most popular models in recent research is the CV Model (Verba *et al.* 1995). Basically, three separate questions arise when explaining levels of political protest:

1. How can fluctuations over time be explained (longitudinal section)?
2. How can fluctuations between countries be explained (cross section)?
3. How can the level in any one country at any one time be explained?

The first question is probably the most difficult one, just because comparable longitudinal data over a sufficient period of time is relatively accessible. The main question is: why does person A participate at the time of t_1 in protest activities, while person B at the time of t_2 does not? Or else, if panel data exists: why does person A participate at the time of t_1 in protest activities, and person A at the time of t_2 does not? Last, but not least, the second question might be paraphrased this way: why does person A in country X participate in protest activities, whilst person B in country Y does not (at a time point t_1)? This question will be the focus of the section below (Protest and institutional analysis). Most studies deal with the last question (even though country comparisons usually only describe similarities and differences without explaining them). The content of this question is: why does person A participate in protest activities in one country, while person B does not? Starting from the benchmark model, which is appropriate for describing protests within one country, a different model is needed to enlarge the benchmark to include aspects capable of addressing inter-country differences.

The differences between France and Germany

In the sections above, the overall levels of political protest emphasised the differences between France and Germany in terms of political protest behaviour – legal and illegal. By means of factor analysis, political protest is operationalised on the basis of WVS findings as an index of signing petitions, attending demonstrations, joining in boycotts, occupying buildings and factories, and joining unofficial strikes. The value margin of the variables ranges between 0 (respondent had not carried out any protest activity) and 1 (respondent had carried out all five protest activities). To assess the country effect upon political protest, a first regression model was conducted with only one country-dummy variable (results are presented in Table 9.5). The country effect 'x', means, in other words, that if a French person lived in Germany, his likelihood of becoming active in protests would increase or decrease by a factor of 'x'. The results are presented in Table 9.4.

Table 9.4: Countries as determinants of political protest

	1990		1999–2000	
	Mean	Std. dev	Mean	Std. dev
France	0.22	0.25	0.28	0.25
Germany	0.19	0.19	0.17	0.19
N	3,761		4,447	
Beta	−.24[a]		−.08[a]	

Notes: a = p:S 0.001; b = p:s 0.01; c = p:s 0.05
Annotation: France = 0; Germany = 1
Source: World Values Survey 1990; World Values Survey 1999–2000; data weighted for Germany; Matthias Sauer's calculations.

In 1990, the country effect was 0.24, which means that French activists would have, on average, 0.24 more chances of becoming involved in political protest if they lived in Germany. Considering that the average for France is 0.22, this is a very impressive effect. Remarkably, the country effect dropped to a value of 0.08 in 1999/2000. This might have been caused by protest behaviour having converged in both countries during those ten years, or by influences other than the country effect in 1999/2000. The first explanation can be dismissed at once: the aggregated differences between France and Germany expanded within those ten years. In 1990, the mean values of political protest differed by a value of 0.03 points; in 1999/2000, those mean values differed by 0.11 points.[5] Hence, effects other than the country effect must have emerged within those years.

Nonetheless, we should note that the gap between the average level of protest

---

5. The slight gap in 1990 should not lead to the assumption that the two countries could not be distinguished during that period. The average figure for protest activities does not give information about the forms and issues of political protest. As stated above: France and Germany display great differences in their forms of political participation.

activities in France and Germany grew in that period. The fluctuations over time and between the two countries shows that political protest rose more in France than in Germany. This may be related to the rise in social movement activities in the 1990s – especially the waves of demonstrations in France from 1995 – and the rising protests over unemployment, housing, and social rights (Sommier 2003, Mouchard 2002). However, as pointed out previously, the country effects in 1999/2000 dropped to a low value, implying that a French activist would have had less chance than before of becoming involved in political protests compared with his German counterpart. This may be due to the fact that the socio-economic characteristics of protest in France and Germany have changed differently over time.

Therefore, the next step is to operationalise those differences between France and Germany, using the CV model in order to explain such variations.

Protest and individual analysis

Sidney Verba, Kay Lehman Schlozman and Henry E. Brady (1995) designed a model aimed at casting light on intra-country causal relations to explain individual political participation in the United States. We aim at applying this CV model to a cross-national comparison of the patterns of political protest in France and Germany, i.e. inter-country relations. To achieve this goal, three different approaches to individual behaviour have been associated:

– the resource-based approach;
– the motivation-based approach; and
– the mobilisation-based approach.

The independence of variables is presented as follows:

The resource-based approach

This follows a simple thesis: the better equipped an individual is with crucial resources, the more likelihood there is of that individual participating in politics (Verba and Nie 1972). Variables such as gender, age, education and income are introduced into the analysis because the WVS data offers a broad range of information on these features, in both France and Germany. Such well-known determinants of political participation as 'education' ('The positive relationship between education and political protest is one of the most reliable results in empirical social science' – La Due Lake and Huckfeldt 1998: 567) or 'age' (younger people seem to participate more in political protest activities than older people – Gabriel and Völkl 2005:566) find an echo within the design of this analysis. Men tend to participate in protest activities more often than women (Schild 2000: 207). One should note that this concept contains social-economic status (SES) variables such as income and employment status, but goes beyond this traditional measurement by including crucial intellectual resources like communication and verbal skills. In this respect, the term resource encompasses material as well as intellectual aspects, i.e. skills, and turns out to be a direct criticism of the rational approach towards political participation (for an example, see Olson 1964). Such intellectual resources are operationalised here under the determinant of 'education', which plays a great role in the production and reproduction of these social skills.

The motivation-based approach

This approach also follows a simple logic: as political activity is voluntary, it therefore requires a choice based upon incentives and stimulations. These incentives have their roots in socialisation processes and foster the disposition and willingness to invest resources in political activities. The more that people internalise participatory norms and values, the more likely they are to become politically active.

The WVS dataset lacks variables such as party identification, internal and external efficacy or norms of participation. But what might sometimes seem somewhat inappropriate at first glance can, on further reflection, prove both theoretically plausible and reasonable. Individuals might ask themselves questions like: Why should I demonstrate? What should I demonstrate against? Why should I become politically active? Not until those questions are answered does an individual become politically engaged. But if those questions are answered positively, such considerations will motivate political activity. Hence, 'political interest' and 'importance of politics' may well be considered as motivating forces to motivate political activity (La Due Lake and Huckfeld 1998: 569). These two items have been combined in one single indicator.[6]

'Internal efficacy' 'relates to the individual's properties of understanding, influencing and controlling political events' (Gabriel 1996: 197); external efficacy resembles political trust. Feelings of efficacy prove to be a relevant determinant of political activity (Milbrath and Goel 1977: 57):

> Feelings of efficacy refer to people's self-image as competent actors in the political game. Individuals viewing themselves as politically efficacious are convinced that they are capable of understanding and interpreting the complexity of the political world, of controlling their own lives, and exerting social and political influence. Finally they think that political leaders are receptive to their influence and will act accordingly when confronted with 'ordinary' people's demands.
>
> (Gabriel 1996: 196)

The statement 'If an unjust law were passed by the government I could do nothing at all about it' (response options: (1) agree completely; (2) somewhat agree; (3) neither agree nor disagree; (4) somewhat disagree; (5) disagree completely) will serve to compensate for the lack of explicit measurement of internal and external

---

6. A pre-test of the model indicated that both items are strongly correlated. This fact vitiates one of the main preconditions for implementing OLS regression: non-correlation of the independent variables. To avoid this multi-collinearity problem, both items have been connected to one single index.

efficacy. Regrettably, the WVS question is not unambiguous: is the unjust law not alterable because the person does not possess the required political understanding (self-assessment)? Or is the unjust law not alterable because the political leaders and the political system do not respond to demands (responsiveness)? But this variable may well compensate for a satisfying measurement of efficacy.

The mobilisation-based approach

Involvement in mobilising networks is a crucial determinant of political participation. The more a person is integrated into social and political networks, and the stronger the mobilisation efforts of those networks are, the more likely it is that the person will become active in politics (Diani and MacAdam 2003; Gabriel and Völkl 2005: 566). This aspect is operationalised by the use of the following variables: frequency of political discussions and efforts to persuade interpersonal trust, church attendance and the fact that people belong to different types of voluntary associations and carry out unpaid work for them. This is because if networks provide crucial skills for becoming active in political life, they can also foster participation by directly requiring involvement (Verba *et al.* 1995: 369). The fact that people belong to various forms of organisations could be a decisive factor for citizen involvement in political life, but this variable is not available. Another question arises. Are all associations alike? That involvement in political non-governmental organisations could foster political participation is perfectly obvious, but what about sports or youth clubs? To start examining this question, a factor analysis (results not presented here) based upon WVS data revealed the following typology of voluntary associations:

- political organisations – labour unions and political parties;
- new social movements – human rights, environment, peace movement;
- leisure organisations – cultural activities, youth work, sports or recreation;
- issue-related organisations – welfare service, church organisations, local political organisations, women's groups and organisations concerned with health.

Accordingly, four indices of associational involvement were established, with the following indices: being a member of or belonging to an association on the one hand, and doing unpaid work for this association on the other hand. While pre-testing this model, the problem of multi-collinearity once more emerged. Although it might be an interesting task to analyse the relationship between mere membership and active involvement and its effects upon political participation, the required independence between the variables – the initial reason for combining both questions – is not given. The fact that factor analysis can be used to detect the effects of group of organisations is surprising, due to the difficulty of measuring social capital as regards political participation (Putnam 1993; Coleman 1990). Indeed, previous indicators of associations and networks often measure individual trends, such as education, income or age, rather than concrete relations between actors. The hypotheses according to the CV model are set out below.

Resource-based approach

1. The higher the incomes of individuals, the better their education and the older they are, the higher their level of political protest.
2. Men tend to participate in protest activities more than women do.

Motivation-based approach

1. The higher the political interest of a person and the more important politics is for a person, the higher the level of political protest.
2. The higher the efficacy of a person, the higher the level of political protest.

Network-based approach

1. The more a person is integrated in social life (frequency of political discussions, ambition to persuade others, interpersonal trust, church attendance and involvement in non-governmental organisations), the higher the level of political protest.

The CV model is able to explain protest activities. The results of OLS regression and features are presented in Table 9.5. The explanatory power of the model presents a 28 per cent explained variance in France and a 25 per cent explained variance in Germany in 1990. It is, however, particularly noticeable that the explained variance declines between 1990 and 1999/2000. All the same, most of the regression coefficients show a decline between the two time points. Obviously, changes must have taken place, i.e. the determinants of political protest must themselves have changed within this decade. Overall, the CV model offers substantial explanatory power for 1990, but considerably less for 1999/2000. Hence, the model has a limited explanatory power for fluctuations over time. However, although we need to be careful about the figures, most of the fluctuations between France and Germany in 1990 can be estimated.

As expected, both France and Germany share education and motivation (interest and importance of politics) as strong determinants of political protest activity. We assume that education is connected with other crucial phenomena: political awareness and efficacy, skills required to become politically active, cognitive mobilisation such as political interest and political knowledge. Our data confirms this hypothesis: the higher the level of education and interest and importance of politics, the greater the likelihood of people being involved in political protest. Similarly, France and Germany show that gender and income were not so relevant in either country in 1990. Political protest seems to occur regardless of such features.

Interestingly, France and Germany show a strong difference with regard to age: the older a person, the less that person participates in protest activities in Germany (at least in 1990), i.e. in Germany, younger people are more likely to protest than older people. Several hypotheses could be tested: this may be due to processes involved in adolescence – younger people tend to challenge the existing values and political attitudes of their parents' generation. According to this line of reasoning, political protest serves as demonstrative action to distinguish younger generations from older ones. In France, age is insignificant. Other hypotheses may well be used to investigate and compare the generation gap in France and Germany.

In addition, France and Germany show a small but decisive difference with regard to political efficiency. A moderate positive correlation is to be observed in France, but not in Germany, which implies that political efficiency does matter for political protest in France. This means that people in France feel more capable of influencing politics, or more inclined to attempt to do so, if political leaders are not receptive. In this respect, one can also point out that this factor was expected to be strongly related to the characteristics of the political context.

One can also assume that, within a political context in France not favourable to political claims, the French would be more likely to feel competent in reacting against a policy, or to refuse the lack of government responsiveness. It would be an interesting point to explore via cultural analysis of France and Germany. It is, however, regrettable that this trend cannot be observed for the years 1999–2000; nor can it be compared with 1990, due to a lack of data.

Finally, France and German present a difference as regards associational involvement. Involvement in political organisations is one of the most substantial determinants for explaining protest behaviour in France, but less significant in Germany. This may well be explained in the case of France by means of involvement there in organisations such as trade unions, centred on traditional issues, and the traditional radicalism of those trade unions. However, the degree of involvement in new social movements and 'new politics' seems quite similar in both countries.

The picture is far from being clear-cut: between 1990 and 1999/2000, in fact, the differences almost disappeared. On the other hand, the regression coefficients lie close together and, therefore, any excessive interpretation should be avoided. Regarding this approach, all coefficients point the same way in both countries – no big differences can be observed. As for the frequency of attending religious services, this exhibits a negative impact upon political protest. Going to church frequently lowers the likelihood of becoming politically active in France and in Germany.

The main result can be considered as follows: education and motivation play a great role in explaining higher levels of political protest in both France and Germany. Age, political efficiency and involvement in various types of associations, however, might explain the higher levels of protest found in France. These features, especially the age of activists, prove to be interesting. However, they do not specifically explain why the level of legal or illegal forms of political protest

Table 9.5: Protest and individual political participation

	France				Germany			
	1990		1999–2000		1990		1999–2000	
	B	Beta	B	Beta	B	Beta	B	Beta
Gender	−.01	−.02	.17	−.05c	.00	.00	.00	.00
Age	.01	.06	.00	.01	−.02	−.17a	.00	−.03
Education	.01	.15a	.01	.06	.01	.17a	.01	.10a
Income	.00	.04	.00	.02	.00	.06b	.01	.06c
Interest and Importance	.14	.16a	.13	.15a	.10	.14a	.11	.16a
Efficacy	.06	.09b	n.a.	n.a.	−.01	−.02	n.a.	n.a.
Political discussion	.09	.11b	.11	.14a	.03	.04	.04	.07c
Persuading friends	.04	.06	n.a.	n.a.	.04	.06a	n.a.	n.a.
Interpersonal trust	.05	.08b	.01	.02	.02	.05b	−.01	−.02
Church attendance	−.11	−.15a	−.08	−.10a	−.03	−.06b	−.03	−.06c
Political org.	.21	.20a	.16	.11a	.07	.13	.11	.11a
Nms.org	.18	.10b	.15	.06b	.17	.14a	.14	.07b
Leisure.org	.02	.02	.11	.11a	.01	.01	.07	.08b
Issue.org	−.06	−.05	.00	.00	.03	.03c	.02	.02
Constant	−.36		.17a		-.05		.03	
R adj	.28a		.16a		.25a		.13a	
N	1,002		1,615		3,437		2,036	

Notes: a = p ≤ 0.001.; b = p ≤ 0.01; c = p ≤ 0.05. n.a. = not available.
Source: World Values Survey 1990; World Values Survey 1999-2000; data weighted for Germany; Matthias Stauer's calculation.

differs between the two countries. This may be because the CV model does not take into account each country's state structure. The next step is, then, to operationalise and test the POS model.

Protest and institutional analysis

In the above section, we have developed a model to explain political protest within countries. However, questions remain: How are these differences to be explained? Why is illegal protest more important in France than in Germany? In other words, what are the underlying factors that determine political protest in France and Germany and explain the differences between these countries?

The CV model neglects the importance of political institutions and state structure in influencing the nature of political participation and political protest. In fact, the relevance of the determinants proposed by the CV model hypotheses also depends on the very dynamics of the political context. The variables 'political interest' and 'importance of politics', as well as the variable political efficiency, for example, might be correlated to the on-going dynamic of the political agenda and the variable capacity of citizens to express their views and be heeded, or otherwise influence public policies.

The added-value of the POS model compared with the CV model is both theoretical – more specific features of each country are introduced – and also empirical – more aspects of political protest are highlighted. To begin with, one can emphasise the openness or closeness of a political system:

> In open, inclusive political systems, where success can be achieved by less demanding conventional strategies, social movements find less need to resort to unconventional protest. If they do, they rely primarily on accepted forms of protest. In closed, exclusive systems, conversely, conventional strategies are not likely to induce authorities to give in to movement demands. Hence, challengers are forced to use radical, unconventional strategies in order to make themselves heard.
>
> (Dekker *et al.* 1997: 229)

What exactly is an open or closed society? The concept of POS has over the past few years been a matter of controversy. Some scholars have used the concept of 'structure of political opportunities' (Kitschelt 1986), but the use of such a model has encountered strong criticism concerning its, so-called, objectivity, the measurement of openness and closeness of POS, and the multiplication of criteria. Other scholars have emphasised the need to explore citizens' perceptions of political opportunities that can be expressed in terms of frames (Gamson and Mayer 1996) or rational options (Koopmans 2004). Such perceptions have been for example defined as follows: 'constraints, possibilities, and threats that originate outside the mobilising group but affect its chances of mobilising and realising its collective interests' (Koopmans 2004). These debates, however, have not yet succeeded in explaining the link between objective structures and subjective perceptions (Crossley 2002; Filleule 2006).

How can these open or closed state structures be measured? A first step is to translate the perceptions of these opportunities into indices. One indicator, for example, of opportunity structure is the perceived responsiveness of the political system. When citizens consider that conventional participation is sufficient to influence the political game, there is no need for them to employ more radical modes of participation (Dekker *et al.* 1997: 235). In open state structures, citizens are expected to use conventional forms of participation or moderate forms of protest because they are appropriate ways of attaining their goals. We can, likewise, expect the legitimacy of radical protest forms to be quite low also. Patterns of perceptions of openness or closure of political systems may therefore explain a great number of inter-country differences as regards political protest.

A second step is to generalise the link between perceptions and an explicit data index. A crucial indicator is the perceived responsiveness of the political elites. A similar line of argumentation can be proposed about trust in the political system: the more trustworthy a political system, the less the need for citizens to protest against it. Other indicators include the level of conventional political participation – the level of unconventional participation as regards our main hypotheses. Another line of argument is important: an open state structure would be able to lower the importance of traditional cleavages and give rise to new political issues; the opposite state of affairs would then characterise closed state structures. Open state structures are supposed to provide enough political access to open the door to new issues and new actors in the political game. These considerations are illustrated in Figure 9.2.

```
                    ┌─────────────────────────────┐
                    │ Nature of political regime  │
                    └──────────────┬──────────────┘
                                   ▼
              ┌──────────────────────────────────────────┐
              │ Perception of political opportunities    │
              └──────────────────────────────────────────┘
               ↙                                        ↘
   ┌──────────────────┐                      ┌──────────────────┐
   │  Open/Inclusive  │                      │ Closed/Exclusive │
   └──────────────────┘                      └──────────────────┘
               ↘                                        ↙
                    ┌─────────────────────────────┐
                    │    Opportunity structure    │
                    └─────────────────────────────┘
                     ↙                           ↘
┌────────────────────────────────────────┐  ┌────────────────────────────────────┐
│ Indicators:                            │  │ Modes of conflict resolutions:     │
│  - Perceived responsiveness            │  │  - Significance of traditional     │
│  - Legitimacy of political protest     │  │    cleavages                       │
│  - Level of conventional participation │  │  - Development of New Social       │
│  - Level of unconventional participation│ │    Movement                        │
│  - Political trust                     │  │                                    │
└────────────────────────────────────────┘  └────────────────────────────────────┘
                      ↘                           ↙
                    ┌─────────────────────────────┐
                    │ Patterns of political protest│
                    └─────────────────────────────┘
```

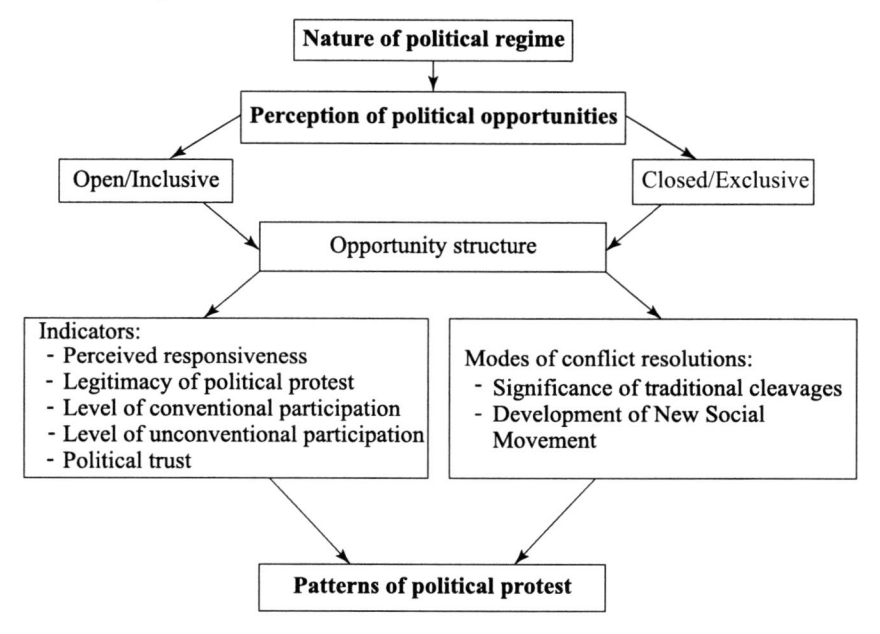

Figure 9.2: Perceptions of political systems

Source: presentation by Matthias Stauer and Emmanuel Rivat.

Table 9.6: Characteristics of open and closed states

	Open states	**Closed states**
Political protest	Low	High
Legitimacy of political protest	Low	High
Responsiveness of the system	High	Low
Trust in government	High	Low
Conventional participation	High	Low
Traditional conflicts (cleavages)	Institutionalised	Still influential

Source: presentation by Matthias Stauer.

Starting from these considerations, the general hypothesis is that the more citizens perceive their political system as open or inclusive, the lower the level of political protest and the lower the level of civil disobedience. Or, put the other way round, the more citizens perceive their political system as closed or exclusive, the higher the level of political protest. Crucial indicators to examine this hypothesis are as defined above: level of political protest, level of conventional participation, perceived responsiveness of the political system, legitimacy of political protest, political trust and the importance of traditional cleavages and the occurrence of new conflict-lines. These indicators may overlap, but they do enable us to address the various perceptions that characterise and distinguish open from closed state structures. Such expectations can be summarised as follows in Table 9.6.

As regards these trends, what are the patterns in France and Germany? How can these hypotheses explain the political protest differences in France and Germany? Herbert Kitschelt (1986) presents further considerations about state structure as follows:

> Political opportunity structures are comprised of specific configurations of resources, institutional arrangements and historical precedents for social mobilisation, which facilitate the development of protest movements in some instances and constrain them in others [...] Comparison can show that political opportunity structures influence the choice of protest strategies and the impact of social movements on their environment.
>
> (Kitschelt 1986: 58)

Kitschelt classified France as being a 'strong' state, partly because the executive branch clearly dominates a weak legislature and the party system tends to be centripetal (Kitschelt 1986: 64). He classified Germany as a 'weak' state because the legislature is central in the nomination of the head of state and the party system more divided (see Table 9.7). As a rule, France is considered as a presidential system with a strong decision-making process, while Germany is seen as a parliamentary system (Lijphart 1992: 6).[7] In other words, the political game is considered to be more open in Germany than France. These results were further completed by Kriesi, who also introduced the concept of 'configuration of power' to describe the strategies of elites towards protest and showed the traditional low degree of responsiveness of French and German elites with regard to political protest (Kriesi et al. 1995). The governmental strategies employed in France and Germany in this respect have been qualified as 'exclusive'.

These hypotheses must be examined very cautiously. As pointed out by Tarrow (1994: 82): 'We must beware of overschematisation. It would be easier if in fact they were constant. But "strength and weakness" are relational values which vary for different sectors and levels of the state.' This theoretical perspective is a generalisation of state structures, while the political opportunities may be very different in specific cases. However, taking into account the point of view of individual perceptions and the collective aggregation of mobilisation may help to give some consistence to such a generalisation.

Table 9.7: Patterns of political opportunity structures

	Weak State	Strong State
Inclusive	X	X
Exclusive	Germany	France

Source: Kitschelt 1986; Kriesi et al.1995; presentation by Emmanuel Rivat.

Kitschelt was interested in social movements, but not in individual protest behaviour. The conflict strategies of such collective actors as new social movements, trade unions, and parties also determine individual protest, according to Schild (2000: 112): collective actors are able to mobilise individual citizens for protest activities. This might be called a mobilisation hypothesis. But collective organisations are not the only determinants of political protest. Put the other way around, individual protest can be explained by individual characteristics (Rosenstone and Hansen 1993). These two references, in fact, describe two sides of the same coin: collective actors choose their conflict strategies according to the opportunity structures prevailing in a political system; individuals are, in turn, geared to the strategies of collective actors.

---

7. In addition, the party systems are quite different: The 'Effective number of parties' index (ENOP) in France averages 3.07 and in Germany 2.68 (base years: 1949–2005 for Germany, and 1958–2002 for France; see Gabriel and Kropp 2008). The ENOP formula shows a difference of 0.39, which is significant.

```
                    ┌─────────────────┐
                    │ Political system│
                    │ (institutional  │
                    │ arrangements,   │
                    │ party system)   │
                    └────────┬────────┘
                             │
                             ▼
┌──────────────────┐    ┌──────────────────┐
│ Conflict         │    │                  │
│ strategies of    │◄───┤ Opportunity      │
│ collective actors│    │ structure        │
│ (trade unions,   │    │                  │
│ social movements)│    └────────┬─────────┘
└────────┬─────────┘             │
         │                       │
  Mobilisation            Perceptions
         │                       │
         ▼                       ▼
    ┌──────────────────────────────┐
    │ Individual process behaviour │
    │ (existence, form, issue)     │
    └──────────────────────────────┘
```

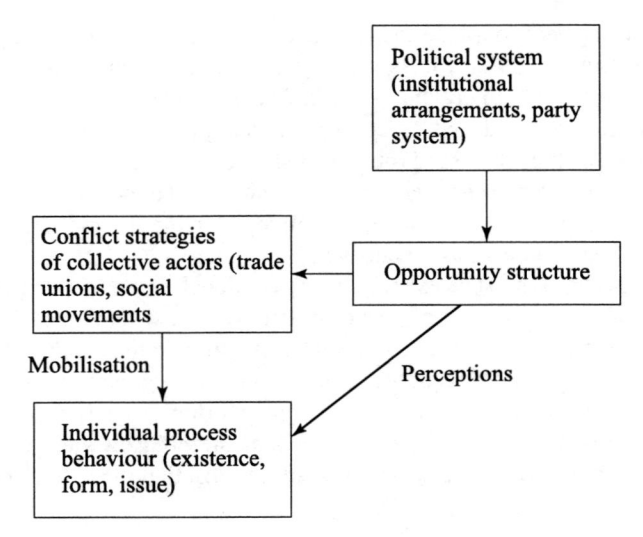

Figure 9.3: Opportunity structures and political protest
Source: presentation by Matthias Stauer.

Bearing in mind our hypothesis, according to which individual citizens orientate themselves in line with opportunity structures – not given ones, but rather perceived ones, depending on whether political systems are considered closed and exclusive or open and inclusive – we can empirically assume the link between individual and collective protests. In accordance with the same line of reasoning, opportunity structures determine individual protest in two respects. On the one hand, individual protest is affected indirectly via collective actors, who consider protest forms in reaction to opportunity structures and mobilise activists for these protest forms. On the other hand, choices of protest are associated with the individual perception of opportunity structures. The factors of collective protest in France and Germany may well depend not only on collective reactions to political opportunity structures, but also on individual reactions (see Figure 9.3).

On the basis of these theoretical considerations, several indicators were introduced. Perceived responsiveness was first operationalised through the items of 'political efficacy': 'external efficacy' as regards the individual feeling of trust in elite responsiveness, and 'internal efficacy' in what concerns the individual feeling of being able to influence politics. Two other indicators of responsiveness were introduced: the likelihood of serious attention concerning political demands and the likelihood of counter-action if an unjust law was passed. General trust in the government, and trust in politicians was operationalised in turn through the item 'political trust'. The question of whether citizens may engage in acts of civil disobedience when they oppose government actions was defined by the indicator for the legitimacy of political protest.

Lastly, two specific collective actors involved in traditional cleavages, trade

Table 9.8: Determinants of context analysis

	France		Germany	
	B	Beta	B	Beta
Trust in government	-.13	-.14a	-.07	-.06c
Trust in politicians	.06	.07c	0.1	.11a
Satisfaction with democracy	.01	.08b	0	-.01
External efficacy	.03	0.02	0.16	.15a
Internal efficacy	.18	.14a	0.31	.28a
Legitimacy of civil disobedience	.14	.14a	0.09	.07b
Unjust law: likelihood of counteraction	.18	.17a	0.15	.14a
Unjust law: likelihood of serious attention	.06	.05a	.08	.07c
Involvement in church	.06	.07	.11	.10b
Involvement in trade union	.14	.13a	.1	.09b
constant		.26a		0
R²adj.		.12a		.21a
N		1,421		1,332

Notes: a = p:S 0.001; b = p:S 0.01; c = p:S 0.05
Source: ISSP 2004; data weighted for Germany; Matthias Stauer's calculations.

unions and churches, were chosen to test the influence of traditional cleavages on political protest.

The analysis was conducted using the International Social Survey Programme (ISSP) data of 2004, and the results are presented in Table 9.8. A different dataset was needed because the new model could not be operationalised with the WVS data, which was too limited with regard to contextual features.

We assumed the following hypotheses regarding the explanatory factors of political protest:

1. The higher the perceived responsiveness of the political system, the lower the level of political protest.
2. The higher the trust in the political system, the lower the level of political protest.
3. Religious involvement and membership in organisations related to old cleavages give rise to political protest.

France and Germany share important similarities, reflecting traditional patterns of political participation. In both countries, government trust lowers political protest, which is not very surprising: why should people rebel when they trust their government? Surprisingly, trust in politicians fosters protest in both countries – but the impact is not that significant. Other indicators highlight similar explanations. The likelihood of counter-action against an unjust law reveals a positive impact throughout the analysis. In both countries, political efficiency fosters political protest, though with some nuances as described below. These results confirm the POS model: both France and Germany are exclusive states.

One can also observe that involvement in organisations related to traditional cleavages in France and Germany facilitates protest, but the influence is only moderate. Churches and trade unions were introduced as proxies for the impact of old, traditional cleavage structures, and we expected these aspects to have a higher impact in France. However, a slight nuance can be observed. The chance for citizens in Germany to involve themselves in political protest is higher when they attend church than is the case in France. This may highlight the fact that activism in Germany has stronger ties with religious beliefs than in France, due to different political traditions of activism.[8]

However, some differences are more significant. 'Internal efficacy' is a strong determinant of political protest in Germany, while its impact in France is considerably lower. 'External efficacy' also fosters protest more in Germany than it does in France. These two results are coherent with the previous sections. They tend to prove that the French political system is perceived as being more closed than in Germany, in the sense that the level of responsiveness is stronger in Germany. As a result, a shift in responsiveness has more effect on 'business as usual' in Germany and, consequently, on the level of protest in Germany. In France, trust in the political system and the feeling of political capability remain fairly low.

These figures of illegal protest may well confirm the fact that Germany is more open than France. France, indeed, presents a higher 'legitimacy of civil disobedience' than Germany. As seen above, external efficacy is a more efficient explanatory variable in Germany than in France: this variable fosters legal protest activities in Germany. The same is true regarding its lower level of illegal political protest in Germany: it can be explained by the feeling of responsiveness of the political system. As regards the high level of civil disobedience legitimacy in France,

---

8. A result also observed in the course of several different interviews conducted with anti-nuclear activists in France, June 2009.

we can assume two kinds of explanation: the low responsiveness of the regime and the fact that legal means of protest, such as demonstrations or signing petitions, are not so effective.

Consequently, the data confirms that the higher the responsiveness of the system, the lower the level of illegal political protest: this actually explains why the level of illegal protest is lower in Germany than it is in France. A further distinction between legal and illegal protest forms would, however, be necessary in the ISSP data. Unfortunately, all available datasets lack a sufficient number of cases with, for example, illegal protesters. Similarly, the divide between traditional and New Social Movement cleavages is not so clear-cut in either France or Germany, and would require further investigation. To conclude, the model has a better explanatory power for Germany than France, since it presents a 12 per cent explained variance in France, but a 21 per cent explained variance in Germany.

Summary and conclusions

This chapter poses the question of whether the level of political protest and the legitimacy of illegal protest, based on the WVS data (1990–2000) and the ESS data (2000–5), were higher in France than in Germany. Basically, our findings support the following: the level of political protest is, overall, much more common in France than in Germany; the forms of protest in France are more radical; and civil disobedience is considered a more legitimate form of action in France than it is in Germany. The findings also underlined common points between France and Germany – signing a petition is by far the most common form of political protest in both countries. Boycotts are also very significant, compared with attending a demonstration. Lastly, civil disobedience in both France and Germany presents very low levels compared with those other forms of protest.

The other research question was: how can these patterns of political protest in France and in Germany be explained? In this respect, we have made the choice of associating two models, the CV model and the perceived POS model, in order to combine an individual and an institutional perspective and extend the spectrum of determinants. Indeed, the CV model presents interesting socio-economic insights into the patterns of political protest, but the relevance of these hypotheses also depends on specific characteristics of the political context. We have presented, therefore, a few key variables: on the one hand, income, gender, age, education, motivation, and social networks and, on the other hand, the level of trust in governments and politicians, internal and external efficiency. What are the results of our analysis?

First, the CV model highlighted the socio-economic determinants of political protest in France and Germany. In line with the literature, education, interest in and the importance of politics, and involvement in political parties or associations from new social movements all proved to have a strong impact on political protest in Germany and France. No surprises emerged here. The only exception, however, was that of age: in Germany, younger people protest more than older people while, in France, the age of a person is almost irrelevant. The CV model exhibits a considerable amount of explanatory power in both countries. But it is worth mentioning that this power decreased significantly within the longitudinal perspective. A closer look at the World Values Survey 1999/2000 may well allow us to assume that determinants other than resources, motivation and mobilisation are at work.

Second, the analysis presented two different types of state structure: open vs. closed societies. This is a typology that refers to a twofold distinction: 'strong/ weak', 'exclusive/inclusive' states; in this respect, we introduce several indicators to measure collective perceptions. The analysis provided some empirical data about the individual perceptions of political opportunities in Germany and France: Germany appeared to be more open because its level of responsiveness was higher. The analysis, however, did not confirm the traditional/new social movements divide between France and Germany. More generally, the analysis failed to establish a link between individual perceptions and collective patterns of political participation. The question remains: why do people perceive their system as open or closed? The answer is to be found in the link between objective structures and subjective perceptions, i.e. the structure/agent debate.

What are the consequences of this analysis? It seems promising to use multi-variable data such as the WVS, the ESS and the ISSP data in order to deal with the individual and collective perceptions of political opportunities. While the theoretical explanation appears plausible, data limitations, however, often complicate the satisfactory utilisation of the indicators. The explanatory models presented here are, accordingly, insufficient to explain these differences: the analysis could not find significant micro-level differences between France and Germany. In our analysis, a first regression with a country dummy revealed a considerable country-specific influence upon political protest. Another option might be to conduct multilevel analyses in order to introduce country-specific macro variables into the analysis. Country specificities seem to matter and need to be observed, measured and compared by further theoretical and empirical research.

political protest | 265

Appendix

Variables and operationalisation, and test runs
Please note: all variables were recoded in a range of 0 to 1, with 0 meaning disagree/don't trust/low income etc.; 1 meaning agree/trust/high income, etc.

World Values Survey

Dependent variable:
'I am going to read out some different forms of political action that people can take, and I'd like you to tell me, for each one, whether you have actually done any of these things, whether you might do it or would never, under any circumstances, do it.'

Gender:
'Sex of respondent: 1= Male; 2= Female.' Recoded: O=Female; 1= Male.

Education:
'At what age did you or will you complete your full time education, either at school or at an institution of higher education? Please exclude apprenticeships. (WRITE IN AGE)'

0= N.A.; 1= Completed formal education at 12 years of age or earlier; 2= Completed education at 13 years of age; 3= Completed education at 14; 4= Completed education at 15; 5= Completed education at 16; 6= Completed education at 17; 7= Completed education at 18; 8= Completed education at 19; 9= Completed education at 20; 10= Completed education at 21 years of age or older; 99. N.A., DK.

Age:
'V 355 b) This means you are   years old.'

Income:
'Here is a scale of incomes and we would like to know in what group your household is, counting all wages, salaries, pensions and other incomes that come in. Just give the letter of the group your household falls into, before taxes and other deductions. (see NATION-SPECIFIC CODES below for categories):'

Political discussion:
'When you get together with your friends, would you say you discuss political matters frequently, occasionally or never?'
1= Frequently; 2= Occasionally; 3= Never; 9= Don't know.

Persuading friends:
'When you yourself, hold a strong opinion, do you ever find yourself persuading your friends, relatives or fellow workers to share your views? IF SO, does it hap-

pen often, from time to time, or rarely?'
1= Often; 2= From time to time; 3= Rarely; 4= Never; 9= Don't know.

Interpersonal trust:
'Generally speaking, would you say that most people can be trusted or that you can't be too careful in dealing with people?'
1= Most people can be trusted; 2= Can't be too careful; 9= Don't know.

Church attendance:
'Apart from weddings, funerals and christenings, about how often do you attend religious services these days?'
1= More than once a week; 2= Once a week; 3= Once a month; 4= Christmas/Easter day; 5= Other specific holy days; 6= Once a year; 7= Less often; 8= Never, practically never

Interest in politics:
'How interested would you say you are in politics?'
1= Very interested; 2= Somewhat interested; 3= Not very interested; 4= Not at all interested; 9= Don't know.

Involvement in organisations:
'Please look carefully at the following list of voluntary organisations and activities and say ...
which, if any, do you belong to?
which, if any, are you currently doing unpaid voluntary work for?'

International Social Survey Programme

Dependent variable:
'Here are some different forms of political and social action that people can take. Please indicate, for each one, whether you have done any of these things in the past year, whether you have done it in the more distant past, whether you have not done it but might do it or have not done it and would never, under any circumstances, do it.'
1= Have done it in the past year; 2= Have done it in the more distant past; 3= Have not done it but might do it; 4= Have not done it and would never do it; 8= Can't choose.

Trust in government:
'To what extend do you agree or disagree with the following statements? Most of the time we can trust people in government to do what is right.' 1= strongly agree; 5= strongly disagree.

Trust in politicians:
'To what extend do you agree or disagree with the following statements? Most politicians are in politics only for what they can get out of it personally.' 1= strongly agree; 5= strongly disagree.

Satisfaction with democracy:
'On the whole, on a scale of 10 to 10 where 0 is very poorly and 10 very well. How well does democracy work (COUNTRY) today?'

Involvement in church and trade unions:
'People sometimes belong to different kinds of groups or associations. For each type of group, please indicate whether you belong and actively participate, belong but don't participate, used to belong but do not any more, or have never belonged to it.' 'A trade union, business, or professional association.'
'A church or other religious organisation.'

External efficacy:
'To what extent do you agree or disagree with the following statements?' 'People like me don't have any say about what government does.'
'I don't think the government cares much what people like me think.' 1= strongly agree; 5= strongly disagree.

Internal efficacy:
'To what extent do you agree or disagree with the following statements?'
'I feel I have a pretty good understanding of the important political issues facing (COUNTRY)?'
'I think most people in (COUNTRY) are better informed about politics and government than I am.'
1= strongly agree; 5= strongly disagree.

Unjust law: likeliness of counteraction
'Suppose a law were being considered by [appropriate national legislature] that you considered to be unjust or harmful. If such a case arose, how likely is it that you, acting alone or together with others, would be able to try to do something about it?' 1= Very likely; 4= Not at all likely

Unjust law: likeliness of serious attention
'Suppose a law were being considered by [appropriate national legislature] that you considered to be unjust or harmful. If you made such an effort, how likely is it that [appropriate national legislature] would give serious attention to your demands?'
1= Very likely; 4= Not at all likely.

European Social Survey

Dependent variable:
'There are different ways of trying to improve things in [country] or help prevent things from going wrong. During the last 12 months, have you done any of the following? Have you ...'
Vote: 'Some people don't vote nowadays for one reason or another. Did you vote in the last [country] national election in [month/year]?'

Runs test before the survey and the one/two index debate

Appendix: Dimensions of political protest participation (1999–2000)

	France			Germany	
	Protest activities	Com-munalities	Legal protest	Civil disobedience	Com-munalities
Signing petition	.61	.38	.92		.78
Lawful demonstration	.79	.63	.81		.70
Joining in boycotts	.75	.57	.60	.33	.59
Joining unofficial strike	.80	.65		.87	.78
Occupying buildings/factories	.75	.60		.91	.81
Explained variance (%)	46.9		41.2	20.9	
Eigen values	2.81		2.47	1.26	

Extraction Method: Principal Component Analysis. Rotation Method: Oblimin with Kaiser Normalisation. Scores under 0.3 were suppressed.
Source: World Values Survey 1999–2000; data weighted for Germany, own calculations.

References

Almond, G. A. and Verba, S. (1989) *The Civic Culture: Political attitudes and democracy in five nations,* London: Sage Publications.

Appelton, A. M. (1999) 'The new social movement phenomenon: Placing France in comparative perspective', *West European Politics,* 22(4): 57–75.

Arendt, H. (1972) *Du Mensonge à la Violence,* Paris: Calman-Levy.

Barnes, S. and Kaase, M. (eds) (1979) *Political Action: Mass participation in five western democracies,* Beverly Hills/London: Sage Publications.

Coleman, J. (1990) *Foundations of Social Theory,* Cambridge: Belknap Press of Harvard University Press.

Crossley, M. (2002) *Making Sense of Social Movements,* Buckingham: Open University Press.

Dahl, R. A. (1971) *Polyarchy: Participation and opposition,* New Haven, London: Yale University Press.

Dekker, P., Koopmans, R. and van den Broek, A. (1997) 'Voluntary associations, social movements and individual political behaviour in Western Europe: A micro-macro puzzle' in J.W. van Deth (ed.) *Private Groups and Public Life: Social participation, voluntary associations and political involvement in representive democracies,* London: Routledge.

Diani, M. and McAdam, D. (2003) *Social Movements and Networks: Relational approaches to collective actions,* New York: Oxford University Press.

Filleule, O. (2006) 'Requiem pour un concept: Vie et mort de la notion de structure des opportunités politiques' in G. Dorronso (ed.) *La Turquie Conteste: Mobilisations sociales et régime sécuritaire,* Paris: CNRS.

Filleule, O. and Jimenez, M. (2003) 'Appendix A: The methodology of protest event analysis and the media politics of reporting environmental protest events' in C. Roots (ed.) *Environmental Protest in Western Europe,* Oxford: Oxford University Press.

Fuchs, D. (1995) 'Die Struktur politischen Handelns in der Übergangsphase' in H.-D. Klingemann, L. Erbing and N. Diederich (eds) *Zwischen Wende und Wiedervereinigung: Analysen zur politischen kultur in West- und Ost-Berlin 1990,* Opladen: Westdeutscher Verlag.

Gabriel, O. W. (1996) 'Distrust, involvement, and political protest in western democracies' in L. Halman and N. Nevitte (eds) *Political Value Change in Western Democracies,* Tilburg: Tilburg University Press.

Gabriel, O. W. and Kropp, S. (eds) (2008) *Die EU-Staaten im Vergleich,* 3rd edn., Wiesbaden: VS Verlag für Sozialwissenschaften.

Gabriel, O. W. and Völkl, K. (2005) 'Politische und soziale Partizipation' in O. W. Gabriel and E. Holtmann (eds) *Handbuch Politisches System der Bundesrepublik Deutschland,* 3rd edn., München: Oldenbourg.

Gamson, W. (1990) *The Strategy of Social Protest,* Belmont: Wadsworth Publishing Company.

— (1975) *The Strategy of Social Protest,* Homewood: Dorsey Press.

Gamson, W. and Meyer, D. S. (1996) 'Framing political opportunity' in D. McAdam, J. D. McCarthy and M. N. Zald (eds) *Comparative Perspectives on Social Movements: Political opportunities, mobilizing structures, and cultural framings,* Cambridge: Cambridge University Press.

Guigni, M. (2002) 'Ancien et nouveau institutionnalisme en sciences politiques', *Politique et Société,* 21(3): 69–90.

Hiez, D. and Villalba, M. (2008) *La Désobéissance Civile, Approche Juridique et Politique,* Villeneuve d'Ascq: Presses universitaires du Septentrion.

Ibarra, P. (2003) *Social Movements and Democracy,* New York: Palgrave Macmillan.

Inglehart, R. (1977) *The Silent Revolution: Changing values and political styles among western publics,* Princeton, N.J.: Princeton University Press.

Kaase, M. and Marsh, A. (1979) 'Political action: A theoretical perspective' in S. Barnes and M. Kaase (eds) *Political Action: Mass participation in five western democracies,* Beverly Hills; London: Sage Publications

Kaase, M. and Newton, K. (1995) 'Political attitudes and political behaviour' in M. Kaase and K. Newton (eds) *Beliefs in Government,* New York: Oxford University Press.

Kitschelt, H. (1986) 'Political opportunity structures and political protest: Anti-nuclear movements in four democracies', *British Journal of Political Science,* 16(1): 57–85.

Koopmans, R. (2004) 'Political opportunity structure: some splitting to balance the lumping' in J. Goodwin and J. Jasper (eds) *Rethinking Social Movements: Structure, meanings and emotions,* Lanham: Rowman and Littlefield Publishers.

Koopmans, R. and Rucht, D. (2002) 'Political event analysis' in B. Klandermans and S. Staggenborg (eds) *Methods of Social Movements Research,* Minneapolis: University of Minnesota Press.

Kriesi, H., Koopmans, R., Duyvendak, J. W. and Guigni, M. (1995) *New Social Movements: A comparative analysis,* London: ULC Press.

La Due Lake, R. and Huckfeldt, R. (1998) 'Social capital, social networks and political participation', *Political Psychology,* 19(3): 567–84.

Lijphart, A. (ed.) (1992) *Parliamentary Versus Presidential Government,* New York: Oxford University Press.

Marsh, A. and Kaase, M. (1979) 'Measuring political action' in S. Barnes and M. Kaase (eds) *Political Action: Mass participation in five western democracies,* Beverly Hills; London: Sage Publications.

Micheletti, M. (2003) *Political Virtue and Shopping: Individualism, consumerism and collective action,* New York: Palgrave Macmillan.

Milbrath, L. W. and Goel, M. L. (1977) *Political Participation: How and why do people get involved in politics?,* 2nd edn., Chicago: Rand McNally College Pub. Co.

Mouchard, D. (2002) 'Le mouvement des sans dans la France contemporaine: L'émergence d'un radicalisme autolimité', *Revue Française de Sciences Politiques,* 52(4): 425–47.

Olson, M. (1964) *The Logic of Collective Action: Public goods and the theory of groups,* Cambridge: Harvard University Press.
Putnam, R. (1993) *Making Democracy Work: Civic traditions in modern Italy,* Princeton: Princeton University Press.
Rosenstone, S. J. and Hansen, J. M. (1993) *Mobilization, participation and democracy in America,* New York: MacMillan.
Rucht, D. (2003) 'Changing role of political protest movements' in H. Kitschelt and W. Streek (eds) *Germany: Beyond the stable state.*
Scaff, L. A. (1975) *Participation in the Western Political Tradition: A study of theory and practice,* 2nd edn., Tucson: University of Arizona Press.
Schild, J. (2000) *Politische Konfliktlinien, individualistische Werte und politischer Protest: Ein deutsch-französischer Vergleich,* Opladen: Leske and Budrich.
Schild, J. and Uterwedde, H. (eds) (2006) *Frankreich: Politik, wirtschaft, gesellschaft,* 2nd edn., Wiesbaden: VS Verlag für Sozialwissenschaften.
Sommier, I. (2003) *Le Renouveau des Mouvements Contestataires à l'Heure de la Mondialisation,* Paris: Flammarion.
Der Spiegel (10 October 2009) *The Renaissance of the Anti-nuclear Movement.* Online. Available http://www.spiegel.de/international/germany/0,1518,589456,00.html (accessed 12 December 2010).
Tarrow, S. (1994) *Power in Movement: Social movements, collective action and politics,* Cambridge: Cambridge University Press.
Tilly, C. (1986) *The Contentious French: Four centuries of popular struggle,* Cambridge: Harvard University Press.
Uehlinger, H. -M. (1988) *Politische Partizipation in der Bundesrepublik: Strukturen und Erklärungsmodelle,* Opladen: Westdeutscher Verlag.
van Deth, J. W. (1997) 'Formen konventioneller politischer Partizipation: Ein neues Leben alter Dinosaurier?' in O. W. Gabriel (ed.) *Politische Orientierungen und Verhaltensweisen im Vereinigten Deutschland,* Opladen: Leske and Budrich.
– (2003) 'Vergleichende politische Partizipationsforschung' in D. Berg-Schlosser and F. Müller-Rommel (eds) *Vergleichende Politikwissenschaft: Ein Einführendes Handbuch,* 7th edn., Opladen: Leske and Budrich.
– (2008) 'Measuring social capital' in D. Castiglione, J. W. van Deth and G. Wolleb (eds) *The Handbook of Social Capital,* New York: Oxford University Press.
van Deth, J. W., Montero, J. R. and Westholm, A. (eds) (2007) *Citizenship and Involvement in European Democracies: A comparative analysis,* London/New York: Routledge.
Verba, S. and Nie, N. H. (1972) *Participation in America: Political democracy and social equality,* New York: Harper and Row.
Verba, S., Schlozman, K. L. and Brady, H. (1995) *Voice and Equality: Civic voluntarism in American politics,* Cambridge, Mass./London: Harvard University Press.

Westle, B. (1994) 'Politische Partizipation' in O. W. Gabriel and F. Brettschneider (eds) *Die EU-Staaten im Vergleich: Strukturen, Prozesse, Politikinhalte*, Opladen: Westdeutscher Verlag.

Other sources

Interview 1: Activist from the network 'Sortir du Nucléaire', previously living in Germany.
Interview 2: Activist from the network 'Sortir du Nucléaire', previously living in Germany.
Interview 3: Former campaigner from Greenpeace France.

chapter ten | new forms of citizen involvement
Ortwin Renn and Pia-Johanna Schweizer

Introduction

Inviting the public to be part of the political decision-making process has long been a noble goal and even a legal requirement in many countries. The popularity associated with the concepts of deliberation and direct democracy, however, obscures the challenge of how to put this noble goal into practice and how to ensure that the resulting policies reflect substantive competence, sensitivity to public concerns and preferences, efficiency, and fair burden-sharing. How can and should policy makers ascertain public preferences, integrate public input into the management process, and assign the appropriate roles to technical experts, stakeholders (socially organised groups that are – or perceive themselves as – affected by the decision) and members of the public? Who represents the public: the elected politicians, administrators, stakeholders, or all those who will be affected by the decision?

This chapter addresses these issues in the context of environmental and technological policies involving decisions made under difficult circumstances. Therefore, it provides a somewhat different perspective on political participation than the other chapters in this volume. It assumes that collectively-binding decisions cannot be steered exclusively by governmental actors adopting the traditional top-down approach. Rather, political decisions need input from heterogeneous actors, thus enabling bottom-up governance (Köck 2006). In this regard, the United States National Academy of Sciences (NAS) has linked environmental protection policies to citizen participation and public involvement to ensure that environmental policies and risk management are more effective, more sensitive to citizens' concerns and more in line with democratic principles (Stern and Fineberg 1996). Their report emphasises the need for a combination of assessment and dialogue, which the authors have termed the 'analytic-deliberative' approach. Unfortunately, however, early public involvement of the public in deliberative processes may either compromise the objective of efficient and effective policy implementation, or else violate the principle of fairness (Okrent 1998).

Another problem is that the public at large is made up of many groups, each with its own different value structure and preferences. There is a great deal of individual variance when lay persons are asked to set environmental priorities (Drottz-Sjöberg 1991; Dake 1991). Without any systematic procedure to reach consensus on values and preferences, the public's position often comes over as unclear (Cross 1998). Participatory processes integrating technical expertise, rational decision-making, cultural values and social preferences are, therefore, indispensable.

It is helpful to distinguish five major theoretical approaches of how to conceptualise participation in public policy making: functionalist, neo-liberal, deliberative, anthropological and post-modern. As each of these perspectives emphasises certain aspects of participation, they have, accordingly, inspired different concepts of participation. Furthermore, the analysis will focus on a variety of views on participation and the degree to which they are embedded in different political cultures. The crucial issue of inclusion (who, what, to which degree of commitment?) and closure (rules of deliberation and decision-making) will be discussed in the light of the perspectives on participation. Additionally, the distinction between co-operation and competition as functional prerequisites of society can also be used as an analytical framework, with competition leading to overall social efficiency and goal attainment, and co-operation providing social cohesion. Another mode of interaction involves hierarchical systems, which are meant to increase effectiveness and accountability. A major emphasis here will be on a comparative review of the application of these concepts in Germany and France.

The second section of this chapter addresses two case studies based on some of the perspectives on participation.

Need for stakeholder involvement and participation

Inclusive governance

A major challenge of our time is the management of ecological and health-related risks that are the result of human intervention in the natural environment. Most of these risks are associated with the development and application of technologies, many of which – such as nuclear power generation, genetically modified organisms, and nanotechnology – are very diverse and complex in what concerns their potential risks. The manifestations of these risks result in major uncertainties and ambiguities (Klinke and Renn 2002), large-scale and long-term effects (Wynne 1996), a wide range of social, political and cultural implications (Taylor-Gooby and Zinn 2006), as well as diverse international and trans-boundary consequences (Kasperson and Kasperson 2005). It is not surprising, then, that there is no agreement among the key actors in the environmental policy arena about the nature and extent of the risks associated with these major interventions, let alone about the appropriate risk management and regulation strategies required.

This heterogeneity and plurality of aspects is mainly due to the fact that risks need to be treated as mental constructs (Jasanoff 1993; OECD 2003: 67): risks are generated in the human mind. Unlike hazards – which are real in the sense that their manifestations actually harm people and objects – risks and their consequences are shaped by human perception. As a consequence, risks are created and selected by human actors: they are framed. Risks, therefore, should be understood as embracing one or more uncertain consequences of an event or activity with respect to something that human's value (Kates and Kasperson 1983). Individual perception and social construction of risks vary from one individual to the other and from one society to another. Accordingly, the values associated with specific risks are subject to inter-individual and inter-cultural variation.

Over time, societies have accumulated experience and knowledge of the potential impacts of certain technologies and natural events. Nevertheless, the social framing of risks implies that only certain possible interventions involve follow-up. Societies are selective as to what they deem risky and, consequently, worth taking into account (Thompson *et al.* 1990; Douglas 1990; Beck 1986, Beck 1994: 9ff.). Specialised organisations have been set up to search for indicators of future problems and provide early warning. The process by which these organisations select signals of potential harm is guided by cultural values (such as the shared belief that each individual life is worth protecting) and by institutional and financial resources (e.g. national government decisions to spend money or not on early warning systems concerning highly improbable but high-consequence events). Systematic reasoning (such as using probability theory to distinguish between more likely and less likely events in order to estimate damage potential or the distribution of hazards in time and space) is also taken into account. Due to the complexity of this signal selection process, there is no simple procedure in place for discovering, evaluating and managing risks, and the conventional management approach of balancing expected costs and benefits will not suffice (Stern and Fineberg 1996; Webler 1999; Renn 2004; Rauschmayer and Wittmer 2006).

What could be an appropriate procedure for dealing with such complex and controversial environmental problems as global climate change, deforestation, loss of biodiversity, and negative technological impacts? Many analysts of modern risks refer to the new term of 'inclusive governance': promoting a joint risk governing effort by all actors of civil society (Tait and Lyall 2005; IRGC 2005). Inclusive (risk) governance is based on the conviction that all four major actors in risk decision-making – political, economic, scientific and civil society – should be involved in problem framing, generating policy options, evaluating those options, and reaching a joint conclusion. Their involvement is meant to ensure that systematic knowledge, public preferences, cultural values and ethical considerations are integral parts of the decision-making process. Such an inclusive governance procedure has two advantages:

1. more information can be amassed and made available to policy makers in governments and civil organisations; and
2. the participation of stakeholders and the public can enhance the quality of the risk regulation process by including different perspectives, concerns, and expectations.

Thus an inclusive governance approach offers a broader perspective for risk governance. Perceptions of increased risk due to technical, ecological and social change, when combined with the desiderata of inclusive governance, go beyond the traditional forms of government and participation in governmental decision-making, and set new objectives for modern governments.

Challenges of participation

Stakeholder involvement and citizen participation are essential elements of an inclusive risk governance process. Any type of decision-making – be it participatory or conventional – needs to address two major aspects: what and whom to include (inclusion), and what and how to select (closure). *Inclusion* and *closure* are, therefore, the two essential parts of any decision- or policy-making activity. Classic decision analysis has, so far, offered formal methods for generating options and evaluating these options in accordance with a set of predefined criteria (von Winterfeldt and Edwards 1986). With the advent of new participatory methods, the two issues of inclusion and selection have become more complex and sophisticated than the conventional strategies of decision analysis.

Inclusion

Participatory decision-making, like any other decision-making process, has to reconcile the two opposing aims of inclusion and closure (Bühl 1984). Although the inclusion of a wide variety of ideas, perspectives and options is certainly helpful for finding creative decisions, a binding framework of selection criteria needs to be established in order to ensure option assessment. In this way, inclusion introduces diversity into the decision-making process. When risk assessment is confronted with complex science, uncertain outcomes and controversial interpretations (Klinke and Renn 2002), a wide spectrum of different forms of input (points of view, types of knowledge, etc.) is required if solutions are to be found in the case of conflicting evidence and values. Inclusion, therefore, should be both open and adaptive. Crucial issues in this respect are:

- Who has been included (stakeholders, scientists, governmental agencies, NGOs, interested citizens)?
- What has been included (options, policies, scenarios, frames, preferences, etc.)?
- What is the scope of the process, and which levels of governance structure have been included (multilevel governance (vertical and horizontal))?
- What is the time frame of the process (time period, future generations)?

Closure

The closure of decision-making processes is at least as challenging as the inclusion of varying perspectives, ideas and participants. Closure sets frames and boundaries for the decision-making process to provide the necessary coherence and goal attainment (Hennen 1994: 465). Thus, closure serves two purposes. First, it limits the scope and heterogeneity of what is included in the process. Secondly, these limits allow for competent problem-solving (Bühl 1984: 98). The quality of the closure process itself can be subdivided into the following dimensions:

- Have all arguments been properly treated? Have all truth claims been fairly and accurately tested against commonly-agreed standards of validation?
- Has all the relevant evidence been collected and processed in accordance with the latest methods?
- Have systematic, experiential and practical knowledge and expertise been adequately included and processed?
- Have all interests and values been considered, and has there been a major effort to arrive at fair and balanced solutions?
- Have all normative judgments been made explicit and thoroughly explained? Have normative statements been deduced from accepted ethical principles or legally-prescribed norms?
- Have all efforts been undertaken to preserve the plurality of lifestyles and individual freedom and to restrict the realm of collectively-binding decisions to those areas in which binding rules and norms are essential and necessary to produce the wanted outcome?

Reconciling inclusion and closure is one of the main challenges of participatory decision-making. The potential benefits from stakeholder and public involvement depend on the careful way in which selection and closure in the participation process is handled. It is not sufficient to gather all interested parties around a table and hope for consent on the most practicable policy option. It is essential, in particular, to treat the time and efforts of the participating actors as spare resources that need to be handled with caution. The participation process should be designed so that the various actors are encouraged to contribute to the process with regard to their areas of expertise, which will lead to improvements in the quality of the final product. Yet, by the same token, the process has to be manageable, efficient and competent.

Perspectives for participation

Inclusive governance has different meanings, depending on the particular meta-theoretical perspective taken towards inclusion and closure. Five different approaches towards participation can be identified: functionalist, neo-liberal, deliberative, anthropological and post-modern. These perspectives have to be considered as abstractions from real-world interaction, in so far as no actual participation process could be attributed exclusively to one of these categories. The perspectives provide the theoretical foundation for participation since they have inspired different participation methods. For instance, the neo-liberal perspective emphasises rational bargaining over scarce resources. As a result, it has influenced the participation method called 'mediation', which focuses on bargaining. The other perspectives have, in like manner, inspired different participation methods. In what follows, we explore the affinities between theoretical perspectives and participation methods.

Functionalist

This approach to citizen participation draws on the functional school of social sciences and evolutionary concepts of social change. Functionalism was originally based on the works of Bronislaw Malinowski and Alfred R. Radcliffe-Brown, the founding fathers of British functionalism (Hillmann 1994, Nassehi 1999). Functionalism conceptualises society as a complex structure realising different essential functions for social survival. Each social action is assumed to be functional in assisting the survival of society (Hillmann 1994: 252).

Structural functionalism, in its later development mainly associated with Talcott Parsons and Robert K. Merton, presumes that a system has to meet functional imperatives (adaptation, goal attainment, integration and latency). As these functions are performed by certain structures, society is, therefore, a stratified system of structures securing functional needs (Ritzer 1996). Social differentiation produces structures that are specialised in the fulfilment of specific functions (Münch 1996: 21). In this sense, participatory exercises are necessary in order to respond to the complex functions of society that require input (knowledge and values) from different constituencies.

The goal of 'functionalist' participation is the improvement of political decision-making in general and of political policies in particular. Functionalist decision-making is clearly oriented towards goal achievement. The main objective is to avoid overlooking important aspects, information, perspectives, etc., for the decision, and to ensure that all knowledge camps are represented. Participation is, therefore, seen as a process of ensuring that all the problem-relevant knowledge and values are incorporated into the decision-making process. The inclusion of all relevant positions is supposed to result in constructive conflict resolution by finding win-win solutions among the various actors. The functionalist perspective assumes that representation and inclusion of diversity will result in the adaptation to new risks and successful risk governance. One method of participation suitable to this approach is negotiated rule making. This participation method is especially suited to the functional perspective since it emphasises the inclusion of various kinds of information for strategic planning.

Neo-liberal

This approach to citizen participation draws on both the philosophical heritage of liberalism and that of Scottish moral philosophy. Neo-liberalism conceptualises social interaction as an exchange of resources. Deliberation is therefore seen as a process of negotiation. Social interaction is generally assumed to be governed by rational action. Roughly speaking, rational action consists of the pursuit of one's (subjective) goals while choosing those options for action that promise to be most advantageous, thereby maximising individual preferences while minimising necessary costs (Coleman 1991). The rational actor paradigm understands humans as resourceful, restricted, expecting, evaluating, maximising men (Lindenberg 1985).

Neo-liberal decision-making, in consequence, focuses on individual interests and preferences. It is assumed that people pursue their individual goals according to their available resources. However, the role of society is not to provide integration, but to grant security for property and personal well-being (Locke 1977; Rawls 2003). The psychic and moral drawbacks of social atomisation have been especially criticised by communitarian debate (e.g. Walzer 1993). Public preferences are seen as miscellaneous and unstable. Stakeholder and citizen participation primarily consist, therefore, in the collection and representation of (well-informed) public preferences.

Within neo-liberal theory, individual preferences are taken as given and stable. Conflicts can only be reconciled if:

(1) all the preferences are known in proportional distribution among all affected parties; and
(2) compensation strategies are available to compensate those who might risk utility losses when the most preferred option is taken (Kaldor-Hicks criterion).

Under these conditions, participation is required to generate a representative picture of public preferences and to provide either win-win solutions for all affected parties or, if that is not feasible, compensation strategies for potential losers. The measurement of preferences is linked to the idea that individuals should have the best knowledge about the likely consequences of each decision option (concept of 'informed consent'). Therefore, public opinion polls are not sufficient to represent the public view on a specific public good or norm. Appropriate methods for revealing informed public preferences are, for instance, focus groups. As regards mediation, the second step in generating win-win solutions or acceptable compensation packages, this is seen as one of the best instrumental choices. This method corresponds to the neo-liberal emphasis on bargaining power and individual interests.

Deliberative

Deliberative citizen participation is mainly influenced by Habermasian discourse theory. Discourse theory and discourse ethics advocate more inclusiveness for legitimate and sustainable political decision-making. Modern societies are characterised by a plurality of values and world views. According to Habermas, conventional politics and political decision-making cannot deal adequately with this heterogeneity. Modern societies lack the moral cohesion that could guide political decision-making (Habermas 1996: 20). Although mutually binding norms and values are non-existent externally, people can allude to their shared reason and experience as human beings. Here, the joint heritage of Habermasian deliberation and communitarism becomes obvious. Consequently, political decision-making has to find mechanisms to serve as guidance instruments to enable joint, rational decisions by citizens.

Habermasian discourse ethics offers a solution to this dilemma. In discourse ethics, only those political and judicial decisions may claim to be legitimate that can find the consent of all affected parties in discursive opinion formation and decision-making processes (Habermas 1992: 169). Accordingly, legitimate political opinion formation is conceptualised as a process of the competition of arguments; thus, the procedure of decision-making decides on its legitimacy. Yet understanding – and, consequently, communicative action – can only be reached under the ideal conditions of non-coercive discourse (Habermas 1991: 113).

Knowledge claims are then settled by alluding to the common rationality of communicative action provided by an appropriate organisational discourse structure. Although no real-world discourse can attain the prerequisites of the ideal speech situation (Gripp 1984), practical discourse can aspire to this goal. Discursive decision-making is therefore oriented towards the common good and seeks the rational competition of arguments. It looks for diversity in participants and perspectives, in the sense that all potentially affected parties should be able to agree with its outcome. The results of discursive decision-making draw their legitimacy, therefore, from the procedural arrangements of the discourse. One method for implementing discursive decision-making involves round tables. This participation method aims at facilitating mutual understanding and transparent decision- making, thus adding legitimacy to the whole process of policy making.

Anthropological

Anthropological citizen participation is mainly influenced by pragmatic Anglo-Saxon philosophy. It is based on the belief that common sense is the best judge for reconciling competing knowledge and value claims. Pragmatism was mainly influenced by the works of Charles S. Peirce and John Dewey. Pragmatism postulates that ideas are to be judged in terms of their consequences in the social world. Peirce states that ideas, theories and hypotheses can be experimentally tested, and inter-subjectively evaluated, according to their consequences (Riemer 1999: 463). For Dewey, the thinking process develops over a series of stages starting from 'defining objects in the social world, outlining possible modes of conduct, imaging the consequences of alternative courses of action, eliminating unlikely possibilities, and finally selecting the optimal mode of action' (Ritzer 1996: 328, quoting Stryker 1980). In this way, science can reach truth by constantly testing and modifying its assumptions. This assumption is equally valid for politics and, generally, for each individual. Dewey assumes that action gains moral validity by contributing ever more meaning to life (Prechtl 1995: 218).

This approach has far-reaching consequences for participatory decision-making: the moral value of policy options can be judged according to their consequences. Furthermore, each citizen is capable of moral judgment, without relying on more than his/her mind and experience. When organising discourses of this kind, however, there is a need for independence as regards judgment: the jury has to be disinterested and there should be some consideration of basic diversity in participants (such as gender, age and class). The goals of decision- making inspired by the anthropological perspective include the involvement of the 'model' citizen, and the implementation of an independent jury system, consisting of non-interested laypersons capable of using their common sense to decide on conflicting interests. One participatory method allowing this kind of common sense judgment is 'consensus conferencing'. This method aims at a quota representation of the population, thereby ensuring that the general attitude of all citizens is taken into account.

Post-modern

This approach to citizen participation is based on Michel Foucault's theory of discourse analysis. Discourse analysis reposes on the three basic concepts of knowledge, power and ethics. Foucault is interested in the constitution of knowledge. He assumes that knowledge formation is the result of social interaction and cultural settings. Truth, then, depends on historically and socially contingent conditions (Foucault 2003).

The archaeology of knowledge shows the underlying sets of rules that determine the formation of knowledge. Power is ubiquitous and permeates society. Power and knowledge are interlinked insofar as power supports the creation of knowledge, whilst knowledge legitimates power structures and their social manifestations (Foucault 1979). By means of genealogy, Foucault provides an examination of the dynamic power structures that permeate society. Ethics and the self-constitution of the individual are Foucault's third topic of interest. It is the task of all people to reflect on the knowledge and power structures surrounding and conditioning them. This type of insight into the restraints and possibilities of knowledge and power, and how they relate to each person, transforms a person into an individual (Foucault 1986). However, individuals need not accept the conditions of society as given once and for all; they have, instead, the power to shape their surrounding social structures.

Thus, ethics and individual 'self-constitution' form the third aspect of discourse analysis. In this respect, discourse analysis provides citizen participation with an analytical focus on social power and knowledge formation. Postmodern decision-making, in this sense, aims at revealing the hidden power and knowledge structures of society, thus deconstructing knowledge and values. Participatory decision-making, in particular, seeks to include dissenting views and social minorities, thereby illustrating the relativity of knowledge and power. The Delphi method is a particularly appropriate participatory method because, rather than setting rigid frames for decision-making, it provides insights into stakeholder interests, knowledge bases and power structures.

Political and regulatory culture

Risk participation, however, not only depends on the perspective taken towards citizen and stakeholder participation, it also reposes on national culture, political traditions and social norms, which influence the mechanisms and institutions for integrating knowledge and expertise in the policy arenas. Policy analysts have developed a classification of governmental styles that highlight different 'cultures' of decision-making. Although these styles have been labelled inconsistently in the literature, they all refer to common procedures in different settings (O'Riordan and Wynne 1987). The culture of decision-making also influences the dominating participatory perspective within a specific country. Political and regulatory culture determines the climate for decision-making. Table 10.1 illustrates these four policy-making approaches: *adversarial, fiduciary, consensual,* and *corporatist.*

The *adversarial approach* is characterised by an open forum in which different actors compete for social and political influence in the respective policy arena. Actors in such an arena need and use scientific evidence to support their positions. Policy-makers pay specific attention to formal proof because their decisions can be challenged by social groups on the basis of insufficient use or neglect of scientific knowledge. Risk participation and communication is essential for risk regulation in an adversarial setting, because stakeholders insist on being informed and consulted. Within this socio-political context, stakeholder and citizen involvement is mandatory.

In the *fiduciary approach*, the decision-making process is confined to a group of patrons who are obliged to make orientation towards the 'common good' the guiding principle of their actions. Public scrutiny and involvement of the affected public are alien to this approach. The public can provide input and arguments for the patrons, but is not allowed to be part of the negotiation or policy formulation process. The system relies on generating trust in the competence and fairness of the patrons involved in the decision-making process. Advisers are selected according to national prestige or personal affiliations. In this political context, stakeholder involvement or even citizen participation may be regarded as either a sign of weakness or a denial of personal accountability.

The *consensual approach* is based on a narrow circle of influential actors who negotiate behind closed doors. Social groups and scientists work together to reach a predefined goal. No controversy is present, and conflicts are reconciled on a one-to-one basis before formal negotiations take place. Risk communication in this context serves two major goals: it is supposed to reassure the public that the 'club' acts in the best interest of the public good; and it also conveys the feeling that the relevant voices have been heard and adequately considered. Stakeholder participation is only required to the extent that the club needs further insights from the groups concerned, or if the composition of the club is challenged.

The *corporatist approach,* although similar to the consensual approach, is far more formalised. Well-known experts are invited to join a group of carefully selected policy-makers representing the major forces in society (employers, unions, churches, professional associations, environmentalists). Risk communication, like the consensual approach, is mainly addressed to outsiders, who should gain the impression that the club is open to all 'reasonable' public demands, and that it tries to arrive at a fair compromise between public protection and innovation. Often, the groups represented within the club are asked to organise their own risk participation and communication programmes, as a means of enhancing the credibility of the whole management process.

Table 10.1: Characteristics of policy-making styles

Style	Characteristics	Risk management
Adversarial approach	open to professional and public scrutiny	main emphasis on mutual agreements concerning scientific evidence and pragmatic knowledge
	need for scientific justification of policy selection	integration of adversarial positions through formal rules (due process)
	precise procedural rules	little emphasis on personal judgment and reflection on the part of the risk managers
	oriented towards producing informed decisions by plural actors	stakeholder involvement essential for reaching communication objectives
Fiduciary approach (patronage)	narrow circle of 'patrons'	main emphasis on enlightenment and background knowledge via experts
	no public control, but public input	strong reliance on institutional in-house expertise
	hardly any procedural rules	emphasis on demonstrating trustworthiness
	oriented towards producing trust in the system	communication focused on institutional performance and 'good record'
Consensual approach	open to members of the 'club'	reputation most important attribute
	negotiations behind closed doors	strong reliance on key social actors (also non-scientific experts)
	flexible procedural rules	emphasis on demonstrating social consensus
	oriented towards producing solidarity with the club	communication focused on support by key actors
Corporatist approach	open to interest groups and experts	main emphasis on expert judgment and demonstrating political prudence
	limited public control, but high visibility	strong reliance on impartiality of risk information and evaluation
	strict procedural rules outside of negotiating table	integration by bargaining within scientifically determined limits
	oriented towards sustaining trust in the decision-making body	communication focused on fair representation of major societal interests

Source: IRGC 2005: 63.

As shown above, the style of political decision-making depends on perspectives concerning participation and political and regulatory culture, but many other contributory factors can be identified. Nevertheless, perspectives concerning participation and political culture do influence political decisions to a great extent because they frame the possibilities and limitations of decision-making. What follows demonstrates how 'real-world' decision processes are framed by these factors. The two case studies below compare French and German political decision-making processes, by paying special attention to the previously introduced factors of political culture and perspective concerning participation, thereby highlighting differences and similarities between France and Germany.

Two case studies: a Franco-German comparison

French case study: Comités Locaux d'Information et de Concentration (CLIC)

In the wake of the AZF explosion that occurred on 21st September 2001 in Toulouse, the French Government decided to conduct risk assessments at all industrial sites with major potential for hazardous incidents. Based on this assessment, the relocation of residents living near these facilities was to be initiated. This plan for relocation was envisaged as being designed and implemented with the participation of major stakeholders and affected populations.

The French government identified approximately 500 sites with potentially dangerous industrial activities or storage of hazardous material. These sites were then divided into three geographic zones. The first – innermost – zone represents a danger zone in which all housing activities should be prohibited. Existing settlements should be relocated at the expense of the regional authorities and the industries concerned. The second zone is characterised as potentially dangerous. In this area, no new settlement should be allowed, and all residents who are willing to move into another, safer area, should receive an offer by the regional authorities to compensate them for their property losses. The third zone, considered a risk zone, is where people are exposed to hazards, but only in very rare circumstances. New settlements here should either be prohibited or at least impeded, while existing settlements should not be affected. However, the populations living in these zones should take part in risk avoidance or disaster management programmes.

The mandate for participation includes the following tasks:

- establishing scientifically-sound and socially-acceptable criteria to distinguish between zones 1, 2 and 3;
- developing appropriate compensation schemes for zones 1 and 2;
- developing risk communication programmes for residents remaining in zones 2 and 3;
- developing a transition plan in terms of timing and implementation.

Each *région* (region) in France was given the task of setting up a participatory body ('Round Table') to meet this mandate. Although the Round Tables, known as CLICs, did not have their structure specified by the central government, most were organised in a similar way. The governor of each region handpicked major stakeholder groups and invited their representatives to negotiate all four tasks at the same time. In addition, a team of scientists, mainly from the Institut National de l'Environnement Industriel et des Risques (INERIS), was asked to provide the scientific risk data at each site and to suggest the best way of defining the demarcation lines between the zones, using scientific evidence. The consultations during the Round Table sessions could best be characterised as 'bargaining'. The representatives of the neighbourhood groups opted for a large amount of compensation, while the spokespeople of industry and government looked for modest compensation sums.

However, during the negotiation process, several surprising developments took place. In contrast to what observers had originally expected, most organised groups in the affected areas tried to keep the innermost zone as small as possible. First, they feared that compensation would probably be lower if a large number of citizens needed to be reimbursed at once, as opposed to the situation in the second zone where a more sequential approach for compensation would be pursued. Secondly, many residents were not willing to move from their houses, even when told that the risks were high. Since moving everyone out of zone 1 was mandatory, all participants shied away from this option, which meant compulsory action to move people to other destinations. Thirdly, zone 1 was soon perceived as a place of high stigmatisation that all participants wanted to avoid. In the end, most of the sites had hardly any territory assigned zone 1 status, other than the hazardous facility itself. A second surprise was that it was almost impossible to justify any demarcation lines between zones 1, 2 and 3. At some sites, GIS techniques were used to demonstrate areas with higher and lower risks, but many participants questioned the rationale of risk analysis in general. They asked the public officials concerned to have just one single zone with voluntary compensation schemes, or else to base the zoning decision on non-risk based criteria (e.g. Is the settlement new or old? How much traditional community life is there in a specific zone?). The Round Tables had a hard time to define criteria for assigning the zoning status (and continue to struggle with this problem). A third surprise was that the expected confrontation between industry and the residents did not occur. On many occasions, industry and residents joined forces against the political administration or questioned the rationale of the entire plan. This was partly due to the fact that many residents made their living directly or indirectly from the hazardous facility, and partly due to the perception that the government was exaggerating the risks after being traumatised by the Toulouse incident.

In terms of the classification developed above, several insights can be drawn from the observation of these Round Tables:

- *Inclusion:* The mandate of the central government was clear – as many stakeholders as possible should be involved in the process. Each *Préfect de Région* (Regional Prefect) interpreted this mandate in a different way, but all felt that they were the ones best suited to select the participants.

Although diverse in composition, there was a strong bias in the selection of most of the Round Table participants. Organised stakeholder groups, such as unions, employers, commercial entities and well-known traditional community forces, were clearly over-represented. Environmentalists, social activist groups and neighbourhood organisations were either not represented at all or only marginally. There was no effort to have non-organised groups join the Round Table. This bias partly explains some of the surprising results, in particular the lack of conflict between hazardous industries and residential groups. The rather homogeneous group composition may have made reaching a consensus easier, but it may also have contributed, in the process, to a lack of legitimacy.

- *Closure:* Although the central government's orientation guidelines mentioned consensus as the desired decision-making mode, most Prefects interpreted this more as advice to listen to all voices and then decide on their own how to reconcile conflicting evidence or values. Very often, however, as the participants gained more influence and power during the course of deliberation, they pressed the Prefect (who normally did not participate in the consultations) to adopt options that were in conflict with his/her own views and preferences. A specifically difficult process was the inclusion of scientific evidence in the deliberation process. Most Prefects had appointed experts to feed in the scientific data with respect to risk, property value and other allegedly factual information. The vast majority of the participants did not, however, accept the findings of these outside experts, unless those experts were themselves involved in the negotiations. Since many experts resided in other regions or were very busy, they were unwilling to participate actively in the deliberations. This meant they had only marginal influence on the outcome of the process.

- *Meta-theoretical approach:* The original guidelines for the regions on how to conduct the participatory exercise was clearly inspired by a functional approach to decision-making. The central government wanted local knowledge and local values to be included in the deliberation process as a means of ensuring that the zoning was accurately established. A second motivation might have been to gain greater acceptance among the population. During the actual consultation, however, it was observed that the discussion moved towards a more deliberative style, in which arguments were exchanged and a sense of community spirit developed. This was often perceived as 'the voice of local territory' resisting the universal truth claims of science and the governance claims of central governments. The more removed the Prefect was from the process and the more people identified with the region, the more the inhabitants (including industry) developed the feeling of 'us' versus 'them'. Lastly, there were elements of the anthropological approach in many of the deliberations, as participants continued to appeal to common sense and anecdotal evidence.

– *Political culture:* The central government's perspective was probably corporatist in intent, but practically all the Prefects interpreted the guidelines as endorsing the traditional French style of fiduciary governance. The Prefects invited the participants without offering any explanation of how they had been selected. Most Prefects expected to be consulted, but did not show the slightest inclination to share power with the group. Again, in the course of the process, the participants themselves reinterpreted their mandate. In several instances, this reinterpretation turned out to be adversarial, with a clear conflict between the Prefect and the group; in others, it turned out to be corporatist, since the organised stakeholders took control of the process. Some Round Tables ended in administrative chaos, as nobody seemed to know who was doing what. Although it is too early to draw conclusions, the traditional fiduciary approach contrasted with the self-perception of the participants, so that something new, and sometimes creative, emerged as a result of this conflict.

The analysis of the CLIC process demonstrates that a process may start out as one model and gradually veer towards another model. It also became clear that early mistakes in the selection process (inclusion) proliferated, persisting throughout the entire process and prejudicing the results. Lastly, it was interesting to note that, despite the many local cultural differences in France and the differences in context, the cause of the risk and composition of the Round Tables, the dynamics of the process developed in similar directions. It moved away from the fiduciary approach, to something more corporatist or even adversarial; away from a merely functional perspective to something more deliberative and anthropological; and away from a highly organised and structured plan into a more iterative and, even, disorganised interaction process.

German case study: Regionaler Gewerbeflächenpool Neckar-Alb – REGENA (The Neckar-Alb Regional Industrial Zoning Pool)

In the region of Neckar-Alb, Baden-Württemberg, the mayors of twenty-four communities formed a Round Table to debate the establishment of a common pool of industrial zones managed and governed by the collective interest of all the participating communities. This case study considers the concept of participation from a different angle than that employed in most of the preceding chapters, insofar as the participants of this case study are not citizens but mayors. The method chosen was the Round Table, with political representatives from all participating communities.

The structure of this participatory project was much simpler than in the French case. The idea was to switch from a competitive to a co-operative arrangement when assigning commercial or industrial zones. Some drawbacks are associated with a competitive style of zoning:

– In the present competitive system, each community is forced to offer a lower bid than the neighbouring community to attract a potential investor; this leads to a situation where, ultimately, not even the costs for building or

maintaining the industrial zone's infrastructure can be recuperated.
- When land is developed for industry and, quite probably, it does not take advantage of this offer (due to the rural character of this region), the land is wasted and biodiversity reduced.

The co-operative system of industrial zoning offers two advantages:

1. a common pool of industrial zones could be placed at the best location in the whole area, thus attracting more powerful investors; and
2. the common pool would provide tax income for all the communities, irrespective of their location and other potential constraints in attracting businesses.

Given these advantages, it is difficult to believe that there has not been even one single case in the whole of Germany in which such a pooled solution has been established. There are four reasons for this. First, there is a long tradition of communities vying with each other for more investors. Many mayors, believing that it is their personal negotiating skills that make the difference, do not want to share revenues with those who, in their eyes, are not clever enough to attract investors. Secondly, the existing legal framework is based on a competitive system, and several legal stipulations would need to be changed to make such a pooled version work. Thirdly, as there are many personal conflicts between the mayors, they have a hard time believing that a co-operative solution could work, given the particular individuals who are participating. Finally, the revenues coming from the pooled land would be distributed among all the communities, thus benefiting those communities that are either unable to set aside land for development or unwilling to do so.

In this situation, the main purpose of the participatory exercise was to build trust among the participants and to find a solution that seemed both fair as regards all the interests involved, and feasible in terms of legal constraints. Between 2001 and 2003, the mayors met more than seven times in plenary sessions, with several of them holding subcommittee meetings in between. The meetings led to a final document in which the main rules for the pooled solution were generated and accepted; there was, however, no consensus as to the legal entity that would be necessary to govern the process. One of the groups wanted a loose form of co-operation based on voluntary agreements without any legally binding structure, while another group opted for a *Zweckverband*, a legally-recognised association (with clear rules, bylaws, and organisational structure). This conflict remained unresolved during the first round of negotiations.

The second round of negotiations started after a year's break, in 2005, for the community elections. The Federal Government had granted funds for this process in order to investigate its feasibility for other regions in Germany. The monetary incentive was certainly one major reason for the mayors to reconvene and look for a consensual solution. The two camps continued to fight for their respective model, but over time it became clear that neither the legal nor the organisational problems could be solved by means of purely voluntary agreements. A compromise was arrived at: temporarily, a voluntary code of co-operative conduct would be in effect until all the by-laws and provisions of the new legal association had been worked out. If setting up such an association proved impossible, the voluntary rules would remain effective.

At present, the Round Table is working on the by-laws and provisions of the association. However, only eleven of the twenty-four mayors initially involved have continued to participate in the process. The others, although they have not withdrawn for good, have opted to wait until a document is drawn up, which they would then evaluate. On the basis of such a document, all the mayors, or at least most of them, might then decide to participate in the association, even though they would not have been part of the team thrashing out all the details of the document.

As in the French case, a few surprises cropped up during the REGENA process. Most mayors showed little interest in actively participating in the discussions, largely adopting the role of observers. They functioned as a sounding board in the fight between the two adversaries, one of whom advocated the voluntary solution, the other that of the legal association. It was obvious who favoured which particular side, although this did change over time. More than 80 per cent of all the Round Table sessions, with twenty-four participants initially involved, took place between four persons. When asked by the facilitator to become more active, they rejected this request. Either they were very satisfied with their remote role, clearly situated as they were in one camp or the other, and feeling well represented by their respective spokespersons; or else they were undecided, and did not want to appear to favour one side rather than the other. The only way to break through this rigid consultation process was to organise small subgroups, with each of them being assigned special tasks that did not require taking sides on the main issue.

A second surprise was the influence of personalities and personal chemistry during the negotiations. In spite of the fact that all the participants were elected mayors, with a certain professional background, personal sympathies and antipathies often governed the process. In particular, the leaders of the two camps were clearly driven by emotional factors in their relations, playing out their satisfaction or dissatisfaction with each other, irrespective of the topic addressed. It often took all of the facilitator's skills to ensure that the process was not derailed and that participants would show willingness to focus on the subject rather than on their personal relations.

In terms of the classification developed above, several insights can be drawn from the observation of this 'Round Table' in Germany:

- *Inclusion:* The mandate to reach an accord among the mayors as representatives of their communities required the participation of the main actors, i.e. the mayors themselves. However, these mayors needed the support of their *Gemeinderat*, their community parliaments. Several mayors were either not courageous enough to face their *Gemeinderat*, or else were not really sure whether they wanted to make the process public and their involvement visible. In several towns, quite a few members of the community parliament found that they were being kept informed by the media about the process and, as a result, were quite annoyed. The facilitator organised an information campaign and visited all the local parliaments that wanted to be informed. Although this campaign did, in certain cases, provide a boost for the idea, it compromised the perceived authority of the mayor. The civil society actors, though they were eager to know more about the process, did not express any immediate desire to take part at an early stage; in fact, their attempt to establish an advisory board failed, due to a lack of interest and controversy in their ranks. As for the interest groups, they favoured the proposal because economic and ecological goals would be better served by co-operation rather than competition.

- *Closure:* The process clearly needs consensus on the part of all participants. Each mayor can either go along with the process or opt out. Since some could not decide, a middle-of-the-road category was introduced: that of observers, for those mayors who did not want to commit themselves but remained interested in the process. These observers cannot vote and, since consensus is always required, are in effect unable to veto an agreement. The consensual decision process is alien to most mayors, but no voting procedure could ever work in this case. In the end, each *Gemeinderat* needs to approve the agreement. So mayors are caught in the middle, between the Round Table with its group pressure and their own *Gemeinderat* with the pressure it could bring to bear.

- *Meta-theoretical approach:* The original Round Table was clearly neo-liberal in its intentions. All participating towns needed to be represented by their mayors. Since consensus was required, there was no necessity for the size of each town to be weighted: equal representation was sufficient to ensure a fair process. The goal was to establish a win-win solution, so that all participants could benefit according to their (predefined) preferences. If problems occurred, compensatory measures would be generated to ensure that potentially negative impacts could be balanced against extra benefits. Similar to what happened in the above-mentioned French case study, the dynamics in the German study changed in what was initially a clear cut meta-theoretical (subconscious) model. First, the personal relations in the groups turned out to be so influential that elements of what Habermas would call a 'therapeutic discourse' needed to be included and applied. This changed the character of the deliberations from bargaining game into a motivational exercise, requiring many appeals to the participants and personal reconfirmations. Secondly, the obvious win-win situations became obscured by procedural difficulties and conflicting values (reliability versus flexibility) when designing the organisational structure. Over time, elements of deliberative argumentation entered the process, although only a few participants were willing to engage in such an argumentative discourse, and capable of doing so. Thirdly, functional elements came into play when conflicts could not be resolved. The advocacy of voluntary agreements collapsed immediately it became clear that this model could

not function within the legal environment of community laws. In essence, the neo-liberal view still dominated the process, but it was enriched by deliberative and functional elements.
- *Political culture:* The mandated Round Table consensual decision-making contrasted with the corporatist expectations of the mayors. They wanted to invite the usual stakeholders, obtain their views and then vote on a set of options. It was quite difficult to convey to the mayors that they would need to generate their own options, argue about them and reach a consensus. In the beginning, many mayors were convinced that without a majority voting procedure, the Round Table would never produce anything. It took months for the participants to become used to a process in which a vote was never taken (although it was demanded several times, in particular when one of the two camps believed it had the majority behind it). The clash between the culture experienced in political life and that demanded for this specific purpose caused a lot of friction. It was certainly one of the reasons why many participants abstained from making any statement, as they felt alienated by the deliberative process. In the course of time, the new style of argumentation and deliberation became more and more visible, yet with a clear emphasis on strategic rather than empathetic reasoning. However, many mayors reported that they had benefited in other political contexts from this new, unfamiliar style of decision- making and that they saw it as a learning experience for a more consensual decision-making culture.

Analysis of the REGENA process demonstrates the difficulties when alien models of decision-making are imposed on an assembly, made up of individuals who had been socialised under different decision-making system. It takes great time and effort to develop a climate in which consensual decision-making can prosper. In the end, most participants felt comfortable with the new rules, but many still have difficulties in participating actively in the debate. The instrument of strategic reasoning and voting according to pooled opinions (party vote) may also be a functional tool to overcome personal antipathies. Emotional factors became much more visible in the consensual mode, with each participant needing to be personally convinced. Several times the process came close to collapse because the group was unable to cope with such personal involvement.

Conclusion

The objective of this chapter has been to address and discuss the implications of inclusive governance in the field of environmental policy making and risk management. Inclusive governance is seen as a necessary requirement since environmental policies demand input from several key society players. Analytic knowledge, social preferences, cultural values and moral norms all serve an important function in environmental risk decision-making; they also need to be integrated into prudent environmental policies as they are being designed. Such integration requires a structure allowing for the systematic inclusion of stakeholders and representatives of the public. Organising and conducting discourses on environmental problems goes beyond mere good intention, that of simply involving the public in decision-making. The mere desire of initiating a two-way communication process and the willingness to listen to public concerns are not sufficient. Discursive processes need a structure that ensures the integration of technical expertise, regulatory requirements and public values. These different inputs should be combined in such a way that they offer the deliberation process the type of expertise and knowledge needed to claim legitimacy within a rational decision-making procedure (von Schomberg 1995). It does not make sense to replace technical expertise with vague public perceptions; nor is it justifiable to have experts insert their own value judgments into what ought to be a democratic process.

An organisational model is needed that assigns specific roles to each contributor while simultaneously ensuring that each contribution is embedded within a dialogue setting. That setting must guarantee the mutual exchange of arguments and information, provide all participants with opportunities to introduce and challenge claims, and create active understanding among all participants (Webler 1999). The key words here are 'inclusion' and 'closure'. The questions are: What is taken up for deliberation? How is a decision made at the end of the deliberation process?

There is no simple answer to these two questions. Depending on context, the political culture and the meta-theoretical framework, different approaches to inclusive government can be taken. In this paper, we have proposed a taxonomy for political culture and for meta-theoretical frameworks that could help those in the participatory procedure understand the processes better, and measure their success or failure in terms of their own propositions and expectations. The political culture taxonomy includes the adversarial, consensual, corporatist and fiduciary approaches; the meta-theoretical approach taxonomy encompasses neo-liberal, functional, deliberative, anthropological and post-modern participation concepts. Each of these approaches and cultural styles is associated with specific models, instruments, and organisational requirements. Participatory research in the social sciences can first analyse each case within the given framework and political style, and then extend this analysis to evaluate the appropriateness of either the selected approach or the regulatory style in relation to each other, and with respect to the requirements of the specific case.

We have applied this taxonomy to two case studies that were part of the *TRUSTNET* project funded by the EU Commission. The analysis revealed that taxonomies provide prototypes of procedures that can never be observed in a pure state. Furthermore, the dynamics or processes lead to sometimes subtle, sometimes dramatic changes in approach and/or style. For example, the French CLIC exercises, designed with a corporatist model in mind, were implemented in a fiduciary spirit, but, in practice, they gradually became more and more adversarial. In addition, the concept of argumentation changed little by little from a functional to a more deliberative model. Although neither the French nor the German case studies fully match any of the categories proposed in this paper, the analysis has shown that they are very useful. They help in characterising components or elements of the process, in describing the beliefs and expectations of actors, and in revealing open or hidden conflicts and problems. Many more case studies are necessary to demonstrate the usefulness of these taxonomies, but an initial examination of the two case studies justifies cautious optimism that the taxonomies explored here can provide useful tools for analysing and interpreting case studies with respect to inclusive governance.

References

Beck, U. (1986) *Risikogesellschaft: Auf dem weg in eine andere moderne*, Frankfurt/Main: Suhrkamp.
— (1994) 'The reinvention of politics: Towards a theory of reflexive modernization' in U. Beck, A. Giddens and S. Lash (eds) *Reflexive Modernization: Politics, tradition and aesthetics in the modern social order*, Stanford: Stanford University Press.
Bühl, W. L. (1984) *Die Ordnung des Wissens*, Berlin: Duncker and Humblot.
Coleman, J. (1991) *Handlungen und Handlungssysteme*, 2nd edn., München: Oldenbourg.
Cross, F. B. (1998) 'Facts and values in risk assessment', *Reliability and Systems Safety*, 59: 27–45.
Dake, K. (1991) 'Orienting dispositions in the perceptions of risk: An analysis of contemporary worldviews and cultural biases', *Journal of Cross-Cultural Psychology*, 22: 61–82.
Douglas, M. (1990) 'Risk as forensic resource', *DAEDALUS*, 119 (4): 1–16.
Drottz-Sjöberg, B. -M. (1991) *Perception of Risk: Studies of risk attitudes, perceptions, and definitions,* Stockholm: Center of Risk Research.
Foucault, M. (1979) *Überwachen und Strafen: Die Geburt des Gefängnisses,* 3rd edn., Frankfurt/Main: Suhrkamp.
— (1986) *Der Gebrauch der Lüste,* Frankfurt/Main: Suhrkamp.
— (2003) *Die Ordnung der Dinge,* Frankfurt/Main: Suhrkamp.
Gripp, H. (1984) *Jürgen Habermas: Und es gibt sie doch – zur kommunikationstheoretischen begründung von vernunft bei Jürgen Habermas*, Paderborn: Schöningh.
Habermas, J. (1991) *Moral Consciousness and Communicative Action*, 2nd edn., Cambridge: MIT Press.
— (1992) *Faktizität und Geltung: Beiträge zur diskurstheorie des rechts und des demokratischen rechtsstaats*, 2nd edn., Frankfurt/Main: Suhrkamp.
— (1996) *Die Einbeziehung des Anderen: Studien zur politischen theorie*, Frankfurt/Main: Suhrkamp.
Hennen, L. (1994) 'Technikkontroversen: Technikfolgenabschätzung als öffentlicher Diskurs', *Soziale Welt*, 45(4): 454–79.
Hillmann, K. -H. (1994) *Wörterbuch der Soziologie,* 4th edn., Stuttgart: Kröner.
IRGC (2005) *Risk Governance: Towards an integrative approach. White Paper No. 1*, written by Ortwin Renn with an Annex by Peter Graham, International Risk Governance Council: Geneva.

Jasanoff, S. (1993) 'Bridging the two cultures of risk analysis', *Risk Analysis*, 13(2): 123–29.
Kasperson, J. X. and Kasperson R. E. (2005) 'Border crossing' in J. X. Kasperson and R. E. Kasperson (eds) *The Social Contours of Risk,* London: Earthscan.
Kates, R. W. and Kasperson, J. X. (1983) 'Comparative risk analysis of technological hazards: A review', *Proceedings of the National Academy of Sciences*, 80: 2027–37.
Klinke, A. and Renn, O. (2002) 'A new approach to risk evaluation and management: Risk-based, precaution-based and discourse-based management', *Risk Analysis*, 22(6): 1071–94.
Köck, W. (2006) 'Governance in der Umweltpolitik' in G. F. Schuppert (ed.) *Governance: Forschung: Vergewisserung über stand und entwicklungslinien,* 2nd edn., Baden-Baden: Nomos.
Lindenberg, S. (1985) 'An assessment of the new political economy: Its potential for the social sciences and for sociology in particular', *Sociological Theory*, 3(1): 99–114.
Locke, J. (1977) *Zwei Abhandlungen über die Regierung* (ed.) W. Euchner and trans. H. Hoffmann, Frankfurt am Main: Suhrkamp.
Münch, R. (1996) *Risikopolitik,* Frankfurt/Main: Suhrkamp.
Nassehi, A. (1999) 'Struktur-funktionale Theorie' in P. Prechtl and F. -P. Burkard (eds) *Metzler-Philosophie-Lexikon: Begriffe und Definitionen,* 2nd edn., Stuttgart: Metzler.
O'Riordan, T. and Wynne, B. (1987) 'Regulating environmental risks: A comparative perspective' in P. R. Kleindorfer and H. C. Kunreuther (eds) *Insuring and Managing Hazardous Risks: from Seveso to Bhopal and beyond,* Berlin: Springer.
OECD (ed.) (2003) *Emerging System Risks*: *Final report on the OECD future project,* Paris: OECD.
Okrent, D. (1998) 'Risk perception and risk management: On knowledge, resource allocation and equity', *Reliability Engineering and Systems Safety*, 59: 17–25.
Prechtl, P. (1995) 'Dewey, John' in B. Lutz (ed.) *Metzler-Philosophen-Lexikon: Von den vorsokratikern bis zu den neuen philosophen,* 2nd edn., Stuttgart: Metzler.
Rauschmayer, F. and Wittmer, H. (2006): 'Evaluation deliberative and analytical methods for the resolution of environmental conflicts', *Land Use Policy*, 23(1) 108–22.
Rawls, J. (2003) *Politischer Liberalismus,* Frankfurt am Main: Suhrkamp Verlag.
Renn, O. (2004) 'The challenge of integrating deliberation and expertise: Participation and discourse in risk management' in T. L. MacDaniels and M. J. Small (eds) *Risk Analysis and Society: An interdisciplinary characterization of the field,* Cambridge: Cambridge University Press.
Riemer, I. (1999) 'Pragmatismus, Neopragmatismus' in P. Prechtl and F. -P.

Burkard (eds) *Metzler-Philosophie-Lexikon: Begriffe und Definitionen*, 2nd edn., Stuttgart: Metzler.
Ritzer, G. (1996) *Sociological Theory*, 4th edn., New York: McGraw-Hill.
Stern, P. C. and Fineberg, H. V. (1996) *Understanding Risk: Informing decisions in a democratic society, national research council, committee in risk characterization*, Washington, D.C.: National Academy Press.
Stryker, S. (1980) *Symbolic Interactionism: A social structural version*, Menlo Park: Benjamin-Cummings Publications.
Tait, J. and Lyall, C. (2005) 'A new mode of governance for science, technology, risk and the environment?' in C. Lyall and J. Tait (eds) *New Modes of Governance*, Aldershot: Ashgate.
Taylor-Gooby, P. and Zinn, J. O. (2006) 'Current directions in risk research: New developments in psychology and sociology', *Risk Analysis*, 26(2): 397–411.
Thompson, M., Ellis, R. and Wildavsky, A. (1990) *Cultural Theory*, Boulder: Westview Press.
von Schomberg, R. (1995) 'Erosion of the value spheres: The ways in which a society copes with scientific, moral and ethical uncertainty' in R. von Schomberg (ed.) *Contested Technology: ethics, risk and public debate*, Tilburg: International Centre for Human Public Affairs.
von Winterfeldt, D. and Edwards, W. (1986) *Decision Analysis in Behavorial Research*, Cambridge: Cambridge University Press.
Walzer, M. (1993) 'Die kommunitaristische Kritik am Liberalismus' in A. Honneth (ed.) *Kommunitarismus: Eine debatte über die moralischen grundlagen moderner gesellschaften*, Frankfurt/Main: Campus.
Webler, T. (1999) 'The craft and theory of public participation: A dialectical process', *Risk Research*, 2(1): 55–71.
Wynne, B. (1996) 'May the sheep safely graze? A reflexive view of the expert-lay knowledge divide' in S. Lash, B. Szerszynski and B. Wynne (eds) *Risk, Environment and Modernity: Towards a new ecology*, Thousand Oaks, CA: Sage Publications.

index

action groups 74, 84, 240
   participation in 73–4, 191
   see also voluntary associations
age 80, *81*, 94
   political participation and 238, 246, 250, 252
   political protest and 254, *255*, 263
   voter turnout and 221, *224*, 225
Ajzen, I. 14–15, 23, 193, 222
Almond, G. A. xv, 1, 3, 6, 21, 72, 100, 128, 190, 195, 237
   civic culture, concept of 1–2
Ansell, C. 23
apathy 6–7, 84
   role of the internet and 89
Appleton, A. M. 49, 212, 217 n.7, 243
Apter, D. E. 168
Arendt, H. 240
Armingeon, K. 18, 20, 84, 192
Arzheimer, K. 209, 220
Asher, H. B. 6
Aubelle, V. 146
Austria *77,* 129, 138 n.1
Ayala, L. J. 82, 95

Bäck, H. 137, 138 n.1, 144, 169 n.5
Bacot, P. 169
Bacqué, M. -H. 161
Barber, B. 168
Barnes, S. 6, 9. 15, 21, 239
Bauer, P. 22
Beck, U. 275
Belgium *77,* 216
Bell, D. xv, 1
Bertelsmann Foundation 22
Besley, J. C. 88, 90, 91
Bimber, B. 89
Blais, A. 120, 127, 214
Blazy, J. -P. 173

Bobbio, N. 184
Bogumil, J. 140
Borraz, O. 129
Bourdieu, P. 23
Bowler, S. 80, 82, 86, 100 n.33
Boy, D. 22, 23
boycotts 242, 243, 246, 249
   French/German comparisons *244,* 245, *247*, 263, *268*
Brady, H. 18, 82 n.18, 83, 86, 114, 193, 194, 200, 221, 248, 250
Bréchon, P. 5, 22
Brubaker, R. 41
Bühl, W. L. 276
Bulgaria *77*
Burhoff, D. 195
Buss, A. 142

Caballero, C. 220
Caillosse, J. 146
Cain, B. E. 6
Campbell, A. 6, 222
Carmines, E. G. 33
Carty, R. K. 120, 127
Castoriadis, C. 168
Caulfield, J. 137
Chirac, J. 175, 212 n.3, 217
Christadler, M. 3
church membership
   participation, political and 82–3, *85*, 95, 222, *224*, 225, 226
   political protest and 254, *255, 261,* 262
civic culture 1, 176
civic duty, sense of 86
civic engagement 4–5, 20, 189, 191, 192, 194, 203
civic rights 2, 5, 6, 35, 36, 40–1
   formalisation and 35, 36

freedom of association and assembly 41, 42, 58, 59
right to vote and 34, 45–6
see also franchise
civic skills 18, 74, 75, 82, 83, 84
civic virtue 20
Civic Voluntarism Model (CVM) 17–19, 79, 194–5, 223,
   mobilisation-based approach and 18–19, 226, 238, 250, 252, 253
   motivation-based approach and 18, 226, 238, 250, 251, 253
   political protest study and 238, 239, 248, 250, 253, 256, 263–4
   resource-based approach and 18, 226, 238, 250–1, 253
   state structure and 255, 256
civil disobedience 8, 75, 181, 237, 238, *240*, 241, 246, 258, 263
   France and 242, 243, 244, 245, 246, 262–3
   Germany and 241, 242, 243, 244, 245, 246
   see also protest, political
Civil Rights Movement (US) 9
Claiborn, M. P. 84
Cnudde, C. F. 1
Coleman, J. 189, 252, 278
common good, notion of 3, 280, 282
communitarianism 279
Costa, O. 157
Council of Europe 120 n.6
Cross, F. B. 273
Crossley, M. 256
culture, political *11*, 128, 202
   participation and 273
Curtis, J. E. 195
Cyprus 77, 216
Czech Republic 138 n.1

Dahl, R. A. 1, 36, 37, 72, 119, 120, 128, 173, 190, 237
   polyarchy, notion of 1
Dake, K. 273
Dalton, R. J. 3, 20, 22, 23, 24, 54, 57, 60, 61, 71, 72, 74, 75, 76, 80, 85, 86, 209, 220
Davidov, E. 90, 105, 106
Day, N. 11
de Gaulle, C. 50, 56, 211 n.2, 216 n.7, 217
Dekker, P. 190, 238, 242, 243, 256, 257
deliberation, concept of 273
democracy 1
   deliberative 137–8, 146
   local 137–8, 144, 146
      institutional framework for 139–44
      tools of 138, 139
   political participation and 1, 40, 45, 85, 137–8, 190, 220
   representative and participatory 146
   trust, role of in 190
   see also direct democracy
demonstrations 35, 72 n.4, 73, 74, 75, 80, 84, 85–6, 87, 91, 94, 181, 237, 240, 242, 246, 248–9
   characteristics of 76
   France and 76, *77*, 92, 93, 99, 101, 243, *244*, 245, *247*, 250, 263, *268*
   Germany and 76, *77*, 79, *93*, 101 n.34, 241, 243, *244*, 245, *247*, *268*
   legitimacy and 75
   see also civil disobedience; protest, political
Denmark *77*, 129, 138 n.1, 220
Denquin, J. -M. 168
Denters, S. A. H. 137
Dewey, J. 280
Dewoghélaëre, J. 173 n.6
Di Palma, G. 85
Diani, M. 252
Die Hanse Federation 5
Dijkstra, B. R. 180
direct democracy 6, 25, 43, 44, 45, 161, 167, 176, 273
   France and 43, 44, 50, 167

Germany and 51, 167
    instruments of 162–4
    popular initiative and 176, 178
    types of practices 50, 161, *163*
    see also referendums
discourse analysis/theory 279–80, 281
Dobrzynska, A. 120, 127, 214
Douglas, M. 275
Downs, A. 13, 14
    An Economic Theory of Democracy 13
Drottz-Sjöberg, B. M. 273
Dunleavy, P. 33
Duverger, M. 211 n.1

education
    political participation and 80, *81*, 94, 97, 98, 202, 209, 221, *224*, 225
    political protest and 238, 250, 251, 252, 253, 254, 263
Edwards, W. 276
Effective number of parties index (ENOP) 259 n.7
Egner, B. 137, 138 n.1, 140, 142, 147, 152
electoral turnout xvi, 113–14, 118
    five factors of contextual difference 114, 119, 130
        analysis of France/Germany and 119–29, 130
    local government analysis (France and Germany) 113–132
        decline in 118–19, 121, 137
        France, turnout in 113, 114, 115–16, 117, 118
        Germany, turnout in 113, 114, 115–16, 117, 118
        institutional differences and 122–4, 130
        local discretion and 128–9, 130
        municipal size and 119–22, 130
        political salience of elections and 124–6, 130

measurement methods and 118, 129
    proportional representation (PR) and 35, 46, 127, 130
    studies of 33, 35, 113–132
    see also voter turnout; voter turnout study, France and Germany
Ellwein, T. 22, 214
employment status 83
    political participation and 83–4, *85*, 95, 96, 222, *224*, 225, 250
Enquete-Kommission
    Bürgerschaftliches Engagement 194
environment protection 182, 183, 185, 273
    citizen participation in 82, 99, 100, 181, 273
    Germany and 180, 252
    voluntary associations and 94, 196, 252
environmental policy making 273–292
    France, case study 284–7
        CLIC (Round Table) process and 284–5, 286, 287, 292
    Germany, case study 287–91
        competitive/co-operative zoning and 287–8
        Round Table process in 287, 289, 290, 291
    inclusive governance and 275, 291–2
        advantages of 275–6
        risk governance and 275, 276, 291
    risks, perception of 274
        social construction of and 275
Ersson, S. O. 3
Estonia 77
Eurobarometer surveys xv, 21, 195 n.4
European Parliament 46, 47, 122
European Social Survey programme (ESS) xv, 21, 71, 72, 76, 77, 79, *81,* 82, 86, *87, 89,* 91–2, *93, 95,* 96, 98, 99, 192 n1, 195, *199, 201,* 238, 241, 246, *247,* 264

European Union
  citizen responsiveness and 72
  country electoral turnout rates 216
  immigrants, status in 36
European Values Survey xv

Falter, J. W. 220
family 81, 83, 84, *85,* 222
Feist, U. 227
Fijalkowski, J. 169
Filleule, O. 241, 256
Filzmaier, P. 216
Fineberg, H. V. 273, 275
Finifter, A. W. 18
Finkel, S. E. 86
Finland *77*
Fishbein, M. 14, 23, 193, 222
Fishkin, J. 161, 163
Foucault, M. 281
France
  bureaucracy in 3, 4
  citizen participation in 2, 3, 4–5, 22, 23, 24–5, 40–4, 46
    basic rights and 40–4, 49, 74
    formalisation of 35, 44, 99
    traditions/culture/values and 4, 91, 92, 93, 95, 96, 98
  Charter of Basic Rights 41
  citizenship laws and 41, 44, 63
  Code Électoral 212
  Communist Party 217
  Constitution of 40, 41, 42, 44, 46, 47, 50, 51, 53, 54, 63, 75 n.9, 162, 211
  Declaration of Human and Civil Rights (1789) 40, 41, 42, 58, 75 n.9
  democracy, development of 4, 44
    direct democracy and 43, 44, 50, 63, 64, 163–4
  electoral participation and 22, 25, 42–3, 45–6, 49, 72 n.3
    active and passive rights and 49
    church attendance and 202, 203, 204
  education and 202, 203, 209
  interest groups and 197
  voter turnout 118, 125, *126,* 215, 219, 227
  see also study under electoral turnout; voter turnout study, France and Germany
  electoral system in 46, 47–9, 63, 124, 127–8, 211–13, 214, 215, 216–19
    registration and 48–9, 118, 129
    electoral law in 211–13, 214
    local systems and 127–8
    majoritarian system and 47–8, 127–8, 130, 211
    mayors and 138
    presidential elections and 46, 47, 63, 72 n.3, 125, *126,* 216–19
    'substitutional' vote and 49
    voter turnout, effect on 211, 212, 214, 215, 216–19
  franchise in 3, 40, 45, 214
  immigrant rights in 41
  interest groups and 53, 58, 60, 61–2
    associations and 58–9, 61–2, 63
    political effect of 60, 62, 63
    see also under trade unions; voluntary associations
  local/regional government in 5, 37, 43, 51, 122–3, 124, 128–9, 140–1, 164, 167–8, 173–4
    elections in 113, 115–32
    electoral turnout analysis *see* under electoral turnout
    mayoral power and 122–3, 124, 129 n.9, 164, 164, 169
    municipal areas in (communes) 120–1, 140–1, 142–3, 167, 175–6, 195
    organisation and power distribution in 122–3, 124, 128–9, 141, 167–8
    referendums and 51, 151, *153,* 162, *163,* 164, 166–7, 169, 175–6

see also local government,
France municipality system
Ministry of Internal Affairs 116,
117, *121*, 122, *126*, 162, 174
National Assembly in 43, 46, 47,
49, 56, 60, 151, 211, 212–13
elections, participation in
212–13, 214–19
participatory systems comparison
study (with Germany) 33–66
four criteria used in 34–8, *39,*
64, *65*
formalisation of 44, 49, 52, 61,
62, *65*
impact of 44, 58, 64, *65*
inclusivity of 64, *65*
participative rights, exhibition
of 64
scope of 44, 49, 57, 62, 63, 64,
65
strength of 44, 52, 62, 64
see also demonstrations; interest
groups; petitions; referendums; voluntary associations
parties, political 53–6, 63
constitutional position of 54
impact of 58, 64
membership and 22, 24, 55, 57
presidential system and 55–6, 58
role and functions of 55–6, 57,
58, 63
political protest in *see* under
demonstrations; petitions;
protest, political;
presidential elections 216–17
1969 216 n.7
2007 35
referendums, national 50, 56, 63,
64, *163*
see also study under referendums
RPR-UDF 217
state system in 3–4, 43, 46, 47, 57,
64, 128–9
as a centralist system 43, 57, 63,
162

decentralisation process and 162,
167, 168, 174
presidential system and 47, 48,
49, 50, 55, 64, 123, 124, 211,
216, 258–9
Unified Socialist Party 163
Frandsen, A. G. 120
Franklin, M. N. 35, 122, 209, 216, 220
Freitag, M. 214
French Revolution 4, 140
Fritz-Thyssen-Stiftung (Cologne) xvi
Frohlich, N. 14
Fuchs, D. 71, 75, 240
Funk, C. L. 91

Gabriel, O. W. 11, 18, 20, 22, 23, 40,
51, 71 n.1, 72, 73, 74, 75, 76 n.10,
77, 80, 81, 82, 83, 86, 87, 98 n.32,
99, 101 n.34, *171*, 178 n.16, 181,
189, 191, 193, 194, 195, 203, 241
n.2, 242, 250, 251, 252, 259 n.7
Gallagher, M. 3, 34
Gamson, W. 237, 239, 256
gender
political participation and 80, *81*, 91
n.25, 94, 221, *224*, 225
political protest 250, 253, *255*
Gensicke, T. 198
German Democratic Republic (GDR)
140, 141
German General Social Survey
(ALLBUS) 20–1
Germany
Basic Law of 41–2, 43, 54, 162
Bundesrat 43, 46, 124
Bundestag 42, 43, 44, 46, 47, 48,
49, 57, 61, 124, 211
elections for 213, 214, 215, *218*,
219–20
Bundesländer 43, 46, 47, 50, 52
Bundeswahlgesetz (*BWG*) 57, 214
Bundeswahlordnung (*BWO*) 213
bureaucracy in 3, 4
civic culture, development of 5–6
citizen participation in 2, 3, 5, 6,

22–3, 24–5, 40–4, 46–7
basic rights and 40–4, 45
church attendance and 202, 203, 204
education and 23, 202, 203, 204
formalisation of 44, 99
interest groups and 196, 198
traditions/culture and values, effect on 4, 90 n.23, 91, 92, 93, 95, 96, 99
voluntary associations and xv
citizenship laws and 41, 44, 63
cleavages in 3–4
Conservative Party (CDU) 54 n.8, 180
Constitution of 40, 41, 42, 44, 47, 48, 55, 62, 72 n.4, 75
democracy, development of 5–6
direct democracy and 163, 168–9, 180
Eastern 120, 202–3, 219
electoral turnout in 115, 116, 117, 118, 210, 219–20, 223, 226, 227, *132*
municipalities in 120 n. 6, 166
party membership in 79
social participation in 203
electoral participation and 22, 25, 43, 45–6, 216
government bodies and 46
voter turnout 23, 118, 124–5, *126*, 209–33
see also study under electoral turnout; voter turnout study, France and Germany
electoral system 43, 46–7, 48, 57, 63, 72 n.3, 124, 127–8, 211, 213–14
active and passive rights in 49
electoral law and 213–14
first-past-the-post 48, 213
local elections and 124, 127–8, 138
parliamentary elections and 214, 215, 216

proportional representation and 48, 127, 130, 211, 213
registration and postal votes 49, 118, 129, 213–14
franchise in 3, 5, 40, 63
Grundgesetz 43, 44, 51, 54, 57, 59, 61
immigrant rights in 41
interest groups in 54, 58, 59
associations and 58, 59–60, 61, 62
political process, effect on 60–1, 62, 63, 64
see also under voluntary associations
local government in 5, 37, 43, 44, 47, 51–2, 120, 123, 129, 140, 164, 165–6
communal assembly 163
direct democracy in 163, 180
elections in 113–129, 130, *132*, 166
forms of 123–4
Länder, function of 46, 51, 140, 141, 142, 164, 166, 169, 185
mayoral role/power in 123–4, 141–2, 157, 169
municipalities in 120, 121, 140, 195
referendums, use of in 51, 142, 147, 151, *153*, 155, 157, 162, *163*, 164, 169, 180
self-government in 118, 129, 140
see also studies under electoral turnout; local government
participatory systems comparison study (with France) 33–66
four criteria used in 34–8, *39*, 64, *65*
formalisation of 44, 49, 52, 57, 61, 62, 64, *65*
impact of 49, 58, 62, 64, *65*
inclusivity of 64, *65*
institutionalised forms and 57, 61
non-institutionalised forms and 66

scope of 44, 52, 57, 62, 63, 64, 65
strong participatory system and 44, 57, 58, 62, 64
see also demonstrations; interest groups; petitions; referendums; voluntary associations
parties, political 54–5, 56–7, 58, 63
impact of 58, 64
membership of 22–3, 24, 55, 57
role and functions of 56–8, 61
regional organisation and 57, 63
petitions in *see* under petitions
plebiscites in 168
reunification (1990) and 120, 123, 162, 216, 219, 220
Reichstag 219
Social-Democratic Party (SPD) 55 n. 8, 180
state system in 3–4, 5, 43, 46, 47, 51, 57, 62, 258, 259
local autonomy and 5, 57
Statistical Election Office *126*
Statistical Offices 116, 117, *121*, 122, *132*
World War I 5
World War II 5, 141
Gesk, A. 173 n.9
Geurts, P. 192
Gingrich, J. 23
Goel, M. L. 15, 18, 193, 221, 251
Goldsmith, M. J. 128
Gosnell, H. F. 33
Graichen, P. R. 180
Greece 138 n.1, 150 n.8
Greenpeace 272
Greiffenhagen, M. 3, 4
Greiffenhagen, S. 3, 4
Gripp, H. 280
Grote, R. 213
Grunberg, G. 22
Guggenberger, B. 176
Guigni, M. 240
Gunlicks, A. B. 5, 123

Habermas, J. 279–80, 290
Haensch, G. 45, 47, 54, 56 n.9, 57
Hansen, J. M. 18, 77, 80, 83, 86, 259
Haus, M. 138 n.1, 142, 146
Hehn, J. 213 n.5
Heinelt, H. 138 n.1, 139, 141, 142
Hennen, L. 276
Herrenschmidt, J.s-D. 164
Hesse, J. J. 113, 118, 128, 129, 137, 214
Hiez, D. 242
Hillman, K. -H. 278
Hlepas, N. K. 141
Hoffman-Martinot, V. 4, 113, 115 n.3, 120, 129, 144, 162, 168
Holtkamp, L. 140, 142, *177*
Holtmann, E. 3, 4
Holtz-Bacha, C. 88, 98
Hooghe, M. 97
Huckfeldt, R. 33, 100 n.33, 250, 251
Humphries, S. 83
Hungary 77, 139 n.1
Huntington, S. P. 72

Ibarra, P. 237
income, political participation and 80, *81*, 94, 97, 98, 221, 250, 252, 253, *255*
ideology 85–6, *87*
Inglehart, R. 2, 9, 18, 90, 100, 182, 193, 222 n.11
Institut National de l'Environnement Industriel et des Risques (INERIS) 285
Institute of Political Studies (Bordeaux) xv
Institute of Social Science (Stuttgart) xv
International IDEA 214
International Social Survey Programme (ISSP) xv, 21, 77, 241, *244*, 261, 264
International Year of Volunteers (IYV) 189
internet, political participation, effect

on 36, 88, 89, 98, 100
class bias and 88
France and *89*, 98, *153, 155*
Germany and *89, 153, 155*
Ireland *77*
IRGC 275, *283*
Ismayr, W. 42, 43, 46, 48, 51, 52, 54, 55, 57, 60 n.16, 61
Italy 138 n.1

Jackman, R. 20, 33, 214
Jankowski, T. B. 77, 100 n.33
Jansen, P. 56 n.9, 59, 60
Jasanoff, S. 274
Jennings, M. K. 9, 29, 83
Jesse, E. 211, 212, 213, 214
Jimenez, M. 241
Jourda, M. -T. 137
Jowell, R. 181 n.17
Jun, U. 55, 56

Kaase, M. 6, 9–10, 15, 21, 34, 72, 75, 161, 193, 239, 246
Kaliwe, S. xvi
Karr, P. 163
Kasperson, J. X. 274
Kasperson, R. E. 274
Kates, R. W. 274
Kempf, U. 46, 47, 48, 49, 50, 51, 54, 59, 60, 176
Kenny, C. 81, 83
Kerrouche, E. 138 n.1, 140, 154, 157
Kersting, N. 113, 137, 138
Kesselman, M. 164, 185
Kim, J. -O. 16–17, 18, 193
Kitschelt, H. 242, 248, 256, 258, *259*
Kjær, A. M. 157
Klein, M. 21, 73, 74
Kleinhenz, T. 118, 221
Klingemann, H. -D. 21, 71, 75
Klinke, A. 274, 276
Knapp, A. *78*, 79 n.13
Knemeyer, F. L. 123, 141
Knoke, D. 82
Koch, A. 22

Köck, W. 273
Kohler, U. 195 n.4
Kooiman, J. 157
Koopmans, R. 240, 242, 256
Korte, K. -R. 213, 214
Kost, A. 141
Kriesi, H. 20, 238, 240, 242, 248, 259
Kropp, S. 43, 46, 59, 61, 63, 259 n.7
Krueger, B. C. 89
Kühnel, S. 15
Kunz, V. 73, 74, 75, 81, 182–3
Kwak, N. 82, 83, 84, 88, 100 n.33

La Documentation Française 195
La Due Lake, R. 250, 251
Laboratoire Européen Associé, LEA-CODE and xv
Lane, J. -E. 3
Lane, R. E. 80, 83, 88, 91
Larsen, H. O. 137
Laux, E. 140
Lazarsfeld, P. F. 6
Le Bart, C. 146
LeDuc, L. 6, 35, 162, 216
Lépinard, E. 150
liberalism 278
  neo-liberal theory 274, 277, 278–9
Lijphart, A. 3, 71, 127, 211, 214, 259
Lindenberg, S. 278
Lipset, S. M. 1, 6
  Political Man 1 n.1
Lithuania 216
lobbying 54, 241
local government, analysis of 137–8
  decentered approach and 138
  democratic dimension of 137–8, 144
  France, municipality (commune) system 140–1, 142–3, 144, 146–7
  council/mayor power balance 143–4, 146, 155
  electoral system in 143, 146–7
  mayor, role of 143–4, 146
  mayoral elections 138, 143, 146, 155, 157

'urban presidentialism' and 144
French and German mayors, study 138–57
   age of mayor and 149, 154, *155*
   attitudes towards local democracy of 144, 146–52
   communication tools used in 152–4, *155*
   gender of mayor and 150, 154, *155*
   mayoral differences and 144, 146, 147, 153–4, 155, 157
   participation, perception of 138–9, 146, 150
   party membership and 147, 148, 151–2, 154
   perception of mayors survey 144–5
   policy making role 138, 139, 146–7, 157
   professionalisation of mayors and 149
   referenda, local and 151, 155, 157
Germany, (Länder) municipality system 140, 141–2, 144
   mayor/council balance of power 142, 144
   mayoral elections 138, 144, 157, 166
   mayors, role of 123–4, 141–2, 146, 147, 169
international survey of mayors, 2003–4 138–9
see also under electoral turnout
Locke, J. 279
Lorrain, D. 137
Loughlin, J.
Lovenduski, J. 74 n.8, 152
Lüdemann, C. 15, 23, 80, 86
Lüsebrink, H. -J. 211 n.2
Luthardt, W. 162
Luxembourg 216
Lyall, C. 275

MacAdam, D. 252
MacClurg, S. 82, 83, 96
Mackie, T. T. 209
MacNeal, R. S. 89
Maier, J. 209
Mair, P. *78*
Malinowski, B. 278
Malta 216
Marburg, University of 178 n.14
Marsh, A. 9–10, 34, 72, 75, 193, 239, 246
Martin, P. S. 84
März, P. 168, 169
Mayer, N. 22, 23, 256
media use 88–9
   for entertainment 88, 98, 100
   'time-displacement' hypothesis 88, 98
   political participation and 88–9, 97–8, 100, 221, 225
   as source of information 88, 89, 100, 221 n.9
   class and 89, 94
   France and *89*, 130, *153,* 226
   Germany and *89, 153,* 226
   media malaise hypothesis 88
   see also internet, political participation, effect on
Mehr Demokratie 175
Mény, Y. 42, 59, 60
Merton, R. K. 278
Meyer, M. 178
Micheletti, M. 242
Milbrath, L. W. 6, 15, 18, 193, 221, 251
Miller, A. H. 87
Mitterand, F. 217
mobilisation, political 16–17, 82, 94, 259
   networks and 114, 252
   political protest and 259, *260,* 261
Morales, L. 192
Moreau, P. 212, 213, 217
Mouchard, D. 250
Mouritzen, P. E. 137, 139

Moyser, G. 11
Muller, E. N. 13, 15, 18
Müller-Brandeck-Bocquet, G. 212, 213, 217
Münch, R. 3, 278
Mutz, D. C. 84

Nagel, J. H. 86
Napoleon, B. 4
Nassehi, A. 278
Négrier, E. 137
NGOs 276
Netherlands, The *77*, 129, 243
Neubauer, D. E. 1
new social movements 9, 238, 243, 252, 254, *257,* 259, *260,* 263, 264
Nie, N. H. 7–10, 15, 16–17, 18, 19, 23, 190, 193, 209, 238, 250
Niedermayer, O. 22
Nohlen, D. 209, 212, 214
Norris, P. 6, 13, 18, 20, 22, 33, 35, 60, 73 n.5, 74 n.8, 82 n.17, 85, 88, 89, 97, 98, 100 n.33, 152, 192, 195, 203, 211, 216, 220
Norway *77,* 129, 138 n.1

occupations 240, 242, 243, *244,* 245, 246, *268*
OECD 274
Ohr, D. 221 n.9
Okrent, D. 273
Oliver, J.-E. 120
Olsen, M. E. 191–2
Olson, M. 13, 14, 251
Opp, K. -D. 15, 23
Oppenheimer, J. A. 14
Ordeshook, P. C. 13
O'Riordan, T. 282
Osselin, J. 180

Page, E. C. 118, 128
Paoletti, M. 146, 167 n.2
Parry, G. 11, 190, 193
Parsons, T. 278
Participation in America 16

participation, political 1–2, 3
 as civic right 1–2, *39*, 40
  individual/organisational rights and 38, 39, 40–4
  strong participatory systems and 38–9
 as a cultural value/norm 2, 90–2, 181–5, 274
 concepts of 274
 community size and 119–22
 conventional and unconventional (Kaase and Marsh) 9–11, 72–3, 75, 239
 definition of 7, 9, 239
 democracy and 1, 40, 45, 85, 137–8, 190, 220
 determinants of 79, 80–101, 221–2
  attitudes, political and 85–8, *95*, 96–7, 100, 138, 221, 222
  class and 89, 94
  factors influencing 80–92, 225–7
  integrated explanatory model of 93–101
  microenvironment and 81–4, *85*, 94–5
  social networks, integration into 18, 221, 222, 223, 225, 226, 252, 263
  value types and 90–2, 95–6, 99, 100
  see also gender; media; social capital theory
 explanation of, approaches to 11–21, 79–101, 194–5, 221, 223
  Civic Voluntarism Model (CVM) (Verba *et al.*) 17, 18, 79, 194–5, 223, 238, 239, 248, 250, 253, 255, 256
  middle-range theories 15–21, 193
  mobilising agencies and 18–19
  neo-institutionalism and 20–1
  social capital, role of 19
  theory of planned behaviour (Ajzen) 14–15

see also rational choice theory; social capital
forms of 73–7, 99, 209
   life-sphere analysis and 99–100
frequency, of 72, 73–4, 75, *76, 77*
horizontal and vertical differentiation 37
indirect and direct 53, 161
non-legal forms and 8, 9, 73
   see also civil disobedience; protest, political
political institutions, role of in 33–4, 38, 64, 66, 173, 256
   formalisation of rules/regulations 34–5, 38, *39*, 44, 49, 64
   inclusive governance and 173, 174–5
   new participatory methods and 276
   see also policy making, participatory processes and
research, development of xv, xvi, 6–11, 193–4
   active/inactive distinction and 8, 10, 18, 192, 193
   macro-level analyses *11,* 12
   micro-level analyses *11,* 12, 18
   multilevel analysis 12
   Political Action Group and 8–9, 15, 34
   regulated/non-regulated 239–40
   social participation and 189, 192–3
   voter turnout and 209
   see also social participation
scope of participation and 36–7, *39*, 44, 49
   extension of participatory tools and 37
socio-economic resource level and (SERL) 16–17
systems (types) analysis of 38, 39
   citizen-initiated contacts and 7–8
   co-operative activities and 7, *8*, 10, 11

impact of 38, *39*, 44, 49
inclusiveness and 35, *39*, 44, 49, 256, *259*, 260, 264
open and closed systems 256–9, 260, 264
strong and weak systems 38, 39, 43, 64, 259, 264
Verba and Nie's classification 7–10, 15, 209
Westerståhl's four types 161
   see also demonstrations; electoral turnout; local government; petitions; referendums; voter turnout
participation, social 53 n.7, 189–207
active and passive 192, 193, 200
determinants of 199–203
concept of 191–3
democracy and 192, 203–4
   skills, acquirement and 192
determinants of 190, 193–4, 203–4
   church attendance and 202, 203, 204
   civic-voluntarism model and 194–5
   education and 202, 203, 204
   socio-economic resources and 193–4
French/German association analysis 191, 193, 194–204, 254
   association types and numbers 196–8, 203
   determinants of membership 201–3, 204
   Eastern Germany and 202–3
   explanatory sets in 194–5, 202
   passive and active involvement and 198–9, 200–3
interpersonal trust and 190, 194, 222
political participation and 53 n.7, 192–3
political role of 189, 192, 203, 204
Verba/Schlozman/Brady model and 193, 194, 200, 202, 204, 222, 223

voluntary associations and 191, 194, 195
party identification 17, 86, 87, 96, 100, 251
  left-right placement and 86, 87, 90, 93, *95,* 96–7, 100
    France and 96, 97 n.30
    Germany and 96 n.29, 97
  voter turnout, effect on 118, 222, 225, 226, 227
party membership 73, 78–9, 227, 259, 263
  active and non-active 73
  characteristics of participation in *76*
  definition of 74 n.7
  France and 76, *77, 78,* 79, *93*
    communist/socialist parties and 79 n.13
  Germany and 76, *77,* 78–9, *93*
  socio-economic factors and 80
  value-types and 91
Pattie, C. 18, 190
Patzelt, W. J. 42
Peirce, C. S. 280
Perea, E. A. 127, 214
Perrineau, P. 22, 23
Petersen, S. H. 82
petitions 40, 45, 50, 73, 74–5, 80, 84, 85, 94, 181, 248
  as protest 237, 240, 242, 246, 260–1
  characteristics of *76*
  European Social Survey data 181
  France and 42, 51, 62, 74–5, 93, 99, *153, 155,* 166, 169, 176, 180, 181, 243, *244,* 245, 246, *247,* 263, *268*
    frequency of participation 76, *77,* 181
  Germany and 42, 44, 74, 75, *153, 155,* 169, 181, 263, *268*
    frequency of participation 76, *77,* 79, 181
Petterson, P. A. 37
Pierce, R. 212
Pierre, J. 113

Pison, G. 78 n.11
plebiscites 50, 52, 63, 64, 162, 169, 181
Poher, A. 217 n.7
Poland *77,* 216
policy making, participatory processes and
  decision-making and 276–7, 280–1
  inclusion and closure processes of 276–7, 285–6, 289–90
  political and regulatory cultures of 282–4, 287, 291, 292
  inclusive governance and 274–93
    advantages of 274
    stakeholder involvement and 276, 279, 282, 292
    risk governance and 275, 276, 278, 281
  participation methods 277
    bargaining and 277, 279, 285, 290
    consensus conferencing 281
    Delphi method 281
    discourse analysis and 281
    focus groups and 279
    jury system 281
    mediation and 277, 279
    'model' citizen and 281
    round table and 280, 284–5, 286, 287
    negotiated rule making 278
  theoretical approaches to 274, 277–81
    anthropological 274, 277, 280–1, 286, 287, 292
    deliberative 274, 277, 279–80, 286, 287, 290, 291, 292
    functionalist 274, 277, 278, 286, 290, 291, 292
    neo-liberal 274, 277, 278–9, 291, 292
    post-modern 274, 277, 281, 292
  styles of 282–4
  see also case studies under environmental policy

Political Action Group 9–10, 15, 34
political behaviour 2, 11, 24
　general theories of 13–15
　political institutions, relationship
　　with 33
　voter turnout research and 209
　see also participation, political;
　　rational choice theory
political culture 21, 282–4, 292
politicians, contacting of 74, *76*, 79,
　91, 181, 240, 246, *247*
　France and *77*, 93
　Germany and 76, *77, 93*
　local government and 74
Pompidou, G. 217 n.7
Portugal *77*, 138 n.1, 150 n.8
Postman, N. 98
Powell, G. B. 18, 127
Prechtl, P. 280
Premat, C. 151
pressure groups 5, 7
　rational choice theory and 13
　single-issue groups and 7
Prewitt, K. 18
Priller, E. 195
Prince-Gibson, E. 90
Prior, M. 88
protest, political xv, xvi, 8–9, 10–11,
　19, 23, 36
　definition of 239–40, 242
　　civil disobedience and 241–2,
　　　243
　democracy, role in 237
　explanations of 248–55, 261–4
　　mobilisation-based approach
　　　250, 252, 253
　　motivation-based approach 250,
　　　251, 253
　　open and closed state systems
　　　and 256–8, 260, 262, 264
　　opportunity structures and 259,
　　　260
　　resource-based approach and
　　　250–1, 253
　　trust of system and 257

France and xv, 21, 23, 24, 25, 75,
　237–8, 241, 242, 246, *249*, 250,
　254, 258, 262
　as 'strong' state 258
　anti-nuclear protest 237, 262 n.8
　illegal protest in 246, *247*, 255,
　　262–3
　participatory type of 243
　student protest (1968) 216 n.7,
　　217
French/German comparison 237–68
　'civic voluntarism model' (CV)
　　and 238, 239, 248, 250, 252,
　　253, 255, 256, 263–4
　civil disobedience differences
　　241, 242, 243, 244, 245,
　　246, 247–8
　differences, explanation of
　　248–55, 256
　legitimacy, measurement of
　　244–5, 260
　main hypotheses and 239, 253,
　　262
　'Political Opportunity Structure'
　　(POS) model and 238, 239,
　　248, 255, 256, 262, 263
　Protest Event Analysis (PEA)
　　and 240
　responsiveness indicators and
　　260, 262, 264
　World Values Survey, use of 241,
　　242, 243, *244, 245,* 246, 247,
　　248, 251–2
Germany and 66, 72 n.3, 237–8,
　241, 243, *249*, 258, 262
　anti-nuclear protest 237
　civil disobedience and 241–2,
　　243, 244, 245, 246, 247, 248
　participatory type of 243
legal/illegal distinction and 11, 240,
　241, 242, 243
objectives of 239
political participation research
　and 8–9, 10, 13, 71 n.1, 73 n.5,
　239–42

referendums and 185
socio-economic resources, link with 238
typologies of *240*, 241–2
values/traditions, role of in 237, 241
see also civil disobedience; demonstrations; new social movements; occupations; strikes
Prussia 5
Putnam, R. 19, 74, 80 n.15, 86, 88 n.22, 91, 98, 100, 189, 190, 192, 194, 195, 203, 252
Pütz, C. 48, 50, 56, 53, 54, 55, 56

Radcliffe-Brown, A. R. 278
Radtke, G. D. 22
Rallings, C. 120
rational choice theory 13
  basic assumptions of 13
  electoral turnout and 119 n.5
  political participation and 250
  voting and 13–14
Rauschmeyer, F. 275
referendums 6, 20, 35, 38, 40, 45, 50–3, 161–2
  direct democracy and 161, 163, 168, 176, 177, 180, 185
  referendums/popular initiatives study 161–85
    approval rate and 167, 178, *182*, 185
    Baden-Württemberg analysis 162, 169, *170, 171,* 172, 173, 174–5, 176–8, 179–80, 183, 184
    France, analysis of 162, 167, 168, 173–4, 175–6, *182,* 184–5
    Germany, analysis of 162, 170–3, 174–5, 177–8, 182, 185
    mayoral attitude and 168
    mobilisation index and 178–9, 180, *182*
    topic analysis and 181–4
    turnout and 162, 165–6, 169, 173–4, 175, 181, *182, 183, 184,* 185
    success, explanation of in 162, 176, 178, 180
    values, relationship with 162, 181, 182–5
  goal of 161
  French system 44, 50, 51, *153,* 162, 166–7, 169, 173, 176, 180
    popular initiatives and *163*, 164, 176, 180, 184
    quorums and 174–5
    turnout, importance of and 175, 176
  German system 50–1, 63, 113, 153, 162, 165–6, 167, 168, 172–3, 180
    East Germany and 166
    popular initiatives and *163*, 164, *165,* 166, 169, 172, 176–7, 178   184
    quorums and 165, 166
  national 50–1, 161
  participatory culture and 181–5
  regional/local 51–2, 161–2, 164, 168
  Sartori's paradox and 161, 162, 175, 180
  types of 50
REGENA (Germany) 287–91
Reidinger, F. *170, 172, 174,* 177 n.13
Reif, K. 122
Reigrotzki, E. 22
Reiser, M. *125*
Renn, O. 274, 275, 276
Reutter, W. 59 n.14, 60, 61
Reynaert, H. 150 n.8, 154
Riemer, I. 280
Riker, W. H. 13
Ritzer, G. 278, 280
Rivat, E. *257, 259*
Rochon, T. 20
Rohrschnieder, R. 209
Rokkan, S. 1, 33, 42
Roller, E. 20

Rosanvallon, H. 177
Rose, L. E. 37, 137
Rosenstone, S. J. 18, 77, 80, 83, 86, 259
Roth, D. 219, 227
Rothstein, B. 33
Rousseau, J. -J. 53
Roussillon, H. 176
Rucht, D. 240, 242
Rudi, T. 20
Rudzio, W. 48, 57, 61, 214
Russian Federation 77

Sadran, P. 174
Sarkozy, N. 117, 219
Sartori, G. 161, 162, 175, 180
Scaff, L. A. 241 n.2
Scarbrough, E. 181
Scarrow, S. E. 22, 73, 74, *78*, 79
Schain, M. A. 3, 5
Scharpf, F. W. 37
Schild, J. 4, 22, 43, 46, 48, 51, 53, 54, 55, 56, 211 n.2, 212, 213, 217, 238, 239, 246, 250, 259
Schiller, T. 61
Schlozman, K. L. 1, 17, 18, 81, 83, 84, 91 n.26, 193, 194, 195, 200, 202, 204, 221, 225, 226, 238, 248, 250
Schmitt, H. 122
Schmitt-Beck, R. 22, 221 n.9
Schrott, P. R. 221 n.9
Schumpeter, J. A. 86, 99
Schwartz, S. H. 90–1, 105, 106
Schwarz, N. 191
Sellers, J. 120
Sharpe, L. J. 113, 118, 128, 129, 137
Slovakia 77
Slovenia 77
Smith, J. 100 n.33
Sniderman, P. M. 33, 222
Sobel, R. 84
social capital theory *11*, 18, 19–20, 81, 189, 190, 191, 194, 195, 203, 252
  interpersonal trust and 194, 195, 252
  social networks and 194
  participation in organisations and 191–2, 252
social engagement 191, 194, 199–203
  determinants of 199
  see also participation, social; voluntary associations
social trust 20, 84–5, 96
  media's effect and 88
socialisation, political *11*, 80, 84, 114
socio-economic resource level (SERL) 16, 17
socio-economic status (SES) 16, 97, 114
  political interest and 97, 250
Sommier, I. 250
sovereignty, principle of popular 1, 35, 40, 45, 146
Spain 77, 138 n.1, 243
Spiegel, Der 237
Stanley, J. W. 89
Statistisches Bundesamt 140 n.3
Stauer, M. *240, 244, 247, 249, 255, 257, 258*
Steinbrecher, M. 117, 118
Stern, P. C. 273, 275
Steyvers, K. 150 n.8, 154
Stoiber, M. 137
Stoker, G. 113
Stoker, L. 83
Stolle, D. 20
Strate, J. M. 100 n.33
strikes 240, 242, 243, *244,* 245, 246, 249, *268*
Stryker, S. 280
Stoker, G. 113
Stuttgarter Zeitung 219
Svara, J. H. 137, 139
Sweden 77, 129, 138 n.1, 220
Sweeting, D. 138, 146
Switzerland 3, 77, 138 n.1, 214, 220
  local municipalities in 120, 129

Tait, J. 275
Taniguchi, M. 181

Tarrow, S. 259
Taylor-Gooby, P. 274
Tchernonog, V. 195
Thoenig, J. -C. 122, 147, 155
Thompson, M. 275
Thrasher, M. 120
Tilly, C. 237, 239
Tingsten, H. 33
Tocqueville, A. de 128, 190
Tolbert, C. J. 88, 89
Topf, R. 21, 209
trade unions
  engagement in 14, 82, 94, 222, 259, 260–1
  France and 42, 44, 54, 58, 217, 254
  right to set up 40, 42
trust, political
  formation of 190
  interpersonal 252
  political protest and 257, *258*, 260, *261*, 262
  social capital theory and 194, 195
  social participation and 202
TRUSTNET project 292
Tsatsos, D. T. 34, 55, 59
Tufte, E. R. 37, 119, 120, 128, 173
Tümmers, H. J. 45, 47, 54, 56 n.9, 57

Uehlinger, H. -M. 11, 22, 240
Ukraine 77
Ulbig, S. G. 91
United Kingdom 77, 138 n.1
United Nations 189
United States
  associations, role of 190
  Civil Rights Movement 8
  local government in 120, 128
  National Academy of Sciences (NAS) 273
  political participation in 3, 18, 220, 250
    church membership and 82, 83, 95
    media, effect of 88 n.22
    research and 21, 24, 80 n.15, 86

n.20, 91 n.26
  social capital and 19
  political protest in 9, 16
  social participation and 190
Uterwedde, H. 4

values 90–2
  value-types (Schwartz) 90, 105
  political participation and 91–2
van Biezen, I. *78*
van den Broek, A. 190
van der Kolk, H. 127, 131
van Deth, J. W. 9, 11, 20, 21, 22, 71, 73, 75, 82 n.16, 84, 86, 87, 114, 181, 190, 191, 192, 194, 195, 222, 238, 240, 241, 242
Verba, S. xv, 1, 6, 7–10, 15, 16–17, 18, 19, 21, 23, 71, 72, 75, *76*, 79, 80, 82, 83, 94, 100, 101, 114, 120, 128, 190, 193–4, 195, 200, 209, 221, 237, 238, 248, 250, 252
  civic culture, concept of 1–2
Vetter, A. 113, 118, 123, 128, 129, 137, 138, 222
Villalba, M. 242
violence, political 11, 239, 240, 241 n.2
Völkl, K. 11, 18, 22, 23, 40, 51, 73, 75, 77, 80, 83, 86, 87, 193, 195, 210, 221, 241 n.2, 242, 250, 252
voluntary associations/organisations 5
  civil rights and 42
  democratic effect of 199, 203
  France and 61, 62, 94, 95–6, 195, 196, 198, 254, *255*
  number and types of 196–7, 198
  Germany and 61, 62, 94, 195–6, 197, 254, *255*
  number and types of 196, 198
  participation in xv, 5, 36, 38, 81–3, 189–90, 222, 252
  passive and active 192, 252
  political mobilisation and 82, 84, 94–5, 252
  social capital theory and 19–20, 81,

191, 192, 194
 social networking and 191
 typology of 252
von Erlach, E. 20
von Schomberg, R. 292
von Winterfeldt, D. 276
voter turnout 33, 35, 127, 209, 214–15
 abstention and 209–10, 220, 221
 compulsory voting and 214, 216
 decrease in 209–10, 215, 216, 227
  France and 215, 219, 227
 democracy, stability of and 220–1
 determinants of 221, 223–7
 electoral law, effect of on 211
 party participation and 6, 86, 190, 225
 qualitative features of (Verba and Nie) 209
 see also electoral turnout
voter turnout study, France and Germany 209–233
 ESS dataset used in 210–11
 determinants of 223–7
  age and *224,* 225, 227
  church attendance *224,* 225, 226
  democracy, satisfaction with and 222, 224, 225, 227–8
  party identification and *224,* 225, 226, 227
  political interest and *224,* 225, 227
  social networks and 225, 226, 227
 France, electoral turnout and 209, 210, 211–13, 214–19, 223, *224,* 225, 227
  decline in 215, 219
  electoral law, effects on 211–13, 214
  parliamentary elections and 210, 215–19
 Germany, electoral turnout and 209, 210, 213–14, 215, 216, 219–20, 223, *224,* 225–7
  East Germany and 210, 219, 220, 223, 226–7
  decline in 219–20
  electoral law, effects on 213–14
  parliamentary elections and 210, 215, 216, 227
  reunification and 219
 non-voter patterns 210
 Verba/Schlozman/Brady model and 221, 223–4, 225, 226–7
voter volatility 209
voting 4, 6, 20, 36, 38, 220
 as a right 42–3
 civic involvement and 4, *8,* 9–10, 11, 34–5
 rational choice theory 13–14
 see also electoral turnout; participation, political

Walter-Rogg, M. 45, 50, 115 n.3, *171*
Walzer, M. 279
Wargny, C. 163
Warren, M. E. 85
Wattenberg, M. P. 74
Weale, A. 176
Weare, C. 89
Webler, T. 279
Weins, C. 22
Weisenfeld, E. 211 n.2, 217
Weixner, B. M. 169
Welzel, C. 2
West, D. M. 74
Westerståhl, J. 161
Westholm, A. 20
Westle, B. 22, 239, 240
Whitehead, L. 166
Widfeldt, A. 74
Wiesendahl, E. 74, *78,* 89, 219
Williams, C. J. 18
Wolf, M. 180
Wollman, H. 129, 141, 144, 157, 165
Wood, D. M. 149
World Values Surveys (WVS) 195 n.4, 238, 241, 242, 243, *244, 245,* 246, 247, 249, 252, *255,* 261, 264, 268

Young, G. 149
Ysmal, C. 21

Zaller, J. 221–2
Zimmer, A. 195
Zinn, J. O. 274
Zintl, R. 51
Zipp, J. F. 100 n.33
Zucherman, A. S. 74
Zukin, C. 11, 18, 20, 36, 189, 194, 195